The Complete Resource Book
for Toddlers and Twos

1

Dedication

To Gabrielle and Madison who are daily reminders of the wonders and joys of "toddlerhood."

The Complete Resource Book for Toddlers and Twos

Over 2000 Experiences and Ideas!

Pam Schiller
Illustrations by Richelle Bartkowiak and Deborah Johnson

Gryphon House
Lewisville, NC

Copyright

Copyright © 2003 Pam Schiller
Published by Gryphon House, Inc.
PO Box 10, Lewisville, NC 27023
800.638.0928 (toll free); 877.638.7576 (fax)

Visit us on the web at www.gryphonhouse.com

Illustrations: Richelle Bartkowiak and Deborah Wright
Cover Photograph: Copyright © 1999 Artville, LLC.

Reprinted September 2019

Library of Congress Cataloging-in-Publication Data

Schiller, Pamela Byrne.
    The complete resource book for toddlers and twos: over 2000 activities for enriching language and developing skills and concepts / Pam Schiller.
    p. cm.
Includes index.
    ISBN 978-0-87659-287-8
    1. Language arts (Preschool) 2. Education, Preschool—Activity programs. I. Title.
LB1140.5.L3S334 2003
372.6--dc21

200215562

Table of Contents

Introduction

Even the casual observer will notice after just a few moments that toddlers and twos are BUSY! But do you know that toddlers and two-year-olds are in the most fertile time of their lives for absorbing the sounds and meanings of words, developing their motor skills, and laying the foundation for their social-emotional well-being? From birth to age three, children have brains that are two and a half times more active than that of adults. They are busy building the foundation for a lifetime of learning.

If children have the right experiences, by the time they are five they will have acquired a working vocabulary of 3000 words, which is 60% of an estimated average adult vocabulary. Toddlers and twos who are surrounded by adults that talk with them, read to them, and sing to them can get a jump on building their vocabulary—a jump that will stay with them as they grow and develop. Toddlers and twos are extremely curious about language and can absorb most of what they are exposed to. They are fascinated with big words and love to use them. Introduce the word *brontosaurus* to them and then watch what they do with it.

These active explorers are also at a prime time for the development of fine and gross motor skills. Once they are on their feet, they will learn to walk, hop, run, jump, gallop, and skip as they practice and perfect the skill of using their legs and feet. Those little hands that struggled so to grasp a rattle during the first year of life will, during the second and third years of life, learn to thread a bead, operate an eyedropper, move a crayon to create an image, turn a ball of playdough into a snake, and build a tower as high as they are tall.

With appropriate experiences in the areas of social and emotional development, toddlers and twos will move from solitary play and total dependence to understanding the subtle nuances of cooperative play and the power of independence. They will learn how to control their impulses and how to communicate their desires effectively.

One of the most neglected areas of development for toddlers and twos is problem solving. While some may think they are too young and too inexperienced to solve their own problems, just the opposite is true. These little ones are eager to solve problems. They just need the opportunity to try. Early brain development research indicates that the wiring for problem solving is established during the first four years of life.

You will find that many of the activities in this book will challenge toddlers and twos to find solutions to simple problems. Every topic has at least one activity under cognitive development that is designated as a problem-solving suggestion. These activities involve looking for solutions, determining cause and effect, putting pieces together, locating matching items, as well as other problem-solving techniques. Occasionally, you will find an activity labeled as a problem-solving suggestion in the physical and social-emotional development areas. After all, problem solving isn't limited to cognitive development.

Allowing toddlers and twos opportunities for risk taking, which is closely related to problem solving, is also crucial to healthy development. Toddlers and twos need opportunities to take child-size risks within a protective environment to develop the disposition to take calculated risks later in life. If they are to learn the difference between throwing caution to the wind and a contemplated risk, they will need experiences that allow practice. This includes physical activities such as climbing, reaching, and throwing; cognitive activities such as experimenting with messy paints and using blunt scissors; and social-emotional activities such as playing with children who are both older and younger than they are.

This book is filled with experiences that target the fertile areas of development for toddlers and twos. Each daily topic is divided into activities and experiences that support:
- Language Enrichment
- Cognitive Development
- Social-Emotional Development
- Physical Development

Because children from birth to age three are in the most fertile period of their lives for language development, this book is rich in suggestions for enhancing and developing language surrounding all areas of development. A list of vocabulary words is offered for each topic and intended for use throughout the day. Story Circle Suggestions are provided to help reinforce each skill or concept. Reading these books will also serve to enhance vocabulary and language development.

You will notice that questions to ask the children are provided for many of the activities in each daily lesson. These questions, which are in quotation marks throughout the book, are intended to be examples of questions you may want to consider asking. Your individual circumstances may suggest other lines of questioning. The important thing is that you ask questions. Questions help children formulate their thinking. They also provide a structure for language. They help children figure out the more difficult part of language development—syntax and grammar. Your questions will also help children increase their vocabulary. Ask questions of all children, even the "not yet talkers." They may not have words yet, but they are listening. They can answer some questions by pointing and others by shaking their head to indicate "yes" or "no." For more complicated questions, you can provide an answer as a model for what these little ones will soon be able to do.

Use the questions two ways:
- **The questions in quotation marks: Ask children these questions to help develop their vocabulary, help them formulate their thinking, and figure out the more difficult part of language development—syntax and grammar.**
- **The questions without quotation marks: Ask yourself these questions to determine what skills the children have developed, what they still need to learn, and how to teach them what they need to learn.**

There are also suggestions for what to look for to evaluate the children's development. These examples, which do not have quotation marks, will help you determine what children have learned, what they still need to learn, and how to teach them what they need to learn.

An important part of teaching is offering children an opportunity to focus on the topic and to reflect on what they have learned. You will find a Getting Started section and a Reflection on the Day section for each skill or concept that is being introduced.

The Complete Resource Book for Toddlers and Twos provides ample suggestions for filling one day and possibly several days. Select activities that meet the developmental needs, abilities, and interests of the children in your care. Because young children learn by repetition, repeat activities and experiences on a regular basis.

The activities and experiences in this book vary in difficulty level to cover the wide range in ability levels found among toddlers and twos. Some activities are targeted for specific age groups such as older twos or "not yet talkers," but ultimately you are the best judge of what each individual child is capable of achieving. You can modify activities easily. For example, if the activity suggests that you teach the children to stand on their toes and they can easily accomplish that task, have them walk on their toes. If they can walk on their toes, have them walk a specific pathway on their toes. You will always be the best judge of what individual children are capable of achieving; the activities may just help stimulate your thinking.

Some activities require advance preparation. If any preparation is needed, it is outlined at the beginning of each skill or concept.

The Appendix provides support pieces for the suggested activities. For example, you will find letters to families requesting photographs or requesting them to collect throwaway items such as coffee cans and tissue boxes for classroom use. There are illustrations in the Appendix to demonstrate the many American Sign Language signs that are introduced. The concept of teaching sign language to little ones is a fairly new concept but has been enjoying a high level of success. It seems that very young children are especially adept at picking up and using the signs. You'll also find an assessment checklist in the Appendix that can be used to track individual children's progress on developing skills and concepts. Last but not least, the Appendix is filled with stories and story patterns (flannel board patterns and puppets) as well as patterns for games and activities.

You play a critical role in development of these young explorers. You actually hold in your hands the power to shape children's futures. The activities and experiences in this book are intended to support your efforts and to make this awesome task a little less overwhelming.

Physical Me

EYES

EARS

NOSE

MOUTH

CHIN

HAIR

HANDS AND FINGERS

ARMS

FEET AND TOES

LEGS

KNEES AND ELBOWS

FACIAL EXPRESSIONS

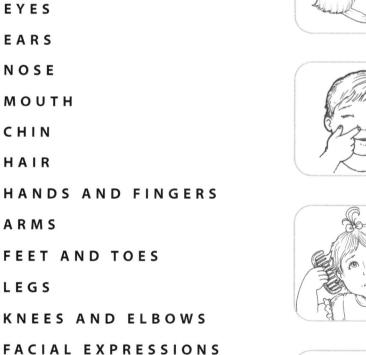

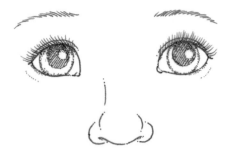

Eyes

WORDS TO PRACTICE

blink	eyelids	hazel eyes
blue eyes	eyes	head
brown eyes	face	look
eyebrows	gray eyes	see
eyelashes	green eyes	wink

GETTING STARTED

- Ask the children to point to their eyes. Ask questions to find out what they know about eyes. "How many *eyes* do you have?" "What can you do with your *eyes?*"
- Tell them that today they will be learning about ways they use their *eyes*.
- Read your favorite book about eyes to the children or select a book from the Story Circle Suggestions below.

STORY CIRCLE SUGGESTIONS

- *Brown Bear, Brown Bear, What Do You See?* by Bill Martin, Jr. and Eric Carle
- *Eyes, Nose, Fingers, Toes* by Judy Hindley
- *I Can Read With My Eyes Shut* by Dr. Seuss

PREPARATION FOR THE "EYES" ACTIVITIES AND EXPERIENCES

- Make the Stick the Tail on the Bunny Game (Appendix p. 469).
- Make the "Little Red Riding Hood" flannel board story (Appendix p. 525-528).
- Become familiar with the story of "Little Red Riding Hood" so you can tell it instead of reading it.

Language Enrichment Choices*

- Play "Peekaboo" with the children. Ask them to cover their eyes and then uncover them when you say, "Peekaboo." After a few rounds, ask them what they can see when they cover their eyes. Then, ask them what they can see when they uncover their eyes.

▨ Sing "Catalina Magnalina" with the older children. Discuss Catalina's funny eyes. Encourage the children to look at their own eyes in the mirror. Don't worry if the children are challenged by learning the words to this song. They will enjoy listening to you sing the silly words in the song.

Catalina Magnalina
She had a peculiar name but she wasn't to blame.
She got it from her mother, who's the same, same, same.

Chorus: Catalina Magnalina, Hootensteiner Bogentwiner
Hogan Logan Bogan was her name.

She had two peculiar eyes in her head,
One was purple and the other was red. (chorus)

▨ Say the poem "My Eyes Can See" with the children. Suit the actions to the words. Talk about things we can see with our eyes. "I see children when I look around the room. What do you see with your eyes?"

My Eyes Can See
My eyes can see.
My mouth can talk.
My ears can hear.
My feet can walk.

My nose can sniff,
My teeth can chew.
My lids can flutter,
My arms hug you.

▨ Encourage children to name the parts of their eyes: lashes, lids, and eyebrows. If you have unbreakable mirrors available, let each child use one to examine his eyes.

▨ Use the word *eyes* in sentences. For example, "Richele has beautiful blue *eyes*."

▨ Present the flannel board story of "Little Red Riding Hood" (Appendix p. 525-528). Children will love the conversation between Red Riding Hood and the wolf when she says, "But Grandmother, what big eyes you have." Because this

* Toddlers and twos present a wide range of developmental needs, abilities, and interests. For each learning area, select among the following activity and experience choices that are appropriate for the children in your care.

story is lengthy for toddlers, you will need to tell it rather than try to read it. Focus on the dialogue between the wolf and Little Red Riding Hood.

▪ Teach the children the American Sign Language sign for *eye* (Appendix p. 431).

Physical Development Choices

▪ Encourage the children to blink their eyes. Teach them "Here Are My Eyes" to go along with their blinking. Show them how to wink. Older children may be able to wink. They will all enjoy watching you wink.

Here Are My Eyes
Here are my eyes, (point to eyes)   *When my eyes are open,* (open eyes wide)
One and two,   *I see the light.*
I can wink, (wink)   *When they are closed,* (close eyes)
So can you.   *It's dark as night.*

▪ Play Stick the Tail on the Bunny. Photocopy and enlarge the illustration of the bunny (see Appendix p. 469). Work with the children one at a time. Place the bunny on a table in front of the child and invite him to close his eyes and try to place the tail (a cotton ball) in the correct spot on the bunny. After the child tries to stick the tail on the bunny with his eyes closed, invite him to try it with his eyes open. "Is it easier with your eyes open or shut?"

▪ Teach the children "Eye Winker." Ask the children to point to their eyes, and then ask them about things they can see. Have them cover their eyes. Point out that now they can't see.

Eye Winker
Eye winker, (point to eye)
Tom Tinker, (touch ears)
Nose smeller, (touch nose)
Mouth eater, (touch mouth)
Chin chopper, (tap chin)
Chin chopper, (tap chin)
Chin chopper chin. (tap chin)

Social and Emotional Development Choices

▪ During the day, select children with different eye colors and say the appropriate "Eye Rhyme" to them. Talk with them about the color of their eyes. "Do you have the same color eyes as your friends?"

Eye Rhymes by Pam Schiller
Brown Eyes
Your eyes are big, and round, and brown.
They must be the prettiest eyes in town.

Green Eyes
When I look at you, know what I see?
Eyes as green as green can be.

Gray Eyes
Blue eyes, green eyes,
Brown eyes, hey.
Your eyes are gray,
And I love them that way.

Blue Eyes
Your eyes are as blue as blue can be
Your eyes are the color of the deep blue sea.

Children With Eyes the Color of Yours
You see me,
I see you.
Your eyes are blue/green/brown,
Mine are, too.

■ Sing "Close Your Eyes" or say "Be Very Quiet" at naptime today. Talk about how we close our eyes when we sleep.

Close Your Eyes by Pam Schiller (Tune: London Bridge)
Close your eyes and go to sleep
Go to sleep, go to sleep.
Close your eyes and go to sleep
Little Madison!

Be Very Quiet
Shhh—be very quiet,
Shhh—be very still.
Fold your busy little hands,
Close your sleepy little eyes.
Shhh—be very quiet.

■ Show the children how to give a Butterfly Kiss. Brush your eyelashes on the back of their hand or on their cheek. Ask the children how Butterfly Kisses feel. "Are they soft? Do they tickle?"

Cognitive Development Choices

■ Look at pictures of people. Encourage the children to point out the eyes in each photo. Discuss how we use our eyes to see. Invite children to name some things they enjoy seeing with their eyes.

■ Go on a nature walk with the children. Stop to admire the beautiful things you see. You may want to make of list of things you might see on your walk and then check off the things that you did see on your walk after you get back.

■ Several times during the day, mention how thankful you are to have your eyes so that you can see where you are going, see what you are trying to read or pick up, see someone's sweet face, or see the beautiful clouds in the sky.

■ Provide some eye equipment such as sunglasses, binoculars, magnifying glasses, and a monocle for the children to explore. Talk with the children about how things look when they use different eye equipment.

■ Problem-solving suggestion: Ask the children to do something with their eyes closed. For example, you might ask them to put the two halves of a plastic egg together or screw on the lid of a jar. Ask them how they are able to work with their eyes closed. Do they use their hands as a guide?

REFLECTION ON THE DAY
Ask the children to think of some things they used their eyes for today. Ask the "not yet talkers" to show you their eyes.

Ears

WORDS TO PRACTICE

earlobes	hear	soft
ears	listen	sounds
face	loud	
head	noise	

GETTING STARTED

- Ask the children to point to their ears. Ask questions to find out what they know about ears. "How do you use your *ears*?" "How many *ears* do you have?"
- Tell the children that today they will be learning about ways they use their *ears*.
- Read your favorite book about ears to the children or select a book from the Story Circle Suggestions below to check out of the library and read.

STORY CIRCLE SUGGESTIONS

- *The Elephants' Ears* by Catherine Chambers
- *Polar Bear, Polar Bear, What Do You Hear?* by Bill Martin, Jr. and Eric Carle

PREPARATION FOR THE "EARS" ACTIVITIES AND EXPERIENCES

- Make Animal Ears, Sound Canisters, Sound Shakers, and Bell Blocks (see pages 22-23).
- Gather animal photos.
- Make earrings, if necessary.
- Make Sound Cards (Appendix p. 467-468).

Language Enrichment Choices *

- Say "Where Do You Wear Your Ears?" with the children several times during the day. Ask the children to point to their ears. Invite them to look in a mirror and smile. Use your finger to trace a line from the corner of their mouths to their ears.

* Toddlers and twos present a wide range of developmental needs, abilities, and interests. For each learning area, select among the following activity and experience choices that are appropriate for the children in your care.

Where Do You Wear Your Ears?
Where do you wear your ears?
Underneath your hat?
Where do you wear your ears?
Yes ma'am, just like that.
Where do you wear your ears?
Say where, you sweet, sweet child.
Where do you wear your ears?
On both ends of your smile!

■ Say "Eye Winker" with the children. "How do we use our ears?" If you have studied eyes already, see who remembers how we use our eyes.

Eye Winker
Eye winker, (point to eye)
Tom Tinker, (touch ears)
Nose smeller, (touch nose)
Mouth eater, (touch mouth)
Chin chopper, (tap chin)
Chin chopper, (tap chin)
Chin chopper chin. (tap chin)

■ Use the word *ears* in sentences. For example, "Elephants have big *ears."*

■ Teach the children the American Sign Language sign for *ear* (Appendix p. 431).

Physical Development Choices

■ Sing and play a modified version of "One Elephant" that appears below. Show the children how to hold their hands by their ears to make large ears. Select one child to be the first elephant. As the children sing "One Elephant," walk with exaggerated steps around in a circle with the first elephant and flap your ears (hands). At the end of the first verse, select a second child to join you and the first child. Continue walking around flapping your ears as the children sing the song again, substituting "two elephants" for "one elephant."

One Elephant
One elephant went out to play.
Out on a spider's web one day.
He had such enormous fun,
He called for another elephant to come.

Two elephants...

- Sing "Do Your Ears Hang Low?" with the children. Show them how to march. Some will be able to do it, and others will enjoy trying. The same is true of the hand motions.

> **Do Your Ears Hang Low?**
> *Do your ears hang low?* (point to ears)
> *Do they wobble to and fro?* (move hands side to side)
> *Can you tie them in a knot?* (make tying motion)
> *Can you tie them in a bow?* (pretend to tie a bow)
> *Can you throw them over your shoulder* (toss hands over shoulder)
> *Like a Continental soldier?* (salute)
> *Do your ears hang low?* (point to ears)

Social and Emotional Development Choices

- Play "Washington Square" with each child. Ask the child to open her hand. Use your index finger to trace a square in her palm as you say the rhyme below. Point out that the part of the ear that you pull is called the earlobe.

> **Washington Square**
> *From here to there* (begin tracing square)
> *To Washington Square.*
> *When I get near*
> *I'll pull your ear.* (gently pull the child's earlobe)

- Display pictures of people on the wall in places where the children will notice. For young children, this may be next to a changing table. For older children, a good spot may be close to where they eat. Throughout the day, talk about the facial features of the people in the pictures. Pay particular attention to the ears.

Cognitive Development Choices

- Invite the children to try on Animal Ears. Cut out mouse ears, elephant ears, and rabbit ears from felt and attach them to headbands. Discuss the size and shapes of the ears. Provide a mirror so the children can look at themselves with the ears on. Provide pictures of animals. Use a marker to make a circle around the ears of the animals.

- Read the listening story, "Humpty's New Ears." Encourage the children to touch their ears when they hear the word ear. Point out that we use our ears for listening.

Humpty's New Ears

Humpty Dumpty sat on a wall,
Humpty Dumpty had a great fall,
And all the king's horses and all the king's men
Couldn't put Humpty back together again.

Humpty Dumpty started to cry,
Humpty said, "Oh, please, won't you try?"
His friend, Jack Horner, knew what to do.
He fixed Humpty Dumpty with his glue.

When Humpty Dumpty saw himself new,
He no longer felt all sad and blue,
He looked in the mirror and said with glee,
"Let's glue some ears to the side of me."

"A pair of ears will look real nice,
Like they do on elephants and mice,
One on the left, and one on the right,
Humpty with ears—what a sight!"

Jack made two ears, and then with his glue,
He carefully attached ear one and ear two.
Humpty looked in the mirror and said with glee,
"I'm a good-looking egg, don't you agree?"

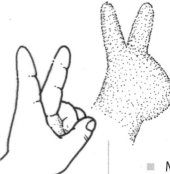

■ Make a rabbit shadow puppet on the wall. Hold up your index finger and middle finger to make a pair of ears. Put your ring finger, pinky, and thumb together to make the face. Place your hand between the wall and a light source, such as an overhead projector or flashlight. Wiggle the rabbit's ears for the children. Talk about shadows. Invite the children to make their own hand shadows on the wall.

■ Make Sound Canisters by putting items such as paper clips, washers, jingle bells, and buttons into film or pill canisters. Glue the lids on securely. Encourage the children to listen to the sounds inside the sound canisters. Discuss the sounds with the children. "Which canisters make loud sounds?" "Which make soft sounds?" "Which canisters make sounds that are similar to each other?"

■ Make Sound Shakers. Fill a half-liter clear soda bottle about one-quarter full with water. Fill a second bottle one-quarter full with white corn syrup. Glue the lids on securely. Encourage the children to shake the bottles. "What sounds do you hear?" "Which bottle makes the loudest sound?"

- Make Bell Blocks. Place jingle bells inside clean half-pint milk cartons. Square off the lids and tape it closed. Encourage the children to build towers with the "jingle blocks." Discuss the sounds the blocks make when they are wiggled. Discuss the sounds the blocks make when the towers fall down. "Is the sound loud?" "Is it soft?"

- Record sounds on a cassette tape and encourage the children to match the sounds to Sound Cards (Appendix p. 467-468). Discuss each sound with the children. "Which sounds are outdoor sounds and which are indoor sounds?" "Do any of the sounds hurt your ears?"

- Problem-solving suggestion: Hide a ticking clock or a music box when the children are not looking. Ask the children to find the item using only their ears. Invite the children to tell you how they found the item.

REFLECTION ON THE DAY
Ask the children to name things they know about their ears. Ask the "not yet talkers" to show you their ears and your ears.

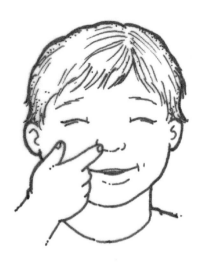

NOSE

WORDS TO PRACTICE

aroma	nose	smell
breathe	nostrils	sniff
face	odor	
head	scent	

GETTING STARTED

- Ask the children to show you their noses. Ask questions to find out what the children know about their noses. "Where is your *nose?*" "How many *noses* do you have?"
- Tell the children that today they will be learning about ways they use their *noses.*
- Read your favorite book about noses to the children or select a book from the Story Circle Suggestions below to check out of the library and read.

STORY CIRCLE SUGGESTIONS

- *Eyes, Nose, Fingers, Toes* by Judy Hindley
- *Frozen Noses* by Jan Carr
- *My Five Senses* by Aliki
- *The Nose Book* by Al Perkins

PREPARATION FOR THE "NOSE" ACTIVITIES AND EXPERIENCES

- Gather pictures of clowns and animals with distinct noses.
- Gather unbreakable mirrors.
- Make the Ring the Nose Game, Feed the Elephant Game, and the Smell Puffs (see p. 27-28).
- If desired, make a clown nose if an actual clown nose is not available (see p. 25).
- Mix the Scratch-and-Sniff paint and the Scented Playdough (see p. 28).

Language Enrichment Choices*

■ Show the children pictures of clowns and animals with distinct noses, such as elephants, dogs, horses, and pigs. Discuss the different kinds of noses and how the clowns and animals use them. You can make a clown nose by cutting a slit into a tennis ball and slipping it over your nose. If desired, paint it red. Ask the children to put their finger on their nose and on your nose.

■ Use the word *nose* in sentences. For example, "When I am cold, my *nose* gets red."

■ Sing "Gray Squirrel" with the children. Talk about the squirrel wrinkling his nose. "Can you wrinkle up your noses?"

Gray Squirrel
Gray squirrel, gray squirrel, (stand with hands on bent knees)
Swish your bushy tail. (wiggle your behind)
Gray squirrel, gray squirrel, (stand with hands on bent knees)
Swish your bushy tail. (wiggle your behind)
Wrinkle up your funny nose, (wrinkle nose)
Hold an acorn in your toes. (pinch index finger and thumb together)
Gray squirrel, gray squirrel, (stand with hands on bent knees)
Swish your busy tail. (wiggle your behind)

■ Say the nursery rhyme, "Sing a Song of Sixpence" with the children. Discuss the humor of the blackbird biting off the maid's nose.

Sing a Song of Sixpence
Sing a song of sixpence,
A pocket full of rye;
Four-and-twenty blackbirds
Baked in a pie!

When the pie was opened
The birds began to sing;
Wasn't that a dainty dish
To set before the king?

The king was in his counting-house,
Counting out his money;
The queen was in the parlor,
Eating bread and honey.

* Toddlers and twos present a wide range of developmental needs, abilities, and interests. For each learning area, select among the following activity and experience choices that are appropriate for the children in your care.

25

The maid was in the garden,
Hanging out the clothes;
When down came a blackbird
And snapped off her nose.

■ Sing "Little Skunk's Hole" to the tune of "Dixie." Discuss unpleasant smells. Can the children think of any unpleasant odors?

Little Skunk's Hole
Oh, I stuck my head
In the little skunk's hole,
And the little skunk said,
"Well, bless my soul!
Take it out! Take it out!
Take it out! Remove it!"

Oh, I didn't take it out,
And the little skunk said,
"If you don't take it out
You'll wish you had.
Take it out! Take it out!"
Phew! I removed it!

■ Teach the children the American Sign Language sign for *nose* (Appendix p. 436).

Physical Development Choices

■ Say the chant, "The Giant's Stomp" and do the actions. Discuss the giant using his nose to sniff out the unwanted visitor in his castle. The children may not be precise with their steps, but they will have a great time stomping like giants.

The Giant's Stomp
"Fee, Fi, Fo, Fum," growled the grumbling giant. (stomp, stomp)
"Fee, Fi, Fo, Fum," roared the restless giant. (stomp, stomp)
"Fee, Fi, Fo, Fum," grumbled the gigantic giant (stomp, stomp)
"Fee, Fi, Fo, Fum! Fee, Fi, Fo, Fum!" (stomp, stomp)

"I smell the feet of an Englishman!" (sniff, sniff) (Repeat 2 times)
Screamed the big, humongous giant. (sniff, sniff)

"Be he here or be he there, (shrug shoulders) (Repeat 2 times)
I'll find him anywhere!" (stomp, stomp)

■ Problem-solving suggestion: Place a ball in the middle of the floor and show the children how to move it by getting down into a crawling position and bumping it with their noses. How else can they move the ball?

■ Play another modified version of "One Elephant." Ask the children to pretend that their arms are elephant noses and that they are going to hold onto each other using their "elephant noses." At the end of each verse, add one child to the line of elephants. If you have a picture of an elephant, show it to the children and ask them to point out the elephant's nose.

One Elephant
One elephant went out to play (child walks in a circle swinging his arm
  as a trunk)
Out on a spider's web one day.
He had such enormous fun,
He called for another elephant to come. (child chooses another child
  to join and uses his arm as a nose to hold the new elephant "nose")

Two elephants...

■ Play the Ring the Nose Game. Cut out a big face from felt (or butcher paper) and place it in the middle of the floor. Put a service bell on the spot where the nose goes. Cover the bell with a piece of round felt. Give the children a beanbag to toss at the nose. Can they ring it?

Social and Emotional Development Choices

■ Ask each child to look individually into a mirror. Discuss their facial features, paying special attention to the nose. Say the rhyme, "I Look in the Mirror" with each child. Ask them to point to their nose on the mirror.

I Look in the Mirror by Pam Schiller
I look in the mirror and what do I see?
I see a funny face looking at me.
A scrunched up nose, twisted mouth, squinty eyes,
And two fuzzy eyebrows—what a surprise!
I look in the mirror and what do I do?
I giggle and laugh at the sight of me.

▪ Show the children how to give nose kisses. "How do the kisses feel?" "Are they gentle?" "What happens if your nose is cold when you give someone a nose kiss?"

Cognitive Development Choices

▪ Give the children Smell Puffs to explore. Scent powder puffs with extracts such as peppermint, vanilla, and lemon. "Which smells do you like best?"

▪ Let the children paint with Scratch-and-Sniff Paints. Mix flavored gelatin as directed, but use only half the amount of water called for. Use the mixture for paint. When it dries, children can scratch and sniff. Discuss the part of the body used for smelling.

▪ Give the children scented markers to draw with. Ask them to describe the aromas they smell. "Which scent do you like best?"

▪ Give the children Scented Playdough to play with. Add 1 teaspoon of scented extract (such as peppermint, lemon, and so on) to your favorite recipe for playdough. You can use scented massage oils in place of extract, if desired. Discuss the aromas.

▪ Encourage the children to play the Feed the Elephant Game. Paint a paper plate and an empty toilet paper tube with gray tempera paint. Cut out large gray ears from construction paper and glue them to the plate. Glue the toilet paper tube to the plate for a nose. Glue on a large pair of wiggle eyes. Ask the children to "feed" the elephant by dropping unshelled peanuts into his nose. Explain that the elephant uses his nose to put food into his mouth.

▪ Problem-solving suggestion: Hide a bag of strongly scented potpourri. Ask the children to find it by using their noses. Ask them how they knew when they were getting close to the potpourri.

REFLECTION ON THE DAY
Ask the children what they smelled with their noses today. Ask the "not yet talkers" to show you their noses and your nose.

Mouth

WORDS TO PRACTICE

chew	mouth	taste
eat	sing	teeth
face	smile	tongue
head	speak	
lips	talk	

GETTING STARTED

- Ask the children to show you their mouths. Ask questions to find out what the children know about their mouths. "How do you use your *mouth?*" "How many *mouths* do you have?"
- Tell the children that today they will be learning about how they use their *mouths*.
- Read your favorite book about mouths to the children or select a book from the Story Circle Suggestions below to check out of the library and read.

STORY CIRCLE SUGGESTIONS

- *Barnyard Banter* by Denise Fleming
- *Lunch* by Denise Fleming
- *Two Eyes, a Nose, and a Mouth* by Roberta Grobel Intrater
- *The Very Hungry Caterpillar* by Eric Carle

PREPARATION FOR "MOUTH" ACTIVITIES AND EXPERIENCES

- Ask families to bring in toothbrushes from home (Appendix p. 441).
- Gather mirrors and empty toilet paper tubes.
- Gather ingredients for Pizza Faces (see p. 33) and for Straw Paint (see p. 32).
- Cut out magazine pictures of faces.
- Get or make Bubble Solution.

physical me • Body parts

Language Enrichment Choices*

- Give each child an unbreakable mirror. Ask them to look at their mouths in the mirror. Suggest that they open their mouths and look at their teeth. Ask them to stick out their tongues. Talk about how we use our mouths.

- Use the word *mouth* in a sentence. For example, "My mother says not to chew with my *mouth* open."

- Sing "My Hand on My Head" with the children. You may want to focus only on the parts of the body you have talked about and leave other parts out of the song so it won't be too long.

   My Hand on My Head
   My hand on my head, (place hand on head)
   What have I here? (open arms, palms up)
   This is my topnotcher, (point to head)
   Mama, my dear.
   Topnotcher, topnotcher, (point to head again)
   Dickie, dickie, doo. (knock on head)
   That's what I learned in school. (shake index finger)
   Boom! Boom!

   My hand on my brow, (place hand on brow)
   What have I here? (open arms, palms up)
   This is my sweat boxer (point to forehead)
   Mama, my dear.
   Sweat boxer, topnotcher, (point to head and then forehead)
   Dickie, dickie, doo. (knock on head)
   That's what I learned in school. (shake index finger)
   Boom! Boom!

(continue adding body parts and suit hand motions to words)
   Eye...eye blinker
   Nose...nose blower
   Mouth...food grinder
   Chin...chin chopper
   Heart...chest ticker
   Stomach...breadbasket
   Knees...knee benders
   Toes...pedal pushers

* Toddlers and twos present a wide range of developmental needs, abilities, and interests. For each learning area, select among the following activity and experience choices that are appropriate for the children in your care.

▥ Sing "Catalina Magnalina" with the children again, adding the verse about Catalina's mouth. Discuss Catalina's funny teeth. Again, don't worry if the words are challenging for the children to learn. They will enjoy listening to you sing the funny words.

Catalina Magnalina
She had a peculiar name but she wasn't to blame.
She got it from her mother, who's the same, same, same.

Chorus: *Catalina Magnalina, Hootensteiner Bogentwiner*
            Hogan Logan Bogan was her name.

She had two peculiar eyes in her head,
One was purple and the other was red. (Chorus)

She had two peculiar teeth in her mouth,
One pointed north and the other pointed south. (Chorus)

▥ Teach the children the American Sign Language sign for *mouth* (Appendix p. 435).

Physical Development Choices

▥ Blow bubbles or invite the children to blow bubbles. Challenge them to keep the bubbles floating by blowing them back up into the air. If commercial bubbles are not available, make homemade Bubble Solution by mixing 1 teaspoon glycerin, $\frac{1}{2}$ cup liquid detergent, and $\frac{1}{2}$ cup water. It is best to make this mixture the night before you want to use it. Talk with the children about how they keep the bubbles afloat.

▥ Teach the children mouth movements such as blowing a kiss, clicking their tongue, and puffing their cheeks.

Social and Emotional Development Choices

▥ At lunchtime or snack time, sing "Chew, Chew, Chew Your Food" to the tune of "Row, Row, Row Your Boat" with the children. Discuss the role of the mouth in eating and the role of the teeth in breaking up our food. Remind the children that it is polite to chew food with their mouth closed.

Chew, Chew, Chew Your Food by Pam Schiller
Chew, chew, chew your food   *Drink, drink, drink your milk*
A little at a time.   *A little at a time.*
Chew it slow, chew it good,   *Drink it slow, drink it fast,*
Chew it to this rhyme.   *Drink it to this rhyme.*

■ Ask families to bring in a toothbrush for each child or ask a dentist to donate toothbrushes to the school. Show the children how to brush their teeth. You may want to make Homemade Toothpaste by mixing 1 tablespoon of baking soda with 2 or 3 drops of peppermint extract. Stir in a small amount of water to make a paste.

■ While the children are brushing, sing the song, "This Is the Way We Clean Our Teeth" to the tune of "The Mulberry Bush."

This Is the Way We Clean Our Teeth
This is the way we clean our teeth,
Clean our teeth, clean our teeth.
This is the way we clean our teeth
Every night and morning.

Take your brush, go up and down,
Up and down, up and down.
Take your brush, go up and down,
Every night and morning.

Don't forget both back and front,
Back and front, back and front,
Don't forget both back and front,
Every night and morning.

Cognitive Development Choices

■ Invite the children to Straw Paint. Cut straws in half. Place a small amount of liquid paint onto each child's paper. Encourage the children to use a straw to blow the paint across their paper to make designs. "How did you make the paint move?"
Safety Warning: Make sure the children blow OUT, not in. Cut a small slit or hole near the blowing end of the straw to prevent the children from sucking paint into their mouths.

■ Sing the "Raindrop Song" (on the next page) with the children. Discuss the humor of catching candy in our mouth. Talk about using our mouths for singing.

Raindrop Song
If all of the raindrops (wiggle fingers in the air)
Were lemon drops and gumdrops, (tap index finger against palm of other hand)
Oh, what a rain it would be. (wiggle fingers in the air)
I'd stand outside with my mouth open wide.
Ah-ah-ah-ah-ah-ah-ah-ah-ah-ah! (stand, looking up with mouth open)

If all of the snowflakes
Were candy bars and milkshakes,
Oh, what a snow it would be.
I'd stand outside with my mouth open wide.
Ah-ah-ah-ah-ah-ah-ah-ah-ah-ah!

▨ Give the children empty toilet paper tubes to use as megaphones. "Do your voices sound different when you use the megaphone?" Encourage the children to sing into their megaphones.

▨ Record children's voices and let them listen to the recording.

▨ Encourage the children to help make Pizza Faces. Give each child half of an English muffin. Brush on pizza sauce and make a face using olives for eyes and a piece of bell pepper for a smiling mouth. Toast the faces in a toaster oven for six to eight minutes (adults only). Ask the children to show you each of the facial features on their Pizza Face. "Which facial feature will you use to eat your Pizza Face?"

▨ Cut out pictures of foods and faces from magazines. Use them as discussion starters for conversations with the children about ways we use our mouths.

▨ Problem-solving suggestions:
1. Talk with the children about using words to tell people what they want. For example, they can use words to tell a friend that they don't want to play or they do want to play. Explain that they can also use words to tell a teacher that they want more juice or milk. Teach the children the American Sign Language signs for *stop* (Appendix p. 438) and *more* (Appendix p. 435). Explain how they can use these sign to help them be better understood.
2. Discuss solutions for not getting our mouths too full of food. For example, eating more slowly and taking smaller bites.

REFLECTION ON THE DAY
Ask children to think of ways they have used their mouths today. Ask the "not yet talkers" to show you their mouths and to smile.

Chin

WORDS TO PRACTICE

bottom   face

chin   head

GETTING STARTED

- Ask the children to point to their chins. Ask the children questions to find out what they know about their chins. "Where is your *chin*?" "How many *chins* do you have?"
- Tell the children that today they will be learning about *chins*.
- Read your favorite book about chins to the children or select a book from the Story Circle Suggestions below to check out of the library and read.

STORY CIRCLE SUGGESTIONS

- *Three Little Pigs* (traditional)
- *Whiskers and Rhymes* by Arnold Lobel

PREPARATION FOR "CHIN" ACTIVITIES AND EXPERIENCES

- Gather pictures of faces.
- Make "The Three Little Pigs" Glove Puppets (Appendix p. 449-452).
- Make whiskers for the children (see p. 37).

Language Enrichment Choices*

- Show the children pictures of faces and point out the chins. Ask each child to point to his chin and then to a friend's chin.

- Use the word *chin* in sentences. For example, "My *chin* moves up and down when I chew."

- Say "Eye Winker" with the children. Point out the "chin chopper."

*Toddlers and twos present a wide range of developmental needs, abilities, and interests. For each learning area, select among the following activity and experience choices that are appropriate for the children in your care.

Eye Winker
Eye winker, (point to eye)
Tom Tinker, (touch ears)
Nose smeller, (touch nose)
Mouth eater, (touch mouth)
Chin chopper, (tap chin)
Chin chopper, (tap chin)
Chin chopper chin. (tap chin)

- Sing "My Hand on My Head." Discuss some of the body parts mentioned in the song, particularly the chin.

My Hand on My Head
My hand on my head, (place hand on head)
What have I here? (open arms, palms up)
This is my topnotcher, (point to head)
Mama, my dear.
Topnotcher, topnotcher, (point to head again)
Dickie, dickie, doo. (knock on head)
That's what I learned in school. (shake index finger)
Boom! Boom!

My hand on my brow, (place hand on brow)
What have I here? (open arms, palms up)
This is my sweat boxer (point to forehead)
Mama, my dear.
Sweat boxer, topnotcher, (point to head and then forehead)
Dickie, dickie, doo. (knock on head)
That's what I learned in school. (shake index finger)
Boom! Boom!

(continue adding body parts and suit hand motions to words)
   Eye…eye blinker
   Nose…nose blower
   Mouth…food grinder
   Chin…chin chopper
   Heart…chest ticker

- Present the "The Three Little Pigs" glove puppet story (Appendix p. 449-452). Encourage the children to repeat the predictable lines with you, especially the line, "not by the hair of my chinny, chin, chin."

- Sing "Michael Finnegan." Discuss the location of Michael Finnegan's whiskers.

Michael Finnegan
There was an old man named Michael Finnegan.
He had whiskers on his chinnegan.
They fell out and then grew in again.
Poor old Michael Finnegan,
Begin again.

▪ Teach the children the American Sign Language sign for *chin* (Appendix p. 431).

Physical Development Choices

▪ Show the children how to hold a tennis ball under their chins. Can they turn in a circle while holding the ball? Can they walk across the room?

▪ Place a ball in the middle of the floor. Encourage the children to roll the ball across the floor using their chins. Show them how to get into a crawling position and use their chins to move the ball. "How else could you move the ball?"

Social and Emotional Development Choices

▪ Play "'Round the House" with each child. "Where does the little mousie live?"

'Round the House
'Round the house (use index finger to trace a circle on the child's open palm)
'Round the house
Goes the little mousie.
Up the stairs (walk index finger and middle finger up the child's arm)
Up the stairs
In his little housie. (tickle the child under his chin)

▪ Sing "Open, Shut Them" with the children. Suit the actions to the words. "Which parts of the body do the fingers walk to?"

Open, Shut Them
Open, shut them.
Open, shut them.
Give a little clap.

Open, shut them.
Open, shut them.
Put them in your lap.

Walk them, walk them, (walk fingers up chest to chin)
Walk them, walk them.
Way up to your chin.

Walk them, walk them, (walk fingers around face, but not into mouth)
Walk them, walk them,
But don't let them in.

▨ Ask the children to stand in front of an unbreakable full-length mirror with their backs to it. Show them how to spread their legs and then bend over and look at their face in the mirror through their legs. "Where is your chin now?"

Cognitive Development Choices

▨ Make whiskers for the children to wear on their chins. Cut a 6" paper plate into a quarter-moon shape. Glue on short pieces of yarn for whiskers. Poke a hole into each side of the plate and insert an 8" piece of elastic thread and tie it into a circle to make ear holders. Help the children attach the whiskers to their chins by placing the elastic thread over their ears.

▨ Invite the children to look at animal photos. "Do animals have chins?" "Do birds have chins?" "What about ducks?"

▨ Problem-solving suggestions:
1. Talk to the children about foods that drip on our chins, such as ice cream and applesauce. Ask the children to think about ways we can keep the foods from dripping (for example, eat slowly or pay attention) and ways to clean our chins if the foods do drip (such as wipe with a napkin, lick our chins with our tongues, and so on).
2. Ask the children to hold a small block in each hand. Offer them a third block and ask them to think of a way to use their chins to help them hold all three blocks at once.

REFLECTION ON THE DAY
Ask the children to tell you something they did with their chins today. Ask the "not yet talkers" to show you their chins and to point to your chin.

Hair

WORDS TO PRACTICE

barrettes	grow	redhead
blonde	hair	ribbons
braid	haircut	shampoo
brunette	pony tail or pig	wash
brush	tail	
comb	red-haired	

GETTING STARTED

▨ Ask the children to point to their hair. Ask the children questions to find out what they know about their hair. "Where is your *hair?*" "What color is it?" "Is it long?" "Is it short?'

▨ Tell the children that today they will be learning about *hair.*

▨ Read your favorite book about hair to the children or select a book from the Story Circle Suggestions below to check out of the library and read.

STORY CIRCLE SUGGESTIONS

▨ *Dandelion* by Don Freeman

▨ *Katy's First Haircut* by Gibbs Davis

▨ *Mop Top* by Don Freeman

▨ *Rapunzel* by the Brothers Grimm

PREPARATION FOR "HAIR" ACTIVITIES AND EXPERIENCES

▨ Gather items (brush and bucket) for Drop the Brush in the Bucket (see p. 39).

▨ Gather scrunchies.

▨ Prepare "The Lion's Haircut" puppet story (Appendix p. 505-506).

▨ Make Gel Bottles, Gel Bags, and Braided Wig (see p. 40).

Language Enrichment Choices*

▨ Say "My Head" with the children. Suit the actions to the words. Discuss hair. "How do we care for it?" "Who cuts it when it gets too long?"

* Toddlers and twos present a wide range of developmental needs, abilities, and interests. For each learning area, select among the following activity and experience choices that are appropriate for the children in your care.

My Head
This is the circle that is my head.
This is my mouth with which words are said.
These are my eyes with which I see.
This is my nose that is part of me.
This is the hair that grows on my head,
And this is my hat I wear on my head.

- Say "All By Myself" with the children. Discuss the things that toddlers are learning to do, such as putting on their shoes and brushing their hair.

All By Myself
These are things I can do,
All by myself. (point to self)
I can comb my hair and fasten my shoe, (point to hair and shoe)
All by myself. (point to self)
I can wash my hands and wash my face, (pretend to wash)
All by myself. (point to self)
I can put my toys and blocks in place, (pretend to put things away)
All by myself. (point to self)

- Use the word *hair* in sentences. For example, "I brush my *hair* each morning."

- Present the puppet story, "The Lion's Haircut" (Appendix p. 505-506) to the children. Discuss the different lengths of hair the children have. Talk about haircuts and also about caring for our hair.

- Teach the children the American Sign Language sign for *hair* (Appendix p. 433).

Physical Development Choices

- Teach the children how to pinch a hair clip. Let them put a hair clip in their hair if it is long enough. Provide small pompoms for them to pick up and transfer from one bowl to another. Talk with them about how hair clips are used.

- Play Drop the Brush (or barrette) in the Bucket. Provide a rubber bucket and a small hairbrush. Challenge the children to hold the brush chest high and drop it into the bucket below them. Discuss how barrettes are used.
  Safety Warning: Be certain all barrettes pass the choke tube test.

- Provide several scrunchies and an empty paper towel tube. Encourage the children to put the scrunchies on the paper towel tube. "How are scrunchies used for the hair?" Demonstrate how scrunchies are used.

Social and Emotional Development Choices

- Take some time with each child to brush her hair. Talk about the way her hair feels, its color, and its length.
  Safety Warning: Be sure to use a clean brush on each child. Sanitize the brush each time you use it on another child, or keep one brush for each child.

- Give the children some beauty supplies such as an old hair dryer with the cord removed, some curlers, a brush, hair clips, an unbreakable mirror, and empty shampoo and conditioner bottles and encourage them to explore the items. Older toddlers may be able to play beauty salon or barber shop. Talk about each item and how it is used to care for the hair.

Cognitive Development Choices

- Make a Braided Wig for the children to wear. Cut the foot off of a pair of pantyhose and cut vertical slits into each leg to make three sections. Braid the three sections of each leg. Children can put the waist part of the hose on their heads and the legs will hang like braids.

- Provide dolls with hair for the children to comb. Talk about gently combing the doll's hair.

- Give the children Gel Bottles to explore. Fill an empty, clear plastic soda bottle with clear hair gel. Add some sequins, buttons, or other interesting items and then securely glue the lid on the bottle. Encourage the children to observe the items in the bottles. "What happens when you wiggle the bottle?" "Roll the bottle?" "Turn the bottle upside down?" "What does hair gel do to our hair?" Describe the substance in the bottle and tell the children why people use it on their hair.

- Provide Gel Bags for the children to use to create designs. Put a cup of hair gel into a quart-size zipper-closure bag. Glue or tape the bag shut. Invite the children to use their index fingers to trace a design or to write their name in the bag. Tell the children about the substance inside the bag and describe why people put it on their hair.

- Give the children paper plates and construction paper cutouts to make a face. Provide pieces of yarn to use for hair.

■ Problem-solving suggestion:

1. Discuss ways to keep your hair out of your face when you are working on something. If possible, show the children some options such as headbands, rubber bands, ribbons, and barrettes.

2. Discuss ways to get tangles out of our hair (conditioner, brushes, and combs). Ask the children how it feels when someone combs tangles out of their hair.

3. Show the children pictures of animals that are covered with hair. Point out how animals use their hair for different purposes, such as keeping warm and keeping insects away.

REFLECTION ON THE DAY

Ask the children how we take care of our hair. Ask the "not yet talkers" to show you their hair and your hair.

Hands and Fingers

WORDS TO PRACTICE

clap	index finger	pointer
fingernails	knuckle	ring
fingers	middle finger	ring finger
fist	palm	snap
hands	pinky	thumb

GETTING STARTED

- Ask the children to show you their hands and fingers. Ask the children questions to find out what they know about hands and fingers. "How many *hands* do you have?" "Where are your *fingers?*" "What can you do with your *hands?*"
- Tell the children that today they will be learning about ways they use their *hands* and *fingers.*
- Read your favorite book about hands and fingers to the children or select a book from the Story Circle Suggestions below to check out of the library and read.

STORY CIRCLE SUGGESTIONS

- *Here Are My Hands* by Bill Martin, Jr.
- *These Hands* by Hope Lynn Price

PREPARATION FOR "HANDS AND FINGERS" ACTIVITIES AND EXPERIENCES

- Make Finger Puppets (Appendix p. 447-448).
- Make the Sensory Glove, Scarf Pull, Feely Box, and Tactile Cylinders (see p. 46-47).
- Make Goop or Gak (see p. 47).

Language Enrichment Choices*

- Say "These Little Hands of Mine" with the children. Discuss all the things hands can do.

* Toddlers and twos present a wide range of developmental needs, abilities, and interests. For each learning area, select among the following activity and experience choices that are appropriate for the children in your care.

These Little Hands of Mine by Pam Schiller
These little hands of mine
Can do things, oh so fine.
They can reach way out,
They can reach way up.
They can hold a crayon,
They can hold a cup.
They can open and close.
They can grab your nose.
These little hands of mine
Can do things, oh so fine.
They can tell what's cold,
They can tell what's hot.
They can tell what's sticky,
They can tell what's not.
They can say, "What's that?"
They can pet the cat.
They can give a big "Hi!"
They can wave good-bye.

- Discuss the parts of the hands: the fist, knuckles, fingernails, palms, and so on.

- Use sentences with the words *hands* and *fingers* in them. For example, "I have ten *fingers* on my *hands*."

- Say the rhyme, "Clap Your Hands" with the children. Suit the action to the words. Discuss the use of hands and fingers in the rhyme.

    Clap Your Hands
    Clap your hands 1-2-3.
    Clap your hands just like me.

    Wiggle your fingers 1-2-3.
    Wiggle your fingers just like me.

- Teach the children the American Sign Language sign for *hands* and *fingers* (Appendix p. 432-433). Review other signs the children have learned.

Physical Development Choices

- Sing "Open, Shut Them" (on the next page) with the children. Discuss the things that the hands do in the song and the things that the fingers do in the song.

Open, Shut Them
Open, shut them.
Open, shut them.
Give a little clap.

Open, shut them.
Open, shut them.
Put them in your lap.

Walk them, walk them, (walk fingers up chest to chin)
Walk them, walk them.
Way up to your chin.
Walk them, walk them, (walk fingers around face, but not into mouth)
Walk them, walk them,
But don't let them walk in.

- Encourage the children to do different things with their fingers. "Can you walk your fingers like a spider?" "Hop your fingers like a bunny?" "Can you make your fingers move like scissors?"

- Say "I Wiggle" with the children. This is a good review of other body parts as well as fingers.

I Wiggle
I wiggle, wiggle, wiggle my fingers. (wiggle fingers)
I wiggle, wiggle, wiggle my toes. (wiggle toes)
I wiggle, wiggle, wiggle my shoulders. (wiggle shoulders)
I wiggle, wiggle, wiggle my nose. (wiggle nose)
Now no more wiggles are left in me, (shake head)
I am sitting as still as still can be. (sit still)

- Encourage the children to toss beanbags at a service bell or into a basket. Discuss the importance of our hands for throwing and tossing.

Social and Emotional Development Choices

- Sing "Where Is Thumbkin?" with the children. The children will probably need your help finding the right fingers to hold up.

Where Is Thumbkin?
Where is Thumbkin? (hands behind back)
Where is Thumbkin?
Here I am. Here I am. (bring out right thumb, then left)

How are you today, sir? (bend right thumb)
Very well, I thank you. (bend left thumb)
Run away. Run away. (put right thumb behind back, then left thumb behind
 back)

Other verses:
  Where is Pointer?
  Where is Middle One?
  Where is Ring Finger?
  Where is Pinky?
  Where are all of them?

- Say "Five Fingers on Each Hand" with each child individually. Help the child
  point to each body part as it is mentioned. In the second verse, some children
  may be able to do the actions. Count each child's fingers.

  Five Fingers on Each Hand
  I have five fingers on each hand, (point to body parts as they are mentioned)
  Ten toes on my two feet.
  Two ears, two eyes,
  One nose, one mouth,
  With which to sweetly speak.

  My hands can clap, (clap)
  My feet can tap, (tap toe)
  My eyes can clearly see. (blink eyes)
  My ears can hear, (cup hand around ear)
  My nose can sniff, (sniff)
  My mouth can say I'm me. (point to self)

- Offer a snack of finger foods such as carrots, raisins, or celery sticks. Encourage
  the children to think about how their fingers help them pick up the food and
  their hands help them get the food to their mouths.

- Teach the children how to shake hands or how to give a high five. Discuss
  why people give high fives and why they shake hands. Encourage them to
  show these new hand signs to their families.

- Talk about individual fingers. "Do you suck your thumb, or do you know
  someone who sucks his/her thumb?" "Which finger is the one on which most
  people wear their rings?" "Which finger do we use to point at something?"
  "Which two fingers do we use to pick up small things?"

■ Teach the children the song "This Is the Way We Wash Our Hands" to the tune of "The Mulberry Bush." Suit actions to words. Talk about the importance of keeping our hands clean.

This Is the Way We Wash Our Hands

This is the way we wash our hands
Wash our hands, wash our hands.
This is the way we wash our hands
Several times each day.

(Other verses)
We put the soap in our hands…and then we go like this. (pretend to wash hands)
We wash between our fingers well…to get off all the dirt.
We use the water to rinse our hands…and then we go like this. (pretend to shake water from hands)
We use a towel to dry our hands…then we put it in the trash.

Cognitive Development Choices

■ Give the children Finger Puppets (Appendix p. 447-448) and encourage them to dance the puppets around. Photocopy the finger puppets, color them, cut them out, and laminate them.

■ Provide fingerpaint. Encourage the children to make handprints and fingerprints with the paint. Show them how to make prints with their knuckles by rolling them in the paint and then rolling them on their paper.

■ Provide a Sensory Glove for the children to explore. Fill a latex glove with GAK (see recipe on the following page) or with sand. Tie it off at the cuff and encourage the children to explore its weight and texture. Ask the children to describe how the glove feels and then point out that they must use their hands to get that information.

■ Give the children a Scarf Pull to enjoy. Tie several scarves together to make one long scarf. Cut a slit into an oatmeal container, stuff the scarves inside of the container, and pull one end of the scarf through the slit. Put the lid on the box. Encourage little ones to pull the scarves through the slit. Discuss how they removed the scarves from the box. Which body part did they use? Discuss the texture of the scarves. "Are they soft?" "Are they smooth?" How do you know how the scarves feel?"

▨ Make Goop or Gak for the children to explore. Discuss how the mixture feels. To make Goop, cook 2 cups salt and ½ cup water for four to five minutes. Remove from heat. Add 1 cup cornstarch and ½ cup water. Return to heat. Stir until the mixture thickens. Store in a zipper-closure bag or covered container. To make Gak, combine 2 cups glue, 1 ½ cups water, and food coloring in a bowl. In a larger bowl, dissolve 2 teaspoons Borax into 1 cup hot water. Slowly add the glue mixture to the Borax mixture. It will thicken quickly and will be difficult to mix. Mix well and drain off any excess water. Let the mixture stand for a few minutes, and then pour it into a shallow tray. Let dry for 10 minutes. Store in zipper-closure plastic bags. (It will keep for two to three weeks.)

▨ Provide mittens for the children to match. "When do we wear mittens?" Ask older children how mittens are different from gloves.

▨ Give the children Tactile Cylinders to explore. Discuss the texture of each cylinder. To make Tactile Cylinders, cover old-fashioned curlers with a textured fabric such as burlap, velvet, fur, satin, art foam, and felt. Use a hot glue gun (teachers only) for best results. Encourage the children to match cylinders that feel the same.

-Top View-

▨ Encourage the children to tear paper and glue it onto a piece of drawing paper to create a Torn Paper Collage. Ask them to describe their work, and then write their descriptions on the back of their collages.

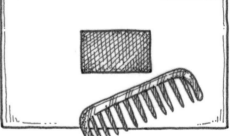

▨ Problem-solving suggestions:
1. Invite the children to explore a Feely Box. Cut a 2" to 3" hole into the lid of a shoebox and then tape the lid on the box. Place a small item that is easy to identify by touch (such as a brush or a comb) inside the box. Encourage the children to stick their hands through the hole to feel the object inside of the box. Can they identify the object in the box just by touching it?
2. Hide a large button in one of your hands. Hold both hands, fists closed, out in front of the children and encourage them to guess which hand is holding the button. Continue this activity several times, changing the object from hand to hand each time. Does anyone catch on to the pattern of the button moving from one hand to the other in an alternating rotation?

REFLECTION ON THE DAY

Ask the children to tell you something they used their hands or fingers for today. Ask the "not yet talkers" to show you their hands and then to show you their fingers.

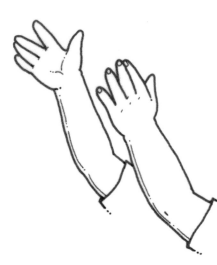

Arms

WORDS TO PRACTICE

armpits	hands	stretch
arms	reach	wrists
elbows	shoulders	

GETTING STARTED

- Ask the children to show you their arms. Ask questions to find out what children know about their arms. "How many *arms* do you have?" "How do you use them?"
- Tell the children that today they will be learning about ways they use their *arms*.
- Read your favorite book about arms to the children or select a book from the Story Circle Suggestions below to check out of the library and read.

STORY CIRCLE SUGGESTIONS

- *Guess How Much I Love You* by Sam McBratney
- *Hug* by Jez Alborough
- *In Grandmother's Arms* by Jayne Shelton
- *Into My Mother's Arms* by Sharon Jennings

PREPARATION FOR "ARMS" ACTIVITIES AND EXPERIENCES

- Make Wrist Bells (see p. 51) and Elastic Bands (see p. 49).
- Prepare "The Strange Visitor" prop story (Appendix p. 559).

Language Enrichment Choices*

- Say the chant, "My Eyes Can See" with the children. Point to the body parts as they are mentioned. Talk about using our arms for hugging. "How do hugs make you feel?"

*Toddlers and twos present a wide range of developmental needs, abilities, and interests. For each learning area, select among the following activity and experience choices that are appropriate for the children in your care.

My Eyes Can See
My eyes can see.
My mouth can talk.
My ears can hear.
My feet can walk.

My nose can sniff.
My teeth can chew.
My lids can flutter.
My arms hug you.

▪ Use sentences with the word *arms*. For example, "I swing my *arms* when I walk."

▪ Tell the children the story "The Strange Visitor" (Appendix p. 559). Discuss the stranger's long, long arms. Use this opportunity to discuss other body parts. You can shorten the story, if necessary, by having two body parts enter at the same time. For example, the feet and the legs can come in together instead of in two different episodes.

▪ Teach the children the American Sign Language signs for *arms* and *hug* (Appendix p. 430, 434). Review signs for hands and fingers.

Physical Development Choices

▪ Show the children how to use their arms to pretend to swim like a fish, fly like a bird, and flap like a chicken (arms tucked under armpits).

▪ Encourage the children to dance creatively with scarves or crepe paper streamers. "How do your arms help you move the streamers so beautifully?"

▪ Give the children Elastic Bands and encourage them to uses their arms and hands to stretch the bands. Elastic Bands are easy to make. Cut ¾" wide elastic into an 18" piece and stitch it into a circle.
Safety Warning: Make sure you supervise the use of the Elastic Bands so that children don't stretch the band and then pop themselves when they let go of it.

▪ Try one of the stretching chants on the next page. "How do your arms help you stretch?"

Stretching Fun
I stretch and stretch and find it fun (stretch)
To try to reach up to the sun. (reach hands up)
I bend and bend to touch the ground, (touch the ground)
Then I twist and twist around. (twist side to side)

Stretching Chant (suit actions to words)
Stretch to the windows,
Stretch to the door,
Stretch up to the ceiling,
And bend to the floor.

■ Sing "Johnny Works With One Hammer" with the children. Encourage them to hammer while you sing. Call attention to the role the arm plays in hammering.

Johnny Works With One Hammer
Johnny works with one hammer,
One hammer, one hammer. (make hammering motion with right hand)
Johnny works with one hammer,
Then he works with two.

Johnny works with two hammers… (motion with left and right hands)
Johnny works with three hammers… (motion with both hands and right foot)
Johnny works with four hammers… (motion with both hands and both feet)
Johnny works with five hammers… (motion with both hands and feet and with head)
Then he goes to bed.

Social and Emotional Development Choices

■ Throughout the day, call the children's attention whenever you see them using their arms to reach for something. "How would you get what you want if you could not reach with your arms?"

■ Discuss hugging. Teach children how to give themselves a hug. Talk about bear hugs. Encourage the children to give a friend a hug. "How do hugs make you feel?"

■ Play "London Bridge Is Falling Down" with the children. Point out how their arms enable them to play the game.

London Bridge Is Falling Down
London Bridge is falling down, falling down, falling down.
London Bridge is falling down,
My fair lady.

Take the key and lock her up, lock her up, lock her up.
Take the key and lock her up,
My fair lady.

(Repeat first verse.)

Cognitive Development Choices

▨ Provide old bracelets and watches for the children to use to decorate their arms. Ask them to describe the jewelry they choose to wear.

▨ Sew jingle bells to scrunchies to make Wrist Bells. Invite the children to wear the Wrist Bells while they play. "When do the bells make the loudest noise?"

▨ Provide beanbags to toss into a basket. "Can you toss without using your arms?"

▨ Provide dress-up clothing with arms, such as shirts and sweaters. Discuss the arms being too long.

▨ Problem-solving suggestions:
   1. Show toddlers how to put on their coats by laying the coats on the floor in front of them, putting their arms in the sleeves, and pulling the coats over their heads.
   2. Try placing an object just barely beyond the children's reach. Can the children find a way to get the item by using their arms?

REFLECTION ON THE DAY
Ask the children how they used their arms today. Ask the "not yet talkers" to show you their arms.

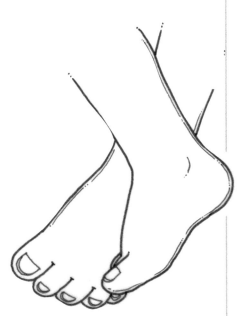

Feet and Toes

WORDS TO PRACTICE

big toe	little toe	toes
dance	run	walk
feet	tiptoe	
heel	toenails	

GETTING STARTED

- Ask the children to show you their feet and their toes. Ask the children questions to find out what they know about feet and toes. "How many *feet* do you have?" "Can you wiggle your *toes?*"
- Tell the children that today they will be learning about ways they use their *feet* and *toes.*
- Read your favorite book about feet and toes to the children or select a book from the Story Circle Suggestions below to check out of the library and read.

STORY CIRCLE SUGGESTIONS

- *Baby Dance* by Ann Taylor
- *The Foot Book* by Dr. Seuss
- *Hello Toes! Hello Feet!* by Ann Witford Paul

PREPARATION FOR "FEET AND TOES" ACTIVITIES AND EXPERIENCES

- Make a Tactile Walk (see p. 54).
- Cut out construction paper footprints and make a trail.

Language Enrichment Choices*

- Ask the children to take off their shoes and socks and look at their feet and toes. Ask them to wiggle their toes. Ask older twos how our toes are like our fingers.

- Use sentences with the words *feet* and *toes.* For example, "I have ten *toes* on my *feet.*"

* Toddlers and twos present a wide range of developmental needs, abilities, and interests. For each learning area, select among the following activity and experience choices that are appropriate for the children in your care.

▨ Say "Terrific Toes" with the children.

> **Terrific Toes**
> *I have such terrific toes,*
> *I take them with me wherever I goes.*
> *I have such fantastic feet.*
> *No matter what, they still smell sweet.*
> *Toes and feet and feet and toes.*
> *There's nothing else as fine as those.*

▨ Teach the children the American Sign Language sign for *feet* and *toes* (Appendix p. 432, 439).

Physical Development Choices

▨ Say the chant, "The Little Ants." Encourage the children to do the actions in the chant. Point out which body parts the children are using for each action. This is a follow-the-leader game. You can play it with children in a line and the leader in front, or with children in a circle and the leader in the middle. The leader makes up movements for each verse. With toddlers, you will be the leader.

> **The Little Ants**
> *Little ants are marching by,*
> *In a line that's mighty long.*
> *With a hip, hop, happy, hi,*
> *Won't you join my song?*
> *Little ants are marching on.*
>
> *Little ants are hopping by,*
> *In a line that's mighty long.*
> *With a hip, hop, happy, hi,*
> *Won't you join my song?*
> *Little ants are hopping on.*

Repeat the chant, replacing "Little ants are marching by" with one of the following:
> *Little ants are spinning by*
> *Little ants are dancing by*
> *Little ants are skating by*
> *Little ants are jumping by*
> *Little ants are waving by*

▨ Show the children how to stand on their toes. If they are able to stand on their toes, then show them how to walk on their toes. If they can walk on their toes, encourage them to try walking on a masking tape line on the floor on their toes.

■ Teach the children how to walk heel to toe. Encourage them to try walking heel to toe along a piece of masking tape place on the floor. "Is it harder or easier to walk this way?"

Social and Emotional Development Choices

■ Teach the children "This Little Piggy." Say the rhyme and wiggle the toes of one child at a time. See if the children can wiggle their own toes. Point out how special toes are.

This Little Piggy
This little piggy went to market, (wiggle big toe)
This little piggy stayed home, (wiggle second toe)
This little piggy had roast beef, (wiggle middle toe)
This little piggy had none, (wiggle fourth toe)
And this little piggy cried,
"Wee-wee-wee!" all the way home. (wiggle little toe)

■ Give the children a foot massage.

■ Sing "Walk, Walk, Walk Your Feet" to the tune of "Row, Row, Row Your Boat."

Walk, Walk, Walk Your Feet
Walk, walk, walk your feet
Everywhere you go.
Walk 'em fast, walk 'em slow,
Walk them heel to toe.

Cognitive Development Choices

■ Set up a Tactile Walk for the children. Cut pieces of fabric and papers with interesting textures into 10" squares and glue them to poster board. Place the squares in a pathway on the floor. Ask the children to remove their shoes and then walk along the path. Discuss the feel of the path under their feet. "Which squares are soft?" "Which squares are rough?" "Which square feels best to you?"

■ Cut out shoe prints from construction paper and make a trail. Invite the children to follow the trail.

■ Provide adult shoes for the children to put on and walk around in. Supervise this activity closely because it is easy for the children to get their feet tangled up when their shoes are too big. "How does it feel to walk in such large shoes?"

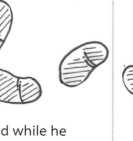

■ This is a messy activity, but it's worth the mess. Ask the children to remove their shoes and then step into a shallow tub of tempera paint. Help each child out of the paint and onto a 10' strip of butcher paper. Hold the child's hand while he walks the length of the paper leaving a trail of footprints behind. Put a tub of soapy water and a towel at the end of the paper. Label one of the child's footprints with his name. "How does the paint feel on your feet?" "Are your footprints large or small?" "Whose footprint is the largest? smallest?"

■ Ask the children to remove their shoes and socks. Challenge them to pick up a spool or a handkerchief with their toes. "Is it difficult to pick up things with your toes?"

■ Problem-solving suggestions:
   1. Provide a basket of shoes for the children to arrange in pairs. "How do you know which shoes match?'
   2. Provide a basket of socks for the children to match. "How do you know which socks go together?"

REFLECTION ON THE DAY
Ask the children to describe how they use their feet and toes. Ask the "not yet talkers" to show you their feet and then their toes.

Legs

WORDS TO PRACTICE

ankles	knees	walk
feet	legs	
jump	run	

GETTING READY

- Ask the children to show you their legs. Ask questions to find out what they know about legs. "How many *legs* do you have?" "What do you use your *legs* for?"
- Tell the children that today they will be learning about ways they use their *legs*.
- Read your favorite book about legs to the children or select a book from the Story Circle Suggestions below to check out of the library and read.

STORY CIRCLE SUGGESTIONS

- *Dance Baby* by Ann Taylor
- *Giraffes Can't Dance* by Giles Andreas
- *Skip to My Lou* by Nadine Bernard Wescott

PREPARATION FOR "LEGS" ACTIVITIES AND EXPERIENCES

- Gather pictures of animals.
- Make Finger Puppets (Appendix p. 447-448).
- Prepare "The Strange Visitor" prop story (Appendix p. 559-560).

Language Enrichment Choices*

- Show the children pictures of people and animals, pointing out the legs. "How are the people and animals using their legs in each picture?" Discuss the parts of the legs.

- Use the word *legs* in a sentence. For example, "Tiffany moves her *legs* fast when she is running."

* Toddlers and twos present a wide range of developmental needs, abilities, and interests. For each learning area, select among the following activity and experience choices that are appropriate for the children in your care.

- Invite the children to play Copycat. Ask them to copy the movements that you make. Use your legs to march, jump, take tiny steps, and kick. Point out how our legs help us with each movement.

- Teach the children the American Sign Language sign for *leg* (Appendix p. 434). Review the signs for *feet* and *toes*.

Physical Development Choices

- Play "Ring Around the Rosie." As you say the chant, hold hands and walk in a circle. Everyone falls down on the words "We all fall down." Ask the children what their legs do when they fall down.

  Ring Around the Rosie
  Ring around the rosie,
  Pocket full of posies.
  Ashes, ashes,
  We all fall down.

- Ask the children to sit in a circle with their legs spread and their feet touching. Encourage them to roll a ball back and forth. Make sure everyone has a turn.

- Place a line of masking tape on the floor. Ask the children to jump over the line. Or place a low candlestick (or use a block to represent a candlestick) on the floor and encourage the children to jump over it while saying the nursery rhyme, "Jack Be Nimble."

  Jack Be Nimble
  Jack be nimble,
  Jack be quick,
  Jack jump over the candlestick.

- Encourage the children to dance between a light source and the wall to create dancing shadows. Point out the movements of their legs.

Social and Emotional Development Choices

- Stand in front of a mirror with each child and point out all the body parts we have been talking about. Start with the legs. "How do you use each body part?"

- Take the children on a walk to visit another classroom. When you return to the classroom, discuss how your legs helped you get from one room to the other.

- Encourage the children to act out "Five Little Monkeys Jumping on the Bed." "How do your legs help you jump?"

    Five Little Monkeys Jumping on the Bed
    Five little monkeys jumping on the bed.
    One fell off and bumped her head.
    Mama called the doctor, and the doctor said,
    "No more monkeys jumping on the bed!"

    Repeat, subtracting a monkey each time.

Cognitive Development Choices

- Ask the children to sit on the floor. Blow bubbles and encourage the children to catch the bubbles they can reach. Then ask them to stand and chase the bubbles. Discuss the use of their legs to get them where they want to go.

- Give the children rubber animals to play with. While they are playing with the animals, talk about the legs on the animals. "How many legs does each animal have?" "Are the legs long? Short?"

- Give the children Finger Puppets (Appendix p. 447-448) to play with. Photocopy the Finger Puppet patterns, color them, and cut out them out. Reinforce the holes for the legs by placing masking tape around the leg openings on the backside of the puppets. Laminate. Discuss the legs on the puppets.

- Teach the children "Fido." It is sung to the tune of "Reuben, Reuben, I've Been Thinking." Encourage the children to sing the song while down on all fours, and then ask them to lift up to their knees when the song says, "If you hold his front legs up."

    Fido
    I have a little dog
    And his name is Fido.
    He is nothing but a pup.
    He can stand up on his hind legs
    If you hold his front legs up.

▪ Tell the children the story "The Strange Visitor" (Appendix p. 559-560). Discuss the stranger's long, long legs. Use this opportunity to review body parts. You can shorten the story, if necessary, by having two body parts arrive at the same time instead of individually.

▪ Problem-solving suggestions:
1. Ask the children to sit on the floor. Place an object just out of the reach of the children. Demonstrate using your leg to reach what you can't reach with your arms. Encourage the children to try it.
2. For older toddlers, you can sort pictures of animals (including humans) and insects into two groups: those with two legs and those with more than two legs.

REFLECTION ON THE DAY
Ask the children how they used their legs today. Ask the "not yet talkers" to show you their legs.

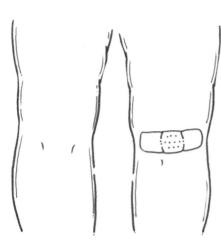

Knees and Elbows

WORDS TO PRACTICE

arms	elbows	legs
bend	joints	
body	knees	

GETTING READY

- Ask the children to show you their knees and their elbows. Ask questions to find out what they know about their knees and elbows. "How many *knees* do you have?" "Where are your *elbows?*"
- Tell the children that today they will be learning about ways they use their *knees* and *elbows*.
- Read your favorite book about knees and elbows to the children or select a book from the Story Circle Suggestions below to check out of the library and read.

STORY CIRCLE SUGGESTIONS

- *Giraffes Can't Dance* by Giles Andreas
- *Whose Knees Are These?* by Anna Ross

PREPARATION FOR "KNEES AND ELBOWS" ACTIVITIES AND EXPERIENCES

- Make a zigzag masking tape line on the floor.

Language Enrichment Choices*

- Show the children full body pictures of people whose knees and elbow are visible. Discuss how our elbows allow us to bend our arms. "How could you hug someone if you couldn't bend your arms?" Explain that our knees help us walk, run, bend, and so forth. "Has anyone ever skinned a knee?" "Has anyone ever skinned an elbow?"

*Toddlers and twos present a wide range of developmental needs, abilities, and interests. For each learning area, select among the following activity and experience choices that are appropriate for the children in your care.

- Sing "Head, Shoulders, Knees and Toes" with the children. Encourage them to point to the body part being named in the song. Change the words of the song to accommodate elbows by replacing the word "shoulders" with "elbows."

> **Head, Shoulders, Knees, and Toes**
> *Head, shoulders, knees, and toes,*
> *Knees and toes.*
> *Head, shoulders, knees, and toes,*
> *Knees and toes.*
> *And eyes and ears and mouth and nose.*
> *Head, shoulders, knees, and toes,*
> *Knees and toes!*

- Use the words *knees* and *elbows* in sentences. For example, "I fell down and skinned my *knees* and *elbows.*"

- Sing "Down by the Bay." Discuss the "bee with the sunburned knee." The words to this song will be challenging for toddlers to sing, but they will love the sound of the rhyming words and listening to you sing the song.

> **Down by the Bay**
> *Down by the bay where the watermelons grow,*
> *Back to my home I dare not go.*
> *For if I do my mother will say,*
> *"Did you ever see a bee with a sunburned knee?"*
> *Down by the bay.*

Additional verses:
> *"Did you ever see a pig dancing a jig?"*
> *"Did you ever see a whale with a polka dot tail?"*
> *"Did you ever see a bear combing his hair?"*

- Teach the children the American Sign Language sign for *knee* and *elbow* (Appendix p. 431, 434). Review the signs for *hand, fingers, toes,* and *feet.*

Physical Development Choices

- Provide a ball outdoors for kicking. Show little ones how to kick. A larger ball makes this an easier task for toddlers. (A beach ball works well.) Discuss how the knees are used when we kick.

■ Encourage the children to march like toy soldiers, keeping their arms and legs straight. Then ask them to march like majorettes, bending their knees and lifting them high. Point out the differences in how they move their legs for each type of march. "How do your knees help you march?"

■ Say the chant "Head, Shoulders, Baby" with the children. Demonstrate moving the body parts as they are named. You can substitute elbows for shoulders. Limit the verses to those that include the shoulders (elbows) and the knees.

Head, Shoulders, Baby
Head, shoulders, baby, 1, 2, 3.
Head, shoulders, baby, 1, 2, 3.
Head, shoulders, head, shoulders,
Head, shoulders, baby, 1, 2, 3.

Shoulders, hip, baby, 1, 2, 3.
Shoulders, hip, baby, 1, 2, 3.
Shoulders, hip, shoulders, hip,
Shoulders, hip, baby, 1, 2, 3.

Additional verses:

Hip, knees.	*Knees, hips.*
Knees, ankle.	*Hip, shoulders.*
Ankle, toes.	*Shoulders, head.*
Toes, ankle.	
Ankle, knees.	

■ Sing "If You're Happy and You Know It" with the children. Change the line, "Clap your hands" to "Slap your knees."

Social and Emotional Development Choices

■ Spend a few minutes alone with each child. Talk about hugging. Show them how to give themselves a hug. Give them one of your hugs. Discuss the role the elbows play in hugging.

■ Say "I Can, You Can" and encourage the children to mimic your motions.

I Can, You Can by Pam Schiller
I can put my hands up high. Can you?
I can wink my eye. Can you?
I can stick out my tongue. Can you?

I can nod my head. Can you?
I can kiss my toe. Can you?
I can pull on my ear. Can you?
I can wrinkle my nose. Can you?
I can give myself a great big hug. Can you?
And if I give my hug to you, will you give yours to me?

- Ask the children to form a line by hooking their elbows. Encourage them to try to walk. "Is it difficult to walk this way?" "Why?"

Cognitive Development Choices

- Collect a variety of cardboard boxes. Cut an arch into two sides of each box. Encourage the children to arrange the boxes from largest to smallest, connecting the arches, to make a tunnel. Invite the children to crawl through the tunnels. Discuss using knees for crawling. Discuss the sizes of the boxes.

- Give the children some Band-Aids or make some pretend Band-Aids using sticky notes. Encourage them to stick the Band-Aids on their knees. Encourage the children to talk about skinned knees they have had. "How did you hurt your knee?"

- Use masking tape to make a zigzag line on the floor. Encourage the children to crawl on the line. Crawl with them and point out how different things look when you are in a crawling position instead of walking. "Which things look bigger?" "Which things look smaller?"

- Have a jumping contest. "Can you jump without bending your knees?"

- Place pictures of animals in the science area for the children to see. Discuss the knees of the animals. "Do they look like your knees?"

- Problem-solving suggestion: Invite the children to put on their shoes without bending their arms or legs. "Does it work?" "Why?" "Why not?"

REFLECTION ON THE DAY
Ask the children to show you their knees and elbows.

Facial Expressions

WORDS TO PRACTICE

afraid	happy	surprised
angry	mad	
face	sad	

GETTING STARTED

- Tell the children that today they will be learning about how their faces show people when they are *happy, sad, surprised,* and/or *afraid.* Ask the children to show you a *happy* face.
- Read your favorite book about facial expressions to the children or select a book from the Story Circle Suggestions below to check out of the library and read.

STORY CIRCLE SUGGESTIONS

- *Baby Faces* by Margaret Miller
- *Copycat Faces* by Deborah Chancellor
- *I See Circles* by Mike Artell
- *If You're Happy and You Know It* by David Carter
- *When You're Mad and You Know It* by Elizabeth Crary

PREPARATION FOR "FACIAL EXPRESSIONS" ACTIVITIES AND EXPERIENCES

- Send a letter home to each family asking for a photograph of their child (Appendix p. 441).
- Make Me Blocks, Happy Face Puzzles, Happy and Sad Face Puppets, and/or Face Puzzles (see p. 67-68).
- Gather cookies, icing, and candies (or peanut butter and raisins) for cookie decorating.
- Cut out facial features from felt.
- Gather magazine photos of people whose faces show different emotions.

Language Enrichment Choices*

- Make faces that express happiness, sadness, fear, and surprise. Ask the children what your face says. If they don't know, tell them. Encourage the children to make faces. If you have some photographs that show facial expressions, show them to the children. Encourage them to talk about the pictures.

- Describe facial expression words in sentences. For example, "I smile when I am *happy*." "My mouth opens when I am *surprised*."

- Sing "If You're Happy and You Know It" with the children. Change all the verses to reflect emotions.

    If You're Happy and You Know It
    If you're happy and you know it, clap your hands. (smile, clap twice)
    If you're happy and you know it, clap your hands. (repeat)
    If you're happy and you know it, then your face will surely show it. (point to smiling face)
    If you're happy and you know it, clap your hands. (smile, clap twice)

Additional verses:
    Sad…say, "Boo-hoo." (look sad, say "boo-hoo", rub eyes)
    Excited…shout, "Hurray!" (look excited, raise hand)

- Teach the children the American Sign Language signs for *happy* and *sad* (Appendix p. 433, 437). Review other signs the children know.

Physical Development Choices

- Play some upbeat music and encourage the children to dance. Point out how music can make us feel happy. Change the music to a more somber tempo and let the children dance. Does the music change they way they dance? Does it change the way they feel? Does it change the expressions on their faces?

- Collect some magazine pictures of people with sad and happy facial expressions. Ask the children to stand in a circle. Explain to them that when you show them a happy face, they should clap their hands and when you show them a sad face, they should stomp their feet.

- Do the following action rhyme, "The Many Faces of Me," with the children. If the children can't make the faces by themselves, make the faces for them.

* Toddlers and twos present a wide range of developmental needs, abilities, and interests. For each learning area, select among the following activity and experience choices that are appropriate for the children in your care.

The Many Faces of Me
My mother says I wear many faces.
When I am happy, I look like this. (turn around and smile)
When I am mad, I look like this. (turn around and look angry)
When I am sad, I look like this. (turn around and look sad)
When I am confused, I look like this. (turn around and look confused)
When I daydream, I look like this. (turn and look pensive)
When my grandmother comes to visit, I look like this. (turn and smile)
When my brother knocks down my sand castle, I look like this. (turn and look angry)
When I can't have a second helping of ice cream, I look like this. (turn and look sad)
When I can't find my shoes, I look like this. (turn and look confused)
When I am thinking about summer vacation, I look like this. (turn and look pensive)
How many faces do you have? (point to another child)

Invite the children to think of other things that might cause them to make faces.

Social and Emotional Development Choices

■ Talk with the children individually. Ask them to show you a happy face. Ask them to tell you what makes them happy. Ask them to show you a sad face. "What makes you sad?"

■ Sit in front of a mirror with the children and make faces with them. Say the rhyme, "I Look in the Mirror" as you make happy, funny, and sad faces. Be expressive.

I Look in the Mirror by Pam Schiller
I look in the mirror
And what do I see?
I see a happy face
Smiling at me.

I look in the mirror   *I look in the mirror,*
And what do I see?   *And what do I see?*
I see a funny face   *I see a sad face*
Staring at me.   *Frowning at me.*

- Say "Inside Out" below for each child individually. Show them how to dance and glide with the words of the second verse.

Inside Out
When I'm happy on the inside,
It shows on the outside.
It is quite impossible, you see,
To hide what's inside of me.

When I am happy I dance,
I lift my feet and prance.
I twirl and spin and glide,
Because I am happy inside.

- Invite the children to help decorate Face Cookies. Put icing on sugar cookies and use small candies to make faces on the cookies. Encourage the children to talk about the expressions on their cookies before they eat them. As a healthier variation, you can use peanut butter and raisins instead of icing and candy. (Be sure to check for allergies.)

Cognitive Development Choices

- Invite the children to build with Me Blocks. Ask the families to provide photographs of the children. Make photocopies of the photographs. Cover small tissue boxes with colored paper and glue each child's photocopied photo on the side of a box. Cover the boxes with contact paper and place them in the block center for building. Ask the children to describe the facial expressions of their friends as they build with the blocks.

- Cut out a large circle from yellow construction paper or butcher paper. Draw a happy face on the circle. Laminate and cut the picture into puzzle pieces. Invite the children to work the Happy Face Puzzle.

- Make Face Puzzles for the children. Draw large faces on poster board or cut out faces from magazines and glue them onto poster board. Cut each face into a two- or three-piece puzzle. You can also use enlarged photocopies of children's photographs to make Face Puzzles. Talk about facial features after they complete the puzzles.

■ Make Happy and Sad Face Puppets for the children to play with. Draw a happy face on one side of a small paper plate and a sad face on the other side. Tape the plate to a tongue depressor. With older twos, play a game of Happy and Sad Face Choices. Provide a scenario and ask the children to show the side of the Happy and Sad Face Puppets that matches the way they feel about that scenario. For example, if you say, "Richele likes ice cream," the child might show you the happy face side of the puppet.

■ Provide magazines pictures of people whose facial expressions are obvious. Help the children sort the pictures by expressions. Discuss each expression.

■ Provide a flannel board and facial features cut from felt. Encourage the children to make faces on the flannel board.

■ Problem-solving suggestion: If you have an infant room available, take the older twos, one or two at a time, for a visit. Encourage them to try to make a baby smile. What strategies do they use?

REFLECTION ON THE DAY
Ask the children to show you happy and sad faces and to tell you something that makes them happy and something that makes them sad.

Which One?

BIG/LARGE	PURPLE
LITTLE/SMALL	ORANGE
SHORT	BLACK
LONG	WHITE
TALL	ROUND
ROUGH	CIRCLE
SMOOTH	SQUARE
SOFT	STRIPES
HARD	SUNNY
LOUD	CLOUDY
THIN/SKINNY	COLD
WIDE/FAT	HOT
RED	RAINY
YELLOW	WINDY
BLUE	ALIKE AND
GREEN	DIFFERENT

Big/Large

WORDS TO PRACTICE

big	large	size
bigger	larger	
biggest	largest	

GETTING STARTED

- Teach the children "The Elephant Song" to the tune of "I'm a Little Teapot." Discuss the size of the elephant.
- Tell the children that today they will be learning how the words *big* and *large* are used to describe things.

> **The Elephant Song**
> *Elephants walk in a line like this.* (children walk in a line)
> *They are terribly big and terribly fat.* (hold hands out to side)
> *They have big ears and great big toes,* (put hands up to ears and wave them)
> *And goodness gracious, what a nose!* (use arm to make a trunk)

- Read your favorite book about big things to the children or select a book from the Story Circle Suggestions below to check out of the library and read.

STORY CIRCLE SUGGESTIONS

- *Daisy: The Little Duck with the Big Feet* by Jane Simmons
- *Go Away, Big Green Monster* by Ed Emberley
- *I'm a Big Brother* by Joanna Cole

PREPARATION FOR "BIG/LARGE" ACTIVITIES AND EXPERIENCES

- Make Paper Bag Blocks (see p. 73).
- Make "The Great Big Pumpkin" flannel board story (Appendix p. 492-494).
- Gather pairs of large and small items.

Language Enrichment Choices*

- Show the children pairs of items that are particularly large, such as big books, big shoes, big boxes, and big balls. Discuss each item. Can the children think of other big things?

- Show the children pictures of big things, such as skyscrapers, planes, buses, mountains, and tall trees. Ask questions to find out what experiences the children have had with big things. "Who has flown in an airplane?" "Has anyone seen the mountains?"

- Make up a sentence that uses *big* as a descriptive word. For example, "This is a *big* ball."

- Present "The Great Big Pumpkin" (Appendix p. 492-494) flannel board story to the children. Discuss the size of the object that Little Bear and his friends found.

- Say "Five Huge Dinosaurs" with the children. Point out that the word huge is a word that means *really big*. Mention fictional dinosaurs that the children might know.

  Five Huge Dinosaurs
  Five huge dinosaurs dancing a jig. (dance five fingers)
  They rumble and grumble and stumble
  Because they are so big. (spread hands apart)

  Five huge dinosaurs floating a barge. (make a boat with hands)
  They jiggle and wiggle and juggle
  Because they are so large. (spread hands apart)

  Five huge dinosaurs singing a song. (put hands beside mouth)
  They bellow and holler and ramble
  Because they sing it wrong. (shake head no)

  Five huge dinosaurs taking a bow. (hold up five fingers and bow)
  They bobble and hobble and tumble
  Because they don't know how. (hold hands out to side)

  Five huge dinosaurs making me laugh. (hold tummy)
  They stumble when they dance— (dance fingers on arm)
  They jiggle when they float— (make boat with hands)
  They ramble when they sing— (place hands beside mouth)

*Toddlers and twos present a wide range of developmental needs, abilities, and interests. For each learning area, select among the following activity and experience choices that are appropriate for the children in your care.

They hobble when they bow— (bow)
But they can make me laugh! (hold tummy—shake head yes)

■ Teach the children the American Sign Language sign for *big* (Appendix p. 430).

Physical Development Choices

■ Invite the children to walk across the room taking big steps. "Does taking big steps help you get where you are going faster than regular steps?" Try it out.

■ Play a game of catch with a big ball (e.g., a beach ball). Say the rhyme, "Three Balls" below with the children. If you have an example of three balls (small, medium, and large), show them. "Which size ball is best for playing catch?" "Why?"

> **Three Balls**
> *A big ball,* (make a circle with your fingers)
> *A bigger ball,* (make a circle with you hands)
> *A great big ball I see.* (make a circle with your arms)
>
> *Are you ready to count them?*
>
> *One,* (make a circle with your fingers)
> *Two,* (make a circle with your hands)
> *Three.* (make a circle with your arms)

Social and Emotional Development Choices

■ Play So Big with each child. Take the child by the hands and ask, "How big is (Austin)? So big!" When you say, "So big," move Austin's arms to a fully extended position to demonstrate the word *big.*

■ Read a story from a big book during story time. Point out that a big book has big pictures, which makes it easy to see everything in the picture even when the child is not sitting close to it.

■ Teach the children "Big, Enormous Spider" which is a variation of "Itsy Bitsy Spider." Sing this song in a big, deep voice. Explain that *enormous* is a word that means *very big.*

Big, Enormous Spider
The big, enormous spider went up the waterspout.
Down came the rain and washed the spider out.
Up came the sun and dried up all the rain,
And the big, enormous spider went up the spout again.

Cognitive Development Choices

- Make Paper Bag Blocks. Fill large paper grocery bags ½ full with crumpled newspaper. Square off the tops of the bags and secure them with duct tape or masking tape to make a set of large blocks. Encourage the children to build with the big blocks. Ask them if the big blocks help them build big buildings or towers faster than they can with the regular blocks.

- Cut a large piece of butcher paper and hang it on a wall. Invite the children to draw on the big paper to make a big picture. How long does it take to cover all the space on the paper?

- Collect large paintbrushes and encourage the children to paint with them. How are the big brushes different from the regular brushes?

- Invite the children to dress up in big people clothing. How do the clothes feel?

- Take the children on a walk outdoors to look for big things, such as trees and buildings. Make a list of the things you find when you return to the room.

- Problem-solving suggestion: Give the children a large (five-pound) coffee can. Cover the opening of the can with duct tape, covering any rough edges. Provide several items that are larger and smaller than the opening of the can. Invite the children to sort the items according to what fits and what doesn't fit. "Which items are too large to fit through the hole?"

REFLECTION ON THE DAY
Ask the children to describe something that is big. Ask the "not yet talkers" to point to something that is big.

Little/Small

WORDS TO PRACTICE

little	smallest	tiny
small	tinier	
smaller	tiniest	

GETTING STARTED

- Tell the children that today they will be learning how the words *little* and *small* are used to describe things. Ask them to show you their little fingers. "Why is this finger called the *little* finger?"
- Read your favorite book about little things to the children or select a book from the Story Circle Suggestions below to check out of the library and read.

STORY CIRCLE SUGGESTIONS

- *Big Sister and Little Sister* by Charlotte Zolotow
- *Daisy: The Little Duck with the Big Feet* by Jane Simmons
- *Hey, Little Ant* by Phillip Hoose
- *In the Small, Small Pond* by Denise Fleming

*Toddlers and twos present a wide range of developmental needs, abilities, and interests. For each learning area, select among the following activity and experience choices that are appropriate for the children in your care.

PREPARATION FOR "LITTLE/SMALL" ACTIVITIES AND EXPERIENCES

- Make the "The Little Ants" flannel board piece (Appendix p. 507-510).
- Gather small items and photos of small things.
- Gather and cover small matchboxes.
- Get seeds and salt.

Language Enrichment Choices*

- Show the children small items such as a dime, a button, a pin, a hook and eye or snap, and a pebble. "Can you think of other small things?" Discuss each item.
  Safety Warning: Supervise closely to prevent children from putting small items into their mouths.

■ Make up a sentence about something little that the children can see. For example, "This is a *little* button."

■ Show the children pictures of little things such as ants, beads, buttons, and a mouse. "Have you seen any of these things?" Encourage them to describe their experiences if they are able.

■ Tell the children the story of "The Little Ants" (see below). Discuss the size of an ant. "Where do ants live?" "What happens if we accidentally step on an ant?" If you can catch an ant or two, put them in a jar for observation. Don't keep them too long—they have work to do outside!

■ Teach the children the American Sign Language sign for *little* (Appendix p. 434). Review the sign for *big*.

Physical Development Choices

■ Show the children how to take little steps. Take little steps across the room. Can the children think of a quicker way to cross the room?

■ Invite the children to play with small balls, such as Ping-Pong balls and super balls, outdoors. Talk with the children about how these balls bounce. "Are they easy to catch or difficult to catch?"

■ Encourage the children to move like "The Little Ants." Demonstrate the moves for each verse.

The Little Ants
Little ants are marching by,
In a line that's mighty long.
With a hip, hop, happy, hi,
Won't you join my song?
Little ants are marching on.

Little ants are hopping by,
In a line that's mighty long.
With a hip, hop, happy, hi,
Won't you join my song?
Little ants are hopping on.

THE COMPLETE RESOURCE BOOK FOR TODDLERS AND TWOS

Repeat the chant, replacing "Little ants are marching by" with one of the following:

Little ants are spinning by   Little ants are jumping by
Little ants are dancing by   Little ants are waving by
Little ants are skating by

Social and Emotional Development Choices

- Visit the infant room. Talk about how little/small the babies are. Remind the children that they used to be babies and discuss how they have grown. Remind them that they used to be as little as the children in the baby room. Encourage the children to compare their hands to one of the babies' hands.

- Ask the children to take off their shoes and show you their little toes. Talk about why they are referred to as *little*. Say "This Little Piggy" with the children.

   This Little Piggy
   This little piggy went to the market, (wiggle big toe)
   This little piggy stayed home, (wiggle second toe)
   This little piggy had roast beef, (wiggle middle toe)
   This little piggy had none, (wiggle fourth toe)
   And this little piggy cried, "Wee-wee-wee!" all the way home. (wiggle little toe)

Cognitive Development Choices

- Select small books from the library and invite the children to look through them. Tell the children that little books are easy to handle because they fit right into their hands.

- During outdoor playtime, hunt for little critters. You may want to take out a few magnifying glasses to assist in the hunt. Ask the children how they think little critters, such as ants, feel when people come near them. "Do you think they think we are giants?"

- Provide clothing items that are too small for the children to wear. Discuss the fact that the clothing is too little for them. If available, use doll clothes.

- Provide small plastic animals for the children to play with. Point out how easy it is to hold and move the small animals. "Can you name the animals?"
   Safety Warning: Make sure the children are closely supervised so that they don't put the animals in their mouths.

- Cover small, sliding matchboxes with contact paper and give one to each child. Help the children find something little enough (such as a piece of paper or ribbon) to fit into their boxes. Discuss the small items. "Will a block fit into the box?"
  Safety Warning: Make sure the items that the children find are not items that might present a choking hazard.

- Invite the children to make a Salt Painting. Place a couple of tablespoons of salt on a paper plate and rub a piece of chalk over it. The salt will pick up the color of the chalk. Place the colored salt into a shaker. Invite the children to make designs with glue and then sprinkle the salt over their design. Help the children look at the tiny grains of salt with a magnifying glass. Talk about how tiny grains of salt and sand are. "Can you pick up a single grain of salt?" "Why or why not?"

- Plant some tiny seeds. Discuss their size with the children. You may want to do the action rhyme "Tiny Seed" to help reinforce the concept of how the seeds grow into plants.

  Tiny Seed
  Tiny seed planted just right, (children tuck themselves into a ball)
  Not a breath of air, not a ray of light.
  Rain falls slowly to and fro,
  And now the seed begins to grow. (children begin to unfold)
  Slowly reaching for the light,
  With all its energy, all its might.
  The little seed's work is almost done,
  To grow up tall and face the sun. (children stand up tall with arms stretched out)

- Problem-solving suggestion: Talk with the children about things we can do with our clothes when they get too small for us. For example, we can give them to a friend who is smaller than we are or donate them to an organization that collects clothing for people who can't afford to buy clothes. We can also make things out of the clothes, such as a quilt or a puppet. Show the children a puppet that is made from a sock.

REFLECTION ON THE DAY
Ask the children to show you something little in the classroom.

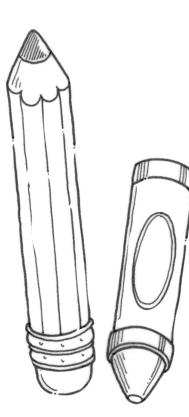

*Toddlers and twos present a wide range of developmental needs, abilities, and interests. For each learning area, select among the following activity and experience choices that are appropriate for the children in your care.

Short

WORDS TO PRACTICE

height	short	shortest
length	shorter	size

GETTING STARTED

- Tell the children that today they will be learning how the word *short* is used to describe things.
- Ask them to look around the room for something that is *short*.
- Read your favorite book about short things to the children or select a book from the Story Circle Suggestions below to check out of the library and read.

STORY CIRCLE SUGGESTIONS

- *Bunny's Tail* by Richard Powell
- *How Tall, How Short, How Faraway* by David Adler
- *I'm a Little Teapot* by Iza Trapani

PREPARATION FOR "SHORT" ACTIVITIES AND EXPERIENCES

- Gather animal pictures and items of things that come in different lengths.
- Get pretzels.
- Cut crepe paper steamers into 6" and 18" lengths.

Language Enrichment Choices*

- Ask two children to stand side by side. Point out that one child is shorter than the other. Is there another child who is shorter than the first child? Explain that the word *short* is used to describe someone or something, not to evaluate one thing as better than another.

- Collect pairs of items that come in different lengths, such as pencils, ribbons, sticks, glasses, straws, and flowers. Show the children the pairs and ask them to identify the shorter item in each pair.

- Say sentences using the word *short* to describe something in the room that the children can see. For example, "Madison's hair is *short*."

- Teach the children the American Sign Language sign for *short* (Appendix p. 437). Review other signs for descriptive words.

Physical Development Choices

- Encourage the children to jump over short blocks or short boxes. "Is it easy to make these jumps?" "Why?"

- Give each child a 6" piece of crepe paper to swirl as the children dance to classical music. Then give each child an 18" piece of crepe paper to dance with. "Which piece is more fun to swirl?"

Social and Emotional Development Choices

- Walk each child around the room in search of things that are shorter than she is. Discuss the sizes of the things you find.

- Say the rhyme "I Am Short" with each child. Talk with the children about growing taller as they grow older.

> **I Am Short** by Pam Schiller
> *I am short. You are tall.*
> *But I am growing day by day.*
> *Soon I won't be so small.*
> *And you may not seem quite so tall.*

- Sing "Where, Oh, Where Has My Little Dog Gone?" with the children. Discuss the dog's ears and tail. "Has anyone ever seen dogs with short ears?"

> **Where, Oh, Where Has My Little Dog Gone?**
> *Oh, where, oh, where has my little dog gone?*
> *Oh, where, oh, where can he be?*
> *With his ears cut short and his tail cut long,*
> *Oh, where, oh, where can he be?*

Cognitive Development Choices

■ Show the children pictures of animals. Help them sort the animals first by the length of their tails and then by the length of their ears. "Which animal do you like the best?" "Do any of the animals have ears or tails that seem too short?"

■ Give the children short straws (about 3" long) to drink from. "Do you like using the short straws?" "Why?"

■ Cut pretzel sticks in half and serve a snack of short pretzels. Discuss the size of the pretzels while the children are eating. "How can you make a short pretzel shorter?"

■ Collect the brushes from old powder and blush containers to use as paintbrushes. Give the children these short brushes to paint with. Talk about how using short brushes is different from using long brushes.

■ Encourage the children to build short buildings with blocks. Discuss the height of the buildings. "How can you make a short building shorter?"

■ Take a walk outdoors and look for short things. When you come back in, you might want to make a list of all the short things you found. "Which item was the shortest?"

■ Problem-solving suggestions:
  1. Attach pull toys to short strings. Discuss how difficult it is to pull the toys when the strings are short, especially while standing. "What can we do to make the strings longer?"
  2. Play Draw the Straw. Cut four straws into different lengths. Hold the straws in your fist. Ask the children to draw the straws from your hand and then measure them to find the shortest one.

REFLECTION ON THE DAY
Ask the children to show you something that is shorter than they are.

Long

WORDS TO PRACTICE

length	longer	size
long	longest	

GETTING STARTED

- Tell the children that today they will be learning how the word *long* is used to describe things.
- Beforehand, hang long streamers from the door jamb or ceiling. Point these out to the children. "Are some streamers *longer* than others?"
- Read your favorite book about long things to the children or select a book from the Story Circle Suggestions below to check out of the library and read.

STORY CIRCLE SUGGESTIONS

- *Hide and Snake* by Keith Baker
- *Kitty's Tail* by Richard Powell
- *Rapunzel* by the Brothers Grimm
- *Where, Oh, Where Has My Little Dog Gone?* by Iza Trapani

PREPARATION FOR "LONG" ACTIVITIES AND EXPERIENCES

- Hang long crepe paper streamers from the door jamb or from the ceiling.
- Get foot-long hot dogs and/or spaghetti.
- Make "The Strange Visitor" prop story (Appendix p. 559-560).
- Make a Braided Wig (see p. 83).
- Gather items that are long.

Language Enrichment Choices*

- Show the children a long piece of yarn that stretches all the way across the classroom. Ask the children to help you stretch it across the room. Discuss how long the yarn is. "What can you do with a long piece of yarn?"

*Toddlers and twos present a wide range of developmental needs, abilities, and interests. For each learning area, select among the following activity and experience choices that are appropriate for the children in your care.

- Collect other long things, such as a piece of rope, yardstick, piece of ribbon, giant straw, or strip of adding machine tape. Discuss the items and their length. Explain that the word *long* is used to describe the length of something.

- Use a sentence with the word *long* in it to describe something in the room that children can see. For example, "Gabrielle has *long* hair."

- Tell the children the prop story "The Strange Visitor" (see Appendix p. 559-560). Discuss the "Something's" long arms and legs.

- Teach the children the American Sign Language sign for *long* (Appendix p. 435).

Physical Development Choices

- Ask the children to join hands and make a long line. Then ask them to stretch their arms to make a longer line.

- Give the children long crepe paper streamers to use as they dance. "Are the long streamers easy to wave or difficult to wave?"

- Make a start line on the floor with masking tape or if outdoors, use a piece of yarn. Place a laundry basket far from the line. Encourage the children to stand at the start line and try to toss a beanbag into the basket. "Would it be easier to hit the target if the distance between the throw line and the target was not so long?"

- Place a long piece of masking tape on the floor and invite the children to walk the long line. Can they walk the long line with a beanbag on their heads?

Social and Emotional Development Choices

- Take off your shoes and compare your feet to the children's feet. Discuss how much longer your feet are compared to their feet.

- Sing "Where, Oh, Where Has My Little Dog Gone?" with the children. Discuss the length of the dog's tail. "Have you seen dogs with long tails?" "What about cats?"

Where, Oh, Where Has My Little Dog Gone?
Oh, where, oh, where has my little dog gone?
Oh, where, oh, where can he be?
With his ears cut short and his tail cut long,
Oh, where, oh, where can he be?

▣ Sing "Do Your Ears Hang Low?" with the children. Invite the children to think of some animals that have long ears. If available, show the children pictures of animals with long ears.

Do Your Ears Hang Low?
Do your ears hang low? (point to ears)
Do they wobble to and fro? (move hands side to side)
Can you tie them in a knot? (make tying motion)
Can you tie them in a bow? (pretend to tie a bow)
Can you throw them over your shoulder (toss hands over shoulder)
Like a Continental soldier? (salute)
Do your ears hang low? (point to ears)

Cognitive Development Choices

▣ Provide long brushes for the children to use to paint. "How does it feel to use a long brush?" Suggest that they paint long lines.

▣ Cut a piece of adding machine tape the same length as the table, roll it out, and ask the children to draw on it to make a long picture.

▣ Use blocks to make a long trail across the room. Encourage the children to walk the length of the trail. "Does it take a lot of steps?"

▣ Give the children a long Braided Wig to wear. Cut the feet off of a pair of pantyhose and slit each leg into three sections. Braid the legs. Children can put the waist part of the hose on their heads and the legs will hang in long braids. Discuss long braids. "Does anyone in the class have long braids?"

▣ Serve a foot-long hot dog for snack. Show the children the long hot dog. Ask them how they would hold such a long hot dog and still be able to eat it. Cut it into bite-sized pieces before you serve it.

83

- Help the children roll playdough into long snake shapes. "How can you make the snakes longer?"

- Problem-solving suggestions:
  1. Tie extremely long strings to pull toys. Discuss how difficult it is to pull the toys on such long strings. "What would make it easier to pull the toys?"
  Safety Warning: Long strings can pose a safety hazard. Remove long strings after this experience, and always supervise children closely while they are using any toy with long strings or cords.
  2. Serve spaghetti for lunch, without cutting the noodles. Encourage the children to try to eat the long noodles. Is it difficult? After everyone has tried eating long noodles, cut them into shorter lengths so the children will be able to eat them more easily.

REFLECTION ON THE DAY
Ask the children to show you something in the classroom that is long.

Tall

WORDS TO PRACTICE

height	tall	tallest
size	taller	

GETTING STARTED

- Ask everyone to stand up. Ask the children to point out the *tallest* person in the room.
- Tell the children that today they will be learning how the word *tall* is used to describe things.
- Read your favorite book about tall things to the children or select a book from the Story Circle Suggestions below to check out of the library and read.

STORY CIRCLE SUGGESTIONS

- *Giraffes Can't Dance* by Giles Andreae
- *How Tall, How Short, How Faraway* by David Adler
- *In the Tall, Tall Grass* by Denise Fleming
- *Rapunzel* by the Brothers Grimm

PREPARATION FOR "TALL" ACTIVITIES AND EXPERIENCES

- Make stilts.
- Gather fruit juice and parfait glasses.
- Gather pictures of tall things.
- Gather paper towel tubes.

Language Enrichment Choices*

- Show the children pictures of tall things, such as trees, skyscrapers, mountains, giraffes, and monuments. Discuss the height of the things in the pictures. "Has anyone ever seen any of these tall things?" Encourage them to discuss their experiences if they are able.

*Toddlers and twos present a wide range of developmental needs, abilities, and interests. For each learning area, select among the following activity and experience choices that are appropriate for the children in your care.

- Show the items that are tall, such as an empty wrapping paper tube, a yardstick, and a measuring tape. Discuss the height of each item.

- Use the word *tall* in several sentences. For example, "The door is *tall.*" "I am *taller* than you." "The tree on the playground is very *tall.*"

- Teach the children the American Sign Language sign for *tall* (Appendix p. 438).

Physical Development Choices

- Do "Sometimes" with the children. Discuss ways to make ourselves taller.

Sometimes
Sometimes I am tall, (stand tall)
Sometimes I am small. (crouch low)
Sometimes I am very, very tall. (stand on tiptoes)
Sometimes I am very, very small. (crouch and lower head)
Sometimes tall, (stand tall)
Sometimes small. (crouch down)
Sometimes neither tall or small. (stand normally)

- For older twos, make a pair of stilts. Poke two holes into the sides of two clean tuna-fish cans and run a 30" piece of twine through the holes in each can to make rope handles. Show the children how to put their feet on the cans and walk. Do this activity outside on the grass. It will be challenging for children because they must coordinate pulling up on the ropes as they lift their feet. They will have a good time trying to do this. Talk about how stilts make us taller.

- Say the chant, "The Giant's Stomp," and do the actions. Discuss the size of the giant. "How tall is he?" The children may not be precise with their steps, but they will have a great time stomping like giants.

The Giant's Stomp
"Fee, fi, fo, fum," growled the grumbling giant. (stomp, stomp)
"Fee, fi, fo, fum," roared the restless giant. (stomp, stomp)
"Fee, fi, fo, fum," grumbled the gigantic giant. (stomp, stomp)
"Fee, fi, fo, fum! Fee, fi, fo, fum!" (stomp, stomp)

"I smell the feet of an Englishman!" (sniff, sniff) (Repeat 2 times.)
Screamed the big, humongous giant. (sniff, sniff)

"Be he here or be he there, (shrug shoulders) (Repeat 2 times.)
I'll find him anywhere!" (stomp, stomp)

Social and Emotional Development Choices

▨ Say "I Measure Myself" with the children. Suit the actions to the words. Measure each of the children to see how tall they have grown.

I Measure Myself
I measure myself from my head to my toes,
I measure my arms, starting right by my nose.
I measure my legs, and I measure me all,
I measure to see if I'm growing tall.

▨ Sing "Where Is Thumbkin?" Discuss the "tall man." Ask the children to look at their hands and decide why the middle finger is called "tall man."

Where Is Thumbkin?
Where is Thumbkin? (hands behind back)
Where is Thumbkin?
Here I am. Here I am. (bring out right thumb, then left)
How are you today, sir? (bend right thumb)
Very well, I thank you. (bend left thumb)
Run away. Run away. (put right thumb behind back, then left thumb
    behind back)

Other verses:
Where is Pointer?
Where is Tall Man?
Where is Ring Finger?
Where is Pinky?

▨ Give each child a ride on your shoulders or a piggyback ride. Walk around the room talking about how things look different when you are taller.

Cognitive Development Choices

▨ Invite the children to make a sculpture using paper towel tubes. Discuss how tall the tubes are.

▨ Encourage the children to build tall towers with blocks or boxes. "What makes the towers tall?"

- Take a walk outdoors to look for tall things. When you return to the classroom, make a list of the tall things that you found.

- Bring the children outdoors to stand in the sun and create a shadow. Show them how to make their shadow grow tall. You can also do this activity indoors by using a light source.

- Place easel paper on the easel in a vertical position and invite the children to paint a tall picture. Encourage the children to describe their picture.

- Cut off a 4' piece of butcher paper, and then cut the piece in half to make a long strip. Turn the strip vertically for the children and invite them to paint a tall picture.

- Serve a fruit juice drink in tall, plastic parfait glasses. Discuss the tall drink.

- Problem-solving suggestion: Help the children stack balls of playdough to make a tall snowman. Discuss ways to make the snowman tall. "How can you keep him from falling down?"

REFLECTION ON THE DAY
Have the children show you something tall.

Rough

WORDS TO PRACTICE

feel	rougher	texture
rough	roughest	touch

GETTING STARTED

- Ask the children to feel the texture of their clothing or the bottoms of their shoes. "Is anyone wearing something that feels *rough*?"
- Tell the children that today they will be learning how the word *rough* is used to describe things.
- Read your favorite book about textures to the children or select a book from the Story Circle Suggestions below to check out of the library and read.

STORY CIRCLE SUGGESTIONS

- *Is It Rough? Is It Smooth? Is It Shiny?* by Tana Hoban
- *My Very First Book of Touch* by Eric Carle
- *Rough Road—Textured Shapes* by Kate Davis
- *Whose Back Is Bumpy?* by Kate Davis

PREPARATION FOR "ROUGH" ACTIVITIES AND EXPERIENCES

- Make a Tactile Path (see next page).
- Gather a variety of items and balls with rough surfaces.
- Gather ingredients and prepare Sand Paint (see p. 91).

Language Enrichment Choices*

- Show the children several items with rough surfaces, such as pieces of sandpaper, burlap, carpet, brick, and tree bark. Let the children touch each item as you discuss the way the surfaces feel. Explain that the word *rough* is used to describe the way something feels.

*Toddlers and twos present a wide range of developmental needs, abilities, and interests. For each learning area, select among the following activity and experience choices that are appropriate for the children in your care.

▓ Use the word *rough* in sentences. For example, "The sidewalk is *rough*."

▓ Teach the children the American Sign Language sign for *rough* (Appendix p. 437). Practice other signs the children have learned.

Physical Development Choices

▓ Invite the children to take off their shoes and walk along a Tactile Path made of four or five rough-textured squares. Cut four or five pieces of poster board into 9" x 12" sheets. Apply glue to one square and then coat it with sand. Glue a piece of burlap, sandpaper, and rough textured wallpaper to the other squares. You can make the walk as long as you want, depending on the materials you have available to create different rough textures. Discuss the feel of each square on children's feet as they step on the squares. "Which square feels the best?"

▓ Invite the children to play with balls that have rough textures, such as basketballs, footballs, and tennis balls. Discuss the texture of the balls and how the texture plays a role in making the ball easier to hold on to, especially if your hands are sweaty or wet.

▓ Encourage the children to play the sand blocks or sticks from the rhythm band set. Discuss the rough texture of these instruments. "How do the rough textures help create the sound?"

Social and Emotional Development Choices

▓ Read *Pat the Bunny* by Dorothy Kunhardt to the children individually. Discuss the various textures in the book. Encourage the children to help you find the rough textures. If you don't have a copy of the book, then look through a wallpaper sample book to find some rough-textured paper.

▓ If there is a male teacher in your school, ask him to let the children feel the texture of his beard. Discuss how men's faces can feel rough when they do not shave.

▓ Just before serving a cup of pudding, stir in some crumbled graham cracker crumbs. Ask the children to describe the texture of the pudding as they are eating it. "Do you like the texture?"

Cognitive Development Choices

- Encourage the children to make sandpaper rubbings. Show the children how to place different textures of sandpaper under drawing paper and rub over the paper with pencils. "What makes the picture appear?" Try putting other rough surfaces such as bark or bricks under the paper.

- Place salt into playdough to create rough-textured dough. Ask the children to describe the dough as they play with it. "How does the playdough feel?"

- Add sand or sawdust to fingerpaint to create a rough-textured paint.

- Take the children outdoors to draw on the sidewalk with chalk. Discuss what happens to the chalk when it is used on the rough sidewalk.

- Invite the children to draw or paint on rough-textured pieces of wallpaper. "How do your pictures look on the rough textures?"

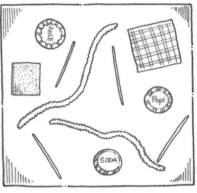

- Make a rough-textured collage by providing bottle caps, pipe cleaners, toothpicks and so forth to glue to a piece of paper. After the glue has dried, encourage the children to rub their hands across their collage and, if able, describe how it feels.

- Encourage the children to investigate items with rough surfaces, such as pinecones, sandpaper, and bark, with a magnifying glass. "What do you see?"

- Invite the children to make Sand Paintings. Color ¼ cup of sand (or salt) by adding ¼ teaspoon powdered tempera to it. Pour the sand into a saltshaker. Make several colors of sand. Invite the children to paint a glue design on a piece of paper and then shake the colored sand over their design. Tap off excess sand and let it dry. Ask the children to feel the surface of their design after it has dried. "How does it feel?"

- Problem-solving suggestion: Place a shallow pan of water on the table. Let the children help you think of ways to make the water get rough. For example, they might stir it with their hands, fan it with a book, or wiggle the tub. Discuss the ways they find to make the water rough. "Has anyone ever been to the beach?" "What did the water look like there?"

REFLECTION ON THE DAY
Ask the children to tell you about something that is rough. Ask the "not yet talkers" to point to something rough.

Smooth

WORDS TO PRACTICE

feel	smoother	texture
smooth	smoothest	touch

GETTING STARTED

- Ask the children to feel the texture of their clothing or the bottoms of their shoes. "Does anyone have on something that feels *smooth?*"
- Tell the children that today they will be learning how the word *smooth* is used to describe things.
- Read your favorite book about textures to the children or select a book from the Story Circle Suggestions below to check out of the library and read.

STORY CIRCLE SUGGESTIONS

- *Is It Rough? Is It Smooth? Is It Shiny?* by Tana Hoban
- *Pat the Bunny* by Dorothy Kunhardt

PREPARATION FOR "SMOOTH" ACTIVITIES AND EXPERIENCES

- Prepare the Tactile Path on the next page.
- Make Gak and Gelatin Jigglers (see p. 94).
- Make a Feely Box and Tactile Cylinders (see p. 94).

Language Enrichment Choices*

- Show the children several items with smooth surfaces, such as pieces of fabric (silk, satin, vinyl, and cotton), a glass, a plate, and a book. Let the children touch each item as you discuss the way the surfaces feel. Ask the children to rub their cheeks. Point out how smooth their skin feels. "Has anybody seen a man's face that needed a shave?" "What did his face look like after a shave?"

*Toddlers and twos present a wide range of developmental needs, abilities, and interests. For each learning area, select among the following activity and experience choices that are appropriate for the children in your care.

■ Use the word *smooth* in sentences. For example, "Evan's skin is *smooth*."

■ Teach the children the American Sign Language sign for *smooth* (Appendix p. 437). Practice other signs the children have learned.

Physical Development Choices

■ Give the children balls with smooth surfaces, such as ping-pong balls and volleyballs, to play with. Discuss the smooth surfaces of the balls.

■ Make a Tactile Path. Invite the children to take off their shoes and walk along a path of four or five smooth-textured squares. Cut four or five pieces of poster board into 9" x 12" sheets. Glue a piece of satin, vinyl, and smooth-textured wallpaper to the other squares. You can make the walk as long as you want, depending on the materials you have available to create different smooth textures. Discuss the feel of each square on children's feet as they step on them. "Which square feels the best?"

Social and Emotional Development Choices

■ Say the poem, "Smooth Things" to each child. Help them think of smooth things that they like to touch.

> **Smooth Things** by Pam Schiller
> *I love smooth things to touch and feel*
> *On my cheek, my hand, my heel.*
> *A marble, a table, a cup, and a dish,*
> *A baby kitten but not a fish.*
> *Mud, paint, clay, and dough,*
> *Books and blocks and fabric to sew.*
> *I love smooth things to touch and feel*
> *On my cheek, my hand, and my heel.*

■ Read *Pat the Bunny* by Dorothy Kunhardt to the children individually. Discuss the various textures in the book. Encourage the children to help you find the smooth textures.

■ Put some body lotion on children's hands and arms to make them smooth.

- Make Gelatin Jigglers by mixing flavored gelatin with half the amount of water suggested on the box. Let it congeal. Cut the gelatin into squares or use cookie cutters to cut out shapes. Encourage the children to pick them up and eat them. Discuss the texture of the Jigglers. Say the poem, "Gelatin Jigglers" below as the children eat their Jigglers.

> **Gelatin Jigglers**
> *Gelatin Jigglers on my tray.*   *Wiggle, giggle, smooth, and cool.*
> *They make me laugh and want to play.*   *What a treat to eat at school.*

Cognitive Development Choices

- Give the children Gak to play with. Combine 2 cups of glue, 1½ cup of water, and several drops of food coloring. Dissolve 2 teaspoons of Borax into 1 cup of hot water. Add the glue mixture to the Borax. It will thicken quickly. Drain off any excess water and store it in zipper-closure plastic bags. As the children play with the Gak, discuss its smooth texture.

- Invite the children to explore a Feely Box. Line two or three empty boxes with fabrics that have a smooth texture. Cut a 2" to 3" hole in each box lid, and then tape the lids to the boxes. Encourage the children to stick their hands into each box to feel the inside of the box.

- Give the children Tactile Cylinders to explore. Glue smooth fabric, such as velvet, fur, and satin, around old-fashioned curlers. Use a hot glue gun (adult only) for best results. Make two of each type of fabric. Encourage the children to match cylinders that feel the same.

- Invite the children to make mud pies. Discuss the texture of the mud. Give the children smooth-textured items (such as stones, seeds, and leaves) to decorate their pies.
  Safety Warning: Be sure that children don't put small items in their mouths.

- Problem-solving suggestion: Invite the children to help you sand a piece of wood to make it smooth. Call attention to the way the rubbing makes the wood feel smooth and warm.

REFLECTION ON THE DAY
Ask the children to describe something in the classroom that is smooth. Ask the "not yet talkers" to point to something that is smooth.

Soft

WORDS TO PRACTICE

feel	softest
soft	texture
softer	touch

GETTING STARTED

- Ask the children to touch their cheeks. "Are your cheeks *soft?*" Ask questions to find out what the children know about the word *soft*.
- Tell the children that today they will be learning how the word *soft* is used to describe things.
- Read your favorite book about textures to the children or select a book from the Story Circle Suggestions below to check out of the library and read.

STORY CIRCLE SUGGESTIONS

- *It Feels Like Fun: A Bumpy, Silky, Smooth, Soft, Furry Book* by Ellen Weiss
- *Pat the Bunny* by Dorothy Kunhardt

PREPARATION FOR "SOFT" ACTIVITIES AND EXPERIENCES

- Make Tactile Box (see p. 97), Paper Bag Blocks (see p. 98), and Ball and Scoop Game on the next page.
- Gather soft items, pantyhose, and pompoms.

Language Enrichment Choices*

- Place several soft items such as cotton, foam, velvet, feathers, and fur inside a soft bag. Take the items out one at a time and pass them around for the children to feel. Discuss the feel of each item.

- Use the word *soft* in sentences. For example, "My mommy's hands are *soft.*"

*Toddlers and twos present a wide range of developmental needs, abilities, and interests. For each learning area, select among the following activity and experience choices that are appropriate for the children in your care.

- Teach the children the American Sign Language sign for *soft* (Appendix p. 438). Practice other signs the children have learned.

- Whisper into the children's ears. Talk about how the sound of a whisper is soft. Invite the children to whisper.

Physical Development Choices

- Play Pass the Cotton Ball. Ask the children to sit in a circle. Give one of the children a cotton ball and ask him to pass the cotton ball around the circle when you start playing some music. When the music stops, the child left holding the cotton ball must stand up and turn around. Start the game again by letting the child who is holding the cotton ball start it around the circle again. Encourage the children to describe how the cotton ball feels. "Is it soft?"

- Invite the children to play the Ball and Scoop Game. Make soft balls by cutting off the feet of a pair of pantyhose and stuffing each foot with the leg and panty portions of the hose. When stuffed, tie off or stitch the feet to make two balls. Using an empty, clean, plastic bleach or similar type bottle, cut off the bottom and half of the sides (up to the handle) to make a scoop. Teach the children how to catch soft balls in the scoop.

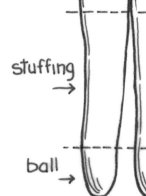

stuffing →

ball →

discard

scoop

Secure with stitching

- Play Tummy Ticklers. Ask the children to lie on the floor on their backs with their heads on a friend's tummy. Make a continuous line of friends. Do something silly to make the children start laughing. "What is making your heads jiggle?" This activity should cause contagious laughter. "Is your friend's tummy soft?"

Social and Emotional Development Choices

▨ Say the poem, "Soft Touches" to the children. Discuss the items in the poem and help children think of other soft things.

Soft Touches by Pam Schiller
I love soft things
Very much.
Soft things to feel,
Soft things to touch.

A feather pillow,
A furry muff,
A baby's cheek,
A powder puff.

My kitten's fur,
A gentle breeze,
A bedtime kiss,
I love all these.

▨ Play some lullaby music at a low volume. Discuss this type of music as *soft music*.

▨ Talk with the children about body parts that are soft, such as their cheeks, hands, and tummies.

Cognitive Development Choices

▨ Provide a Tactile Box with soft items inside for the children to explore. Cut a hand-size hole into the top or side of a shoebox. Fill the box with two or three soft items that are easily identified by touching. Invite the children to stick their hand through the hole in the box and identify the object inside by feeling it. Ask them to describe the things they feel.

▨ Using a sheet, make a tent and fill it with pillows. Encourage the children to read books inside their soft tent. "Is your reading area 'comfy'?"

▨ Invite the children to toss pompoms into a bucket. "Do the pompoms make a noise when they land?" "Why or why not?"

- Place several small, soft things such as a feather, tissue, cotton ball, and pompom on the table. Let the children explore them. "Are they light?" "Are they heavy?" "Can you make them move by blowing on them?" "Which items make a sound when dropped on the table or floor?"

- Make Paper Bag Blocks. Stuff small lunch sacks ¾ full with crumpled newspaper, square off the tops, and tape them shut with duct tape or masking tape. Encourage the children to build with these soft blocks. "What happens if the blocks fall on top of you?" "Do they hurt?" "Why not?"

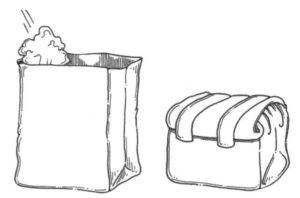

- Provide a spray bottle of water and a cookie sheet. Set the spray nozzle on a mist setting and ask the children to spray the water on the cookie sheet. "What kind of sound does the water make?"

- Problem-solving suggestion: Place a soft feather on the table. Ask the children to think of a way to get the feather off the table without touching it. "Is the feather difficult or easy to move?"

REFLECTION ON THE DAY
Have the children show you soft things in the room.

Hard

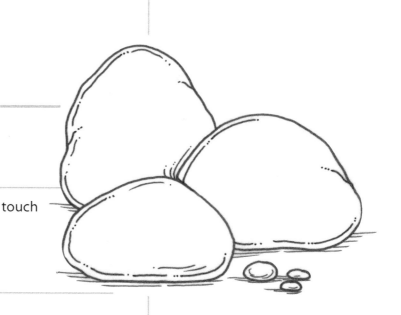

WORDS TO PRACTICE

feel	hardest	touch
hard	hardness	
harder	texture	

GETTING READY

- Ask the children to show you something *hard* on their bodies. This might be clothing (such as the sole of a shoe) or a body part (such as a fingernail).
- Tell the children that today they will be learning how the word *hard* is used to describe things.
- Read your favorite book about textures to the children or select a book from the Story Circle Suggestions below to check out of the library and read.

STORY CIRCLE SUGGESTIONS

- *Brush Your Teeth, Please* by Leslie McGuire
- *Looking at Rocks* by Jennifer Drussling

PREPARATION FOR "HARD" ACTIVITIES AND EXPERIENCES

- Prepare the "Henny-Penny" flannel board story (Appendix p. 498-501).
- Make Baker's Clay (see p. 101).
- Dye rock salt.

Language Enrichment Choices*

- Place several hard objects such as a block, book, plate, spoon, and large button in a box. Take the items out and pass them around for each child to touch and feel. Describe the items while the children explore them. Explain that the word *hard* is used to describe how something feels.

*Toddlers and twos present a wide range of developmental needs, abilities, and interests. For each learning area, select among the following activity and experience choices that are appropriate for the children in your care.

▪ Make up sentences with the word *hard*. For example, "The buttons on my shirt are *hard*."

▪ Present the flannel board story, "Henny-Penny" (Appendix p. 498-501). Discuss what hit Henny-Penny on the head (an acorn). "Was it hard?" If you have acorns available, let the children hold one and feel its surface.

▪ Teach the children the American Sign Language sign for *hard* (Appendix p. 433). Review other signs that children have learned.

Physical Development Choices

▪ Invite the children to take off their shoes and "sock skate" on a hard surface. You may want to hold the little skaters' hands while they "skate," especially the younger ones.

▪ Tape washers to the bottoms of the children's shoes and invite them to tap on a hard surface. Discuss the sound the washers make on the floor. "What happens if you tap on a surface that isn't hard?"

Social and Emotional Development Choices

▪ Walk around the room with each child and look for things that are hard. Encourage them to touch the items.

▪ Explain to the children that some of their body parts have hard surfaces: teeth, fingernails, and toenails. Discuss the reason why these body parts have hard surfaces.

Cognitive Development Choices

▪ Give each child a large, flat rock to paint. Discuss the texture of the rock.

▪ Challenge the children to drop beads into a can. "Do the hard beads make a loud noise?"

▪ Encourage the children to build with building blocks. Talk about the hard surface of the blocks. Ask what happens if the building falls and they accidentally get hit with one of the blocks. "Does it hurt?" Make a pathway with the blocks and ask the children to walk along the path. Discuss the hard surface of the path they created.

▧ Leave playdough uncovered for an hour or two. "What happens to the dough?"

▧ Make Baker's Clay. Mix 1 cup of white flour and 1 cup of salt in a bowl. Add water, a little at time, until the mixture becomes soft clay. Knead until smooth. If the clay is too wet, add more flour. If the clay is too dry, add more water. Encourage the children to create designs (pendants, charms, sculptures, and so on). When the children are done, bake the creations in the microwave or a conventional oven. In the microwave, heat the creations for 30 seconds at a time, checking for hardness. In the conventional oven, bake the creations at 225°, checking every 15 minutes for hardness. Baking time will vary depending on the density of the item. Turn the item over when it is halfway through baking. When the creations are cool, the children can paint them with poster paint. Discuss the hardness of the clay after cooking.

▧ Take a walk outdoors to look for hard items. Gather a "hard item collection" for the science area. When you return to the room, make a list of the hard things you found.

▧ Invite the children to make a dyed rock salt collage. To dye the rock salt, mix a few drops of food coloring with 2 tablespoons of alcohol in a jar and then add 1 cup of rock salt. Put the lid on the jar and shake for 30 seconds. Pour the salt on a paper towel to dry. As the children are gluing the rock salt onto their collages, ask them to describe how the salt feels.

▧ Problem-solving suggestion: Give the children several sizes of large nuts and bolts or several pots and lids. Challenge them to find the matching nut and bolt or pot and lid. Discuss the feel of the surface of these objects. **Safety Warning:** Make sure that the children do not put nuts or bolts in their mouths.

REFLECTION ON THE DAY
Ask the children to name some things that are hard. Ask the "not yet talkers" to show you something that is hard.

Loud

WORDS TO PRACTICE

loud	loudly	volume
louder	noise	
loudest	noisy	

GETTING READY

- Tell the children that today they will learn how the word *loud* is used to describe sounds. Ask the children to say, "Hello," in a loud voice.
- Read your favorite book about sound to the children or select a book from the Story Circle Suggestions below to check out of the library and read.

STORY CIRCLE SUGGESTIONS

- *Loudmouse* by Richard Wilbur
- *Please Be Quiet* by Mary Murphy
- *The Banging Book* by Bill Grossman

PREPARATION FOR "LOUD" ACTIVITIES AND EXPERIENCES

- Gather noisemakers.
- Make Sound Canisters (see p. 104) and drums.
- Get bubble wrap, oatmeal boxes, and washers.
- Purchase crunchy snacks.

*Toddlers and twos present a wide range of developmental needs, abilities, and interests. For each learning area, select among the following activity and experience choices that are appropriate for the children in your care.

Language Enrichment Choices*

- Pass around noisemakers such as horns, whistles, and shakers. Use them all together to create a loud noise. Discuss the word *loud*. "Do loud sounds hurt your ears?"

- Use sentences with the word *loud*. For example, "These noisemakers are too *loud*."

- Teach the children the American Sign Language sign for *loud* (Appendix p. 435).

Physical Development Choices

- Encourage the little musicians to play rhythm band instruments to moderately high-volume music. Discuss the loud sound of the music. Do the children know someone who plays music at a loud volume?
  Safety Warning: Make sure the music is not so loud that it may damage children's sensitive ears.

- Give the children sheets of large bubble wrap to stomp on. "What kind of noise do the popping bubbles make?"

Social and Emotional Development Choices

- Many children are frightened by loud noises such as sirens and thunder. Talk to the children about loud noises. Find out if there are noises that frighten them and help them understand the source of the noise. This often helps diminish the fear. For sources that are too difficult for the children to understand, make up a fanciful source. For example, tell them that thunder happens when giants are dancing on the clouds.

- Read "My Noisy House" to the children. Discuss loud noises that are part of the home environment.

  My Noisy House

  My house is always noisy | *Television blares,*
  Sound stirs all around. | *And the radio too.*
  We're hustling, bustling, on the move, | *Vacuum roars.*
  We're making lots of sound. | *What can I do?*

  Telephone rings, | *My house is always noisy,*
  Doorbell buzzes, | *And busy as can be.*
  Someone's knocking, | *We're never ever quiet here*
  Toilet flushes. | *We're loud and nois-eeeeee!*

- Talk with the children about taking care of their ears. Point out that it is a good idea to stay away from loud noises. Discuss how to wash your ears.

Cognitive Development Choices

▨ Make Sound Canisters. Fill empty film canisters or potato chip cans with items that make a loud noise such as washers or pennies. Make two canisters with each item. Seal the lids on with tape or glue and give them to the children to shake. Help the children find the two loud sounds that match. Use descriptive words to describe the sounds.

▨ Serve a crunchy snack such as cereals, pretzels, or crackers. Discuss the loud sound the children make when chewing.

▨ Take a walk outdoors and listen for loud sounds. When you return to the classroom, discuss the loud sounds that you heard.

▨ Invite the children to make drums. Collect oatmeal containers. Cut the boxes in half and glue or tape the lids on the half-size containers. Encourage the children to paint their boxes. Provide cardboard coat hanger tubes (from the dry cleaner) for drumsticks. Invite the children to beat their drums loudly. Talk about the noise they make. Ask the children to beat their drums one at a time, and then ask them to beat their drums all at the same time. "Is it louder when everyone is beating their drums at the same time?"

▨ Take the children outdoors and encourage them to run and yell. Discuss the volume of their "outdoor voices." "How are outdoor voices different from indoor voices?"

▨ Invite the children to toss washers or other metal objects into a metal bucket. Ask them to describe the sound.

▨ Problem-solving suggestion: Build a building with blocks on a hard surface floor. Encourage the children to knock the building down. Discuss the loud noise the blocks make as they hit the floor. Talk about ways to soften the noise. Provide carpet squares for the children to build on. "When the buildings fall down, is the sound less loud?"

REFLECTION ON THE DAY
Ask the children to describe a loud sound. Ask the "not yet talkers" to make a loud sound.

Thin/Skinny

WORDS TO PRACTICE

size	thin	thinnest
skinny	thinner	

GETTING STARTED

- Tell the children that today they will be learning about how the words *thin* and *skinny* are used to describe things.
- Read your favorite book about size to the children or select a book from the Story Circle Suggestions below to check out of the library and read.

STORY CIRCLE SUGGESTIONS

- *Fat, Thin, and Other Opposites* by Ingrid Godon
- *Mouse's Tail* by Richard Powell
- *Square, Triangle, Round, Skinny* by Vladimir Radunsky

PREPARATION FOR "THIN/SKINNY" ACTIVITIES AND EXPERIENCES

- Gather skinny items.
- Get thin crackers.
- Make the Drop Slot Can (see p. 107) and chips.

Language Enrichment Choices*

- Show the children some skinny/thin items, such as money (dimes and dollars), pieces of ribbon, fabric, straws, and paper. Pass the items around so the children can examine them. Explain that the words *skinny* and *thin* are used to describe the size of something. For older children, you might explain that some people might be hurt if you say they are skinny or thin.

- Use the words *skinny* and *thin* in sentences. For example, "These straws were too *skinny*." "The piece of paper is *thin*."

*Toddlers and twos present a wide range of developmental needs, abilities, and interests. For each learning area, select among the following activity and experience choices that are appropriate for the children in your care.

- Present the prop story, "The Strange Visitor" (Appendix p. 559-560), in which the visitor has long, skinny arms and long, skinny legs.

- Teach the children the American Sign Language signs for *thin* and for *skinny* (Appendix p. 439).

Physical Development Choices

- Sing "Six White Ducks" with the children. Show them how to waddle like a duck (walk in a squatted position). Point out that some of the ducks are skinny. "Is it easier for fat ducks or skinny ducks to waddle?"

  Six White Ducks
  Six white ducks that I once knew, (hold up six fingers)
  Fat ducks, skinny ducks, they were, too. (hold hands out to show fat and skinny)
  But the one little duck with the feather on her back, (hold up one finger, then point to your back)
  She ruled the others with a quack, quack, quack! (shake finger)

  Down to the river they would go, (walk fingers out in front of you)
  Wibble, wobble, wibble, wobble all in a row. (sway side to side)
  But the one little duck with the feather on her back, (hold up one finger, then point to your back)
  She ruled the others with a quack, quack, quack! (shake finger)

- Make a thin line on the floor with masking tape. Invite the children to walk along the skinny line. Challenge them to walk along the line with a beanbag on their head. Do they find it difficult to stay on the line?

Social and Emotional Development Choices

- Tour the room in search of thin things, such as mini-blinds, posters, fabrics, brushes, blocks, and so on. Discuss the size of the things you find.

- Talk with the children about their fingers. Discuss the thinness of their fingers. "Which finger is the thinnest?"

- Serve thin crackers for snack. Discuss the thinness of the crackers.

Cognitive Development Choices

▨ Show the children how to make thin lines on easel paper using thin brushes and thinned paint (mix paint with water). Encourage the children to draw a picture. Ask them to describe their work.

▨ Give the children a box of thin things, such as a piece of silk, a piece of paper, a ribbon, and a pipe cleaner to explore. Ask them to describe the items.

▨ Invite the children to use a rolling pin to roll playdough into a thin, flat circle. "Is it easy to pick up the thin, flat circle?" "What happens?"

▨ Provide thin boxes (e.g., spaghetti boxes) for the children to build with. Other skinny/thin box suggestions are Q-tip boxes, match boxes, and candle boxes. Ask the children to describe their thin sculptures or buildings.

▨ Serve pretzel sticks for snack. Ask the children to describe the pretzels. "Are they thin?" Provide a drink and let the children drink it through skinny straws.

▨ Take the children outdoors to gather some leaves. Discuss the thinness of the leaves.

▨ Problem-solving suggestion: Give the children a Drop Slot Can. Cut a 1½" slot in the lid of an empty coffee can. Replace the lid. Provide thin poker chips (regular chips) and fat chips (three poker chips glued together) for children. Challenge the children to sort the chips by those that will fit through the slot and those that won't fit through the slot. Encourage them to check their sorting by trying to push the chips through the slot. "Which chips fit through the slot?"

REFLECTION ON THE DAY
Ask the children to show you something thin.

Fat/Wide

WORDS TO PRACTICE

chunky	fatter	size
fat	fattest	wide

GETTING STARTED

- Teach the children "The Elephant Song" to the tune "I'm a Little Teapot." Discuss the size of the elephant.

  The Elephant Song
  Elephants walk in a line like this (children walk in a line)
  They are terribly big and terribly fat. (hold hands out to side)
  They have big ears and big, fat toes, (put hands up to ears and wave them)
  And goodness gracious what a nose! (use arm to make a trunk)

- Tell the children that today they will be learning about how *fat* and *wide* are used to describe things.
- Read your favorite book about size to the children or select a book from the Story Circle Suggestions below to check out of the library and read.

STORY CIRCLE SUGGESTIONS

- *Barnyard Tails* by Chris Tougas
- *Big Fat Hen* by Keith Baker
- *Farmer Smart's Fat Cat* by James Sage
- *Fat Cat on a Mat* by Phil Roxbee Cox

PREPARATION FOR "FAT/WIDE" ACTIVITIES AND EXPERIENCES

- Gather fat items.
- Make the "One, Two, Buckle My Shoe" flannel board rhyme (Appendix p. 601-602).
- Get fat pretzels.
- Get books about animal tails.
- Make chunky crayons, if needed.

Language Enrichment Choices*

▨ Show the children some fat things, such as chubby crayons, giant straws, and thick yarn. If available, show the children pictures of animals that are considered fat, such as an elephant, a hippo, and a pig. You may want to explain that we do not use the word *fat* to describe people who are large because saying someone is fat may hurt their feelings. It is better to say *large*.

▨ Use the words *fat* and *wide* in sentences. For example, "The elephant was too *fat* to make it through the door." "The room is *wide*."

▨ Teach the children the American Sign Language sign for *fat* and *wide* (Appendix p. 432, 439). Review other signs the children have learned.

Physical Development Choices

▨ Sing "Six White Ducks." Teach the children to waddle like a fat duck by walking while in a squatting position.

> **Six White Ducks**
> *Six white ducks that I once knew,* (hold up six fingers)
> *Fat ducks, skinny ducks, they were, too.* (hold hands out to show fat and skinny)
> *But the one little duck with the feather on her back,* (hold up one finger, then point to your back)
> *She ruled the others with a quack, quack, quack!* (shake finger)
>
> *Down to the river they would go,* (walk fingers out in front of you)
> *Wibble, wobble, wibble, wobble all in a row.* (sway side to side)
> *But the one little duck with the feather on her back,* (hold up one finger, then point to your back)
> *She ruled the others with a quack, quack, quack!* (shake finger)

▨ Say the rhyme, "To Market, To Market." Ask the children to join hands to form a circle. On the first verse, have them walk around to the left, speeding up on the last two lines. Change direction for the second verse. Point out, to older children, the difference between a pig and a hog. A hog is raised for market and weighs more than 120 pounds, and a pig is generally younger and weighs less than 120 pounds. Hogs are fatter than pigs. Gather four children together in a group and explain that a hog weighs more than all of them together.

*Toddlers and twos present a wide range of developmental needs, abilities, and interests. For each learning area, select among the following activity and experience choices that are appropriate for the children in your care.

To Market, To Market

To market, to market,   *To market, to market,*
To buy a fat pig.   *To buy a fat hog.*
Home again, home again,   *Home again, home again,*
Jiggety-jig.   *Jiggety-jog.*

- Play Duck, Duck, Goose with older children. Change "goose" to "fat goose." Suggest the goose run as if he is fat—hands out to the side and with wide steps.

Social and Emotional Development Choices

- Teach the children the rhyme, "One, Two, Buckle My Shoe." Use the flannel board patterns to illustrate the rhyme as you say it (Appendix p. 601-602). Point out the big, fat hen at the end of the rhyme. Explain that the hen is not as fat as she looks. She just has a lot of feathers.

One, Two Buckle My Shoe

One, two, buckle my shoe. (hold up one, then two fingers and then point to shoe)
Three, four, shut the door. (pretend to shut a door)
Five, six, pick up sticks. (pretend to pick up sticks)
Seven, eight, lay them straight. (pretend to lay sticks on the ground)
Nine, ten, a big fat hen. (hold hands out to each side of your body to indicate fat)

- Take a walk around the room looking for fat and wide things. Ask the children to describe the items that they find.

- Teach the children the song, "Five Fat Turkeys Are We."

Five Fat Turkeys Are We

Five fat turkeys are we.
We spent the night in a tree.
When the cook came around,
We couldn't be found
And that's why we're here, you see—gobble, gobble!
Oh, five fat turkeys are we.
We spent the night in a tree.
It sure does pay
On Thanksgiving Day
To sleep in the tallest tree—gobble, gobble!

Cognitive Development Choices

■ Give the children chunky crayons to draw with. Talk to them about how the fat crayons feel in their hands. You can make chunky crayons by peeling the paper off old crayons, sorting them by color into a muffin tin, and then placing the muffin tin on a warming tray. After the crayon pieces have melted, let them cool and set, and then remove them from the muffin tin.

■ Serve fat pretzels for snack. Provide a drink and let the children drink it through fat straws. Discuss the size of the pretzels and the straws. "Do you get more juice through a fat straw?"

■ Provide fat paintbrushes and thick paint. Invite the children to paint fat/wide stripes on easel paper. What can the children paint with fat brushes? Invite them to describe their pictures.

■ Use butcher paper to make a wide path. Ask the children to walk on the wide path. Then ask them to walk on the path with their legs spread out wide. "Can you spread your legs as wide as the path?"

■ Read a book about animal tails, such as *Let's Talk Tales* by June English or *Animal Tales* by Ken Kawata. Pick out the animals that have fat tails such as a beaver. If a book is unavailable, show the children photos of animals.

■ Stack several fat pillows in a corner and invite the children to use the corner as a reading area. Point out the coziness of the pillows and what makes them so cozy.

■ Problem-solving suggestion: Cut a wide river out of blue butcher paper. Give the children a toy car to cross over the river. Help the children build a bridge over the river with blocks. Encourage them to drive the car over the wide river. "What does it take to make a bridge wider?"

REFLECTION ON THE DAY

Ask the children to tell you about something that is fat or wide. Ask the "not yet talkers" to show you something that is fat or wide.

Red

WORDS TO PRACTICE

bright	shades
colors	warm
red	

GETTING STARTED

- Wear red clothes. Invite the children to wear red (Appendix p. 443). Discuss the color of everyone's clothing. Ask the children questions to find out what they know about the color *red*.
- Tell them that today they will be learning about the color *red* and how it is used to describe things.
- Read your favorite book about the color red (or other colors) to the children or select a book from the Story Circle Suggestions below to check out of the library and read.

STORY CIRCLE SUGGESTIONS

- *Big Red Barn* by Margaret Wise Brown
- *Big Red Fire Truck* by Ken Wilson-Max
- *Is It Red? Is It Yellow? Is It Blue?* by Tana Hoban
- *Little Red Hen* by Paul Galdone
- *My Little Red Tool Box* by Stephen Johnson
- *Rudolph the Red-Nosed Reindeer* by Robert Lewis May
- *Ted in a Red Bed* by Jenny Tyler

PREPARATION FOR "RED" ACTIVITIES AND EXPERIENCES

- Send letter home to families inviting children to wear red (see color schedule letter, appendix p. 443).
- Gather red items.
- Get strawberry jelly, bread, strawberries, and apples.
- Prepare Scratch-and-Sniff Paint (see p. 112).
- Make Color Hoops and Red Puzzle (see p. 115).

Language Enrichment Choices*

- Collect red items such as scarves, flowers, cherries, apples, and crayons. Show them to the children. Discuss them and pass them around so the children can look at the things more closely. Lay the items on a special "color table" so that the children can look at them throughout the day.

- Sing the red verse of "The Color Song" to the tune of "I've Been Workin' on the Railroad." You will add a new verse each time you introduce a new color. Ask the children to think of other red things to add to the song.

    The Color Song
    Red is the color of an apple to eat.
    Red is the color of cherries, too.
    Red is the color of strawberries.
    I like red, don't you?

- Use the word *red* in a sentence. For example, "Sam looks handsome in his *red* shirt."

- Teach the children the American Sign Language sign for *red* (Appendix p. 437).

Physical Development Choices

- Play a toddler version of Red Rover. Place a sheet of red construction paper or a red streamer on the floor. Invite the toddlers, one at a time, to jump over the paper or streamer as you chant, "Red Rover, Red Rover, let (Abby) jump over." Encourage the children to tell you what color the paper or streamer is after they have made their jump.

- On a sunny day, give each child a 12" x 24" sheet of red cellophane. Show them how to make red shadows outside by allowing the sun to shine through their paper. Encourage them to run with the paper as if it were a kite. A red shadow will follow them.

- Teach the children the fingerplay, "Little Red Apple." "What other colors do apples come in?"

    Little Red Apple
    A little red apple grew high in a tree. (point up)
    I looked up at it. (shade eyes and look up)
    It looked down at me. (shade eyes and look down)

*Toddlers and twos present a wide range of developmental needs, abilities, and interests. For each learning area, select among the following activity and experience choices that are appropriate for the children in your care.

"Come down, please," I called. (use hand to motion downward)
And that little red apple fell right on my head. (tap the top of your head)

Social and Emotional Development Choices

■ Serve strawberry jelly on bread for snack. Let the children help spread the jelly on their bread (as much as possible) using a tongue depressor or a plastic knife. As you sit and eat your snack, discuss the color and taste of the jelly. "Where does jelly come from?"

■ Discuss how the color red makes you feel. It is a bright, warm color. According to brain research, the color red makes us more alert. It also increases our appetites. Give the children sheets of red construction paper to use for placemats.

■ Sing "My Little Red Wagon." "Does anyone have a little red wagon?"

> **My Little Red Wagon**
> *Bumping up and down in my little red wagon,*
> *Bumping up and down in my little red wagon,*
> *Bumping up and down in my little red wagon*
> *Won't you be my darlin'?*

Cognitive Development Choices

■ Paint with Scratch-and-Sniff red paint. Mix cherry or strawberry flavored gelatin as directed, but use only half the amount of water called for. Encourage the children to use the mixture for paint. When it dries, children can scratch and sniff.

■ Serve apples or strawberries for snack. "Is an apple red on the inside?" "Is a strawberry red on the inside?"

■ Invite the children to make red collages. Provide red fabric swatches, ribbon, rickrack, buttons, tissue paper, and so on. Encourage the children to glue the red items to a piece of red paper.

■ Provide several shades of red paint and encourage the children to experiment with painting with each shade. Add peppermint extract to the paint for added fun. Encourage the children to talk about their painting. Did they paint something that is red?

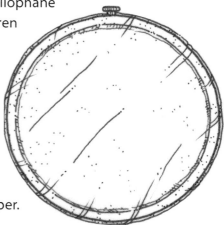

■ Give the children red Color Hoops to explore. Place colored cellophane or plastic wrap inside embroidery hoops. Encourage the children to look through the hoops to see what happens to the world around them. Ask them to describe what they see.

■ Ask the children to build something using only red Legos. If Legos are not available, spray paint small boxes red or cover them with red paper. Encourage the children to talk about their buildings.

■ Encourage the children to draw with red crayons on white paper. Ask them to describe their drawing.

■ Provide red dress-up clothes for the children to explore.

■ Take a walk outdoors in search of red things. When you return to the classroom, make a list on chart paper of the things you found.

■ Give the children a basket of large stringing beads. Help them sort out the red beads. "Which color of beads do you like best?"

■ Provide a bucket of red wrapping bows. Encourage the children to spill the bows and pick them up again.

■ Problem-solving suggestion: Invite the children to work on a Red Puzzle. Make the puzzle by cutting a sheet of red poster board into three or four puzzle pieces. Is it more difficult for the children to work a puzzle that has no picture on it?

REFLECTION ON THE DAY
Ask the children to show you something or name something that is red.

Yellow

WORDS TO PRACTICE

colors   yellow
warm

GETTING STARTED

- Wear yellow clothes. Invite the children to wear yellow (Appendix p. 443). Discuss the color of everyone's clothing. Ask the children questions to find out what they know about the color *yellow*.
- Tell them that today they will be learning about the color *yellow* and how it is used to describe things.
- Read your favorite book about yellow (or other colors) to the children or select a book from the Story Circle Suggestions below to check out of the library and read.

STORY CIRCLE SUGGESTIONS

- *Fuzzy Yellow Ducklings* by Matthew Van Fleet
- *Red, Blue, Yellow Shoe* by Tana Hoban
- *Yellow and You* by Candace Whitman
- *Yellow Hippo* by Alan Rogers

PREPARATION FOR "YELLOW" ACTIVITIES AND EXPERIENCES

- Send a letter home to families inviting children to wear yellow (see color schedule letter, Appendix p. 443).
- Gather yellow items.
- Get bananas, vanilla, milk, and buttermilk.
- Make Color Hoops (see p. 118).

Language Enrichment Choices*

- Collect yellow items such as scarves, flowers, bananas, a toy "yield" sign, a pencil, and crayons. Show them to the children. Discuss them and pass them around so the children can look

*Toddlers and twos present a wide range of developmental needs, abilities, and interests. For each learning area, select among the following activity and experience choices that are appropriate for the children in your care.

at the things more closely. Lay the items on a special "color table" so that the children can look at them throughout the day.

▦ Sing the yellow verse of "The Color Song" to the tune of "I've Been Workin' on the Railroad." Review the red verse. "What other yellow things can you think of that could be added to the song?"

> **The Color Song**
> *Yellow is the color of the great big sun.*
> *Yellow is the color of lemonade, too.*
> *Yellow is the color of a baby chick.*
> *I like yellow, don't you?*

▦ Use the word *yellow* in a sentence. For example, "I like *yellow* flowers."

▦ Teach the children the American Sign Language sign for *yellow* (Appendix p. 440).

Physical Development Choices

▦ Invite the children to dance with yellow streamers to upbeat music.

▦ Play Bellow Yellow. Ask the children to find different things in the room. When the thing they find is yellow, they should "bellow" out the word yellow (explain that "bellow" means to shout). For example, you might say, "Find a chair." If the chair is yellow, it is time to bellow. If the chair is any other color, the children say nothing.

Social and Emotional Development Choices

▦ Make and serve Banana Milk Shakes. Let the children help you peel and smash two fully ripe bananas. Point out the color of the banana peel and the banana inside. Put the bananas into the blender with 1 cup of chilled milk, 1 tablespoon of sugar, and ¼ teaspoon of vanilla. Blend and serve (serves four). Discuss the color and taste of the shake.

▦ Talk with the children about how the color yellow makes them feel. Yellow is a vibrant and warm color that, according to brain development research, energizes us. Research also indicates that yellow is the optimum color for learning.

▦ Teach the children "Yellow Chicks." "Who has seen a baby chick?"

Yellow Chicks
Yellow chicks say, "Peep, peep, peep,"
As they wake from sleep, sleep, sleep. (rub eyes)
Yellow chicks say, "Peep, peep, peep,"
And hear the birds go "cheep, cheep, cheep." (repeat "cheep, cheep, cheep")
Yellow chicks say, "Peep, peep, peep,"
As they leap, leap, leap. (jump up and down)
Yellow chicks say, "Peep, peep, peep,"
And now it's time to sleep, sleep, sleep. (lay head in hands)

Cognitive Development Choices

- Invite the children to draw with yellow Buttermilk Chalk. Place about a tablespoon of buttermilk on each child's paper and encourage each child to use yellow chalk to make designs.

- Give the children yellow Color Hoops to explore. Place yellow colored cellophane or plastic wrap in embroidery hoops. Ask them to describe what they see.

- Give the children a basket of large stringing beads. Have them sort out the yellow beads. "Which color bead is your favorite?"

- Hide yellow objects in the sand table and challenge the children to find them.

- Use yellow vinyl tape to make a 10' line on the floor. Encourage the children to walk on the yellow line.

- Problem-solving suggestion: Encourage the children to work Happy Face Puzzles. Make the puzzles by cutting a large circle out of yellow poster board. Draw a happy face on the circle, laminate it, and cut it into simple puzzle pieces. Make a few two- and three-piece puzzles and some five- and six-piece puzzles so that you have a range of difficulty. Put colored stick-on dots on the backs of the puzzle pieces to make the pieces of each puzzle easy to identify.

REFLECTION ON THE DAY
Ask the children to show you something or name something that is yellow.

Blue

WORDS TO PRACTICE

blue	cool
calm	shades
colors	

GETTING STARTED

- Wear blue clothing. Invite the children to wear blue (Appendix p. 443). Discuss the color of everyone's clothing. Ask the children questions to find out what they know about the color *blue*.
- Tell them that today they will be learning about the color *blue* and how it is used to describe things.
- Read your favorite book about blue or colors to the children or select a book from the Story Circle Suggestions below to check out of the library and read.

STORY CIRCLE SUGGESTIONS

- *Big Blue Engine* by Ken Wilson-Max
- *Blue Hat, Green Hat* by Sandra Boynton
- *Is It Red? Is It Yellow? Is It Blue?* by Tana Hoban

PREPARATION FOR "BLUE" ACTIVITIES AND EXPERIENCES

- Send a letter home to families inviting children to wear blue (see color schedule letter, appendix p. 443).
- Gather blue items.
- Get blueberries and coconut flavoring.
- Make Wave Machine and blue Colorscopes (see p. 121).

Language Enrichment Choices*

- Collect blue items such as scarves, hats, blueberries, balls, and crayons. Show them to the children. Discuss them and pass them around so the children can look at the things more closely. Lay the items on a special "color table" so that the children can look at them throughout the day.

*Toddlers and twos present a wide range of developmental needs, abilities, and interests. For each learning area, select among the following activity and experience choices that are appropriate for the children in your care.

- Sing the blue verse of "The Color Song" to the tune of "I've Been Workin' on the Railroad." Review the red and yellow verses. Ask the children to think of other blue items to add to the song.

   The Color Song
   Blue is the color of the big blue sky.
   Blue is the color of baby things, too.
   Blue is the color of my sister's eyes.
   I like blue, don't you?

- Use the word *blue* in a sentence. For example, "The sky is really *blue* today."

- Teach the children the American Sign Language sign for *blue* (Appendix p. 430). Review other color signs.

Physical Development Choices

- Invite the children to dance creatively to some mellow music with blue scarves or streamers. "How do the streamers and the music make you feel?"

- Play Blue Thunder. Ask the children to join hands and make a circle. Select one child to be IT ("the wind"). Ask the children in the circle to raise their hands to make arches and chant, "Blue Thunder, Blue Thunder, let (Rose) go under." Rose, "the wind," then goes in and out of the arches as fast as she can. You may need to assist the child who is "the wind" for the first few times. When the wind goes all the way around the circle, she can select the next child to be the wind.

- Give the children blue cellophane or blue tissue paper to crumple. "What sounds can you make?"

Social and Emotional Development Choices

- Invite the children to sample blueberries. Discuss how they look, taste, and feel. "Are they blue through and through?"

- Talk about how the color blue makes you feel. It is a calming and cool color that should make us feel calm, according to brain development research.

- Teach the children "Little Boy Blue." "Why do you think they call him Little Boy Blue?"

Little Boy Blue

Little Boy Blue, come blow your horn,
The sheep are in the meadow, the cow is in the corn.
But where is the boy who looks after the sheep?
He's under a haystack, fast asleep.

▧ Make blue snow cones. Chip or shave (adult only) some ice and put it into cups. Encourage the children to squeeze a small amount of coconut flavoring (which is usually blue) or another flavor that is blue to the ice to create blue snow cones. Discuss the color of the ice and then enjoy tasting it. "How does the color *blue* taste?"

Cognitive Development Choices

▧ Make Wave Machines and invite the children to explore them. Fill clear plastic bottles ¼ full with mineral oil or clear vegetable oil. Finish filling with denatured alcohol and a few drops of blue or green food coloring. Glue on the lids securely and invite the children to rotate the bottle to create waves. If desired, make individual wave machines using 20-ounce bottles. These bottles make nice wave machines for the science center. Ask the children how they feel as they watch the water run back and forth.

▧ Give the children blue Colorscopes to explore. Cover one end of an empty toilet paper tube or paper towel tube with blue cellophane or plastic wrap. Secure with glue or masking tape. Invite the children to view the word through colored glasses. Ask them to describe what they see.

▧ Give the children several different shades of blue paint. Point out the subtle differences between shades of blue.

▧ Give the children large stringing beads and ask them to sort out the blue beads. "Which color of beads do you like best?"

- Hang blue streamers from the ceiling or door jamb. Make them long enough so that they brush toddlers' faces as they walk through them. Encourage the children to walk and dance through the streamers.

- Fill the water table with blue water (plain water mixed with several drops of food coloring). Provide funnels, basters, cups, and spoons. Talk about the color of the water as they children play.

- Problem-solving suggestion: Give the children three or four sheets of blue construction paper in a variety of shades. Challenge them to arrange the blue paper from the lightest to the darkest shade of blue.

REFLECTION ON THE DAY

Ask the children to show you something or name something that is blue.

Green

WORDS TO PRACTICE

calm	cool	shades
colors	green	

GETTING STARTED

- Wear green clothes. Invite the children to wear green (Appendix p. 443). Discuss the color of everyone's clothing. Ask the children questions to find out what they know about the color *green*.
- Tell them that today they will be learning about the color *green* and how it is used to describe things.
- Read your favorite book about green (or other colors) to the children or select a book from the Story Circle Suggestions below to check out of the library and read.

STORY CIRCLE SUGGESTIONS

- *Blue Hat, Green Hat* by Sandra Boynton
- *Green Eyes* by Abe Birnbaum
- *Little Green* by Keith Baker
- *Little Green Tow Truck* by Ken Wilson-Max

PREPARATION FOR "GREEN" ACTIVITIES AND EXPERIENCES

- Send a letter home to families inviting children to wear green (see color schedule letter, Appendix p. 443).
- Gather green items.
- Make the Lily Pad Hop game and Green Gobblers on the next page.
- Gather ingredients for Green Gelatin Gigglers (see p. 125) and prepare in advance.

Language Enrichment Choices*

- Collect green items such as scarves, leaves, grass, a lime, a dollar bill, and crayons. Show them to the children. Discuss

*Toddlers and twos present a wide range of developmental needs, abilities, and interests. For each learning area, select among the following activity and experience choices that are appropriate for the children in your care.

them and pass them around so the children can look at the things more closely. Lay the items on a special "color table" so that the children can look at them throughout the day.

■ Sing the green verse of "The Color Song" to the tune of "I've Been Workin' on the Railroad." Review the verses about the colors red, yellow, and blue. "What other green things could be added to the song?"

The Color Song
Green is the color of the leaves on the trees.
Green is the color of green peas, too.
Green is the color of a watermelon.
I like green, don't you?

■ Use the word *green* in a sentence. For example, "I love playing in the *green* grass."

■ Teach the older children the song, "Great Green Gobs" to the tune of "Row, Row, Row Your Boat." Even if children are challenged by learning the words, they will still enjoy hearing the sounds of the words in this song.

Great Green Gobs
Great green gobs of grass,
Great green gobs of peas,
Grass and peas, peas and grass,
All in great green gobs.

Great green gobs of frogs,
Great green gobs of leaves,
Frogs and leaves, leaves and frogs,
All in great green gobs.

■ Teach the children the American Sign Language sign for *green* (Appendix p. 433). Review other color signs.

Physical Development Choices

■ Play Lily Pad Hop. Cut out large green lily pads from green poster board, vinyl, or bulletin board paper. Laminate and place them on the floor about 1' apart. Encourage the children to jump like frogs from lily pad to lily pad. Be sure to tell the children what lily pads are and where they are found.

- Play Drop the Handkerchief using a green handkerchief. Choose one child to be IT while the other children sit in a circle facing the center. The child who is IT skips or walks around the outside of the circle and casually drops the green handkerchief behind one of the children sitting in the circle. This child picks up the handkerchief and chases IT around the circle. IT tries to run around the circle and sit in the second child's spot without being tagged. If IT is not tagged, then he sits in his new spot in the circle and the child with the handkerchief is now IT. If IT is tagged, then he is IT for another round. Depending on the age of your group, you may need to offer assistance to each child as he is IT while a second adult helps the runner.

Social and Emotional Development Choices

- Make Green Gelatin Gigglers. Mix flavored gelatin using half the amount of water suggested on the box. Let it congeal. Cut it into interesting shapes or use a cookie cutter to cut. Serve as a finger food. Discuss the color and texture of the gelatin. Teach the children the rhyme, "Gelatin Gigglers in My Tummy."

  Gelatin Gigglers in My Tummy
  Gelatin Gigglers in my tummy,
  Gelatin Gigglers, oh, so yummy!
  Wiggle, giggle—giggle, wiggle,
  Oh, what a delight to nibble!

- Discuss how the color green makes you feel. It is a cool, calm color. Brain research suggests that the color green calms us.

Cognitive Development Choices

- Mix a few drops of green food coloring with water. Give the children large eyedroppers and encourage children to drop the food coloring mixture onto coffee filters. Children will need some assistance at first but will soon be able to operate the eyedroppers. This is a great activity to encourage finger coordination. Point out the different shades of green that form on their filters.

- Give the children a Green Gobbler to pick up green pompoms. Spray paint a meatball press green (adult only). Glue on two wiggle eyes (or felt pieces for younger children). It will look like a big-mouth frog. Invite the children to use the gobblers to pick up green pompoms or other green objects.

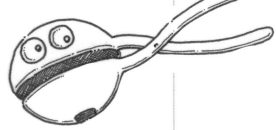

- Cut green grapes into pieces and serve them for snack. Discuss their color as you eat them. "Are they green on the inside?"
  Safety Warning: To prevent choking, do not serve whole grapes to young children.

- Place a service bell in the center of the floor. Cut a small hole into a piece of green felt and place it over the knob on the top of the service bell. Encourage the children to toss green beanbags at the green square. "Who can ring the bell?"

- Encourage the children to fingerpaint with green fingerpaint. Slowly add a small amount of yellow fingerpaint to the green paint. "What happens?" Slowly add a small amount of blue fingerpaint to the green paint. "What happens?"

- Give the children large stringing beads and encourage them to find the green ones. Ask them which color of bead is their favorite.

- Provide green wrapping bows for the children to put into pails and pour out again.

- Problem-solving suggestion: Fill all 12 compartments of a Styrofoam egg carton half full with water. Put blue food coloring into one of the compartments at the top of the carton and yellow food coloring into the other compartment at the top. Give the children an eyedropper and encourage them to explore mixing blue and yellow food coloring into the other compartments. How many colors of green can they make?

REFLECTION ON THE DAY
Ask the children to show you something or name something that is green.

Purple

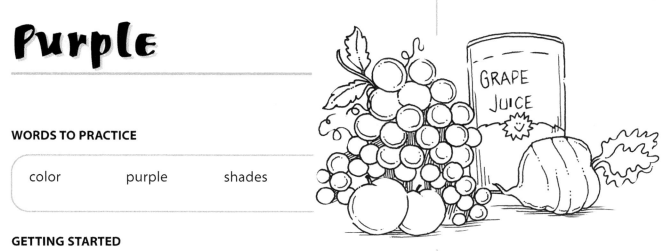

WORDS TO PRACTICE

color	purple	shades

GETTING STARTED

- Wear purple clothes. Invite the children to wear purple (see color schedule letter, Appendix p. 443). Discuss the color of everyone's clothing. Ask the children questions to find out what they know about the color *purple*.
- Tell them that today they will be learning about the color *purple* and how it is used to describe things.
- Read your favorite book about purple (or other colors) to the children or select a book from the Story Circle Suggestions below to check out of the library and read.

STORY CIRCLE SUGGESTIONS

- *Harold and the Purple Crayon* by Crockett Johnston
- *I Like Colors* by Margaret Miller
- *Mr. Pine's Purple House* by Leonard Kessler

PREPARATION FOR "PURPLE" ACTIVITIES AND EXPERIENCES

- Send a letter home to families inviting children to wear purple (see color schedule letter, appendix p. 443).
- Make "The Great Big Turnip" flannel board story (Appendix p. 495-497).
- Gather purple items.
- Gather ingredients to make Purple Cow Shakes on the next page.
- Gather ingredients and make purple Gak (see p. 129).
- Cut purple crepe paper streamers.

Language Enrichment Choices*

- Collect purple items such as scarves, flowers, turnips, and crayons. Show them to the children. Discuss them and pass them around so the children can look at the things more closely. Lay the items on a special "color table" so that the children can see them throughout the day.

- Sing the purple verse of "The Color Song" to the tune of "I've Been Workin' on the Railroad." Review the red, yellow, blue, and green verses. Ask the children if they can think of other purple things to add to the song.

> **The Color Song**
> *Purple is the color of a bunch of grapes.*
> *Purple is the color of grape juice, too.*
> *Purple is the color of a violet.*
> *I like purple, don't you?*

- Use the word *purple* in a sentence. For example, "Grape juice is *purple.*"

- Teach the children the American Sign Language sign for *purple* (Appendix p. 436). Review other color signs.

Physical Development Choices

- Play Purple, Purple, Burple as you would Duck, Duck, Goose.

- If you happen to have access to a copy of the old record "Purple People Eater," play it for the children and encourage them to dance to the music with purple streamers. If you don't have this specific piece of music, any music will do.

Social and Emotional Development Choices

*Toddlers and twos present a wide range of developmental needs, abilities, and interests. For each learning area, select among the following activity and experience choices that are appropriate for the children in your care.

- Make Purple Cow Shakes. Place 1 small scoop of vanilla ice cream, 2 tablespoons of grape juice concentrate, and 2 tablespoons of milk in a baby food jar. Close the lid and let the children shake, shake, shake! As the children are drinking their shakes, discuss the color, taste, temperature, and so forth. Teach the rhyme, "I Never Saw a Purple Cow" to the children. "Has anyone ever seen a purple cow?"

> **I Never Saw a Purple Cow** by Gelett Burgess
> *I never saw a purple cow,*
> *I never hope to see one.*
> *But I can tell you anyhow,*
> *I'd rather see than be one.*

- Discuss how the color purple makes you feel. It is a cool and subdued color. Brain research indicates that purple makes us feel calm.

- Serve frozen purple grapes for snack. Discuss the color of the grapes as you eat them. "Are they the same color inside as outside?"
  Safety Warning: Whole grapes are a choking hazard for toddlers. Cut grapes into quarters before freezing them.

Cognitive Development Choices

- Invite the children to make a purple collage. Provide purple fabric, ribbon, tissue paper, and so on. Encourage the children to glue the purple items onto purple paper. Encourage them to talk about the purple things they use on their artwork.

- Encourage the children to play with Purple Gak. Discuss its texture and its color. To make Gak, combine 2 cups of glue, 1½ cups of tap water, and a few drops of red and blue food coloring in a bowl. In a larger bowl, dissolve 2 teaspoons of Borax in 1 cup of hot water. Slowly add the glue mixture to the Borax. It will thicken quickly and be difficult to mix. Mix well and drain off excess water. Let stand for a few minutes, and then pour into a shallow tray. Let dry for 10 minutes. Store in zipper-closure plastic bags. This mixture will keep for two or three weeks.

- Encourage the children to draw with a purple crayon on white paper. Ask them to describe their drawings.

- Mix several shades of purple paint and encourage the children to experiment painting with them. Discuss the different shades. "Does anyone have a favorite shade?"

- Present the story of "The Great Big Turnip" (Appendix p. 495-497). Discuss the color of the turnip. If you have a real turnip available, show it to the children.

- Problem-solving suggestion: Hide purple construction paper hearts around the room. Give the children clues about where to find the purple hearts. For example, you might say, "Look under the art table," or "Look beside the library books."

REFLECTION ON THE DAY
Ask the children to show you something or name something that is purple.

Orange

WORDS TO PRACTICE

color   shades

orange   warm

GETTING READY

- Wear orange clothes. Invite the children to wear orange (Appendix p. 443). Discuss the color of everyone's clothing. Ask the children questions to find out what they know about the color *orange*.
- Tell them that today they will be learning about the color *orange* and how it is used to describe things.
- Read your favorite book about orange (or other colors) to the children or select a book from the Story Circle Suggestions below to check out of the library and read.

STORY CIRCLE SUGGESTIONS

- *Orange in My World* by Joanne Winne
- *Oranges* by Claire Llewellyn
- *The Runaway Orange* by Felicity Brooks
- *What Color Is It? Orange* by Mary Elizabeth Salzmann

PREPARATION FOR "ORANGE" ACTIVITIES AND EXPERIENCES

- Send a letter home to families inviting children to wear orange (see color schedule letter, Appendix p. 443).
- Make "The Great Big Pumpkin" flannel board story (Appendix p. 492-494).
- Gather orange items.
- Cut orange crepe paper streamers.
- Get oranges.
- Gather ingredients for Orange Sherbet (see p. 132).
- Make orange Colorscopes (see p. 133).
- Cut sponges into fish shapes.

Language Enrichment Choices*

▨ Collect orange items such as scarves, flowers, oranges, and crayons. Show them to the children. Discuss them and pass them around so the children can look at the things more closely. Lay the items on a special "color table" so that the children can see them throughout the day.

▨ Sing the orange verse of "The Color Song" to the tune of "I've Been Workin' on the Railroad." Review red, yellow, blue, green, and purple. Ask the children if they can think of other orange things that could be added to the song.

> **The Color Song**
> *Orange is the color of oranges.*
> *Orange is the color of carrots, too.*
> *Orange is the color of a jack-o-lantern.*
> *I like orange, don't you?*

▨ Use the word *orange* in a sentence. For example, "John's favorite color is *orange*."

▨ Teach the children the American Sign Language sign for *orange* (Appendix p. 436). Review other color signs.

Physical Development Choices

▨ Give the children an orange and show them how to hold it between their chin and their neck. Make a 10' walking line using orange vinyl tape. Challenge the children to walk on the line holding the orange between their chin and neck.

▨ Encourage the children to dance with orange streamers or scarves to a selection of upbeat music.

▨ Teach the children the fingerplay, "Five Little Pumpkins." Discuss the color of pumpkins.

> **Five Little Pumpkins**
> *Five little pumpkins sitting on a gate.* (hold up five fingers)
> *First one said, "It's getting late."* (wiggle first finger)
> *Second one said, "There's witches in the air."* (wiggle second finger)
> *Third one said, "We don't care."* (wiggle third finger)
> *Fourth one said, "Let's run, let's run."* (wiggle fourth finger)
> *Fifth one said, "Oh, it's just Halloween fun."* (wiggle fifth finger)

*Toddlers and twos present a wide range of developmental needs, abilities, and interests. For each learning area, select among the following activity and experience choices that are appropriate for the children in your care.

But "Whooo" went the wind and out went the light (hold hands sides of your
   mouth and blow)
And five little pumpkins rolled out of sight. (roll hand over hand)

Social and Emotional Development Choices

■ Invite the children to help make Orange Sherbet. Place one can of condensed
   milk in a clean 1-pound coffee can. Add ½ cup of pineapple juice and then fill
   the remainder of the can with orange soda. Place the lid on the can and put it
   inside of a 5-pound coffee can. Fill the remainder of the 5-pound can with ice
   and rock salt and then place the lid on it. Ask the children to roll the coffee
   can back and forth across the floor for about 20 minutes. Remove the smaller
   can from the larger can, open it, and serve the sherbet. Discuss the color,
   smell, texture, and taste of the sherbet.
   Allergy Warning: Check with families to make certain no one is allergic to
   milk.

■ Discuss how the color orange makes us feel. It is a bright, warm color.
   According to brain research, it should make us feel more alert.

■ Serve orange slices for snack. Discuss the color, smell, and taste of the
   oranges. "Are oranges orange inside and out?"

Cognitive Development Choices

■ Add orange extract to orange paint to make orange-scented paint. Encourage
   the children to paint orange pictures. Ask them to describe their work.

- Add orange extract to orange playdough to make orange-scented playdough. Encourage the children to roll, pound, and model it. Discuss the color and the smell of the dough. What orange things do the children make?

- Give the children orange Colorscopes to explore. To make Colorscopes, cover one end of an empty toilet paper tube or paper towel tube with orange cellophane or plastic wrap. Secure with glue or masking tape. Invite the children to view the word through colored glasses. Ask them to describe what they see.

- Give the children orange cellophane or tissue paper to crush and crunch. "How does it sound?" "How does it feel?"

- Give the children large stringing beads and ask them to pick out the orange beads. Ask the children which beads are their favorite.

- Cut sponges into simple fish shapes. Cut blue paper into the shape of a fish bowl. Encourage the children to sponge paint orange fish onto the blue fish bowls. Clip clothespins to the sponges so that the children can handle them more easily.

- Tell the children the story of "The Great Big Pumpkin" (Appendix p. 492-494). If the children have heard the story "The Great Big Turnip," point out the similarities and differences between the two stories. Ask the children if they have ever seen a pumpkin. "Where did you see it?" "What color was it?"

- Problem-solving suggestion: Fill all 12 compartments of a Styrofoam egg carton half full with water. Place red food coloring in one compartment and yellow in another. Encourage the children to use a large eyedropper to mix red coloring and yellow coloring in the other compartments. "What color does it make?" Point out all the shades of orange that are created.

REFLECTION ON THE DAY
Ask the children to show you something or name something that is orange.

Black

WORDS TO PRACTICE

black	dark
color	shades

GETTING STARTED

- Wear black clothes. Invite the children to wear black (Appendix p. 443). Discuss the color of everyone's clothing. Ask the children questions to find out what they know about the color *black*.
- Tell the children that today they will be learning about the color *black* and how it is used to describe things.
- Read your favorite book about black or colors to the children or select a book from the Story Circle Suggestions below to check out of the library and read.

STORY CIRCLE SUGGESTIONS

- *Black on White* by Tana Hoban
- *It Looked Like Spilt Milk* by Charles Shaw
- *Ten Black Dots* by Donald Crews
- *White on Black* by Tana Hoban

PREPARATION FOR "BLACK" ACTIVITIES AND EXPERIENCES

- Send a letter home to families inviting children to wear black (see color schedule letter, Appendix p. 443).
- Gather black items.
- Cut black crepe paper streamers.
- Make black Paper Bag Blocks (see p. 136) and black and white sacks for Black Sack game on the next page.
- Mix black Puff Paint (see p. 136).
- Make Black Puzzles (see p. 136).
- Gather black-eyed peas.

Language Enrichment Choices*

- Collect black items such as scarves, shoes, hats, licorice, and crayons. Show them to the children. Discuss them and pass them around so the children can look at the things more closely. Lay the items on a special "color table" so that the children can look at them throughout the day.

- Use the word *black* in a sentence. For example, "Mary has a *black* kitten."

- Teach the children the American Sign Language sign for *black* (Appendix p. 430). Review other color signs.

Physical Development Choices

- Play Black Sack. Hide four sacks—one black and the other three white or brown. Ask the children to find the sacks. The child who finds the black sack is the winner and gets to help hide the sacks the next time the game is played.

- Encourage the children to dance between a light source (such as a flashlight or overhead projector) and the wall to make black shadows. Discuss the shadows they make. "Can you make scary shadows?" "Funny shadows?" Show them how.

Social and Emotional Development Choices

- Invite the children to try a black (licorice) jellybean. "What does it taste like?" "Who likes it?"

- Discuss how the color black makes you feel. Play some somber classical music and encourage the children to dance to the music with black streamers.

- Teach the children the song/chant, "Two Little Blackbirds." "Has anyone seen a blackbird?"

    Two Little Blackbirds
    Two little blackbirds (hold up index finger of each hand)
    Sitting on a hill.
    One named Jack. (hold right hand/finger forward)
    One named Jill. (hold left hand/finger forward)
    Fly away, Jack. (wiggle right finger and place behind your back)
    Fly away, Jill. (wiggle left finger and place behind your back)
    Come back, Jack. (bring right hand back)
    Come back, Jill. (bring left hand back)

*Toddlers and twos present a wide range of developmental needs, abilities, and interests. For each learning area, select among the following activity and experience choices that are appropriate for the children in your care.

Cognitive Development Choices

▪ Provide black dress-up clothes for exploration. Be sure to have a mirror available. Help the children describe the ensembles they create.

▪ Invite the children to build with black Paper Bag Blocks. Fill black paper bags about ¾ full with crumpled newspaper, square off the tops, and seal them closed with black vinyl tape. Discuss the color of the blocks as the children play with them. "What can you build with black blocks?"

▪ Invite the children to draw with black markers on white paper. Encourage the children to describe their work.

▪ Encourage the children to paint with black Puff Paint. Mix ⅓ cup of white glue with 2 tablespoons of black tempera paint and 2 cups of shaving cream. Encourage the children to use it like fingerpaint. "How does the paint feel?"

▪ Encourage the children to use white chalk on a chalkboard or on black construction paper. Ask the children to describe their pictures.

▪ Invite the children to shell black-eyed peas. "Can you find the black eye on the pea?" If possible, cook the peas and serve with lunch.

▪ Problem-solving suggestion: Invite the children to work Black Puzzles. Laminate pieces of black poster board and then cut them into simple puzzle pieces. Make some puzzles that have two or three pieces and some that have five or six pieces.

REFLECTION ON THE DAY
Ask the children to show you something or name something that is black.

White

WORDS TO PRACTICE

color

white

light

GETTING STARTED

- Wear white clothes. Invite the children to wear white (Appendix p. 443). Discuss the color of everyone's clothing. Ask questions to find out what the children know about the color *white*.
- Tell them that today they will be learning about the color *white* and how it is used to describe things.
- Read your favorite book about white (or other colors) to the children or select a book from the Story Circle Suggestions below to check out of the library and read.

STORY CIRCLE SUGGESTIONS

- *Black on White* by Tana Hoban
- *It Looked Like Spilt Milk* by Charles Shaw
- *White on Black* by Tana Hoban

PREPARATION FOR "WHITE" ACTIVITIES AND EXPERIENCES

- Send a letter home to families inviting children to wear white (see color schedule letter, Appendix p. 443).
- Make the "Frosty the Snowman" (Appendix p. 475-478) flannel board story.
- Gather white items.
- Get bread, soda, peppermint extract, marshmallow cream, and graham crackers.
- Ask families to bring in toothbrushes.
- Gather ingredients and make Cloud Dough (see p. 140) and Goop (see p. 141).

Language Enrichment Choices*

- Collect white items such as handkerchiefs, socks, coconut, marshmallows, paper, and crayons. Show them to the children. Discuss them and pass them around so the children can look at the things more closely. Lay the items on a special "color table" so that the children can explore them throughout the day.

- Use the word *white* in a sentence. "I like to wear my *white* socks."

- Present the flannel board story/song, "Frosty the Snowman" (Appendix p. 475-478). Discuss Frosty's color. Ask the children if they have seen snow. Encourage the children who have to describe their experiences.

- Teach the children the fingerplay, "Five Little Snowmen." Discuss the color of snow.

  Five Little Snowmen
  Five little snowmen happy and gay, (hold up five fingers and move one
      for each snowman)
  The first one said, "What a nice day!"
  The second one said, "We'll cry no tears."
  The third one said, "We'll stay for years."
  The fourth one said, "But what happens in May?"
  The fifth one said, "Look, we're melting away!" (hold hands out as if saying "gone")

- Teach the children the American Sign Language sign for *white* (Appendix p. 439). Review other color signs.

Physical Development Choices

- Play White Light. Turn off the classroom lights and use a flashlight to make a spot on the floor. Encourage the children, one at a time, to try to step on the light as you move it around on the floor.

- Take a walk outdoors to look at the clouds. Discuss their color and their shape.

- Take a large white sheet outdoors to use as you would a parachute. Ask the children and other adults in the class to stand around the perimeter of the sheet. As one group raises and lowers the sheet, another group can run under and back out as the sheet goes up and down. Or bounce white wads of paper on the sheet.

*Toddlers and twos present a wide range of developmental needs, abilities, and interests. For each learning area, select among the following activity and experience choices that are appropriate for the children in your care.

■ Teach the children the song, "Six White Ducks." Talk about the colors of the ducks. Show the children how to wobble like a duck. Encourage them to squat and then walk.

Six White Ducks
Six white ducks that I once knew, (hold up six fingers)
Fat ducks, skinny ducks, they were, too. (hold hands out to show fat and skinny)
But the one little duck with the feather on her back, (hold up one finger, then point to your back)
She ruled the others with a quack, quack, quack! (shake finger)

Down to the river they would go, (walk fingers out in front of you)
Wibble, wobble, wibble, wobble all in a row. (sway side to side)
But the one little duck with the feather on her back, (hold up one finger, then point to your back)
She ruled the others with a quack, quack, quack! (shake finger)

Social and Emotional Development Choices

■ Work with the children one at a time. Give the child a piece of white bread. Encourage the child to take bites of the bread around the edges. Look at the resulting shape. "Does it look like anything?"

■ Discuss how the color white makes us feel.

■ Invite the children to help make Homemade Toothpaste by mixing 1 tablespoon of baking soda with 2 or 3 drops of peppermint extract. Stir in a small amount of water to make a paste. Teach the children how to brush their teeth. Discuss how brushing their teeth will help keep them pretty and white. Sing the following song, "This Is the Way We Clean Our Teeth," to the tune "The Mulberry Bush."

This Is the Way We Clean Our Teeth
This is the way we clean our teeth,
Clean our teeth, clean our teeth.
This is the way we clean our teeth
Every night and morning.
Take your brush, go up and down
Up and down, up and down.
Take your brush, go up and down,
Every night and morning.

Don't forget both back and front,
Back and front, back and front,
Don't forget both back and front,
Every night and morning.

■ Sing "Three White Mice" to the tune of "Three Blind Mice." "Has anyone ever seen a white mouse?"

Three White Mice
Three white mice, three white mice,
See how they dance, see how they dance.
They danced and danced for the farmer's wife,
Who played for them on a silver fife.
Did you ever see such a sight in your life,
As three white mice!

■ Serve a snack of marshmallow cream on graham crackers. Discuss the color of the cream on their crackers. You might also discuss the texture of the cream and the taste of the snack.

Cognitive Development Choices

■ Spray shaving cream on a tabletop and encourage the children to use their hands to create designs in the cream. Talk about the color of the shaving cream. "How does the shaving cream feel?"

■ Provide Styrofoam chips in a shallow tub and encourage the children to fill and spill containers full of chips. Talk with the children about the color and weight of the Styrofoam.

■ Build a tent with a white sheet. Invite the children to look at books inside the tent. Sit inside with them and read a book.

■ Give the children Cloud Dough to play with. Mix 1 cup of oil, 6 cups of flour, and 1 cup of water. Use just enough water to bind the mixture. Start with 1 cup of water as called for in the recipe, and then add 1 tablespoon at a time as needed. Knead the mixture. Cloud dough is very oily, but provides a different tactile experience. Encourage the children to talk about the feel of the dough.

- Invite the children to play with Goop. To make Goop, gradually add 2 cups of warm water to 3 cups of cornstarch. Mix the ingredients together with your hands. Goop is ready when it has a satin-like texture. Goop hardens in the air and turns to liquid when held. It resists punching, but a light touch causes a finger to sink in. Ask the children to describe the feel of the goop.

- Problem-solving suggestion: Encourage the children to blow ping-pong balls across a table. "Are there other ways to move the ball across the table without blowing on it or touching it?"

REFLECTION ON THE DAY

Ask the children to name or show you something that is white.

Round

WORDS TO PRACTICE

circle   round   shape

GETTING STARTED

- Ask questions to find out what the children know about the word *round*. Ask them to show you something that is round.
- Tell them that today they will be learning about the word *round* and how it is used to describe things.
- Read your favorite book about round things/shapes to the children or select a book from the Story Circle Suggestions below to check out of the library and read.

STORY CIRCLE SUGGESTIONS

- *Big, Small, Little Red Ball* by Emma Dodd
- *Carousel* by Donald Crews
- *Goodnight Moon* by Margaret Wise Brown
- *Round Is a Mooncake* by Roseanne Thong
- *What Is Round?* by Rebecca Kai Dotlich

PREPARATION FOR "ROUND" ACTIVITIES AND EXPERIENCES

- Gather several sizes of balls and several round objects.
- Get ingredients for Orange Ball Cookies (see p. 144).
- Mix Cloud Dough (see p. 144).
- Make "Frosty the Snowman" (Appendix p. 475-478) and "The Great Big Pumpkin" flannel board stories (Appendix p. 492-494), if not already made.
- Prepare "The Strange Visitor" prop story, if not already made (Appendix 559-560).

Language Enrichment Choices*

- Fill a basket with balls of all sizes and types. Use the balls to discuss things that have a round shape. Show some other

*Toddlers and twos present a wide range of developmental needs, abilities, and interests. For each learning area, select among the following activity and experience choices that are appropriate for the children in your care.

round things (or photos of round things) such as a globe, an ornament, an orange, and a pumpkin. (There are separate suggestions for *circle* found on page 146-150.) Although a round item is circular, the activity and experiences will focus on three-dimensional round items.

▨ Use the word *round* in a sentence. For example, "The beach ball is big and *round.*"

▨ Present the "Frosty the Snowman" flannel board story/song (Appendix 475-478). Discuss the three round balls that make up Frosty's body. You can also use this story to review facial features.

▨ Tell the flannel board story, "The Great Big Pumpkin," (Appendix p. 492-494) to the children. Discuss the roundness of the thing the bear and his friends are trying to take home. "Would the pumpkin roll if it was square?"

▨ Tell the children the prop story, "The Strange Visitor" (Appendix p. 559-560). Discuss the round, round head of the visitor.

▨ Teach the children the American Sign Language sign for *round* (Appendix p. 437).

Physical Development Choices

▨ Ask the children to sit in a circle with their legs spread out in front of them, touching the feet of the child next to them so that the entire circle is enclosed. Give the children a ball and encourage them to roll it back and forth to each other. Encourage the child who is rolling the ball to call the name of the child she is rolling the ball to. Make sure everyone gets a turn to roll and to catch.

▨ Show the children how to roll a ball across the floor using their heads. Ask them to get into a crawling position and then use a nodding motion with their head to roll the ball.

▨ Give the children wads of paper shaped into round balls to toss into a basket. Discuss the shape of the paper balls.

▨ Encourage the children to chase bubbles. "What shape are the bubbles?"

Social and Emotional Development Choices

▨ Let the children help you make Orange Ball Cookies. Crush 35 vanilla wafers by placing them into a zipper-closure plastic bag and pounding them with a block. Pour the vanilla wafers into a bowl and add ¼ cup of orange juice and 2 tablespoons sugar. Mix well. Moisten your hands with water and roll the mixture into balls, and then roll the balls in powdered sugar. Talk about the shape of these delicious cookies as you roll them (makes 24 balls).

▨ Say the following action rhyme, "A Big Round Ball" with each of the children. Suit the actions to the words and talk about making our bodies into a round ball.

A Big Round Ball
I like being really tall. (stand up tall)
I like being very small. (squat down)
But when I'm tired of being tall, (stand up tall)
And tired of being very small, (squat down)
Onto the floor I will fall (lay on the floor)
And make myself a big round ball. (bring knees to chin to make a ball)

▨ Serve grapes for snack. "What shape are the grapes?" "What other fruit is round?" **Safety Warning:** Cut the grapes into quarters before serving them. Whole grapes are a choking hazard for toddlers.

▨ Sing "This Is the Way We Bounce the Ball" to the tune of "Mulberry Bush." Demonstrate how to bounce a ball as you sing. Encourage the little ones to try to bounce a ball. They will all be able to throw a ball and watch it bounce.

This Is the Way We Bounce the Ball
This is the way we bounce the ball
Bounce the ball, bounce the ball.
This is the way we bounce the ball
Across the classroom floor.

Cognitive Development Choices

▨ Give the children Cloud Dough to play with. Mix 1 cup of oil, 6 cups of flour, and 1 cup of water. Use just enough water to bind the mixture. Start with 1 cup of water as called for in the recipe, and then add 1 tablespoon at a time as needed. Knead the mixture. Cloud dough is very oily, but provides a different tactile experience. Encourage the children to roll the dough into round balls. Show them how to make a snowman.

- Invite the children to roll ping-pong balls across a table and into a basket on the other side of the table. Try rolling an object that isn't round, such as a block.

- Invite the children to make marble paintings. Place a piece of drawing paper in the bottom of a shallow box. Place a couple of marbles into a cup of tempera paint and coat them with paint. Remove the marbles with a spoon and drop them into the box. Show the child how to rotate the box to make the marbles move back and forth. A great design will result. Discuss the roundness of the marbles and how being round helps the marbles roll.

- Provide playdough and encourage the children to roll the dough into balls. Show the children how to roll two balls together to make a larger ball.

- Encourage the children to pop the bubbles in a sheet of large bubble wrap. Ask the children what shape the bubbles are before they pop.

- Problem-solving suggestion: Construct a ramp. Give the children things that will roll down the ramp such as a ping-pong ball, tennis ball, can, and crayon, and things that won't roll down the ramp such as a block, book, and stuffed animal. Help the children see that all of the things that roll are round.

REFLECTION ON THE DAY
Ask the children to show you something that is round.

Circle

WORDS TO PRACTICE

circle	round
circular	shape

GETTING STARTED

- Make a large circle on the floor using masking tape. Ask the children to sit on the circular line for group activities. Call attention to the shape they are creating by their seating arrangement. Ask questions to find out what the children know about circles.
- Tell them that today they will be learning about how the words *circle* and *circular* are used to describe things.
- Read your favorite book about circles or shapes to the children or select a book from the Story Circle Suggestions below to check out of the library and read.

STORY CIRCLE SUGGESTIONS

- *I See Circles* by Mike Artell
- *So Many Circles, So Many Squares* by Tana Hoban
- *What Is Round?* by Rebecca Kai Dotlich

*Toddlers and twos present a wide range of developmental needs, abilities, and interests. For each learning area, select among the following activity and experience choices that are appropriate for the children in your care.

PREPARATION FOR "CIRCLE" ACTIVITIES AND EXPERIENCES

- Make a masking tape circle on the floor.
- Gather circular items.
- Make Circular Rings on the next page, Wrist Bells (see p. 148), and Concentric Circles (see p. 149).
- Make "Smart Cookie's Best Friend: Gabby Graham" flannel board story (Appendix p. 556-558).
- Get English muffins or cookies.
- Cut drawing paper into circles.

Language Enrichment Choices*

- Place several circular items such as a plate, bowl, clock, button, ring, and hat in a box (a round hat box, if available).

Take the items out of the box one at a time and discuss each shape. Show the children how a plate will roll.

■ Use the word *circle* in a sentence. For example, "We sit in a *circle* when we sing."

■ Present the flannel board story, "Smart Cookie's Best Friend, Gabby Graham" (Appendix p. 556-558). Discuss Smart Cookie's shape. Talk with the children about the shapes of their favorite cookies.

■ Teach the children the American Sign Language sign for *circle* (Appendix p. 431).

Physical Development Choices

■ Play "Ring Around the Rosie" with the children. Ask the children to hold hands and walk in a circle. Everyone falls down on the words, "We all fall down." While the children are in a circle, call their attention to the fact they are in a circle.

Ring Around the Rosie
Ring around the rosie
Pocket full of posies.
Ashes, ashes,
We all fall down.

■ Place a circular basket in the middle of the floor and challenge the children to toss small paper plates into it. Call attention to the circular basket and plates.

■ Cut the center out of several plastic lids, such as those found on coffee cans, to make Circular Rings. Encourage the children to place the Circular Rings over a half-liter soda bottle. Discuss the circular shape of the rings. Encourage children to trace it with their finger.

Social and Emotional Development Choices

■ Say the action rhyme, "My Head" with each of the children. Discuss the "circle that is our head." Have a circular hat (see cognitive activities) available to put on the child's head.

My Head
This is the circle that is my head.
This is my mouth with which words are said.
These are my eyes with which I see.
This is my nose that is part of me.

This is the hair that grows on my head,
And this is my hat I wear on my head.

▪ Play "'Round the House" with the children. Point out the circle you make on their hands as the game begins.

'Round the House
'Round the house, (use index finger to trace a circle on the child's open palm)
'Round the house,
Goes the little mousie.
Up the stairs, (walk index finger and middle finger up the child's arm)
Up the stairs,
In his little housie. (tickle the child under his chin)

▪ Place a colored stick-on dot on each child's hand. Discuss the shape of the dot.

▪ Serve circular snacks such as English muffins with jelly or cookies. Discuss the shape of the snack.

Cognitive Development Choices

▪ Invite the children to make circular hats. Cut out the center of a few paper plates, one for each child. Provide tissue paper, plastic flowers, lace, bows, rickrack, and so on to glue to the outer rim of the plate (the hat). Staple ribbon or yarn to each side of the rim to use as ties. Encourage the children to put on their hats and take a look in the mirror. "How do they look?"

▪ Cut sponges into circles and invite the children to make circular sponge prints on a piece of paper. "Do the circular designs look like anything?"

▪ Provide several scrunchies and an empty paper towel tube. Encourage the children to put the scrunchies on the paper towel tube. Discuss the circular shape of the scrunchies.

▪ Sew jingle bells to scrunchies to make Wrist Bells. Invite the children to wear the Wrist Bells while they play. Discuss the circular shape of the Wrist Bells.

- Invite the children to make paper chains. Cut construction paper into 1" x 12" strips. Show the children how to glue (or paste) the first strip into a circle and then how to continue the chain by threading the remaining strips and gluing each of them into a circle. Younger toddlers will need your help with the threading. They will enjoy the pasting and will love the finished product. Discuss the circles they are making.

- Provide stick-on dots and encourage the children to stick them on a piece of paper, a box, or an empty paper towel tube. "What shape are the stick-on dots?"

- Give the children circular sheets of paper on which to draw. Ask them to describe their work. "Is it more fun to draw on circular paper?"

- Provide a box of buttons for the children to play with. Discuss the shape of the buttons and the holes in the buttons. Commercial buttons, such as Attribute Buttons, are perfect for toddler play.
  Safety Warning: Supervise this activity closely to make sure that little ones don't put buttons into their mouths.

- Cut circles out of wallpaper sample books or out of construction paper. Invite the children to glue the circles onto a piece of drawing paper to make a circle collage.

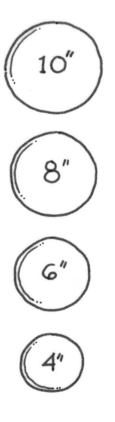

- Problem-solving suggestion: Provide Concentric Circles for the children to explore. Cut four circles out of different colors of construction paper. Cut the first circle 10" in diameter, the second one 8" in diameter, the third one 6" in diameter, and the last circle 4" in diameter. Laminate the circles. Encourage the children to arrange the circles in descending order from largest to smallest, laying each circle on top of the one just larger. "Which circle is the largest? Smallest?"

REFLECTION ON THE DAY
Show the children several objects and ask them to point out the ones that are circles.

Square

WORDS TO PRACTICE

shape   square

GETTING STARTED

- Use masking tape to make a large square on the floor. Ask the children to sit on the perimeter of the square. Discuss the shape they are creating.
- Tell the children that today they will be learning about how the word *square* is used to describe things.
- Read your favorite book about squares/shapes to the children or select a book from the Story Circle Suggestions below to check out of the library and read.

STORY CIRCLE SUGGESTIONS

- *I See Squares* by Mike Artell
- *Shapes* by Alvin Granowsky
- *Shapes, Shapes, Shapes* by Tana Hoban
- *Squares* by Jennifer Burke
- *Squares* by Sophie Fatus

*Toddlers and twos present a wide range of developmental needs, abilities, and interests. For each learning area, select among the following activity and experience choices that are appropriate for the children in your care.

PREPARATION FOR "SQUARE" ACTIVITIES AND EXPERIENCES

- Make "Smart Cookie's Best Friend: Gabby Graham" flannel board story, if not already made (Appendix p. 556-558).
- Gather square items.
- Cut paper, sandpaper, and sponges into squares.
- Gather bread, jelly, and/or graham crackers.
- Make a memory game with square playing cards.

Language Enrichment Choices*

- Fill a box with square items such as a hot pad, a book, a pan, and a bandana. Take the items out of the bag one at a time and discuss their shape. Ask the children if they can think of other things with a square shape.

- Use the word *square* in a sentence. For example, "I like the *square* blocks."

- Present the flannel board story, "Smart Cookie's Best Friend: Gabby Graham," (Appendix p. 556-558). Discuss Gabby Graham's shape. "Has anyone eaten graham crackers before?"

- Teach the children the American Sign Language sign for *square* (Appendix p. 438). Review other shape signs.

Physical Development Choices

- Make a big square on the playground with yarn or rope. Encourage the children to walk, run, and crawl around the square.

- Invite the children to toss square beanbags into a square box. Encourage them to use their fingers to trace around the perimeter of the square box or beanbag.

Social and Emotional Development Choices

- Take a tour of the room in search of square things.

- Do "Washington Square" with each child. Have the child open his or her hand. Use your index finger to trace a square in his or her palm as you say the rhyme below.

    Washington Square
    From here to there (begin tracing square)
    To Washington Square.
    When I get near
    I'll pull your hair. (gently pull the child's hair)

- Serve square snacks such as graham crackers or jelly sandwiches. Point out the shape of the snack. "What happens to the square when you take a bite out of your snack?"

Cognitive Development Choices

- Give the children several square boxes that fit inside of each other. Encourage them to place the boxes inside of each other. Ask the children to rub their fingers around the perimeter of the boxes.

- Provide large square boxes for the children to play in.

- Encourage the children to play with the square blocks. What things can they build with the squares? Can they build a square with the square blocks?

- Give the children square sheets of paper on which to draw. Ask the children to identify the shape of their paper. Encourage them to tell you about their picture.

- Cut squares out of construction paper or from wallpaper sample books. Invite the children to glue the squares onto a sheet of square paper to make a square collage.

- Cut squares out of sandpaper. Place the sandpaper squares under drawing paper and encourage the children to make crayon rubbings by rubbing a crayon over the squares. Discuss the shapes as the children create their pictures.

- Provide a tub of water and square sponges. Invite the children to play with the sponges. Discuss their shape. "Can you change the shape of the sponge by squeezing it?"

- Problem-solving suggestion: Play a memory game using square cards. Cut index cards into squares. Use stickers to create two of each card design. For toddlers, six cards make a good game; eight cards are challenging. If you would like to use a shape memory game, just draw circles on two cards, triangles on two cards, and squares on two cards. Sit with the children while they play and ask them about their choices. Help them learn how to make good choices.

REFLECTION ON THE DAY
Ask the children to show you square things in the classroom.

Stripes

WORDS TO PRACTICE

designs	striped
patterns	stripes

GETTING STARTED

- Wear clothing that is striped. Hang strips of crepe paper from the top of the door jamb so that the children pass through them on their way into the classroom, or from the top of the windows. If you hang the paper from the top of the windows, you will probably have striped shadows sometime during the day. Discuss the stripes you are wearing and the stripes you have added to the classroom.
- Tell the children that today they will be learning about how the word *stripes* is used to describe things.
- Read your favorite book about stripes/patterns to the children or select a book from the Story Circle Suggestions below to check out of the library and read.

STORY CIRCLE SUGGESTIONS

- *Spots and Stripes: A Baby Soft Book*
- *Who Is the Beast?* by Keith Baker

PREPARATION FOR "STRIPES" ACTIVITIES AND EXPERIENCES

- Hang crepe paper streamers from the door jamb.
- Gather striped items and empty paper towel tubes.
- Gather ingredients for cheese bread (see p. 155).
- Mix two colors of playdough.

Language Enrichment Choices*

- Show the children striped pieces of fabric, wallpaper samples, candy, flags, and plastic or stuffed animals. Show them pictures of things that have stripes such as zebras and clothing. Talk about the stripes. "What color are they?" "Are they wide or narrow?"

*Toddlers and twos present a wide range of developmental needs, abilities, and interests. For each learning area, select among the following activity and experience choices that are appropriate for the children in your care.

Which One! • Words That Describe

■ Share the poem, "The Zebra." Show the children a picture of a zebra.

The Zebra by Pam Schiller
The zebra looks just like a horse
Except for all those stripes, of course.
I wonder if he's black with stripes of snowy white,
Or is he snowy white with stripes as black as night?

■ Use the word *stripes* in a sentence. For example, "Steve has on a shirt with green *stripes.*"

■ Teach the children the American Sign Language sign for *stripes* (Appendix p. 438). Review other signs that the children have learned.

Physical Development Choices

■ Cut out several squares of striped wallpaper and several squares of solid wallpaper. Tell the children that you are going to show them the squares. When they see striped paper, they should jump up and down. When they see a solid, they should turn around in a circle. Show the squares in random order.

■ Play Drop the Handkerchief with a striped handkerchief. Choose one child to be IT while the other children sit in a circle facing the center. The child who is IT skips or walks around the outside of the circle and casually drops the green handkerchief behind one of the children sitting in the circle. This child picks up the handkerchief and chases IT around the circle. IT tries to run around the circle and sit in the second child's spot without being tagged. If IT is not tagged, then he sits in his new spot in the circle, and the child with the handkerchief is now IT. If IT is tagged, then he is IT for another round. Depending on the age of your group, you may need to offer assistance to each child who is IT while a second adult helps the runner.

Social and Emotional Development Choices

■ Play a memory game with each child. Cut out squares from a wallpaper sample book. Cut two squares of striped paper, two squares of a solid color paper, and two squares of polka dot paper. Glue the squares to index cards. Turn the cards face down. Encourage the child to choose two cards to turn over. If they match, pick them up and move them to the side. If they don't match, try again.

- Help the children make striped cheese toast. Butter a piece of bread. Cut a square of cheese into stripes and invite the children to arrange it on the bread so that there is a space between each strip. Toast the bread. Point out the stripes on the toast as the children eat it. "Does it taste better than plain toast?"

Cognitive Development Choices

- Invite the children to paint stripes on easel paper. Provide different widths of brushes, if desired. Encourage the children to discuss their paintings.

- Cut construction paper into 1" x 12" strips. Help the children glue them to a piece of paper to create stripes. Discuss the stripe pattern they are making.

- Provide striped dress-up clothing for the children to explore. Discuss the pattern on the clothing.

- Make two different colors of playdough. Show the children how to roll snakes in each color and then place them in alternating rows to create stripes. "What happens if you twist two different colored snakes into one?"

- Help the children make a striped pathway by placing white and red Legos in columns.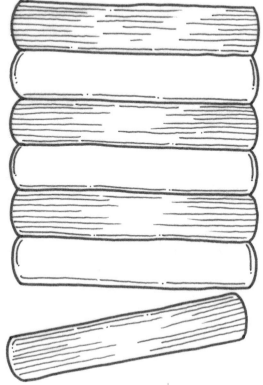

- Place strips of masking tape on a table, leaving the table showing through between strips. Invite the little ones to peel off the stripes. Call attention to the stripes on the table before they start removing them.

- Problem-solving suggestion: Spray paint (adult only) 8-10 empty paper towel tubes, or cover them with contact paper. Make half of the tubes red and the other half white. Challenge the children to arrange the tubes in a striped pattern. Discuss the results and assist if necessary.

REFLECTION ON THE DAY
Ask the children to show you something that is striped.

Sunny

WORDS TO PRACTICE

bright	sunny	weather
hot	sunshine	
summer	warm	

GETTING STARTED

- Make a Weather Wheel (Appendix p. 474). If the weather is sunny, go outside and discuss how the weather feels and how things look on a sunny day. "Is it bright outside?" "Is it warm?" "Can you feel the warmth of the sun?" "Does the sun hurt your eyes?" "Do you have to squint?" Show the children the Weather Wheel. Point out the symbol that represents a sunny day. Set the wheel to the symbol for "sunny." If the weather isn't sunny, you may want to wait for a sunny day to teach these activities.
- Tell the children that today they will be learning about how the word *sunny* is used to describe the weather.
- Read your favorite book about weather to the children or select a book from the Story Circle Suggestions below to check out of the library and read.

STORY CIRCLE SUGGESTIONS

- *Barney's Weather Book* by Mary Ann Dudko
- *Bear in the Sunshine* by Stella Blackstone
- *Kipper's Book of Weather* by Mick Inkpen
- *Rain or Shine* by Alvin Granowsky

PREPARATION FOR "SUNNY" ACTIVITIES AND EXPERIENCES

- Prepare Weather Wheel (Appendix p. 474).
- Make Sunshine Puzzles (see p. 159).
- Make the Magnetic Dress-Me Dolls (Appendix p. 455-466).
- Freeze ice cubes.
- Gather items for Hairy Creatures (see p. 159).
- Find pictures of sunny days. (Look in magazines and catalogs.)

Language Enrichment Choices*

▧ Sing "Sunny, Sunny" to the tune of "Clementine." Talk about things to do on a sunny day.

> **Sunny, Sunny**
> *Sunny, sunny,*
> *Sunny, sunny,*
> *It is sunny in the sky.*
> *Sunny, sunny,*
> *Sunny, sunny,*
> *It is sunny in the sky.*

▧ Show the children pictures of sunny days, if available. Ask questions about what the children see in the photos. Encourage descriptive words.

▧ Use the word *sunny* in a sentence. For example, "I love *sunny* days."

▧ Teach the children the American Sign Language sign for *sunny* (Appendix p. 438).

Physical Development Choices

▧ Show the children how to play shadow tag. Help them find another child's shadow and then try to step on it. "Does it hurt when someone steps on your shadow?" Explain that this game only works on a sunny day.

▧ Invite the children to paint with water on the sidewalk and/or wooden fence. When the "paint" (water) evaporates, explain that the sun is so warm it dries the water right off the fence and/or sidewalk.

▧ Do the action rhyme, "Tiny Seed." Talk about the role of the sun in helping seeds to grow.

> **Tiny Seed**
> *Tiny seed planted just right,* (children tuck themselves into a ball)
> *Not a breath of air, not a ray of light.*
> *Rain falls slowly to and fro,*
> *And now the seed begins to grow.* (children begin to unfold)
> *Slowly reaching for the light,*
> *With all its energy, all its might.*
> *The little seed's work is almost done,*
> *To grow up tall and face the sun.* (children stand up tall with arms stretched out)

*Toddlers and twos present a wide range of developmental needs, abilities, and interests. For each learning area, select among the following activity and experience choices that are appropriate for the children in your care.

Social and Emotional Development Choices

- Talk with the children about the importance of wearing sunscreen when they are out in the sun. If appropriate, spread some on them when they play outdoors today.

- Sing "It Is Sunny" to the tune of "Are You Sleeping?" with the children. Talk to each one of them about what they might like to do on a sunny day.

    It Is Sunny
    It is sunny,
    It is sunny.
    Yes it is,
    Yes it is.
    Let's go out and play.
    Let's go out and play.
    We'll have fun!
    We'll have fun!

- Sing "Mister Sun" to the tune of "Mister Moon" with the children. Point out that it is the sun that creates a sunny day.

    Mister Sun
    Oh, Mister Sun, Sun, Mister Golden Sun,
    Won't you please shine down on me?
    Oh, Mister Sun, Sun, Mister Golden Sun,
    Hiding behind that tree.
    These little children are asking you
    To please come out so we can play with you.
    Oh, Mister Sun, Sun, Mister Golden Sun,
    Won't you please shine down on me?

Cognitive Development Choices

- Provide some bright, sunny colors of tempera paint. Invite the children to paint a sunny day picture. Ask them to describe their painting.

- Provide several pairs of sunglasses for the children to explore. "How do sunglasses change the way things look?"

- Give the children sun hats to try on. Provide a mirror. Ask the children to describe how they look. Talk about how important it is to wear a sun hat on sunny days. It protects our skin and our heads.

■ Let the children dress the Magnetic Dress-Me Dolls (Appendix p. 455-466) in sunny-day clothes. You can also use the dolls to tell a story about a sunny day. Discuss the clothes as the children dress the dolls.

■ Provide sunny-day clothing for dress-up play. Be sure to include some sun hats and a mirror.

■ Hang prisms in the window and call attention to the rainbows created by the sun shining through the crystals. Spin the crystals to make spinning rainbows. Invite the children to try to hop on the rainbows. "Which color do you like best?"

■ Make Hairy Creatures. Cut off the feet from pairs of pantyhose. You will need one foot portion per child. Help each child place the toe of the hose inside a Styrofoam cup and then fold the cut edge of the hose around the mouth of the cup. This is to hold the hose in place while the children stuff it. Stuff the hose with potting soil and rye grass seeds. Remove from the cup and tie off the open end of the hose. Sew on bead eyes or glue on wiggle eyes. Hang the creatures in a sunny window. In a few days the seeds will sprout and the creatures will become "hairy." Encourage the children to name the creatures.

cut

hose

styrofoam cup

Potting Soil and seeds

Hairy Creature!

■ Give each child an ice cube in a cup to take out to the playground. Encourage them to watch the ice melt in the sun.

■ Problem-solving suggestion: Give the children Sunshine Puzzles to work. Cut out large circles from yellow construction paper. Draw a face on the circles, if desired. Laminate and cut them into puzzle pieces. Cut some puzzles into two or three pieces and others into four or five pieces to create a range of difficulty. You can keep track of which puzzle pieces go to which puzzles by color coding them with colored stick-on dots on the back of each piece of the same puzzle.

REFLECTION ON THE DAY
Ask the children to describe something that happens on a sunny day. Show the children some weather pictures and invite your "not yet talkers" to show you a picture of a sunny day.

Cloudy

WORDS TO PRACTICE

cloudy

gray

weather

GETTING STARTED

- If the sky is cloudy, go outside and discuss how the weather feels and what things look like on a cloudy day. "Is the sky gray or blue?" "Are the clouds puffy?" "Is it dry or damp?" If it is sunny and cloudy, point out the whiteness of the clouds. Show the children the Weather Wheel (Appendix p. 474). Point out the symbol on the wheel that represents a cloudy day. Set the Weather Wheel to the cloudy symbol. If the weather isn't cloudy, you may want to wait for a cloudy day to use these activities.
- Tell the children that today they will be learning about how the word *cloudy* is used to describe the weather.
- Read your favorite book about weather to the children or select a book from the Story Circle Suggestions below to check out of the library and read.

STORY CIRCLE SUGGESTIONS

- *Barney's Weather Book* by Mary Ann Dudko
- *It Looked Like Spilt Milk* by Charles Shaw
- *Kipper's Book of Weather* by Mick Inkpen

PREPARATION FOR "CLOUDY" ACTIVITIES AND EXPERIENCES

- Prepare Weather Wheel, if not already made (Appendix p. 474).
- Cut out clouds from white poster board or vinyl.
- Gather ingredients and mix Cloud Dough and white Puff Paint (see p. 162).
- Make Shadow Match game (see p. 163).
- Find pictures of cloudy days to share with the children.

Language Enrichment Choices*

▦ Sing "It Is Cloudy" to the tune of "Clementine." Ask the children to think of things to do on a cloudy day. Many people think that cloudy days are good days for yard work.

It Is Cloudy
Cloudy, cloudy,
Cloudy, cloudy,
It is cloudy in the sky.
Cloudy, cloudy,
Cloudy, cloudy,
It is cloudy in the sky.

▦ Show the children pictures of cloudy days, if available.

▦ Use the word *cloudy* in a sentence. For example, "The sky is *cloudy,* and it looks like it will rain."

▦ Teach the children the American Sign Language sign for *clouds* (Appendix p. 431).

Physical Development Choices

▦ Play Musical Clouds as you would Co-operative Musical Chairs. Cut out clouds from white vinyl or poster board. If you use poster board, laminate the clouds. Make one less cloud than children playing the game. Play some music and ask the children to march around in a circle until the music stops. When it stops, instruct the children to find a cloud to stand on. In this version of the game, it is okay if more than one child stands on the same cloud. No one is ever "out." Take a cloud away each time you stop the music, until there is only one cloud left. "Can all the children stand on one remaining cloud?"

*Toddlers and twos present a wide range of developmental needs, abilities, and interests. For each learning area, select among the following activity and experience choices that are appropriate for the children in your care.

▦ Play Cloud Hop. Tape the clouds you made for Musical Clouds to the floor and encourage the children to jump from cloud to cloud.

Social and Emotional Development Choices

▢ Give each child a piece of bread. Ask them to take bites around the perimeter to create a cloud. Talk with them about the shape of their cloud. "Does it look like something that is recognizable?" "Does it look like a cloud?"

▢ Say "April Clouds" with the children.

> **April Clouds**
> *Two little clouds one April day* (hold both hands in fists)
> *Went sailing across the sky.* (move fist from left to right)
> *They went so fast that they bumped their heads* (bump fists together)
> *And both began to cry.* (point to eyes)
>
> *The big round sun came out and said,* (make circle with arms)
> *"Oh, never mind, my dears,*
> *I'll send all my sunbeams down* (wiggle fingers downward like rain)
> *To dry your fallen tears."*

Cognitive Development Choices

▢ Take the children outdoors to watch the clouds. What shapes do they find?

▢ Place shaving cream on a tabletop and encourage the children to make clouds.

▢ Give the children Cloud Dough to play with. Mix 1 cup of oil, 6 cups of flour, and 1 cup of water. Use just enough water to bind the mixture. Start with 1 cup of water as called for in the recipe, and then add one tablespoon at a time as needed. Knead the mixture. Cloud dough is very oily, but provides a different tactile experience. Challenge the children to shape clouds with the dough.

▢ Give the children sheets of gray construction paper. Ask them to tear the paper to make a cloud. They will enjoy simply tearing the paper—any resulting shape can simulate a cloud.

▢ Provide white Puff Paint and gray or blue construction paper. Mix $\frac{1}{3}$ cup of white glue with 2 tablespoons of black tempera paint and 2 cups of shaving cream. Encourage the children to use it like fingerpaint. Encourage the children to paint some clouds on their blue or gray sky. Ask them to describe their work.

■ Place bubble bath or dishwasher soap in a water play table. Stir up the bubbles and let the children pick up handfuls of "clouds."

■ Problem-solving suggestion: Invite the children to play Shadow Match. Ask them to match white clouds to their shadows. Cut six white and black clouds out of white and black construction paper at the same time so you have a matching white and black clouds. Try to make each of the six cloud shapes distinctively different. Glue the black clouds inside a manila folder and laminate the folder. Laminate the white clouds. As the children match the clouds, talk with them about the shadows that clouds make on the ground on a sunny day.

REFLECTION ON THE DAY
Ask the children to describe a cloudy day. Show the children some weather pictures and invite the "not yet talkers" to show you a picture of a cloudy day.

Cold

WORDS TO PRACTICE

chilly	freezing	winter
cold	weather	

GETTING STARTED

- If it is a cold day (but not too cold to go outside), go outside and discuss how the weather feels. "Does 'smoke' come out of your mouth?" "Do your hands and feet tingle?" "Is it damp?" "Is it dry?" If it is too cold to go outdoors, go to a window to discuss the weather. You should be able to touch the window and feel that it is cold outside. Show the children the Weather Wheel (Appendix p. XX). Point out the symbol on the wheel that represents cold weather. Set the Weather Wheel to the cold symbol. If the weather isn't cold, you may want to wait for a cold day to offer these activities.
- Tell the children that today they will learn about how the word *cold* describes the weather.
- Read your favorite book about weather to the children or select a book from the Story Circle Suggestions below to check out of the library and read.

STORY CIRCLE SUGGESTIONS

- *Frosty the Snowman* by Diane Muldrow
- *Frozen Noses* by Jan Carr
- *Snowy Day* by Ezra Jack Keats
- *Snowy, Flowy, Blowy* by Nancy Tafuri

PREPARATION FOR "COLD" ACTIVITIES AND EXPERIENCES

- Make Weather Wheel, if not already made (Appendix p. 474).
- Cut white crepe paper streamers.
- Cut out a white snowflake.
- Gather ingredients for hot chocolate.
- Make a cold weather Observation Bottle (see p. 167).

- Freeze a small toy in a bowl of ice.
- Make the Magnetic Dress-Me Dolls (Appendix p. 455-466).
- Make Ice Brushes (see p. 168).
- Make "Frosty the Snowman" flannel board story (Appendix p. 475-478).

Language Enrichment Choices*

- Sing "It Is Chilly" to the tune of "Clementine." Help the children think of things to do on a chilly day.

    It Is Chilly
    Chilly, chilly,
    Chilly, chilly,
    It is chilly in the air.
    Chilly, chilly,
    Chilly, chilly,
    It is chilly in the air.

- Show the children pictures of a cold day. Ask them to describe what they see in the photograph. Encourage descriptive words.

- Use the word *cold* in a weather-related sentence. For example, "When it is *cold* outside, I wear my mittens."

- Present the flannel board story, "Frosty the Snowman" (Appendix p. 475-478). Remind the children that Frosty needs cold weather to keep him from melting.

- Teach the children the American Sign Language sign for *cold* (Appendix p. 431). Review the other weather signs.

Physical Development Choices

- Invite the children to dance like snowflakes with white streamers or scarves.

- Teach the children some warming-up exercises. Explain that when we are cold, exercising helps keep us warm.

- Play Musical Freeze. Encourage the children to dance freely until the music stops. Then have them freeze. Be patient—as easy as this sounds, it requires listening, coordination, and balance.

*Toddlers and twos present a wide range of developmental needs, abilities, and interests. For each learning area, select among the following activity and experience choices that are appropriate for the children in your care.

■ Play Hot and Cold Hide and Seek. Cut out a snowflake from white construction paper. Show it to the children so they will know what they are looking for. Hide the snowflake so part of it is visible and invite the children to find it. Use the word "hot" to indicate that the children are close to the snowflake and "cold" to indicate they are not close. Little ones will have to learn to respond to these clues with a lot of help from you.

■ Invite the children to take off their shoes and pretend to ice skate. Play some waltz music for effect. Encourage them to try skating on a hard surface and then on the rug. "Which skating is easier?"

■ Invite the children to chase bubbles outdoors. The bubbles will float away faster in the cold air than they do on a warm day. "Does anyone notice?"

Social and Emotional Development Choices

■ Show the children how to blow on their hands or rub their hands together to keep them warm. Discuss how good warm hands feel when you are cold.

■ Make Hot Chocolate. Serve it after it cools down, but is still warm. As the children drink their warm drink, discuss how it warms their tummy.

■ Talk with the children about winter- or cold-weather clothing. Say the rhyme, "All By Myself" as a springboard to putting on cold-weather clothing.

All By Myself
Hat on head, just like this
Pull it down, you see.
I can put my hat on
All by myself, just me.

One arm in, two arms in,
Buttons one, two, three.
I can put my coat on
All by myself, just me.

Toes in first, heels down next,
Pull and pull, then see.
I can put my boots on
All by myself, just me.

Fingers here, thumbs right here,
Hands warm as can be.
I can put my mittens on
All by myself, just me.

▨ If appropriate, sing "Winter's Coming" to the tune of "The Muffin Man." Discuss the signs of winter.

Winter's Coming by Pam Schiller
Can you feel the wind blow cold?
The wind blow cold?
The wind blow cold?
Can you feel the wind blow cold?
Winter's coming soon.

Other verses:
Can you see the darker skies?
Can you hear the cold wind blow?
Can you see the trees all bare?
Can you button up your coat?
Can you put your mittens on?

Cognitive Development Choices

▨ Give the children cold-weather Observation Bottles to explore. Fill a clean, half-liter soda bottle with white crayon shavings and water. Fill another bottle with cold weather items, such as dried berries, moss, bark, and acorns. Glue the lid on both bottles to secure the contents. Invite the children to examine and name the items inside each bottle.

▨ Place white Styrofoam packing chips in a small plastic pool or a large box. Encourage the children to play in the "snow." Be prepared for static electricity as well as a mess to clean up.

▨ Invite the children to make designs in white shaving cream on a tabletop. Encourage them to pretend the shaving cream is snow.
Safety Warning: Be sure children do not put the shaving cream into their mouths.

▨ Provide white tempera paint, coarse sponges, and blue paper. Encourage the children to sponge paint a snowy scene. Attach clothespins to the sponges to make them easier to manipulate. Ask the children to describe their paintings.

- Invite the children to dress the Magnetic Dress-Me Dolls (Appendix p. 455-466) in winter clothes. You can also use the dolls to tell a story about a wintry day.

- Provide winter dress-up clothes such as sweaters, hats, mittens, and coats for the children to explore.

- Give the children pairs of mittens to match. Talk about how mittens are different from gloves.

- Encourage the children to draw on blue paper with white crayons. Ask them to describe their drawings. "Does it look like a wintry day?"

- Invite the children to make ice paintings with Ice Brushes. Make ice brushes by placing craft sticks into partially frozen ice cubes, and then freezing them completely. Give each child an ice cube to use as a paintbrush. Place some powdered tempera paint on their paper and encourage them to paint. "How is using an ice brush different from using a regular brush?"

- Problem-solving suggestion: Freeze a favorite toy in a bowl of ice. Place the chunk of ice in a sunny or warm spot in the room. Encourage the children to guess what is in the ice as they watch it melt.

REFLECTION ON THE DAY
Ask the children to tell you what they have learned about cold weather. Show the children some weather pictures and invite your "not yet talkers" to show you a picture of a cold day.

Hot

WORDS TO PRACTICE

hot	summer	weather
muggy	sweating	

GETTING STARTED

- If it is a hot day, go outside and discuss how the weather feels. "Is it muggy?" "Can you feel the heat of the sun?" "Is it bright?" "Does the sun hurt your eyes?" There is not a specific symbol on the Weather Wheel (see page 474) to represent hot weather. However, some of the other symbols may apply (perhaps sunny). Move the pointer on the Weather Wheel to any other symbols that are appropriate. If the weather isn't hot, you may want to wait for a hot day to offer these activities.
- Tell the children that today they will learn how the word *hot* is used to describe the weather.
- Read your favorite book about weather to the children or select a book from the Story Circle Suggestions below to check out of the library and read.

STORY CIRCLE SUGGESTIONS

- *Barney's Weather Book* by Mary Ann Dudko
- *Kipper's Book of Weather* by Mick Inkpen
- *On a Hot, Hot Day* by Nicki Weiss
- *Hotter Than a Hot Dog* by Stephanie Calmenson

PREPARATION FOR "HOT" ACTIVITIES AND EXPERIENCES

- Make a Weather Wheel, if not already made (Appendix p. 474).
- Make a yellow construction paper sun.
- Cut orange and red streamers.
- Gather ingredients for lemonade and Baggie Ice Cream (see p. 171).
- Make hot weather Observation Bottles (see p. 171-172).
- Make the Magnetic Dress-Me Dolls (Appendix p. 455-466).
- Gather beach props.

Language Enrichment Choices*

▪ Sing "It Is Sunny," to the tune of "Are You Sleeping?" with the children. Discuss the fact that it can be sunny without being hot, but most of the time when it is hot it is also sunny.

It Is Sunny
It is sunny,
It is sunny,
Yes, it is.
Yes, it is.
Let's go out and play.
Let's go out and play.
We'll have fun!
We'll have fun!

▪ Show the children hot-weather pictures, if available. Ask the children to describe what they see in the photographs. Encourage descriptive words.

▪ Use the word *hot* in a weather-related sentence. For example, "I love to eat ice cream on a *hot* day."

▪ Teach the children the American Sign Language sign for *hot* (Appendix p. 434). Review other weather signs.

Physical Development Choices

▪ Play Hot and Cold Hide and Seek. Cut out a sun from yellow construction paper. Show it to the children so they are familiar with what they are looking for during the game. Hide the sun so part of it is visible and invite the children to find it. Use the word "hot" to indicate that the children are close to the sun and "cold" to indicate they are not close. Little ones will have to learn to respond to these clues with your help.

▪ Invite the children to dance creatively with orange and red streamers.

▪ Invite the children to chase bubbles outdoors. The bubbles will float slowly on the air currents on a hot day because warm air is lighter than cold air.

*Toddlers and twos present a wide range of developmental needs, abilities, and interests. For each learning area, select among the following activity and experience choices that are appropriate for the children in your care.

Social and Emotional Development Choices

▨ Encourage each child to draw a picture on a piece of paper to help create a fan. When they have finished drawing, ask their permission to fold their picture into a fan. Show them how to use the fan and talk about how it helps us keep cooler.

▨ Make Lemonade. As the children drink their hot-weather drink, discuss why it is a good drink on a hot day.

▨ Make Baggie Ice Cream with the children. To make one serving, pour ½ cup of milk, 1 tablespoon of sugar, and ¼ teaspoon of vanilla into a small zipper-closure bag and seal it. Place the small bag, with rock salt, inside a large zipper-closure bag and seal. Shake the bag for approximately 10 minutes. Let the children help. "Why is ice cream so tasty on a hot day?" Teach the children "I Scream for Ice Cream."

I Scream for Ice Cream
You scream, I scream,
We all scream for ice cream!

▨ Explain why it is important to apply sunscreen and why we need to protect our skin on hot days. If appropriate, apply a little sunscreen to each child's hands and face.

▨ If appropriate, sing "Summer's Coming" to the tune of "Are You Sleeping?" Discuss the signs of summer.

Summer's Coming
Summer's coming,
Summer's coming,
Yes, it is!
Yes, it is!
Fun is in the air.
Sunshine here and there.
Summer's here.
Summer's here.

Cognitive Development Choices

▨ Give the children hot-weather Observation Bottles to explore. Fill an empty, clean half-liter soda bottle with blue water, sand, and plastic fish. Fill another bottle with dried flowers, insects, and grass. Glue the lids onto both bottles to secure the contents. Invite the children to examine and name the items in each bottle.

- Let the children dress the Magnetic Dress-Me Dolls (Appendix p. 455-466) in summer clothes. You can also use the dolls to tell a story about a hot day. Talk with the children about the clothes as they dress the dolls.

- Encourage the children to paint hot-weather pictures. Provide blue paper and yellow, orange, and green paints. Encourage them to describe their paintings.

- Provide flowers and insects for the children to examine with a magnifying glass. Help them notice the tiny details of each item.

- Provide dress-up clothes such as shorts, T-shirts, bathing suits, sandals, and sun hats for the children to explore. Discuss the importance of sun hats when the days are hot.

- If the weather is warm and families approve, set up a water-play day. Toddlers love the sprinkler.

- Provide beach props such as beach towels, sun hats, sunglasses, empty sunscreen bottles, a cooler, and so on for the children to explore. Discuss the beach as a great spot on a hot day.

- Melt crayons in muffin tins on a warming tray. Allow the children to watch the crayons melt under your close supervision. Discuss the word *hot*. Discuss the heat of the tray and the results of placing the crayons on the heat.
  Safety Warning: Supervise closely to make sure that the children don't touch the hot tray.

- Problem-solving suggestion: Go outside on a nature hike. Point out things we see when the weather is hot that we do not see when the weather is cold, such as leaves, insects, flowers, and animals.

REFLECTION ON THE DAY
Ask the children to tell you something they have learned about hot weather. Show the children some weather pictures. Invite your "not yet talkers" to show you a picture of a sunny day.

Rainy

WORDS TO PRACTICE

damp	rainy	weather
pour	shower	wet
rain	soggy	

GETTING STARTED

- If the day is rainy, go to a window where the children can look outside. Discuss the sound of the rain, the feel of the rain, the taste of the rain, and the appearance of the sky. If it is gray and cloudy outside, point that out. Show the children the Weather Wheel (Appendix p. 474). Point out the symbol on the wheel that represents a rainy day. Set the wheel to rainy. If the weather isn't rainy, you may want to wait for a rainy day to offer these activities.
- Tell the children that today they will learn about how the word *rainy* is used to describe the weather.
- Read your favorite book about weather to the children or select a book from the Story Circle Suggestions below to check out of the library and read.

STORY CIRCLE SUGGESTIONS

- *Duck Is Dirty* by Satoshi Kitamura
- *Listen to the Rain* by Bill Martin, Jr.
- *Pete's Puddle* by Joanne Foster
- *The Puddle* by David McPhail
- *Splish, Splash* by Marcia Leonard
- *Splish, Splashy Day* by Liza Alexander

PREPARATION FOR "RAINY" ACTIVITIES AND EXPERIENCES

- Make a Weather Wheel, if not already made (Appendix p. 474).
- Cut large puddles out of blue or brown poster board, vinyl, or bulletin board paper.
- Make Magnetic Dress-Me Dolls (Appendix p. 455-466) with rainy-day clothing.

- Cut easel paper into raindrops.
- Make Raindrop Puzzles (see p. 177).
- Gather pictures of rainy day scenes.

Language Enrichment Choices*

- Sing "It Is Rainy" to the tune of "Clementine."

   It Is Rainy
   Rainy, rainy,
   Rainy, rainy,
   It is rainy in the sky.
   Rainy, rainy,
   Rainy, rainy,
   It is rainy in the sky.

- Show the children rainy-day pictures. Ask the children to describe what they see in the photographs. Encourage them to use descriptive words.

- Use the word *rainy* in a sentence. For example, "I love to look at books on *rainy* days."

Physical Development Choices

*Toddlers and twos present a wide range of developmental needs, abilities, and interests. For each learning area, select among the following activity and experience choices that are appropriate for the children in your care.

- Play a modified game of Drop the Handkerchief. Cut out a raindrop from construction paper to use instead of a handkerchief. Choose one child to be IT while the other children sit in a circle facing the center. The child who is IT skips or walks around the outside of the circle and casually drops the raindrop behind one of the children sitting in the circle. This child picks up the raindrop and chases IT around the circle. IT tries to run around the circle and sit in the second child's spot without being tagged. If IT is not tagged, then she sits in her new spot in the circle and the child with the raindrop becomes IT. If IT is tagged, then she is IT for another round. Depending on the age of your group, you may need to offer assistance to each child as they are IT while a second adult helps the runner.

- Play Puddle Hop. Cut out large puddles from blue or brown poster board, vinyl, or bulletin board paper. Laminate the puddles and place them on the floor about a foot apart. Encourage the children to "splash" (hop) like raindrops from puddle to puddle. "Has anyone hopped in a real puddle?" "What happens when you hop in a real puddle?"

■ Encourage the children to participate in the following action story, "Weather." Discuss what happened when the children felt the first raindrops.

Weather

The children were excited. They jumped up and down with delight (jump up and down). *It was time to go outdoors.*

They put on their coats (pretend to put on a coat). *They put on their mittens* (pretend to put on mittens). *And then put on their hats* (pretend to put on a hat).

They opened the door (pretend to open door) *and out they ran.*

The wind was strong. It blew hard against them (pretend to walk against the wind). *The children walked more slowly toward the swings and the slide. They swung awhile* (pretend to swing). *The wind blew their swings crooked* (pretend to go crooked). *They decided to try the slide. They climbed up the ladder* (pretend to climb). *When they went down the slide the wind pushed them faster* (pretend to slide and land on bottom).

Next, some of the children rode on the tricycles (pretend to pedal) *while others played ball* (pretend to catch a ball).

Soon the children noticed that the wind had died down. They began to feel warm (fan yourself). *The children took off their mittens* (pretend to take off mittens). *Then they went to play in the sand* (pretend to hold sand in your hand).

The children were still hot (fan). *They took off their hats* (pretend to take off hat). *They took off their coats* (pretend to take off coat). *They went back to play on the swings* (pretend to swing) *and the slide* (pretend to slide).

Just then they began to feel raindrops (hold out hand as if feeling for rain). *The children picked up their mittens, their coats, and their hats and ran inside. They got in just in time because when they looked out the window* (shade eyes as if looking) *they saw a big black cloud and lots and lots of raindrops.*

Social and Emotional Development Choices

■ Teach the children "Rain, Rain, Go Away." Talk about why children might not enjoy the rain. Point out how much the flowers, trees, and grass do enjoy the rain.

Rain, Rain, Go Away

Rain, rain, go away.
Little children want to play.

Additional verses by Pam Schiller:
Clouds, clouds, go away
Little children want to play.

Thunder, thunder, go away
Little children want to play.

Rain, rain, come back soon
Little flowers want to bloom.

■ Do the action rhyme, "Tiny Seed." Talk about the role of the rain in helping seeds to grow.

Tiny Seed
Tiny seed planted just right, (children tuck themselves into a ball)
Not a breath of air, not a ray of light.
Rain falls slowly to and fro,
And now the seed begins to grow. (children begin to unfold)
Slowly reaching for the light,
With all its energy, all its might.
The little seed's work is almost done,
To grow up tall and face the sun. (children stand up tall with arms stretched out)

■ Teach the children "The Raindrop Song."

The Raindrop Song
If all of the raindrops (wiggle fingers in the air)
Were lemon drops and gumdrops, (tap one index finger against palm of other hand)
Oh, what a rain it would be! (wiggle fingers in the air)
I'd stand outside with my mouth open wide.
Ah-ah-ah-ah-ah-ah-ah-ah-ah-ah! (stand, looking up with mouth open)
If all of the raindrops (wiggle fingers in the air)
Were lemon drops and gumdrops, (tap one index finger against palm of other hand)
Oh, what a rain it would be! (wiggle fingers in the air)

Cognitive Development Choices

- Cut easel paper into large raindrops. Invite the children to paint the raindrops with blue tempera paint.

- Invite the children to dress the Magnetic Dress-Me Dolls (Appendix p. 455-466) in rainy day clothes. You can also use the dolls to tell a story about a rainy day. Talk with the children about the clothing they chose for dressing the dolls.

- Collect rainwater and invite the children to help you use the rainwater to water the indoor plants.

- Encourage the children to squirt spray bottles of water on a shower curtain liner. Encourage them to watch the water drops travel down the liner. Talk with them about how the drops fall. "Are they fast or slow?"

- Give the children a spray bottle with an adjustable nozzle and a cookie sheet. Encourage them to create rain showers. Ask them to spray the water on the cookie sheet in a fine mist. "How does the 'rain' sound?" Ask them to spray with a more direct spray. "Now how does the 'rain' sound?" Try several adjustments.

- Place an umbrella upside down in the middle of the floor. Invite the children to toss wadded paper balls into the umbrella.

- Problem-solving suggestion: Invite the children to work Raindrop Puzzles. Cut big raindrops out of white or blue poster board. Laminate them and cut them into simple puzzle pieces.

REFLECTION ON THE DAY
Ask the children to tell you something they have learned about rainy weather. Ask the "not yet talkers" to make the sound of rain.

Windy

WORDS TO PRACTICE

blow	wind
weather	windy

GETTING STARTED

- If the weather is windy, go outside and discuss how it feels and what things look like on a windy day. "How does the wind feel on your face?" "What are the trees doing?" "What happens to your clothing?" Show the children the Weather Wheel (Appendix p. 474). Point out the symbol on the wheel that represents a windy day. Set the Weather Wheel to the windy symbol. If the day is not windy, you may want to wait for a windy day to offer these activities.
- Tell the children that today they will learn about how the word *windy* is used to describe the weather.
- Read your favorite book about weather to the children or select a book from the Story Circle Suggestions below to check out of the library and read.

STORY CIRCLE SUGGESTIONS

- *Kipper's Book of Weather* by Mick Inkpen
- *Snowy, Flowy, Blowy* by Nancy Tafuri
- *Who Took the Farmer's Hat?* by Joan Nodset
- *Wind* by Monique Felix

PREPARATION FOR "WINDY" ACTIVITIES AND EXPERIENCES

- Make Weather Wheel, if not already made (Appendix p. 474).
- Gather materials for Paper Bag Kites (see p. 181).
- Find windy-day pictures.

Language Enrichment Choices*

▦ Sing "It Is Windy" to the tune of "Clementine." Discuss good windy day activities.

It Is Windy
Windy, windy,
Windy, windy,
It is windy in the sky.
Windy, windy,
Windy, windy,
It is windy in the sky.

▦ Show the children windy-day pictures. "How can you tell it is a windy day?"

▦ Use the word *windy* in a sentence. For example, "I like to fly my kite on *windy* days."

Physical Development Choices

▦ Blow bubbles for the children and invite them to chase the bubbles. If you blow the bubbles outdoors, try holding the wand in the wind and letting the wind blow the bubbles. If you blow the bubbles indoors, try waving the wand in the air to create a wind.

▦ Play Whistle Stop. Give the children a series of movements to do, such as jumping up and down, marching, and twisting. Have them continue to do the activity until they hear you blow a whistle. Talk about the wind it takes to blow the whistle.

▦ Encourage the children to dance like leaves being pushed by the wind. Say the poem, "Falling Leaves" as a springboard.

Falling Leaves by Pam Schiller
Leaves are drifting softly down,
They make a carpet on the ground.
Then, swish! The wind comes whistling by
And sends them dancing in the sky!

*Toddlers and twos present a wide range of developmental needs, abilities, and interests. For each learning area, select among the following activity and experience choices that are appropriate for the children in your care.

Social and Emotional Development Choices

▨ Encourage the children to participate in the action story, "Weather" (see Rainy Weather, page 175). "What did the wind do in the story?"

▨ Encourage the children to rock baby dolls and sing them the lullaby, "Rock-a-Bye Baby."

Rock-a-Bye Baby
Rock-a-bye baby
In the tree top.
When the wind blows,
The cradle will rock.
When the bough breaks,
The cradle will fall,
And down will come baby
Cradle and all.

Cognitive Development Choices

▨ Invite the children to Straw Paint. Place a small amount of liquid tempera paint on each child's paper. Give each child a wide straw cut to a 3" length. Discuss the way they can move the paint with their breath.

▨ Read older children the listening story, "The Wind and the Sun." Discuss the role of the sun and the role of the wind.

The Wind and the Sun
The Wind and the Sun were disputing which was stronger.

Suddenly they saw a traveler coming down the road, and the Sun said, "I see a way to decide our dispute. Whichever of us can cause that traveler to take off his cloak shall be regarded as the stronger. You begin."

So the Sun retired behind a cloud, and the Wind began to blow as hard as it could upon the traveler. But the harder he blew, the more closely did the traveler wrap his cloak around him, till at last the Wind had to give up in despair.

Then the Sun came out and shone in all his glory upon the traveler, who soon found it too hot to walk with his cloak on.

■ Encourage the children to fly Paper Bag Kites. Give each child a paper bag. Invite them to color on the bag, making any designs they choose. When they are finished, place masking tape around the opening of the bag to reinforce it. Then punch a hole through the tape in one side of the bag. Tie an 8' piece of yarn through the reinforced hole. Ask the children if they can feel the wind pulling their kite as they run with it.

■ Blow bubbles for the children. Challenge them to keep the bubbles from hitting the ground. Show them how to keep the bubbles aloft by blowing the bubbles upward.

■ Place a feather on a tabletop and encourage the children to blow the feather off the table. "What happens when you blow softly?" "What happens when you blow hard?"

■ Problem-solving suggestion: Place a fan in a safe area of the room. Toss objects such as a feather, a cotton ball, a tissue, a scarf, a leaf, a penny, a small block, and a string bead into the path of the air. Ask the children to watch. Let the children examine the objects after the experiment. Help them determine that the wind was able to blow the lightweight objects.
Safety Warning: Supervise closely at all times.

REFLECTION ON THE DAY
Ask the children to tell you something they have learned about windy weather. Ask your "not yet talkers" to make the sound of the wind.

Alike/Same and Different

WORDS TO PRACTICE

alike

different

same

GETTING STARTED

- Show the children two items that are exactly alike, such as two red crayons, and then two items that are different, such as a red crayon and a blue crayon. Look for items the children may be wearing that can demonstrate alike and different such as shoes or socks. Point out any clothing you find that is alike and then compare the items that are alike to an item that is different. For example, "Jeanne and Pat both have on the *same* tennis shoes; their shoes are exactly *alike*. John's tennis shoes are *different* from Jeanne's and Pat's shoes. John's shoes have a different picture on them and they have a *different* color of laces."
- Tell the children that today they will be learning about things that are *alike/same* and things that are *different*.
- Read your favorite book about things that are alike and different to the children or select a book from the Story Circle Suggestions below to check out of the library and read.

STORY CIRCLE SUGGESTIONS

- *We Are All Alike. . .We Are All Different* by the Cheltenham Elementary School Kindergarteners (Scholastic)
- *What's Alike? What's Different? The Book of Comparing* by Dennis Smith

PREPARATION FOR "ALIKE/SAME AND DIFFERENT" ACTIVITIES AND EXPERIENCES

- Gather set of items that have two members that are alike and one that is different.
- Gather simple, uncluttered stickers.
- Make the Hit the Shape Game (see p. 184) and the Alike and Different Matching Game (see p. 185).

Language Enrichment Choices*

- Lay three items on the floor, two of them alike and one of them different. Ask the children which two items are alike and which one is different. Repeat this activity several times.

- Show the children two simple stickers that are alike and two stickers that are different. Talk about how the matching pair of stickers are exactly the same and point out the differences in the other pair. Place a sticker on each child's arm. Use pairs of stickers so that later, each child will be able to find a child who has the same sticker he has. Tell the children to leave the sticker on their arms because they will play a game using the stickers a little later in the day.

- Use the words *alike* and *different* in a sentence. For example, "Your shoes and my shoes are *alike,* but Sam's are *different.*"

- Present the "Sam and Pam" listening story to the children. "Who can remember how Pam and Sam are alike?" "Who can remember how Pam and Sam are different?"

Pam and Sam

Pam and Sam are best friends. They are so much alike. Pam and Sam both love to be outdoors. Pam and Sam both like peanut butter and jelly sandwiches better than any other food. They both love to swim and love to dance. They love to watch movies, and they love to blow bubbles. They hate rainy days. They love puppy dogs, ice cream, sunshine, baseball, trips to Mexico, bicycle riding, and nature hikes. There is even something about their names that is the same. Do you know what it is?

As much as Sam and Pam are alike, they are also very different. In many ways they are opposites. Sam is tall, but Pam is short. Sam has short hair, but Pam's hair is long. Sam has brown eyes, but Pam's eyes are blue. Sam hates to work puzzles, but Pam enjoys working puzzles. Sam likes to ride his bike fast, but Pam prefers to ride slowly. Sam likes the weather when it is hot, but Pam likes the weather better when it is cold.

Now it is easy to see that, as much as Pam and Sam are alike, they are still very different. There is something else different about Pam and Sam. Do you know what it is? (If necessary, give the children hints to help them determine that Sam is a boy and Pam is a girl.)

*Toddlers and twos present a wide range of developmental needs, abilities, and interests. For each learning area, select among the following activity and experience choices that are appropriate for the children in your care.

Physical Development Choices

■ Play the Hit the Shape Game. Make six playing cards by drawing red circles on two 5" x 7" index cards, blue squares on two of the cards, and yellow triangles on the last two cards. Place one of each type of card on the floor. Give the children a beanbag and the remainder of the cards. Ask them to draw a card and then try to toss the beanbag on the matching card on the floor. Let each child have a turn trying to hit the match of each of the shapes. Use alike and different vocabulary with this game.

■ Play a game of Copycat. You do an action, and the children copy your action. Point out that everyone is doing the same action. Add a variation to the game. Ask another teacher to join the game but to keep "messing up" (doing a different action than the leader is doing) the actions. Say, "Mrs. Marotta is not doing the same thing we are. She is doing something different. Try harder Mrs. Marotta." Do a new action and have Mrs. Marotta get it right. Say, "Good job. Now you are doing the same thing we are." Then have her mess up again. Continue for three or four rounds. For older twos, play a game of Your Way, My Way. You do an action and your partner or the group must do something that is different.

Social and Emotional Development Choices

■ In very simple terms, talk with the children about how people are alike in many ways and yet different in others. Point out that people generally have the same body parts, but those parts may be different in color, shape, size, and texture. For example, even when two people have the same body parts, such as eyes, their eyes can be a different color. The same is true for hair and skin color. Same body parts can also be different in size. Demonstrate by comparing your hand to a child's hand.

■ Say the following "I Have Five Fingers" action rhyme with all the children, and then say one of the "Eye Rhymes 1-4" (whichever is appropriate) to each child individually. Explain that our differences make us unique and special. Unless you have a physically challenged child in your classroom, you may want to leave the discussion of these differences to a later time.

I Have Five Fingers
I have five fingers on each hand,
Ten toes on my two feet.
Two ears, two eyes,
One nose, one mouth,
With which to sweetly speak.

My hands can clap, my feet can tap,
My eyes can clearly see.
My ears can hear,
My nose can sniff,
My mouth can say I'm me.

Additional Eye Rhymes by Pam Schiller:

Eye Rhyme #1
You see me,
I see you.
Your eyes are blue/green/brown,
Mine are, too.

Eye Rhyme #2
Your eyes are big and round and brown.
They must be the prettiest eyes in town.

Eye Rhyme #3
When I look at you, know what I see?
Eyes as green as green can be.

Eye Rhyme #4
Blue eyes, green eyes,
Brown eyes, hey.
Your eyes are gray,
And I love them that way.

- Help the children search for a friend who has a sticker that matches hers. As you encounter children with different stickers, point out what is different about that child's sticker. When you find the correct match, point out the ways in which the stickers are the same. Say, "Your stickers are just alike."

Cognitive Development Choices

- Use stickers to make Alike and Different Matching Cards. Place two stickers side by side on an index card. On some cards, use two of the same sticker. On other cards, use two different stickers. Laminate the cards. Encourage the children to sort the cards by those that have stickers that are alike and those that have stickers that are different. For older twos, you can make the differences less obvious but for younger toddlers, use stickers that are really different.

■ Show the children three beanbags, two that are alike and one that is different. Ask them to cover their eyes as you hide two of the three beanbags. Encourage the children to find the two missing beanbags and when they bring them back to you, ask them to tell you if they have found one that is the same as the one you still have or if it is different.

■ Take the children outdoors for a leaf hunt. Let them bring a few leaves back indoors. Select a leaf from the pile that is distinct, yet similar to other leaves left in the pile. Ask the children to sort the rest of the leaves by whether they are like the one you took from the pile or different from the one you took from the pile.

■ Place several blocks on the floor. Make sure that there is more than one type of block but multiple copies of each block. Select one block from the pile and ask the children to help you find the other blocks that are the same as the one you have selected.

■ Problem-solving suggestion: Provide socks for the children to match. Ask them how they know which socks go together.

REFLECTION ON THE DAY
Ask the children to show you two things in the room that are alike and two things that are different.

Who or What Is Where?

IN/INSIDE

OUT/OUTSIDE

ON

OFF

UP

DOWN

OVER/ABOVE

UNDER/BELOW

TOP, MIDDLE, AND BOTTOM

FIRST, NEXT, LAST

In/Inside

WORDS TO PRACTICE

in	location
inside	where
into	

GETTING STARTED

- Place a large box in the middle of the circle area and invite the children to get into the box, one at a time. "Can everyone fit *inside* the box?" Ask a few children to get out of the box and then discuss who is still *in* the box.
- Tell the children that today they will learn how the words *in* and *inside* describe where someone or something is located.
- Read your favorite book about spatial relationships to the children or select a book from the Story Circle Suggestions below to check out of the library and read.

STORY CIRCLE SUGGESTIONS

- *Cat in the Hat* by Dr. Seuss
- *Inside Outside Upside Down* by Stan & Jan Berenstain
- *The Mitten* by Jan Brett

PREPARATION FOR "IN/INSIDE" ACTIVITIES AND EXPERIENCES

- Locate a large cardboard box.
- Make the "What's In the Box?" flannel board story (Appendix p. 579-583).
- Make a Drop Slot Can (see p. 192), Tactile Box (see p. 191), and Dog and Bone Game (Appendix p. 445-446).

Language Enrichment Choices*

▨ Sing "Good Morning to You." Discuss the place that each child is in.

Good Morning to You
Good morning to you!
Good morning to you!
We're all in our places
With bright shining faces.
Oh, this is the way to start a great day!

▨ Use the words *in* and *inside* in sentences. For example, "Look how many children can fit *inside* the box," and "How many children are *in* your family?"

▨ Tell the children the flannel board story, "What's In the Box?" (Appendix p. 579-583). Discuss the location of the object mentioned in the story.

▨ Teach the children the American Sign Language signs for *in* and *inside* (Appendix p. 434).

Physical Development Choices

▨ Play a simplified version of "Birdie, Birdie, Where Is Your Nest?" Make a big "nest" by placing a large sheet (brown or gray would be good) on the floor. Ask the children to flap their arms like wings as they circle the nest. When you get to the line of the song, "In the tree that I love best," the children run to get into the nest.

Birdie, Birdie, Where Is Your Nest?
Birdie, birdie, where is your nest?
Birdie, birdie, where is your nest?
Birdie, birdie, where is your nest?
In the tree that I love best.

▨ Encourage children to toss beanbags into a box or basket. Discuss the location of the beanbags.

▨ Do "The Hokey Pokey" (on the next page) with the children. Discuss the position of their body parts when they are "in."

*Toddlers and twos present a wide range of developmental needs, abilities, and interests. For each learning area, select among the following activity and experience choices that are appropriate for the children in your care.

The Hokey Pokey
You put your right hand in, (form a circle and act out the words)
You take your right hand out.
You put your right hand in,
And you shake it all about.
You do the Hokey Pokey, (hold hands in the air and shake them)
And you turn yourself around.
That's what it's all about.

Repeat, using other body parts.

◾ Invite the children to toss or drop large pompoms into a bucket. Do all the pompoms land *in* the bucket?

Social and Emotional Development Choices

◾ Play "'Round the House" with the children. Discuss the mousie going "in" the little housie.

'Round the House
'Round the house, (use index finger to trace a circle on the child's open palm)
'Round the house,
Goes the little mousie.
Up the stairs, (walk index finger and middle finger up the child's arm)
Up the stairs,
In his little housie. (tickle the child under his or her chin)

◾ Show the children a Jack-in-the-Box. Say the following "Jack-in-the-Box" poem to coax Jack out of his box.

Jack-in-the-Box by Pam Schiller
Hey, Jack, what are you doing in that box?
Are you awake? Do you hear my knocks?
Are you singing? What do you say?
Will you come out and play today?
Hey, Jack, what are you doing in that box?
Are you dressing? What color are your socks?
Is it dark inside? Can you see?
Will you come out and play with me?

- During lunch or snack time, call attention to the food that is going into the children's mouths. You might also discuss not talking while food is in the mouth.

- Sing "I Have Something in My Pocket." Discuss things that could be in your pocket. "What is in your pocket?"

  I Have Something in My Pocket
  I have something in my pocket,
  It belongs across my face.
  I keep it very close at hand
  In a most convenient place.

  I bet you could not guess it,
  If you guessed a long, long while.
  So I'll take it out and put it on.
  It's a great big happy SMILE!

Cognitive Development Choices

- Provide mittens and shoes. Discuss putting hands inside of mittens and feet in shoes. Encourage the children to look at the insides of their shoes. Turn a mitten inside out so the children can see the inside of a mitten.

- Encourage the children to put baby dolls into buggies and push them around.

- Make a Tactile Box. Cut a hole in the top or side of a shoebox. Fill the box with hard and soft items such as small blocks, feathers, cotton balls, fabric scraps, and so on. Put the lid on the box and encourage children to reach inside and try to identify the objects. Discuss the feel of each item.

- During outdoor play, give the children a ride in the wagon. Ask them if they prefer to ride in the wagon or pull the wagon.

- Provide tempera paints and a small box, such as a shoebox. Invite the children to paint the inside of the box.

- Give the children a Drop Slot Can and encourage them to drop chips into the can. Cut a 1½" slot in the lid of an empty coffee can. Replace the lid. Provide poker chips or very large buttons for children to push through the Drop Slot Can. This is great practice for buttoning. Point out the location of the chips. "Can you see the chips when they are inside the can?"

- Make a tent by draping a large sheet over tables and chairs and invite the children to play inside the tent. "How many children can fit inside the tent?"

- Give the children an old purse and some fun items to put into their purse, such as a handkerchief, an empty compact, an empty lipstick tube, and a change purse. "What does Mommy carry in her purse?"

- Give the children the Dog and Bone Game (Appendix p. 445-446) and ask them to place a bone in each dog's mouth. Color code the dog's collar and the bones and encourage the children to give each dog the bone that matches his collar. "What do dogs have inside their mouth?" (For example, teeth, tongue, and so on.)

- Problem-solving suggestions:
  1. Make a circle about 4' in diameter with masking tape. Give the children a handful of pompoms. Ask them to stand inside the circle and toss the pompoms into the air. Encourage the children to pick up the pompoms that land outside the circle and toss them again. Continue until all the pompoms are inside the circle. Do the children figure out that the more gently they toss the pompoms, the more likely they are to land inside the circle?
  2. Give the children a small cup of water, a large eyedropper, and a soda bottle. Challenge the children to remove the water from the cup and put it into the bottle without pouring it or spilling it. Guide them to the conclusion that the water will not spill if they place the eyedropper inside the bottle before releasing the water.

REFLECTION ON THE DAY

Show the children a box and ask them to show you the inside of the box. Then give them directions to get into the box.

Out/Outside

WORDS TO PRACTICE

location	outside
out	where

GETTING STARTED

- Use masking tape to make a large circle on the floor. Ask the children to stand inside the circle and then step outside the circle. Continue to play the game by asking specific children to step outside the circle. Discuss who is inside the circle and who is *outside* the circle.
- Tell the children that today they will learn how the words *out* and *outside* tell us where someone or something is located.
- Read your favorite book about spatial relationships to the children or select a book from the Story Circle Suggestions below to check out of the library and read.

STORY CIRCLE SUGGESTIONS

- *Inside Outside Upside Down* by Stan Berenstain
- *Outside* by Joseph Bonsall
- *Outside Inside* by Kathleen Fain

PREPARATION FOR "OUT/OUTSIDE" ACTIVITIES AND EXPERIENCES

- Make a masking tape circle on the floor.
- Prepare "The Great Big Turnip" flannel board story (Appendix p. 495-497), if not already made.
- Make the Scarf Pull and Colored Sand (see p.196-197).

Language Enrichment Choices*

- Show the children a Jack-in-the-box and discuss Jack's location after he pops out of the box. Teach the children one of the "Jack-in-the-Box" fingerplays below.

* Toddlers and twos present a wide range of developmental needs, abilities, and interests. For each learning area, select among the following activity and experience choices that are appropriate for the children in your care.

Jack-in-the-Box
Jack-in-the-box (tuck thumb into fist)
Oh, so still.
Won't you come out? (raise hand slightly)
Yes, I will. (pop thumb out of fist)

Jack-in-the-box, jack-in-the-box, (suit actions to words)
Wake up, wake up, somebody knocks.
One time, two times, three times, four.
Jack pops out of his little round door.

■ Use the words *out* and *outside* in sentences. For example, "I keep my puppy *outside* of the house." "I can stick my tongue *out.*"

■ Present the flannel board story, "The Great Big Turnip" (see Appendix p. 495-497). Discuss the location of the turnip and discuss the farmer's and his friend's efforts to get the turnip out of the ground.

■ Sing "Little Skunk's Hole" to the tune of "Dixie." Discuss the request the skunk makes.

Little Skunk's Hole

Oh, I stuck my head
In the little skunk's hole,
And the little skunk said,
"Well, bless my soul!
Take it out! Take it out!
Take it out! Remove it!"

Oh, I didn't take it out,
And the little skunk said,
"If you don't take it out
You'll wish you had.
Take it out! Take it out!"
Pheew! I removed it!

■ Teach the children the American Sign Language signs for *out* and *outside* (Appendix p. 436).

Physical Development Choices

■ Do "The Hokey Pokey" with the children. Point out the position of their body parts when they are out.

The Hokey Pokey
You put your right hand in, (form a circle and act out the words)
You take your right hand out.
You put your right hand in,
And you shake it all about.

You do the Hokey Pokey, (hold hands in the air and shake them)
And you turn yourself around.
That's what it's all about.

Repeat, using other body parts.

▪ Play a modified game of Run, Rabbit, Run. Create a safe area called a hutch. It can be a circle of masking tape or it can be a cardboard box large enough for several children to stand inside. Ask all the "rabbits" (children) to stand inside the hutch. You will be the wolf. Call the children, one at a time, out of the hutch and ask them to run to the "briar patch" and back. The briar patch can be a tree, a base, or any item you choose. The wolf will chase the rabbit to the briar patch and back again to the hutch. Point out the location of the "rabbits" when they are in the outside hutch.

▪ Sing "Five Little Ducks" with the children. Discuss going outside to play.

Five Little Ducks
Five little ducks went out one day,
Over the hills and far away.
Papa duck called with a "quack, quack, quack."
Four little ducks came swimming back.

Repeat, losing one more duck each time until you are left with one duck. Have momma duck call and end with "five little ducks came swimming back."

▪ Invite the children to act out "Five in the Bed," which is a variation of "Ten in the Bed." Use a beach towel or a sheet of paper to represent the bed. Ask the children to roll over each time the song says to roll over, until there is only one child left. Discuss rolling out of the bed. "Has anyone ever rolled out of your bed at home?"

Five in the Bed
There were five in the bed, (hold up ten fingers)
And the little one said,
"Roll over! Roll over!" (roll hand over hand)
So they all rolled over,
And one rolled out. (hold up one finger)

There were four in the bed... (repeat hand motions)
Three in the bed...
Two in the bed...

There was one in the bed,
And the little one said,
"Alone at last!" (place head on hands as if sleeping)

Social and Emotional Development Choices

- Show the children how to stick out their tongues. Provide an unbreakable mirror so they can see the silly faces they can make.

- Have snack outside.

- Sing "I Have Something in My Pocket." "What things does Daddy take out of his pocket?"

   I Have Something in My Pocket

   I have something in my pocket.   *I bet you could not guess it,*
   It belongs across my face.   *If you guessed a long, long while.*
   I keep it very close at hand   *So I'll take it out and put it on.*
   In a most convenient place.   *It's a great, big, happy SMILE!*

Cognitive Development Choices

- Give the children a Scarf Pull and encourage them to pull the scarves out of the container. Talk with the children as they pull the scarves out of the can. Tie or sew the corners of three or four small scarves (in different colors and textures, if possible) together to make one long scarf. Cut a slit in the lid of a potato chip canister or oatmeal box. Stuff the scarf inside the can, pull an end through the lid, and place the lid on the can. Securely fasten the lid with tape.

- Ask the children to stand in a box with three or four beanbags inside. Encourage them to toss the beanbags out of the box. "How many beanbags are outside of the box?" "Is it easier to toss bags into a box or out of a box?"

- Take the children to a window and discuss what the weather looks like outside. "Where is the sun?" "Are there clouds?" "Is the wind blowing?" "What animals do you see outside?"

■ Invite the children to shake Colored Sand out of a shaker to create a sand painting. Place 2 tablespoons of sand (or salt) on a paper plate. Rub a piece of colored chalk over the sand and it will gradually turn the color of the chalk. Fill a saltshaker with the Colored Sand. Encourage the children to make a design with glue on their paper and then shake the Colored Sand over their design.

■ Problem-solving suggestions:
1. Provide a large cardboard box and challenge the children to cover the outside of the box with paint. Provide brushes in a variety of widths. Does anyone notice that the wider brushes cover more territory?
2. Make a circle about 4' in diameter with masking tape. Give the children a handful of pompoms. Ask them to stand just outside the circle and toss the pompoms into the air. Encourage the children to pick up the pompoms that land inside the circle and toss them again. Continue until all the pompoms are outside the circle. Does anyone figure out that the higher they toss the pompoms, the more likely they are to land outside the circle?

REFLECTION ON THE DAY
Ask the children to show you the outside of their shoes.

On

WORDS TO PRACTICE

location
on
where

GETTING STARTED

- Discuss the kinds of hats the children are wearing on their heads. Ask questions to find out what the children know about the word *on*.
- Tell them that today they will learn how the word *on* is used to describe where something is located.
- Read your favorite book about spatial relationships to the children or select a book from the Story Circle Suggestions below to check out of the library and read.

STORY CIRCLE SUGGESTIONS

- *The Farmer's Hat* by Joan L. Nodset
- *Mrs Honey's Hat* by Pam Adams
- *Old Hat, New Hat: The Berenstain Bears* by Stan and Jan Berenstain

PREPARATION FOR "ON" ACTIVITIES AND EXPERIENCES

- In advance, send a note home to families inviting children to wear a hat to school today. Gather some extra hats for children who may forget and do not have a hat to wear. Be sure to wear a hat yourself.
- Make the "Little Miss Muffet" (Appendix p. 597-599) flannel board story, if not already made.
- Get bread and jelly.

Language Enrichment Choices*

- Provide carpet squares or spread out a blanket or quilt for the children to sit on. Discuss sitting on the carpet squares or blanket.

* Toddlers and twos present a wide range of developmental needs, abilities, and interests. For each learning area, select among the following activity and experience choices that are appropriate for the children in your care.

- Use the word *on* in a sentence. For example, "Jon has a bandage *on* his hand."

- Teach the children "Little Miss Muffet." Where was Miss Muffet sitting? Act out the rhyme. Ask the children to sit on a "tuffet" (chair or stack of pillows) and you pretend to be the spider that frightens them away.

  Little Miss Muffet
  Little Miss Muffet sat on her tuffet
  Eating her curds and whey.
  Along came a spider
  And sat down beside her.
  And frightened Miss Muffet away.

- Teach the children the American Sign Language sign for *on* (Appendix p. 436).

Physical Development Choices

- Encourage the children to walk on a masking tape line with a beanbag on their head. Is it difficult for the children to stay on the line?

- Invite the children to participate in a hat parade. Play some marching music and march around the room with hats on the heads.

Social and Emotional Development Choices

- Offer a bread and jelly snack. Invite the children to help you spread jelly on their bread. Talk with them about things that are spread on bread.

- Sing "My Hand on My Head" with the children. Discuss the position of their hand as you sing about the different body parts.

  My Hand on My Head
  My hand on my head, (place hand on head)
  What have I here? (open arms palm up)
  This is my topnotcher, (point to head)
  Mamma, my dear.
  Topnotcher, topnotcher, (point to head again)
  Dickie, dickie, doo. (knock on head)
  That's what I learned in school. (shake index finger)
  Boom! Boom!

Continue, adding body parts and suit hand motions to words:

Eye... eye blinker
Nose... nose blower
Mouth... food grinder
Chin... chin chopper
Heart... chest ticker
Stomach... bread basket
Knees... knee benders
Toes... pedal pushers

- During lunch or snack time, describe placing the food on plates and the plates on the table.

Cognitive Development Choices

- Take chalk outdoors and encourage the children to draw on the sidewalk. Discuss the location of their drawings. "Can you stand on your drawing?"

- Provide dolls and doll clothing and invite the children to put clothes on the dolls, or use the Magnetic Dress-Me Dolls (Appendix p. 455-466).

- Invite the children to use eyedroppers to take colored water from a bowl and drop it on a coffee filter. "What happens when the water lands on the coffee filter?"

- Invite the children to explore putting on mittens and gloves. "Which is easier to put on?"

- Provide collage materials such as ribbon, yarn, rickrack, buttons, beads, and colored tissue paper. Encourage the children to glue the various items on their paper. When they have finished their collages, invite them to help you hang them on the wall. "Do you have pictures on your refrigerator at home?"

- Sit in a circle with the children and shine a flashlight on different items in the room and on the children's bodies (e.g., their shoes, hands, and so on). Let each child have a turn shining the flashlight on something in the room.

- Problem-solving suggestion: Show the children how to balance a book on their hands. Discuss getting the book situated before removing their hands. Older twos can try to walk with the book balanced on their head.

REFLECTION ON THE DAY
Ask the children to place a block or book on the table.

Off

WORDS TO PRACTICE

location	position
off	where

GETTING STARTED

▨ Teach the children the fingerplay, "Four Little Leaves." Discuss jumping and falling off the leaves. Ask questions to find out what the children know about the word *off*.

> **Four Little Leaves**
> *Four little leaves high in a tree,*
> *One fell off and then there were three.*
> *Three bright leaves covered in dew,*
> *Another jumped off, and then there were two.*
> *Two trembling leaves looking for fun,*
> *"I'm off," said two, and then there was one.*
> *One last leaf hanging by a thread*
> *Said, "Jumping off is something I dread."*
> *Then shoosh went the wind and off flew the leaf.*
> *Now the jumping off is over. What a relief!*

▨ Tell the children that today they will be learning about how the word *off* is used to describe the location of things.

▨ Read your favorite book about spatial relationships to the children or select a book from the Story Circle Suggestions below to check out of the library and read.

STORY CIRCLE SUGGESTIONS

▨ *Hey! Get Off Our Train* by John Burningham
▨ *Lights On! Lights Off!* by Angela C. Santamero
▨ *On and Off* by Kate Davis
▨ *Pants Off First!* by Ruth Ohi

PREPARATION FOR "OFF" ACTIVITIES AND EXPERIENCES
- Make "The Three Billy Goats Gruff" flannel board story (Appendix p. 561-567).
- Gather plastic jars and bottles.
- Cut out a construction paper heart and tape it to the bottom of a tray or tub.

Language Enrichment Choices*

- Encourage the children to sit in a circle and take off their shoes. Discuss their shoes being off, and then talk about other things that they take off, such as their coats and mittens. Talk about turning off the lights and water after we use them.

- Use the word *off* in a sentence. For example, "I turn *off* the lights when I leave a room."

- Present "The Three Billy Goats Gruff" flannel board story (Appendix p. 561-567). "What did the troll tell the goats to do?"

- Teach the children the American Sign Language sign for *off* (Appendix p. 436).

Physical Development Choices

- Encourage the children to act out "Five Little Monkeys." Discuss the monkeys falling off the bed.

    Five Little Monkeys
    Five little monkeys jumping on the bed.
    One fell off and bumped her head.
    Mamma called the doctor, and the doctor said,
    "No more monkeys jumping on the bed!"

  Repeat, subtracting a monkey each time. You can say the rhyme using fingers or let children act it out.

- Play Musical Freeze. Have the children dance freely until the music is turned off. When the music stops, they should freeze until the music starts again.

- Play the following game after presenting "The Three Billy Goats Gruff" flannel board story. Make a bridge out of blocks. Encourage the children to walk across the bridge saying, "Trip, trap, trip, trap" as they walk. You be the troll and say the verse below. After you have said the verse, chase the "little goats" around the room.

* Toddlers and twos present a wide range of developmental needs, abilities, and interests. For each learning area, select among the following activity and experience choices that are appropriate for the children in your care.

Who is traipsing on my bridge?
Trip, trap, trip, trap! Get off my bridge!
No one should be traipsing there.
Get off! Get off! Don't you dare!

Social and Emotional Development Choices

▨ Invite the children to take off their shoes. Play "This Little Piggy" with their toes. "Which piggy do you like best?" "Which piggy is the largest?" " Which piggy is the smallest?"

This Little Piggy
This little piggy went to market, (wiggle big toe)
This little piggy stayed home. (wiggle second toe)
This little piggy had roast beef, (wiggle middle toe)
This little piggy had none. (wiggle fourth toe)
And this little piggy cried,
"Wee-wee-wee!" all the way home. (wiggle little toe)

▨ Talk with the children about making sure to turn off the water when they are done washing their hands.

▨ Sing "Little Ant Hill" below to the tune of "Dixie." "Why would someone want to hurry to get his foot off of an anthill?"

Little Ant Hill
Oh, I stuck my foot on a little ant hill.
The little ant said, "You better be still.
Take it off, take it off.
Remove it."
Well, I didn't take it off and the little ant said,
"If you don't take it off, you're gonna wish you had.
Take it off, take it off."
Ouch! I removed it.

Cognitive Development Choices

▨ Give the children plastic jars and bottles and encourage them to take off the lids.

▨ Invite the children to drop beads on a carpet square. Discuss how many of the beads land off of the carpet. Does anyone notice that the easier they drop the bead, the more likely it is to stay on the carpet square?

- Make a line of masking tape on the floor and invite the children to walk on the line on their tiptoes without falling off. Does anyone fall off the line?

- Glue a construction paper heart inside a shallow tray or plastic tub. Cover the bottom of the tray with a small amount of sand. Provide a pastry brush and invite the children to brush the sand off the heart. Can anyone guess what is under the sand before they start brushing?

- Invite the children to peel off pieces of masking tape from a tray or tabletop. "Is it easy or difficult to remove the tape?"

- Problem-solving suggestion: Place a feather on a table and invite the children to think of ways to get the feather off the table without touching it. They can blow the feather or fan the feather off the table. Discuss the options.

REFLECTION ON THE DAY

Ask the children to tell you something they learned about off today. Ask the "not yet talkers" to show you something that can be turned off.

Up

WORDS TO PRACTICE

high
up
where

GETTING STARTED

▧ Hang colorful streamers from the ceiling over the circle time area. Ask the children to lie on their backs and look up at the streamers. Discuss the location of the streamers. Ask the children questions to find out what they know about the word *up*.

▧ Tell the children that today they will be learning how the word *up* is used to tell where something is located.

▧ Read your favorite book about spatial relationships to the children or select a book from the Story Circle Suggestions below to check out of the library and read.

STORY CIRCLE SUGGESTIONS

▧ *Baby Dance* by Ann Taylor
▧ *Itsy Bitsy Spider* by Pam Schiller
▧ *Mrs. McNosh Hangs Up Her Wash* by Sarah Weeks

PREPARATION FOR "UP" ACTIVITIES AND EXPERIENCES

▧ Gather empty toilet paper tubes and pictures of animals.
▧ Get a pulley (optional).

Language Enrichment Choices*

▧ Sing "Itsy Bitsy Spider" with the children. "What was the spider doing before the rain came?" "What did she do when the rain stopped?"

* Toddlers and twos present a wide range of developmental needs, abilities, and interests. For each learning area, select among the following activity and experience choices that are appropriate for the children in your care.

Itsy Bitsy Spider
The itsy bitsy spider
Went up the waterspout.
Down came the rain
And washed the spider out.
Up came the sun
And dried up all the rain.
And the itsy bitsy spider
Went up the spout again.

▪ Use the word *up* in a sentence. For example, "I watched the kite soar *up* in the air."

▪ Teach the children the American Sign Language sign for *up* (Appendix p. 439).

Physical Development Choices

▪ Blow bubbles for the children to chase. Challenge them to blow the bubbles to keep them up in the air.

▪ Show the children how to toss beanbags up into the air.

▪ If space is available outdoors, let the children help you fly a kite. Discuss the location of the kite when it is up in the air.

▪ Sing "The Grand Old Duke of York" with the children. "Where did the Duke march his soldiers?"

The Grand Old Duke of York
The grand old Duke of York (salute)
He had ten thousand men. (hold up ten fingers)
He marched them up to the top of the hill, (point up)
And he marched them down again. (point down)
And when they're up, they're up. (stand tall)
And when they're down, they're down. (squat)
But when they're only halfway up, (stoop down)
They're neither up nor down. (open arms and shrug)

Social and Emotional Development Choices

▪ Place little ones on your shoulders and take them on a tour of the room. "What can you see from your high-up perch?"

- Do "'Round the House" with the children. Discuss the mouse's walk up the stairs. If there are stairs in the school take the children for a walk up and down the stairs. Count the stairs or say "up, up, up we go" as you climb the stairs.

> **'Round the House**
> *'Round the house,* (use index finger to trace a circle on the child's open palm)
> *'Round the house,*
> *Goes the little mousie.*
> *Up the stairs,* (walk index finger and middle finger up the child's arm)
> *Up the stairs,*
> *In his little housie.* (tickle the child under the chin)

Cognitive Development Choices

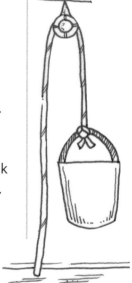

- Take the children outdoors to watch the clouds. Discuss the location of the clouds up in the sky. Watch for airplanes and discuss their location, as well.

- Tie a piece of yarn or string to the ceiling. Show the children how to string empty toilet paper tubes up the string. It is a good idea to use a long string that will curve a bit before the tubes start to fall. You can use this activity to discuss the effect of gravity and the concept that down is the opposite of up. Ask the children what happens to the tubes when they try to string them up the string. Even though the concept of gravity may be too difficult for little ones to understand, you can still mention that it is gravity that makes this task difficult. Explain that gravity is what makes a ball fall down when you toss it up.

- If available, attach a pulley to the ceiling and then run a rope through it. Attach a bucket to one end of the rope. Show the children how to make the bucket go up by pulling the rope through the pulley.
  Safety Warning: Do not let children play with the pulley unattended. If a child lets go of the rope, it can fall and hit that child or another child.

- Invite the children to toss wadded paper up in the air. "Why won't it stay up?"

- Problem-solving suggestion: Show the children pictures of animals, including some that fly. Help them decide which animals are seen up in the sky. "What body part do flying animals have that we don't?"

REFLECTION ON THE DAY
Ask the children to tell you something they have learned about up. Ask your "not yet talkers" to show you something that is up.

Down

WORDS TO PRACTICE

direction	position
down	where

GETTING STARTED

▦ Show the children a Jack-in-the-Box. Have Jack down in his box. Say the "Jack, Jack" action rhyme with the children. Point out that Jack is *down* in his box when the action rhyme begins.

Jack, Jack
Jack, Jack, down you go, (crouch down low)
Down in your box, down so low.
Jack, Jack, there goes the top. (pop up)
Quickly now, up you pop.

▦ Make Jack pop up and then press him down again. Describe the movements verbally as the children watch you work the Jack-in-the-Box. Ask questions to find out what the children know about the word *down*.

▦ Tell them that today they will be learning about how the word *down* is used to describe the location of something.

▦ Read your favorite book about spatial relationships to the children or select a book from the Story Circle Suggestions below to check out of the library and read.

STORY CIRCLE SUGGESTIONS

▦ *Down by the Bay* by Raffi

▦ *Inside, Outside, Upside Down* by Jan Berenstain

▦ *Up, Down, All Around* by Matt Mitter

PREPARATION FOR "DOWN" ACTIVITIES AND EXPERIENCES

▦ Make the "Hickory Dickory Dock" flannel board story, if not already made (Appendix p. 600).

▦ Gather squirt bottles and Floaters and Droppers (see p. 212).

Language Enrichment Choices*

- Sing "Are You Listening?" to the tune of "Are You Sleeping?" with the children. Sit down at the end of the song. Repeat if necessary.

   Are You Listening?
   Are you listening?
   Are you listening?
   Boys and girls, girls and boys.
   Come and join our circle,
   Come and join our circle,
   Sit right down.
   Sit right down.

- Use the word *down* in a sentence. For example, "I love to slide *down* the sliding board."

- Teach the children "Hickory Dickory Dock" (Appendix p. 600). Using the flannel board patterns will help the children see the difference between up and down.

   Hickory Dickory Dock
   Hickory dickory dock
   The mouse ran up the clock.
   The clock struck one,
   The mouse ran down.
   Hickory dickory dock.

- Teach the children the American Sign Language sign for *down* (Appendix p. 431).

Physical Development Choices

- Play "Ring Around the Rosie" with the children. Ask the children to hold hands and walk in a circle. Everyone falls down on the words, "All fall down." Discuss falling down. "Does it hurt when you fall down gently?" "What about when you fall down hard?"

   Ring Around the Rosie
   Ring around the rosie
   Pocket full of posies,
   Ashes, ashes,
   We all fall down.

* Toddlers and twos present a wide range of developmental needs, abilities, and interests. For each learning area, select among the following activity and experience choices that are appropriate for the children in your care.

■ If available, encourage the children to go down the sliding board.

■ Sing "The Grand Old Duke of York" with the children. Discuss the down position of the soldiers.

> **The Grand Old Duke of York**
> *The grand old Duke of York* (salute)
> *He had ten thousand men.* (hold up ten fingers)
> *He marched them up to the top of the hill,* (point up)
> *And he marched them down again.* (point down)
> *And when they're up, they're up.* (stand tall)
> *And when they're down, they're down.* (squat)
> *But when they're only halfway up,* (stoop down)
> *They're neither up nor down.* (open arms and shrug)

■ If wagons are available, take each of the children for a ride. Sing "My Little Red Wagon" while each child is riding.

> **My Little Red Wagon**
> *Bumping up and down in my little red wagon,*
> *Bumping up and down in my little red wagon,*
> *Bumping up and down in my little red wagon*
> *Won't you be my darlin'?*

■ Play a modified version of "London Bridge Is Falling Down" with the children. Instead of two children forming "the bridge," the teachers can make the bridge.

> **London Bridge Is Falling Down**
> *London Bridge is falling down,*
> *Falling down, falling down.*
> *London Bridge is falling down,*
> *My fair lady.*
>
> *Take the key and lock her up,*
> *Lock her up, lock her up.*
> *Take the key and lock her up,*
> *My fair lady.*

Repeat first verse.

■ Teach the children "Here We Go" (on the next page).

Here We Go
Here we go—up, up, up. (stand up on toes)
Here we go—down, down, down. (crouch down)
Here we go—moving forward. (take a step forward)
Here we go—moving backward. (take a step backward)
Here we go—round and round and round. (spin)

- Invite the children to do Log Rolls. Ask them to lie down on the ground and roll like a log. If you have an inclined area, encourage them to roll down the incline. Discuss the position they need to get in before rolling.

Social and Emotional Development Choices

- Sing "The Ants Go Marching" with the children. Discuss what the sentence, "They all go marching down to the ground…" means.

The Ants Go Marching

The ants go marching one by one
Hurrah, hurrah.
The ants go marching one by one
Hurrah, hurrah.
The ants go marching one by one,
The little one stops to suck his thumb.
And they all go marching down
To the ground
To get out
Of the rain.
BOOM! BOOM! BOOM! BOOM!

Two…tie her shoe…
Three…climb a tree…
Four…shut the door…
Five…take a dive…

- If there are stairs in the building, take the children to walk up and down them. Count the stairs or say "down, down, down we go!" as you go up or down the stairs.

- Sing "Itsy Bitsy Spider" with the children. "What happened to the spider when the rain came?" "Did she stay down?"

Itsy Bitsy Spider

The itsy bitsy spider
Went up the waterspout.
Down came the rain
And washed the spider out.

Up came the sun
And dried up all the rain.
And the itsy bitsy spider
Went up the spout again.

■ If a rocking chair is available, use it to rock each child. Sing "Rock-a-Bye Baby" while you rock. When you are finished, invite the little ones to rock doll babies and sing them to sleep.

Rock-a-Bye Baby

Rock-a-bye baby
In the tree top.
When the wind blows,
The cradle will rock.

When the bough breaks,
The cradle will fall.
And down will come baby
Cradle and all.

Cognitive Development Choices

■ Give the children squirt bottles filled with water and encourage them to spray the water on plastic sheeting, a large cookie sheet, or outdoors on the walls. Encourage them to watch the water drops as they run down the surface they are spraying.

■ Use a plank to make an inclined ramp and encourage the children to roll cars down the ramp. Discuss the direction the cars are going.

■ Invite little ones to play Drop the Clothespin. Provide a bucket and some clothespins and encourage the children to hold the clothespins waist high and then drop them into the bucket below. Discuss the downward fall of the clothespins.

■ If you use these activities in the fall, the children can watch the leaves falling down. If you use these activities on a rainy day, the children can watch the raindrops falling down.

■ Problem-solving suggestion: Give the children some Floaters (e.g., tissue, feather, paper) and Droppers (e.g., washer, block, crayon). Encourage them to drop each item and watch to see how quickly or slowly the item falls down to the ground. "Which items are floaters?" "Which items are droppers?"

REFLECTION ON THE DAY

Ask the children to sit down. Ask them to name or show you something that can fall down.

Over/Above

WORDS TO PRACTICE

above	over
location	where

GETTING STARTED

▨ Sing "The Bear Went Over the Mountain" with the children.

The Bear Went Over the Mountain
The bear went over the mountain,
The bear went over the mountain,
The bear went over the mountain
To see what he could see.

To see what he could see,
To see what he could see.
The bear went over the mountain
To see what he could see.

▨ Ask questions to find out what the children know about the words *over* and *above*.
▨ Tell the children that today they will be learning how the words *over* and *above* are used to describe where something is located.
▨ Read your favorite book about spatial relationships to the children or select a book from the Story Circle Suggestions below to check out of the library and read.

STORY CIRCLE SUGGESTIONS

▨ *Fraggles Over, Under and Between* by Laurie Berns
▨ *Over, Under, and Through and Other Spatial Concepts* by Tana Hoban

PREPARATION FOR "OVER/ABOVE" ACTIVITIES AND EXPERIENCES

▨ none

Language Enrichment Choices*

■ Hang colorful crepe paper streamers, sun catchers, cut-out animals, interesting small toys, and so on above your circle time area. Ask the children to lie on their backs and look at the things that are hanging over their heads or above their heads. Discuss the items and their location.

■ Use the words *over* and *above* in sentences. For example, "The light is *above* the table," or "The streamers are hanging *over* my head."

■ Teach the children the American Sign Language signs for *over* and *above* (Appendix p. 436). Review other signs that the children have learned.

Physical Development Choices

■ Say "Jack Be Nimble" with the children. Provide a block or an empty toilet paper tube for a candle and encourage the children to jump over the "candlestick" as they say the rhyme.

Jack Be Nimble
Jack be nimble,
Jack be quick.
Jack jump over the candlestick.

■ Play a modified game of "Red Rover, Red Rover." Make a short wall of pillows in the middle of the floor. You stay on one side of the wall and ask the children to go on the other side of the wall. Call the children, one at a time, to come over the wall. Say, "Red Rover, Red Rover, let Mandy come over." When you call the children, they should climb over the wall of pillows and come to you. Be sure to comment on the fact that they are climbing over the pillows.

■ With older twos, sing "Grasshopper" to the tune of "The Battle Hymn of the Republic" with the children. Have the children jump one hand over the other as each line of the song is sung. Older twos may enjoy trying a game of Leap Frog after they finish singing the song.

Grasshopper
The first grasshopper jumped right over the second grasshopper's back.
Oh, the first grasshopper jumped right over the second grasshopper's back.
The first grasshopper jumped right over the second grasshopper's back.
Oh, the first grasshopper jumped right over the second grasshopper's back.
They were only playing leapfrog,

* Toddlers and twos present a wide range of developmental needs, abilities, and interests. For each learning area, select among the following activity and experience choices that are appropriate for the children in your care.

They were only playing leapfrog,
They were only playing leapfrog,
When the first grasshopper jumped over the second grasshopper's back.

Do the action story, "Going on a Bear Hunt" with the children. Discuss all the things that you could and couldn't go over.

Going on a Bear Hunt
We're going on a bear hunt.
Want to come along?
Well, come on then.
Let's go! (walk in place)
Look! There's a river.
Can't go over it.
Can't go under it.
Can't go around it.
We'll have to go through it. (pretend to walk into river, through the water, and onto other bank, then resume walking in place)
Look! There's a tree.
Can't go under it.
Can't go through it.
We'll have to go over it. (pretend to climb up and over tree; then resume walking in place)
Look! There's a wheat field.
Can't go over it.
Can't go under it.
Can't go around it.
We'll have to go through it. (pretend to walk through field, make swishing sounds with hands against thighs, then resume walking in place)

Add verses to make the story as long as you want.

Look! There's a cave.
Want to go inside?
Ooh, it's dark in here. (look around, squinting)
I see two eyes.
Wonder what it is. (reach hands to touch)
It's soft and furry.
It's big.
It's a bear! Let's run! (retrace steps, running in place, through wheat field, in place, over tree, in place, across river, in place, then stop)
Home safe. Whew!

Social and Emotional Development Choices

- Serve the children ice cream with different toppings. Discuss the fact that the topping goes over the ice cream.

- Sing "Five Little Ducks" (p. 195) with the children. Discuss the ducks going over the hill.

- Sing "Five in the Bed" with the children. You can use a sheet or towel to represent the bed and invite the children to act out the song or sing it using the hand motions described below. Discuss rolling over.

  Five in the Bed
  There were five in the bed, (hold up five fingers)
  And the little one said,
  "Roll over! Roll over!" (roll hand over hand)
  So they all rolled over
  And one rolled out. (hold up one finger)

  There were four in the bed... (repeat hand motions)
  There were three in the bed...
  There were two in the bed...

  There was one in the bed
  And the little one said,
  "Alone at last!" (place head on hands as if sleeping)

Cognitive Development Choices

- Suspend a beach ball from the ceiling at a height that is just above the children's heads. Invite them to bat the ball by reaching their hands over their heads. "Is the ball over your head?"

- Sing "Twinkle, Twinkle, Little Star" with the children. Talk about the stars up above the world. Give the children rock salt and let them glue it to black construction paper to make a starry night picture.

  Twinkle, Twinkle, Little Star
  Twinkle, twinkle, little star,
  How I wonder what you are!
  Up above the world so high,
  Like a diamond in the sky.

Twinkle, twinkle, little star,
How I wonder what you are!

■ Go outside and watch the clouds pass over the ground. Discuss the location of the clouds. You may want to share the following fingerplay while you are enjoying the clouds.

Two little clouds one April day (hold both hands in fists)
Went sailing across the sky. (move fist from left to right)
They went so fast
That they bumped their heads, (bump fists together)
And both began to cry. (point to eyes)

The big round sun came out and said, (make circle with arms)
"Oh, never mind, my dears,
I'll send all my sunbeams down (wiggle fingers downward like rain)
To dry your fallen tears."

■ Take a squirt bottle of water outdoors and invite the children to spray the water over the fence.

■ Give the children wadded pieces of paper to toss over a table or over a box.

■ Build a bridge with blocks. Invite the children to drive small cars over the bridge.

■ Problem-solving suggestion: Provide a piece of blue paper to represent a river. Give the children some blocks and a car. Tell them that the people in the car want to get across the river. Ask them how that can happen. They may need some hints. They can build a bridge or a boat with the blocks.

REFLECTION ON THE DAY
Ask the children to show you something that is over their heads.

Under/Below

WORDS TO PRACTICE

below   under
location where

GETTING STARTED

▨ Provide carpet squares for the children to sit on. Place cut-out shapes or stickers under the carpet squares. Begin by asking the children what is *under* their bottoms. Then ask them to pick up the carpet squares to see what is *under* them. Ask the children questions to determine what they know about the words *under* and *below*.

▨ Tell the children that today they will be learning how the words *under* and *below* are used to describe where something is located.

▨ Read your favorite book about spatial relationships to the children or select a book from the Story Circle Suggestions below to check out of the library and read.

STORY CIRCLE SUGGESTIONS

▨ *Fraggles Over, Under and Between* by Laurie Berns
▨ *Over, Under, and Through and Other Spatial Concepts* by Tana Hoban

PREPARATION FOR "UNDER/BELOW" ACTIVITIES AND EXPERIENCES

▨ Find and laminate a photo to place at the bottom of the sand table or tub.
▨ Cut out shapes from contact paper.
▨ Make Mystery Pictures Folders and Tactile Walk (see p. 220).

Language Enrichment Choices*

▨ Show the children three small toys. Then cover the toys with a blanket and point out that the toys are located under the blanket. Secretly remove one of the toys. Uncover the toys and see if the children can tell you which toy is missing from under the blanket. Try the game again.

▨ Use the words *under* and *below* in a sentence. For example, "The car went *under* the bridge," or "My friend lives in the apartment *below* ours."

▨ Teach the children the American Sign Language signs for *under* and *below* (Appendix p. 439). Review the signs for *above* and *over*.

Physical Development Choices

▨ If you have a parachute, bring it outdoors and play games that allow the children to run under it. If you do not have a parachute, use a large sheet. Give the children directions, such as "all the boys run under the sheet" or "all the girls crawl under the sheet."

▨ Encourage the children to walk on a masking tape line with a ball or an orange under their chin. Have them try walking on the line with a book under their arms. Which is easier?

▨ Encourage the children to stand with their legs spread apart, and then roll a ball through their legs (by bending over) to a friend who is standing behind them. Discuss rolling the ball under their bodies and under their legs.

Social and Emotional Development Choices

▨ Sing "Under the Spreading Chestnut Tree." Take the children outdoors and read a book under a tree.

> **Under the Spreading Chestnut Tree**
> *Under the spreading chestnut tree,*
> *There I held her on my knee.*
> *We were happy, yesiree,*
> *Under the spreading chestnut tree.*

▨ Place a sticker on the underside (bottom) of a lunch or snack plate or cup. Encourage the children to "clean their plates" so they can see the surprise under the plate.

* Toddlers and twos present a wide range of developmental needs, abilities, and interests. For each learning area, select among the following activity and experience choices that are appropriate for the children in your care.

Cognitive Development Choices

- Build a bridge with blocks. Invite the children to drive small cars under the bridge.

- Make a tent by placing a sheet over a table. Invite the children to get under the tent.

- Tape a piece of drawing paper under the art table and invite the children to go under the table and draw a picture.

- Tape a picture to the bottom of the sand table or sand tub. Encourage the children to find what is under the sand.

- Ask each child to show you something he is wearing that is located below his knees. Children may answer their shoes, their socks, or both.

- Cut out several shapes from contact paper and stick them to the top of a table. Cover the table with shaving cream. Encourage the children to find the shapes under the shaving cream. Can they name the shapes?

- Invite the children to explore Mystery Pictures Folders. Glue pictures to the inside of file folders. Cut small flaps on the outside of the folders. Encourage the children to look under the flaps, one at a time, to identify the pictures inside the folder. You should be able to include four or five pictures in each folder. Ask the children to describe or name the mystery pictures.

- Set up a Tactile Walk for the children. Find fabric and papers with interesting textures and cut them into 10"-square pieces. Glue the squares to poster board and place them in a pathway on the floor. Encourage the children to walk on the path. Discuss the feel of the pathway under their feet.

- Problem-solving suggestion: Show the children two identical caps or hats. Hide a small toy under one of the hats. Move the hats around and challenge the children to show you which hat they think the toy is under.

REFLECTION ON THE DAY

Ask the children to name what is under their feet. Ask the children to show you a body part that is below their knees.

Top, Middle, Bottom

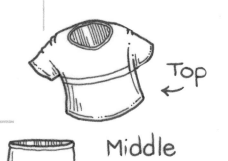

WORDS TO PRACTICE

top	middle	bottom

GETTING STARTED

- Using three different colors of blocks, stack the blocks in a tower with one color on the top, another in the middle, and the third on the bottom. "Can you name the color of the blocks on the *top* of the tower, in the *middle* of the tower, and on the *bottom* of the tower?" Ask questions to find out what the children know about the words *top, middle,* and *bottom*.

- Tell the children that today they will be learning how the words *top, middle,* and *bottom* are used to describe the location of someone or something.

- Read your favorite book about spatial relationships to the children or select a book from the Story Circle Suggestions below to check out of the library and read.

STORY CIRCLE SUGGESTIONS

- *All About Where* by Tana Hoban
- *Construction Zone* by Tana Hoban
- *Mop Top* by Don Freeman

PREPARATION FOR "TOP, MIDDLE, BOTTOM" ACTIVITIES AND EXPERIENCES

- Gather pudding, cookie crumbs, and whipped topping.
- Make Dress-Me Dolls (Appendix p. 455-466) and the Top, Middle, and Bottom Monster Puzzles (Appendix p. 470-472).

Language Enrichment Choices*

- Show the children some items that have a distinct top, middle, and bottom section such as a jar, a box of cereal, a milk carton, a flower (if you can see the roots), and a house.

* Toddlers and twos present a wide range of developmental needs, abilities, and interests. For each learning area, select among the following activity and experience choices that are appropriate for the children in your care.

Discuss what is on the top of the item, what is in the middle, and what is on the bottom.

■ Use the words *top, middle,* and *bottom* in a sentence. For example, "I keep my socks in my *top* drawer, my shirts in my *middle* drawers, and my toys in my *bottom* drawer."

■ Teach the children the American Sign Language signs for *top, middle,* and *bottom* (Appendix p. 430, 435, and 439).

Physical Development Choices

■ Sing "Head, Shoulders, Knees, and Toes" with the children. Touch the body parts as they are mentioned. Ask the children to identify which body part mentioned in the song is at the top of their bodies, which ones are in the middle, and which ones are at the bottom.

Head, Shoulders, Knees, and Toes
Head, shoulders, knees and toes,
Knees and toes.
Head, shoulders, knees and toes,
Knees and toes.
And eyes and ears and mouth and nose.
Head, shoulders, knees and toes
Knees and toes!

■ Take the children on a walk outdoors and point out the top, middle, and bottom of things you see on your walk. Try to get the children looking for things they can describe by noting the top, middle, and bottom of the item.

Social and Emotional Development Choices

■ Invite the children to help make a Three-Layer Dessert. Provide clear plastic cups, cookie crumbs, vanilla pudding, and a whipped topping. Show the children how to put the cookie crumbs on the bottom of their cup, the pudding in the middle, and the whipped topping on the top. If you want to try something simpler, just help the children fix cheese and crackers and discuss what is on the bottom, in the middle, and on the top.

- Take the children on a tour of the room or the building. Look for items that have a top, middle, and bottom. Encourage the children to help you find the items and identify the parts.

- Sing "On Top of Spaghetti" with the children. "What was on top of the spaghetti?"

Cognitive Development Choices

- Invite the children to build a house with blocks. Ask them to show you the house's top, middle, and bottom.

- Give the children plastic jars and pots and pans with which to play. As the children remove and replace the tops, label the top, middle, and bottom of each pot and pan.

- Give the children the Dress-Me Dolls (Appendix p.455-466) to dress. Discuss which clothing items go on the top of the dolls, which go in the middle, and which go on the bottom.

- Draw three horizontal lines across pieces of drawing paper and invite the children to draw something at the top of their papers, something in the middle of their papers, and something on the bottom of their papers.

- Encourage the children to build a tower using several colors of blocks. Challenge them to name the color of the block at the top and the bottom of the tower. "What color blocks are in the middle?"

- Problem-solving suggestion: Invite the children to work the Top, Middle, and Bottom Monster Puzzles (Appendix p. 470-472). Discuss the parts of each monster. For extra fun, try mixing and matching the parts to create new monsters.

REFLECTION ON THE DAY
Show the children a carton of milk and ask them to show you the top, the middle, and the bottom of the carton.

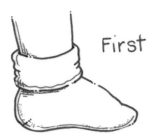
First

Next

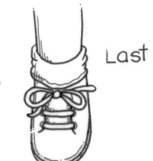
Last

First, Next, Last

WORDS TO PRACTICE

first
last
next

GETTING STARTED

- Talk with the children about what they have done prior to coming to school. You will probably have to prompt them. For example, you can ask, "What was the *first* thing you did after you woke up? What did you do *next?*" If the children are too young to describe the events of their morning, briefly tell them about your morning.

- Tell the children that today they will be learning how the words *first, next,* and *last* can be used to describe where something is or when something happens.

- Read your favorite book about temporal and positional relationships to the children or select a book from the Story Circle Suggestions below to check out of the library and read.

STORY CIRCLE SUGGESTIONS

- *All About Where* by Tana Hoban
- *Peanut Butter and Jelly: A Play Rhyme* by Nadine Bernard Westcott

PREPARATION FOR "FIRST, NEXT, LAST" ACTIVITIES AND EXPERIENCES

- Make the "Madison's Day" flannel board story (Appendix p. 529-531).
- Gather peanut butter and jelly sandwich ingredients.
- Make the Glove Puppet and fingerplay characters (Appendix p. 447-454).
- Gather three large cardboard boxes and cut arches in each side of each box.

Language Enrichment Choices*

▪ Put a child's tennis shoes on the child while the other children are watching. Describe your actions. Say, "First I put your foot in the shoe. Next I tighten your laces. The last thing I do is tie your laces." Repeat your description while putting on the second shoe.

▪ Ask the children about their daily routine at school. "What do we do first each morning? What do we do next? What is the last thing we do before going home each day?"

▪ Use the words *first, next,* and *last* in a sentence. For example, "The *first* thing I do when I get up in the morning is wash my face. The *next* thing I do is eat my breakfast. The *last* thing I do is brush my teeth."

▪ Present the "Madison's Day" flannel board story (Appendix p. 529-531). "What made Madison sad?" "What made Madison happy?"

▪ Teach the children the American Sign Language sign for *first,* and *last* (Appendix p. 432, 434).

Physical Development Choices

▪ Sing "Peanut Butter" with the children. "What happens first in the song? What happens next? What happens last?" Note that some of the words have been altered to reflect next and last.

Peanut Butter
Chorus:
Peanut, peanut butter, jelly!
Peanut, peanut butter, jelly!

First you take the peanuts and (pretend to dig peanuts)
You dig 'em, you dig 'em.
Dig 'em, dig 'em, dig 'em.
Then you smash 'em, you smash 'em. (pretend to smash peanuts)
Smash 'em, smash 'em, smash 'em.
Then you spread 'em, you spread 'em. (pretend to spread the peanuts)
Spread 'em, spread 'em, spread 'em.

Chorus

* Toddlers and twos present a wide range of developmental needs, abilities, and interests. For each learning area, select among the following activity and experience choices that are appropriate for the children in your care.

225

Next you take the berries and (pretend to pick berries)
You pick 'em, you pick 'em.
Pick 'em, pick 'em, pick 'em.
Then you smash 'em, you smash 'em. (pretend to smash berries)
Smash 'em, smash 'em, smash 'em.
Then you spread 'em, you spread 'em. (pretend to spread berries)
Spread 'em, spread 'em, spread 'em.

Chorus

Last you take the sandwich and
You bite it, you bite it. (pretend to bite a sandwich)
Bite it, bite it, bite it.
Then you chew it, you chew it. (pretend to chew a sandwich)
Chew it, chew it, chew it.
Then you swallow it, you swallow it. (pretend to swallow peanut butter
  sandwich)
Swallow it, swallow it, swallow it.

Hum chorus.

- Play "One Elephant." To play the game, ask the children to sit in a circle. Choose a child to be the elephant. The child places one arm out in front to make a trunk, and walks around the circle while the group sings the song below. When the group sings, "He called for another elephant to come," the first child chooses another child to become an "elephant." The first child takes the hand of the second elephant and continues to walk around the room. After all the elephants have been chosen, ask about the positions in the line. "Which elephant is first in line?" "Which elephant is next in line?" "Which elephant is last in line?"

  One Elephant
  One elephant went out to play.
  Out on a spider's web one day.
  He had such enormous fun,
  He called for another elephant to come.

  Two elephants...

- Cut out an arch from both sides of three large cardboard boxes of graduated sizes. Place the boxes in a row.

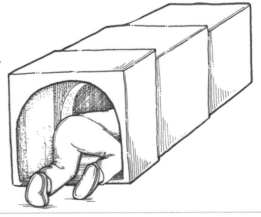

Encourage the children to crawl though the first box (the smallest box), then the next box (the medium box), and then the last box (the largest box). If you can't locate boxes large enough to crawl through, use smaller boxes and ask the children to roll a ball through the boxes in the same order.

Social and Emotional Development Choices

- Say one or more of the following fingerplays that focus on position and ordinal numbers: "Five Little Pumpkins," "Five Waiting Pumpkins," or "Five Little Snowmen." Make a Glove Puppet so that the children are actually able to see the characters as they speak and as they disappear. Discuss what happened to the pumpkin and/or snowman in the first position, the next position, and the last position.

Five Little Pumpkins
Five little pumpkins sitting on a gate. (hold up five fingers)
First one said, "It's getting late." (wiggle first finger)
Second one said, "There's witches in the air." (wiggle second finger)
Third one said, "We don't care." (wiggle third finger)
Fourth one said, "Let's run, let's run." (wiggle fourth finger)
Fifth one said, "Oh, it's just Halloween fun." (wiggle fifth finger)
But whooo! went the wind and out went the light (hold hands sides of your
   mouth and blow)
And five little pumpkins rolled out of sight. (roll hand over hand)

Five Waiting Pumpkins (suit actions to words)
Five little pumpkins growing on a vine.
First one said, "It's time to shine!"
Second one said, "I love the fall"
Third one said, "I'm round as a ball."
Fourth one said, "I want to be a pie."
Fifth one said, "Let's say good-bye."
"Good-bye," said one!
"Adios," said two!
"Au revoir," said three!
"Ciao," said four!
"Aloha," said five!
And five little pumpkins were picked that day!

Five Little Snowmen

Five little snowmen happy and gay, (hold up five fingers and move one for
    each snowman)
The first one said, "What a nice day!"
The second one said, "We'll cry no tears,"
The third one said, "We'll stay for years."
The fourth one said, "But what happens in May?"
The fifth one said, "Look, we're melting away!" (hold hands out as if saying
    all gone)

- Talk with the children about the sequence of some of the things they do, such as putting on their clothing or brushing their teeth.

- As you work with children individually today (putting on shoes and socks, helping wash their hands, and so on), use the first, next, and last vocabulary to describe what you are doing.

Cognitive Development Choices

- Give the children a set of simple sequential directions for an activity. Give the directions one at a time. For example, "The first thing I want you to do is to get a crayon." Pause. "Next I want you to pick up a piece of paper." Pause. "The last thing I want you to do is color a picture."

- When the children line up, discuss their position in the line. "Who is first? Last?" "How many children are in the middle?"

- Invite the children to help make peanut butter and jelly sandwiches. "What do you do first when making the sandwich?" "What happens next?" "What is the last thing you do?"

- Provide baby dolls and bath accessories. Invite the children to pretend to bathe the baby. "What is the first thing you do when bathing the baby?" "What do you do next?" "What do you do last?"

- Problem-solving suggestion: Ask the children to tell you what they do to get ready for bed and when they get up in the morning.

REFLECTION ON THE DAY

When the children are in line, ask them to identify who is first in line, who is next in line, and who is last in line.

Sing a Song of Opposites

BIG AND SMALL

TALL AND SHORT

LONG AND SHORT

UP AND DOWN/HIGH AND LOW

IN AND OUT/INSIDE AND OUTSIDE

OVER AND UNDER

FRONT AND BACK/FORWARD AND
    BACKWARD

FAT AND SKINNY

DAY AND NIGHT

HARD AND SOFT

FAST AND SLOW

THICK AND THIN

LOUD AND SOFT

LIGHT AND HEAVY

Big and Small

WORDS TO PRACTICE

big	larger	smallest
bigger	largest	tinier
biggest	small	tiniest
large	smaller	tiny

GETTING STARTED

- Ask questions to find out what the children know about *big* and *small*. Show them a big book and a small book of the same story. Ask which book they would prefer you to read. "Which book will provide better pictures to see?" Read a story from a big book.
- Tell the children that today they will be learning about the opposites *big* and *small*.
- Read your favorite book about opposites to the children or select a book from the Story Circle Suggestions below to check out of the library and read.

STORY CIRCLE SUGGESTIONS

- *Berenstain Bears, Big Bear, Small Bear* by Stan and Jan Berenstain
- *Panda Big, Panda Small* by Jane Cabrera
- *Sing a Song of Opposites* by Pam Schiller

PREPARATION FOR "BIG AND SMALL" ACTIVITIES AND EXPERIENCES

- Gather big and small pairs of items.
- Prepare "The Lion and the Mouse" (Appendix p. 502-504) and/ or the "Peanut" flannel board story (Appendix p. 545-548).
- Make rings and weighted soda bottles.
- Gather snack items that come in large and small sizes.
- Make a large puzzle if you don't have a commercial one.
- Get popcorn.

Language Enrichment Choices*

■ Show the children a variety of objects that come in big and small sizes such as cups, books, spoons, socks, and shoes. Discuss the items one pair at a time. Explain that big and small are opposites.

■ Sing "Sing a Song of Opposites" to the tune of "Mary Had a Little Lamb," using the pairs of opposites you have just shown the children.

This Is Big and This Is Small
This is big and this is small,
This is big; this is small.
This is big and this is small,
Sing along with me.

■ Use the words *big* and *small* in a sentence. For example, "I like *big* books better than *small* books."

■ Present the flannel board story, "The Lion and the Mouse" (Appendix p. 502-504) to the children. "What size is the lion?" "What size is the mouse?"

■ Present the flannel board story, "Peanut" (Appendix p. 545-548) to the children. "What size is Peanut at the beginning of the story?" "What size is he at the end of the story?"

■ Teach or review the American Sign Language signs for *big* and *small* (Appendix p. 430, 437).

Physical Development Choices

■ Invite the children to do the action rhyme, "Big and Small." Can the children name something that is big? Small?

Big and Small
I can make myself real big (stand up on toes)
By standing up straight and tall.
But when I'm tired of being big,
I can make myself get small. (stoop down)

■ Encourage the children to play with big and small balls. "Which balls are easier to catch?" "Which balls are easier to throw?" "Which balls do you like best?"

* Toddlers and twos present a wide range of developmental needs, abilities, and interests. For each learning area, select among the following activity and experience choices that are appropriate for the children in your care.

- Fill two big and two small clear soda bottles with sand. Cut out the centers of plastic lids (e.g., coffee can lids) to make rings. Encourage the children to toss or drop a ring on one of the bottles and then tell you if that bottle is large or small.

Social and Emotional Development Choices

- Teach the children the following adapted version of the fingerplay, "When I Was One."

   When I Was One
   When I was one I was so small, (hold up one finger)
   I could not speak a word at all. (shake head)
   When I was two, I learned to talk. (hold up two fingers)
   I learned to sing; I learned to walk. (point to mouth and feet)
   When I am three, I'll learn and grow, (hold up two fingers)
   There's no telling what I'll know. (point to head)

- Take the children on a visit to a classroom with children who are older than they are and then to a classroom with children who are younger than they are. Discuss the size of the children in each classroom. Remind the children that they used to be smaller than they are now and that they will grow even bigger than they are now.

- Compare the children's hands to your hands. Talk to them about how small their hands are in comparison to yours.

- Trace your hand and then a child's hand next to your hand. Ask the child which hand is big and which hand is small.

- Read the poem "What Size Am I?" to the children. Discuss their size in relationship to members of their family.

   What Size Am I?
   I'm little beside my mother,
   But big next to baby brother.
   Beside my dad I am little.
   I guess when it comes to my size,
   I am somewhere in the middle.

Cognitive Development Choices

- Provide some big and small shoes for the children to try on. Make sure to have some shoes that are too small for the children to put on their feet. If available, doll shoes work well.

- Provide pictures of animals that are big (such as elephants, giraffes, and hippos) and animals that are small (such as ants, mice, and squirrels). Invite the children to sort the animals by their size. "Has anyone see a real giraffe? Elephant? Hippo?"

- Provide a magnifying glass and some small objects such as a button, a penny, and a seed. Invite the children to examine the items through a magnifying glass. Discuss how much bigger these things look when looking at them through the magnifying glass.
  Safety Warning: Supervise closely so children do not put small objects into their mouths.

- Give the children big and small books to look at. "Which book is easier to handle?" "Which book do you prefer to look at?"

- Give the children big and small sheets of paper to draw on. "Which paper is easier to draw on?"

- Serve items for snack that come in big and small sizes such as marshmallows and pretzels. Discuss the sizes of the snacks.

- Pop popcorn. "What size is the corn before it pops?" "What size is it after it pops?"

- Problem-solving suggestions:
  1. Give the children large and small items to sort.
  2. Provide large and small puzzles for the children to work. If you don't have large puzzles (floor puzzles), you can make one by drawing a simple item such as a sun or a heart on a large piece of poster board. Cut it out, laminate it, and then cut it into three or four large puzzle pieces.

REFLECTION ON THE DAY
Ask the children to tell you something they have learned about big and small. Ask younger toddlers to show you something that is big and something that is small.

Tall and Short

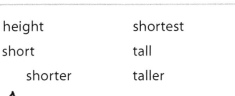

WORDS TO PRACTICE

height	shortest	tallest
short	tall	
shorter	taller	

GETTING STARTED

- Stand up and select a child to stand beside you. Ask the children which of you is *tall* and which of you is *short*. Ask the children questions to determine what they know about *tall* and *short*.
- Tell them that today they will be learning more about *tall* and *short*.
- Read your favorite book about opposites to the children or select a book from the Story Circle Suggestions below to check out of the library and read.

STORY CIRCLE SUGGESTIONS

- *Short and Tall (Animal Opposites)* by Rod Theodorou
- *How Tall, How Short, How Faraway* by David A. Adler
- *Tall Body, Short Body, Everybody's Somebody* by Mary Hollingsworth
- *Toddy Bear's Tall and Short Book* by V. Gilbert Beers

PREPARATION FOR "TALL AND SHORT" ACTIVITIES AND EXPERIENCES

- Make the "Madison's Day" flannel board story, if not already made (Appendix p. 529-531).
- Gather pairs of tall and short items.
- Get tall and short pretzels.

Language Enrichment Choices*

- Show the children a variety of objects that come in tall and short heights, such as cups, bottles, measuring sticks, and boxes. Discuss the items one pair at a time. Explain that tall and short are opposites.

- Sing "Sing a Song of Opposites" to the tune of "Mary Had a Little Lamb" using the pairs of opposites you have just shown the children. You can sing a verse about *big* and *little* if you have already introduced these concepts.

    Sing a Song of Opposites
    This is short and this is tall,
    This is short; this is tall.
    This is short and this is tall,
    Sing along with me.

- Use the words *short* and *tall* in a sentence. For example, "My sister is *tall* for her age. My mother says I am *small*."

- Present the flannel board story, "Madison's Day" (Appendix p. 529-531) to the children. Discuss the height of the people in Madison's family.

- Teach or review the American Sign Language signs for *short* and *tall* (Appendix p. 437-438).

Physical Development Choices

- Teach the children "Sometimes."

    Sometimes
    Sometimes I am tall, (stand tall)
    Sometimes I am small. (crouch low)
    Sometimes I am very, very, tall. (stand on tiptoes)
    Sometimes I am very, very small. (crouch and lower head)
    Sometimes tall, (stand tall)
    Sometimes small. (crouch down)
    Sometimes neither tall or small. (stand normally)

- Invite the children to toss beanbags over short and tall walls of blocks or into short and tall boxes. "Is it easier to toss beanbags into tall or short boxes?"

* Toddlers and twos present a wide range of developmental needs, abilities, and interests. For each learning area, select among the following activity and experience choices that are appropriate for the children in your care.

Social and Emotional Development Choices

▦ Examine the children's hands with them. "Which fingers are short?" "Which fingers are taller?"

▦ Serve juice in tall and short glasses. Discuss the size of the glasses. "Which one holds more juice?"

▦ Serve tall and short pretzel sticks. "Do they taste different?"

▦ Problem-solving suggestion: Ask each of the children to find someone who is taller than he is. This should be possible for all the children, including the tallest child, because you will be taller than her.

Cognitive Development Choices

▦ Provide photos of animals and encourage the children to sort them into tall and short categories. "Do short animals have short legs?"

▦ Provide empty toilet paper tubes and empty wrapping paper tubes for the children to play with. Encourage them to talk through the tubes. "Does your voice sound different when you speak through different length tubes?"

▦ Invite the children to build tall and short towers with blocks. "Which towers are more fun to build?"

▦ Provide tall (cut easel paper lengthwise) and short sheets of paper. Invite the children to paint tall and short pictures.

▦ Measure the children. Talk about how tall they are today (which is taller than they were a couple of months ago) and how tall they will grow in the future (which is taller than they are today). Say the poem "My Father Is Extremely Tall." Ask them about the sizes of the different members of their family. "Which family members are tall?" "Which ones are short?"

My Father Is Extremely Tall
My father is extremely tall
When he stands upright like a wall.
But I am very short and small.
Yet I am growing, so they say,
A little taller every day.

■ Give the children pairs of tall and short items, such as measuring sticks, blocks, unbreakable drinking glasses, and so on, and encourage them to sort them by size.

■ Problem-solving suggestion: Provide a light source such as an overhead projector and show the children how to make tall and short shadows on the wall. Can they figure out how to make their shadows grow without your help?

REFLECTION ON THE DAY
Ask the children to tell you something they have learned about tall and short. Ask younger toddlers to show you something in the classroom that is tall and something that is short.

Long and Short

WORDS TO PRACTICE

length	longest	shortest
long	short	
longer	shorter	

GETTING STARTED

- Place two strips of masking tape on the floor—one long and one short. Invite the children to walk on both lines. Ask them which line is longer and which line is shorter. Explain that *long* and *short* are opposites.
- Tell the children that today they will learn more about the opposites *long* and *short*.
- Read your favorite book about opposites to the children or select a book from the Story Circle Suggestions below to check out of the library and read.

STORY CIRCLE SUGGESTIONS

- *The Long and the Short of It* by Lisa McCourt
- *Sesame Street Characters: Long and Short* by Jane Beethoven
- *Short Train, Long Train* by Frank Asch

PREPARATION FOR "LONG AND SHORT" ACTIVITIES AND EXPERIENCES

- Make "The Lion's Haircut" flannel board story (Appendix p. 505-506).
- Gather pairs of items that come in long and short lengths.
- Get animal pictures and carrots or pretzels.

Language Enrichment Choices*

- Show the children a variety of objects that come in short and long lengths, such as ribbons, bottles, measuring sticks, and straws. Discuss the items one pair at a time. Remind the children that long and short are opposites.

Sing a Song of Opposites

* Toddlers and twos present a wide range of developmental needs, abilities, and interests. For each learning area, select among the following activity and experience choices that are appropriate for the children in your care.

- Sing "Sing a Song of Opposites" to the tune of "Mary Had a Little Lamb" using the pairs of opposites you have just shown the children. You can sing a verse about *big* and *little* if you have already introduced this concept.

  Sing a Song of Opposites
  This is long and this is short,
  This is long; this is short.
  This is long and this is short,
  Sing along with me.

- Use the words *short* and *long* in a sentence. For example, "My mother likes my hair *short,* but my grandmother likes it *long.*"

- Present the flannel board story, "The Lion's Haircut" (Appendix p. 505-506) to the children. Discuss the length of Leo's mane when he was young and when he was older.

- Teach or review the American Sign Language signs for *short* and *long* (Appendix p. 435, 437). Review the sign for *tall*.

Physical Development Choices

- Ask the children to do some jumps. Encourage them to try some long jumps and some short jumps. Use masking tape to mark start and finish lines for each type of jump.

- Problem-solving suggestion: Show the children how to take long and short steps/strides. Walk across the room using both kinds of steps. "Which steps get you across the room faster?"

Social and Emotional Development Choices

- Give the children long and short straws to use to drink their juice. "Which straw do you like best?"

- Sing "Where, Oh, Where Has My Little Dog Gone?" Discuss the length of the dog's ears and the dog's tail.

  Where, Oh, Where Has My Little Dog Gone?
  Where, oh, where has my little dog gone?
  Where, oh, where can he be?

With his ears cut short and his tail cut long,
Oh, where, oh, where can he be?

- Sing long and short songs. For example, you can use "Rain, Rain, Go Away" for a short song and "The Ants Go Marching" for a long song.

  Rain, Rain, Go Away
  Rain, rain, go away.
  Little children want to play.

  Ants Go Marching
  The ants go marching one by one
  Hurrah, hurrah.
  The ants go marching one by one
  Hurrah, hurrah.
  The ants go marching one by one,
  The little one stops to suck his thumb.
  And they all go marching down
  To the ground
  To get out
  Of the rain.
  BOOM! BOOM! BOOM! BOOM!

  Two... tie her shoe...
  Three... climb a tree...
  Four... shut the door...
  Five... take a dive...

- Read a long and a short story. Any of the nursery rhymes make good short stories. *Brown Bear, Brown Bear, What Do You See?* by Bill Martin Jr. and Eric Carle makes a good long story for little ones.

- When the children wake up from their naps, discuss the length of their nap. "Was it a long or short nap?"

- Problem-solving suggestion: Cut cooked carrots or pretzel sticks into long and short lengths. Serve them for snack and discuss the length of the carrots with the children. "Does it take longer to eat a long or short carrot stick?" **Safety Warning:** Raw carrots pose a choking hazard for young children; therefore, it is a good idea to cook them first.

Cognitive Development Choices

▨ Provide playdough and encourage the children to roll long and short snakes. Provide blunt knives, such as butter knives, or blunt scissors and let the children cut long snakes into short snakes.

▨ Invite the children to make a collage with long and short straws. "Have you tried drinking from long and short straws?" "Which is more fun to drink from?"

▨ Encourage the children to make long and short roads with the blocks. "Which road requires more blocks?"

▨ Take the children outdoors in search of long and short things. Make a list of the things you find.

▨ Place long and short lines of masking tape on the floor and invite the children to walk on them. "Which line takes longer to walk?"

▨ Show the children pictures of animals and ask them to decide if the animal has a long or short tail, long or short ears, and long or short legs.

▨ Provide pull toys with long and short strings. "Which length of string makes it easier to pull the toy?"

▨ Invite the children to paint with long and short paintbrushes. Discuss the difference in using each type of brush. "Can you reach further with one brush than the other?"

▨ Provide a long sheet of butcher paper and invite the children to paint a long mural. Provide a sheet of easel paper and encourage the children to paint a short mural. "Which mural takes longer to paint?"

▨ Provide dress-up clothing in long and short sizes. For example, you can use long and short pants, long and short socks, and long and short dresses. Encourage the children to explore both sizes of each item.

▨ Problem-solving suggestion: Give the children the pairs of long and short items you collected and ask them to sort the items by their length.

REFLECTION ON THE DAY
Ask the children to show you something in the classroom that is long and something that is short.

Up and Down/ High and Low

WORDS TO PRACTICE

down	opposites
high	position
location	up
low	

GETTING STARTED

■ Do the action rhyme, "Jack, Jack" with the children. Find out what the children know about up and down. Explain that up and down are opposites. You may want to mention any other pairs of opposites that the children have learned about.

Jack, Jack
Jack, Jack, down you go, (crouch down low)
Down in your box, down so low.
Jack, Jack, there goes the top. (pop up)
Quickly now, up you pop.

■ Tell the children that today they will be learning more about the opposites *up* and *down*.
■ Read your favorite book about opposites to the children or select a book from the Story Circle Suggestions below to check out of the library and read.

STORY CIRCLE SUGGESTIONS

■ *Berenstain Bears Go Up and Down* by Jan and Stan Berenstain
■ *Up and Down on the Merry-Go-Round* by John Archambault
■ *Go, Dog, Go!* by Philip D. Eastman

PREPARATION FOR "UP AND DOWN/HIGH AND LOW" ACTIVITIES AND EXPERIENCES

▨ Make the "The Mouse and the Clock" (Appendix p. 600) and the "Jack and Jill" flannel board stories, if not already made.

▨ Ask families to provide a toothbrush for school use.

▨ Gather Floaters and Droppers (see p. 247).

▨ Get raisins and lemon-lime soda, such as Sprite.

▨ Make Paper Bag Blocks (optional)(see p. 247).

Language Enrichment Choices*

▨ Point out things in the classroom that are *up high* and things that are *down low*. Remind the children that the words *up* and *down* are opposites.

▨ Sing "Sing a Song of Opposites" to the tune of "Mary Had a Little Lamb," pointing to things in the classroom as you sing. If desired, add verses about other opposites that you have studied.

> **Sing a Song of Opposites**
> *This is up and this is down,*
> *This is up; this is down.*
> *This is up and this is down,*
> *Sing along with me.*

▨ Use the words *up* and *down* in a sentence. For example, "I like going *down* the slide better than climbing *up*."

▨ Do the action rhyme, "High and Low" with the children. Discuss the ways they move with the rhyme.

> **High and Low**
> *I reach my hands way up high.* (reach high)
> *I can almost touch sky.* (wave hands)
> *Then I bend way down low,* (bend down)
> *And touch the floor just so.* (touch the floor)

▨ Say "The Mouse and the Clock" (Appendix p. 600) or "Jack and Jill" (Appendix p. 592-594) with the children. Use the flannel board illustrations so that the children can see the difference in up and down. Discuss the up and down run of the mouse, or the upward climb and downward fall of Jack and Jill.

* Toddlers and twos present a wide range of developmental needs, abilities, and interests. For each learning area, select among the following activity and experience choices that are appropriate for the children in your care.

- For older twos, tell the action (participation) story of Mr. Wiggle and Mr. Waggle (Appendix p. 534). Discuss the up and down pathway between Mr. Wiggle's house and Mr. Waggle's house. "Has anyone ever walked up a hill?"

- Teach or review the American Sign Language signs for *up* and *down* and *high* and *low*. (Appendix p. 431, 433, 435, and 439). Review the other signs for opposite words.

Physical Development Choices

- Teach the children "Here We Go." Discuss the movements in the chant.

   Here We Go
   Here we go—up, up, up. (stand up on toes)
   Here we go—down, down, down. (crouch down)
   Here we go—moving forward. (take a step forward)
   Here we go—moving backward (take a step backward)
   Here we go round and round and round. (spin)

- Sing "The Grand Old Duke of York" with the children.

   The Grand Old Duke of York
   The grand old Duke of York, (salute)
   He had ten thousand men. (hold up ten fingers)
   He marched them up to the top of the hill, (point up)
   And he marched them down again. (point down)
   And when they're up, they're up. (stand tall)
   And when they're down, they're down. (squat)
   But when they're only halfway up, (stoop down)
   They're neither up nor down. (open arms and shrug)

- Sing "Open, Shut Them" with the children. Discuss the movement of the fingers as they walk them up and then down.

   Open, Shut Them
   Open, shut them.
   Open, shut them.
   Give a little clap.

   Chorus
   Open, shut them.
   Open, shut them.
   Put them in your lap.

Walk them, walk them, (walk fingers up chest to chin)
Walk them, walk them.
Way up to your chin.
Walk them, walk them, (walk fingers around face, but not into mouth)
Walk them, walk them,
Right down to your shin.

Chorus

Crawl them, crawl them,
Crawl them, crawl them,
Right up to your nose.
Crawl them, crawl them,
Crawl them, crawl them,
Right down to your toes.

Chorus

- Encourage the children to walk standing up on their toes. Encourage them to get down on their knees and walk. "Which way of walking is the most difficult?"

- Show older twos how to bounce a beach ball. Talk about the up and down movement of the ball.

- Encourage the little ones to jump up and down. Say, "We're up, we're down," while jumping.

Social and Emotional Development Choices

- Sing "This Is the Way We Clean Our Teeth" to the tune of "The Mulberry Bush" with the children. Encourage them to use their fingers as a pretend toothbrush. At a later time, help each child brush his teeth with the toothbrush he brought from home or one that you supply. Remind them of the proper way to brush their teeth or sing the song as they brush.

  This Is the Way We Clean Our Teeth
  This is the way we clean our teeth,
  Clean our teeth, clean our teeth.
  This is the way we clean our teeth
  Every night and morning.

Take your brush, go up and down
Up and down, up and down.
Take your brush, go up and down,
Every night and morning.

Don't forget both back and front,
Back and front, back and front.
Don't forget both back and front,
Every night and morning.

■ Sing "Itsy Bitsy Spider" with the children. Discuss the spider's travels up and down and the motions of the sun and the rain. Try singing the song in a high voice and in a low voice.

Itsy Bitsy Spider

The itsy bitsy spider
Went up the waterspout.
Down came the rain
And washed the spider out.

Up came the sun
And dried up all the rain.
And the itsy bitsy spider
Went up the spout again.

■ Sing "My Little Red Wagon." Discuss riding in a wagon. "Has anyone had this experience?" "Did you bump up and down?" "What makes the ride so bumpy?"

My Little Red Wagon

Bumping up and down in my little red wagon,
Bumping up and down in my little red wagon,
Bumping up and down in my little red wagon
Won't you be my darlin'?

■ Teach the children "Whoops, Johnny." Say the rhyme individually to each child and tap the child's fingertips with your index finger, starting with the pinky and moving toward the thumb on each "Johnny." As you say, "Whoops, Johnny," trace the curve of the hand between the index finger and the thumb. Finish with "Johnny" at the top of the thumb. Call attention to the up and down movement of your fingers as you say, "Whoops Johnny." Repeat backwards to the pinky.

Whoops, Johnny

Johnny, Johnny, Johnny, Johnny,
Whoops, Johnny.

Cognitive Development Choices

■ Invite the children to paint a picture on paper that is up on the easel and then on paper that is down on the floor. In which position do the children prefer to paint?

▦ Ask the children to work puzzles up on the table and then down on the floor. "Is it more fun to work the puzzles when you are on the table or on the floor?"

▦ Give the children a ride up on your shoulders. "What does it look like looking down from such a high place?"

▦ Tie a piece of yarn or string to the ceiling and let it drape down onto the floor. Give the children empty toilet paper tubes and invite them to try to push them up the string. "Why do the tubes keep falling down?" Can they keep them from falling down?

▦ Give the children Floaters and Droppers to explore. Provide items such as cotton balls, pompoms, tissue paper, beads, crayons, and feathers. Encourage the children to drop the items and watch them fall down to the ground. "Which items drop down fast?" "Which items float down?"

▦ Invite the children to build towers up and then knock them down. You may want to use Paper Bag Blocks because they are quieter when they fall. To make Paper Bag Blocks, fill grocery sacks about three-quarters full with crumpled newspaper, then square off, and tape down the opening of the bag.

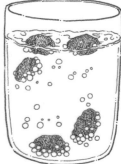

▦ Prepare Up and Down Raisins so the children can enjoy watching them rise and fall. Put four or five raisins in a clear glass of lemon-lime soda, such as Sprite. The raisin will go up and down in the glass. Here's how it works: As the carbonated water forms air bubbles around the raisins, they are lifted to the surface. When they hit the surface, the bubbles pop and the raisins fall back down to the bottom of the glass. The explanation for how this works is too complicated for toddlers and twos. They will be fascinated just watching the raisins move up and down. Describe the movement of the raisins as they watch.

▦ Problem-solving suggestion: Blow bubbles up in the air and encourage the little ones to figure out how to keep the bubbles up and not let them come down.

REFLECTION ON THE DAY
Encourage the children to tell you something they have learned about up and down and high and low. Ask younger toddlers to show you something that is up and something that is down and something that is high and something that is low.

In and Out/ Inside and Outside

WORDS TO PRACTICE

in	out	outside
inside	opposites	
inside	out	

GETTING STARTED

- Do the "Jack-in-the-Box" fingerplay with the children. Discuss the position of the thumb inside the fist and outside the fist. Ask the children questions to find out what they know about the opposite positions of *in* and *out*. Explain that the words *in* and *out* are opposites. Remind the children of other pairs of opposites they have learned about.

  Jack-in-the-Box
  Jack-in-the-box (tuck thumb into fist)
  Oh, so still.
  Won't you come out? (raise hand slightly)
  Yes, I will. (pop thumb out of fist)

- Tell them that today they will be learning more about the opposites *in* and *out*.
- Read your favorite book about opposites to the children or select a book from the Story Circle Suggestions below to check out of the library and read.

STORY CIRCLE SUGGESTIONS

- *In and Out (Baby Bug Pop-Up Book)* by David Carter
- *In and Out* by Bob Filipowich
- *In, Out and Other Places* by Ingrid Godon

PREPARATION FOR "IN AND OUT/INSIDE AND OUTSIDE" ACTIVITIES AND EXPERIENCES

- Gather an item and the containers you will place the item inside of and outside of (e.g., a purse, a box, a jar, and so on).

- Make the "My Little Red Wagon" (Appendix p. 542-544) and "The Runaway Cookie Parade" (Appendix p. 550-554) flannel board stories.
- Make Nesting Boxes and the Caterpillar/Butterfly Puppet (see p. 252).

Language Enrichment Choices*

- Place an object in several different types of containers such as a box, a purse, and a bag and then take it out. Explain that in and out are opposites.

- Sing "Sing a Song of Opposites" to the tune of "Mary Had a Little Lamb," putting objects in and out of a box or jar as you sing. You can stick your tongue in and out for one of the verses. Add verses about other opposites that you have studied.

    Sing a Song of Opposites
    This is in and this is out,
    This is in; this is out.
    This is in and this is out
    Sing along with me.

- Use the words *in* and *out* in a sentence. For example, "I keep my best toys *in* the toy basket and my stuffed animals *out* on my bed."

- Present the "My Little Red Wagon" flannel board story (Appendix p. 542-544). Talk about all the things the child loaded inside the wagon. "How did the things get outside the wagon?" "What was the last thing that Aunt Linda put inside the wagon?"

- Present "The Runaway Cookie Parade" flannel board story (Appendix p. 550-554). Discuss the cookies being placed in the jar and then talk about how they got out of the jar.

- Sing or say "A Fuzzy Caterpillar." Accompany the song/chant with a Caterpillar/Butterfly Puppet. Place a piece of cardboard inside an old black or brown sock. Glue two wiggle eyes to the toe of the sock. When dry, turn the sock inside out and glue two eyes to the toe of the sock and a pair of multi-colored felt wings at the heel of

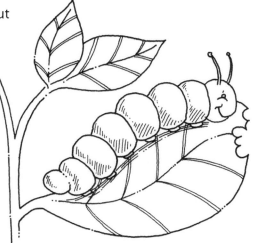

* Toddlers and twos present a wide range of developmental needs, abilities, and interests. For each learning area, select among the following activity and experience choices that are appropriate for the children in your care.

the sock. When the glue is dry, turn the sock back to the caterpillar side. When you sing or say "A Fuzzy Caterpillar," turn the sock inside out on the last two lines.

A Fuzzy Caterpillar
A fuzzy caterpillar went out for a walk.
His back went up and down.
He crawled and he crawled
And he crawled and he crawled
'til he crawled all over town.
He wasn't disappointed
Not a bit to be a worm.
Not a tear was in his eye.
Because he knew that he'd become
A very, very pretty butterfly.

With older children, talk about the caterpillar making a cocoon and staying inside for several days. Explain that when the caterpillar comes out of the cocoon, it is a butterfly.

■ Teach or review the American Sign Language signs for *in* and *out* (Appendix p. 434, 436). Review other opposite signs.

Physical Development Choices

■ Play "Go In and Out the Windows" with the children. Discuss their movements in and out. Select one child to be IT. Ask the other children to form a circle, hold hands, and raise their arms. For younger toddlers, you may want to do the first verse only. IT walks around the circle, weaving in and out between the children.

Go In and Out the Windows
Go in and out the windows.
Go in and out the windows.
Go in and out the windows,
As we have done before.

Stand and face your partner... (IT chooses a partner)
Now follow her/him to London... (IT and partner weave through circle)
Bow before you leave her/him... (IT leaves partner [new IT] and joins circle)

■ Do the "Hokey Pokey" with the children. Form a circle and act out the words.

> **Hokey Pokey**
> *You put your right hand in.*
> *You take your right hand out.*
> *You put your right hand in,*
> *And you shake it all about.*
> *You do the Hokey Pokey,* (hold hands in the air and shake them)
> *And you turn yourself around.*
> *That's what it's all about.*

Repeat verses, using other body parts. Talk about the movements *in* and *out*.

■ Make a circle on the floor using masking tape. Ask the children to stand inside the circle and throw beanbags outside the circle. Talk to the children about where they are standing and where the beanbags are landing.

Social and Emotional Development Choices

■ With older twos, say the poem "Inside Out" to the children. Discuss how the feelings we have on the inside can show on the outside of us.

> **Inside Out** by Pam Schiller
> *When I'm happy on the inside,*
> *It shows on the outside.*
> *It is quiet impossible you see*
> *To hide what's inside of me.*
>
> *When I am happy I dance.*
> *I lift my feet and prance.*
> *I twirl and spin and glide,*
> *Because I am happy inside.*

■ Do the action rhyme, "Wake Up, Jack-in-the-Box" with the children. Suit the actions to the words. Discuss Jack's in and out position. "What is it like inside Jack's box?"

> **Jack-in-the-Box**
> *Jack-in-the-box, jack-in-the-box,*
> *Wake up, wake up, somebody knocks.*
> *One time, two times, three times, four.*
> *Jack pops out of his little round door.*

■ Discuss the difference in voices appropriate to use inside the classroom and voices appropriate to use outside the classroom.

Cognitive Development Choices

■ Provide several containers that the children can fill with sand or water. Discuss filling the containers with sand and water and then emptying them.

■ Give the children a Jack-in-the-Box to play with. Talk about Jack's location as they play. "Where is Jack?"

■ Provide old purses or sacks with handles for the children to play with. Provide items that they can put into their purses or sacks. Ask them to take the items out of the purse and show you what they have.

■ Let the children play with the Caterpillar/Butterfly Puppet. Talk to them about which puppet is on the inside and which puppet is on the outside.

■ Provide dump trucks that children can load and unload. Discuss putting the blocks or animals inside the truck and then taking them out of the truck.

■ Problem-solving suggestion: Give the children Nesting Boxes (several small boxes that fit inside of each other) to place inside of each other. Discuss which boxes are on the inside and which are on the outside.

REFLECTION ON THE DAY

Ask the children to put a beanbag in a box and then take the beanbag out of the box.

Over and Under

WORDS TO PRACTICE

opposites	under
over	where

GETTING STARTED

▤ Create a simple maze that requires the children to go under and over some obstacles. Take the children through the maze, saying the words *over* and *under* as you move through the obstacles. Ask questions to find out what the children know about *over* and *under* and explain that they are opposites. Remind the children of other pairs of opposites they have learned about.

▤ Tell the children that today they will be learning more about the opposites *over* and *under*.

▤ Read your favorite book about opposites to the children or select a book from the Story Circle Suggestions below to check out of the library and read.

STORY CIRCLE SUGGESTIONS

▤ *Over, Under, and Through and Other Spatial Concepts* by Tana Hoban

▤ *The Three Billy Goats Gruff* by Paul Galdone

PREPARATION FOR "OVER AND UNDER" ACTIVITIES AND EXPERIENCES

▤ Create a maze.

▤ Make the "Three Billy Goats Gruff" (Appendix p. 561-567) flannel board story.

▤ Gather the ingredients for the Banana Pudding (see p. 255).

▤ Gather animal pictures.

Language Enrichment Choices*

▪ Ask the children to raise their hands over their heads and then put their hands under their chin. Tell the children that when their hands are up, they are *over* their heads and when their hands are below their chin, they are *under* their heads. Remind the children that *over* and *under* are opposites.

▪ Sing "Sing a Song of Opposites" to the tune of "Mary Had a Little Lamb." Use your hand to demonstrate things that are over and under, such as a table, your leg, and a book.

> **Sing a Song of Opposites**
> *This is over and this is under,*
> *This is over; this is under.*
> *This is over and this is under*
> *Sing along with me.*

▪ Use the words *over* and *under* in a sentence. For example, "I love the grass *under* my feet and the sky *over* my head."

▪ Present the "Three Billy Goats Gruff" flannel board story (Appendix p. 561-567). Discuss the goats going over the bridge and the troll living under the bridge.

▪ Teach or review the American Sign Language signs for *over* and *under* (Appendix p. 436, 439). Review other opposite signs.

Physical Development Choices

▪ Invite the children to participate in the "Going on a Bear Hunt" action rhyme. Talk about the things that you can't go over and you can't go under.

> **Going on a Bear Hunt**
> *We're going on a bear hunt.*
> *Want to come along?*
> *Well, come on then.*
> *Let's go!* (walk in place)
> *Look! There's a river.*
> *Can't go over it.*
> *Can't go under it.*
> *Can't go around it.*
> *We'll have to go through it.* (pretend to walk into river, through the water, and onto other bank, then resume walking in place)

* Toddlers and twos present a wide range of developmental needs, abilities, and interests. For each learning area, select among the following activity and experience choices that are appropriate for the children in your care.

Look! There's a tree.
Can't go under it.
Can't go through it.
We'll have to go over it. (pretend to climb up and over tree; then resume walking in place)
Look! There's a wheat field.
Can't go over it.
Can't go under it.
Can't go around it.
We'll have to go through it. (pretend to walk through field, make swishing sounds with hands against thighs, then resume walking in place)

Add verses to make the story as long as you want.

Look! There's a cave.
Want to go inside?
Ooh, it's dark in here. (look around, squinting)
I see two eyes.
Wonder what it is. (reach hands to touch)
It's soft and furry.
It's big.
It's a bear! Let's run! (retrace steps, running in place, through wheat field, in place, over tree, in place, across river, in place, then stop)
Home safely. Whew!

- Play a toddler game of Leap Frog. Cut out lily pads from green construction paper. Encourage the children to jump from pad to pad. Ask them what is under their feet when they land on a pad.

- Problem-solving suggestion: Invite the children to play in a maze that you create. Can they navigate it by themselves?

Social and Emotional Development Choices

- Let the children help make Banana Pudding. Provide graham cracker crumbs, pudding, and whipped topping. Ask the children to place the crumbs on the bottom of their cups and then add a scoop of pudding. Ask them to place whipped topping on the top. Talk about what is under the pudding and what is over the pudding.

- Invite the children to go outside to do some cloud watching. As you are lying on the grass, ask the children what is over their heads and what is under their backs.

- If there are trees on the playground, take the children outdoors for story time under a tree. Point out that you are having story time under the tree. Discuss what is over your head and what is under your bottom.

- Say the rhyme, "Over, Under, Over Again" with toddlers who are still small enough for you to lift.

  Over, Under, Over Again
  Up, up you go, over my head. (lift the child overhead)
  Down, down you go, under my chin. (bring the child to your chest and hug him or her)
  Now, up, up and over my head again! (lift the child overhead again)

Cognitive Development Choices

- Tape a piece of paper under the table and invite the children to draw on the paper. Tape a sheet of butcher paper over the table and let the children draw on it.

- Blow bubbles for the children to chase. Blow some over the table and some under the table.

- Invite the children to throw wadded paper balls over the table and under the table.

- Help the children build a bridge for cars to go over and boats to go under. Provide toy cars and boats for the children to maneuver.

- Problem-solving suggestion: Give the children pictures of animals that fly overhead and animals that live under the sea. Discuss where the animals live and how they move. Ask them to sort the pictures by animals that live under the sea and animals that live over our heads.

REFLECTION ON THE DAY
Ask the children to place their hands under the table and then over the table.

Front and Back/ Forward and Backward

Front

Back

WORDS TO PRACTICE

back	direction	front
backward	forward	opposites

GETTING STARTED

- Ask the children to stand. Ask them to point to a friend's back and then point to the front of their friend. Ask them to take a step backward and then a step forward. Ask questions to find out what the children know about *front* and *back* and *forward* and *backward*. Tell the children that *front* and *back* are opposites and *forward* and *backward* are opposites. Encourage the children to tell you another pair of opposites that they have learned about.

- Tell the children that today they will be learning more about the opposites *front* and *back* and *forward* and *backward*.

- Read your favorite book about opposites to the children or select a book from the Story Circle Suggestions below to check out of the library and read. Point out the front and the back of the book.

STORY CIRCLE SUGGESTIONS

- *Backward Day* by Ruth Krauss
- *Front Frog Fred and Back Frog Jack* by Mr. Sunshine
- *The Little Engine That Could* by Watty Piper

PREPARATION FOR "FRONT AND BACK/FORWARD AND BACKWARD" ACTIVITIES AND EXPERIENCES

- Make the "Little Engine Ninety-Nine" puppet story (Appendix p. 511-517).
- Make the Tactile Path (see p. 90) and Two-Sided Teddy Bear Puppet (Appendix p. 473).

Language Enrichment Choices*

- Show the children the Two-Sided Teddy Bear Puppet (Appendix p. 473). Talk about the features you see on the front of the bear and then the features you see on the back of the bear. Move the bear forward and then backward to demonstrate this pair of opposites. Remind the children that both front and back and forward and backward are pairs of opposites.

- Read a short book to the children. Point out the front (cover) and the back of the book. Explain that when you turn the pages of the book, you are moving forward through the pages and the story. Show them how you could turn the pages backward but that then the story would be backward and it wouldn't make sense.

- Use the words *front* and *back* and *forward* and *backward* in sentences. For example, "When I color, I like to use the *front* and the *back* of my paper," and "The train can move *forward* and *backward* on the train tracks."

- Present the "Little Engine Ninety-Nine" puppet story (Appendix p. 511-517) to the children. Point out the front and the back of the train and forward and backward motion of the train.

- Teach the children the American Sign Language signs for *front* and *back* and *forward* and *backward* (Appendix p. 430, 432).

Physical Development Choices

- Do the action rhyme, "I'm a Choo-Choo Train" with the children. Point out the direction of the movements of the train.

   I'm a Choo-Choo Train
   I'm a choo-choo train, (bend arms at side)
   Chugging down the track. (rhythmically move arms)
   First I go forward, (move forward)
   Then I go back. (move backward)

   Now my bell is ringing. (pretend to pull bell)
   Hear my whistle blow.
   What a lot of noise I make (cover ears)
   Everywhere I go!

- Do the action rhyme, "Here We Go" with the children.

*Toddlers and twos present a wide range of developmental needs, abilities, and interests. For each learning area, select among the following activity and experience choices that are appropriate for the children in your care.

Here We Go
Here we go—up, up, up. (stand up on toes)
Here we go—down, down, down. (crouch down)
Here we go—moving forward. (take a step forward)
Here we go—moving backward (take a step backward)
Here we go round and round and round. (spin)

▦ Ask the children to take steps forward and backward on a Tactile Path (see p. 90).

▦ Play Follow the Leader. Point out the person at the front of the line and the person at the back of the line. Change the children in the back of the line position a few times as you play. With children this young, you will need to be the leader, which keeps you at the front of the line. Point out the movements you are making in a forward position and be sure to do some backward movements.

▦ Do the following "Little Ants" chant and actions with the children. Ask the children to form a line behind you and follow your lead.

Little Ants
Little ants are marching by,
In a line that's mighty long.
With a hip, hop, happy, hi,
Won't you join my song?
Little ants are marching on.

Little ants are hopping by,
In a line that's mighty long.
With a hip, hop, happy, hi,
Won't you join my song?
Little ants are hopping on.

Repeat the chant, replacing "Little ants are marching by" with one of the following:
Little ants are spinning by
Little ants are dancing by
Little ants are jumping by
Little ants are waving by

Social and Emotional Development Choices

▦ Sit with each child individually to read a book. Encourage the child to show you the front and the back of the book. Let the child help turn the pages forward. When you have finished reading, ask the child to turn the pages backward.

■ Stand in front of an unbreakable mirror. Show the children the backs of their hands, backs of their knees, and the back of their heads. Give the children the correct word for the front of each of these areas of the body (e.g., palm, knee, and face). Show them the front and the back of their legs and the front and the back of their ears.

Cognitive Development Choices

■ Invite the children to draw a picture on both the front and the back of their paper. Display their artwork on the front and the back of the classroom door.

■ Make a front/back pattern using the children. Ask them to stand in a line with one child facing forward and the next child facing backward. Let one child at a time stand outside the line and look at the pattern. Verbalize the pattern (e.g., front, back, front, back, and forward, backward, forward, backward).

■ This is a messy activity but worth the mess. Ask the children to remove their shoes and then step into a shallow tub of tempera paint. Help them out of the paint and onto a 10' strip of butcher paper. Hold their hand while they walk the length of the paper leaving a trail of footprints behind. When they reach the end of the paper, ask them to walk backwards to their starting place. Have a tub of soapy water and a towel available at the end of the walk. Point out the forward and the backward footprints.

■ Give the children cars and trucks that they can move forward and backward over a road made of blocks. Sit with them and point out the direction they are moving their vehicles.

■ Create an inclined plank. Give the children cars to roll forward and backward down the plank."Do the cars go the same speed no matter what direction they are rolling?"

■ Give the children the Two-Sided Teddy Bear Puppet (Appendix p. 473) to play with. Ask them to show you the front and the back of the bear and have them move the bear in a forward and backward direction.

REFLECTION ON THE DAY
Ask the children to tell you something they learned about front and back and forward and backward. Ask the "not yet talkers" to show you how to move forward and backward and have them show you their fronts and their backs.

Fat and Skinny/ Wide and Narrow

WORDS TO PRACTICE

fat	opposites	wide
narrow	skinny	

GETTING STARTED

- Ask the children to sit in two lines facing a partner. Leave a narrow space between the lines and point out to the children that the space between the lines is *narrow* or *skinny*. Ask the children to back up several spaces to create a *wide* or *fat* space between the lines. Call attention to the new width of the space. Ask the children questions to determine what they know about *fat* and *skinny* and *wide* and *narrow*. Explain that *fat* and *skinny* and *wide* and *narrow* are pairs of opposites. Give examples of other opposites that the children have learned about.

- Tell the children that today they will be learning more about the pair of opposites *fat* and *skinny*.

- Be aware that children may bring up body weight at some point during these activities. If they do, explain that being called fat or skinny can hurt someone's feelings. Explain that it is nicer to refer to people as *large* and *small*. (Note: Be especially sensitive if you have heavy and/or thin children in your class. You may want to use wide and narrow and not include fat and skinny in these activities.)

- Read your favorite book about opposites to the children or select a book from the Story Circle Suggestions below to check out of the library and read. Discuss the width of the book. Compare it to a book that is fatter.

STORY CIRCLE SUGGESTIONS

- *Dragon's Fat Cat* by Dav Pilkey
- *Fat Cat Sat on a Mat* by Nurit Karlin

PREPARATION FOR "FAT AND SKINNY/WIDE AND NARROW" ACTIVITIES AND EXPERIENCES

- Gather pairs of fat and skinny and wide (e.g., crayons, yarn, and pencils) and narrow items (e.g., ribbon, fabric, or belts).
- Make "The Strange Visitor" prop story (Appendix p. 559-560).
- Gather pretzels, carrot sticks, or cookies.
- Cut wide and narrow streamers.
- Find animal photos.
- Make Fishing Game.

Language Enrichment Choices*

- Show the children pairs of items that come in fat and skinny sizes, such as crayons, pencils, yarn, and books. Show them pairs of items that are wide and narrow, such as pieces of ribbon, fabric, and belts. Remind the children that fat and skinny are opposites.

- Sing "Sing a Song of Opposites" to the tune of "Mary Had a Little Lamb" using either the items you have gathered objects in the room (or use your hands) for examples of fat and skinny and wide and narrow.

Sing a Song of Opposites
This is fat and this is skinny,
This is fat; this is skinny.
This is fat and this is skinny,
Sing along with me.

This is wide and this is narrow,
This is wide; this is narrow.
This is wide and this is narrow,
Sing along with me.

- Use the words *fat* and *skinny* and *wide* and *narrow* in a sentence. For example, "The legs of the hippopotamus are *fat* and the legs of the giraffe are *skinny*. The road is *narrow* by my house, but it is *wide* by my school."

- Present "The Strange Visitor" prop story (Appendix p. 559-560). Discuss the Somebody's fat, fat hands and his long, skinny legs and arms.

- Teach or review the American Sign Language signs for *fat* and *skinny* (Appendix p. 432, 439). Teach the signs for *wide* and *narrow* (Appendix p. 435, 439).

* Toddlers and twos present a wide range of developmental needs, abilities, and interests. For each learning area, select among the following activity and experience choices that are appropriate for the children in your care.

SING A SONG OF OPPOSITES

Physical Development Choices

- Play some "heavy" music and invite the children to dance like fat animals (e.g., an elephant, hippo, and a gorilla). Then play some "light" music and invite the children to dance like skinny animals (e.g., an ant, a tiger, and a spider monkey).

- Give the children wide and narrow streamers to dance with.

Social and Emotional Development Choices

- Sing and act out "Six White Ducks" with the children. Discuss the "fat ducks, skinny ducks" in the song.

     Six White Ducks
     Six white ducks that I once knew, (hold up six fingers)
     Fat ducks, skinny ducks, they were, too. (hold hands out to show fat and skinny)
     But the one little duck with the feather on her back, (hold up one finger, then point to your back)
     She ruled the others with a quack, quack, quack! (shake finger)

     Down to the river they would go, (walk fingers out in front of you)
     Wibble, wobble, wibble, wobble all in a row. (sway side to side)
     But the one little duck with the feather on her back, (hold up one finger, then point to your back)

     She ruled the others with a quack, quack, quack! (shake finger)

- Serve fat and skinny snacks, such as pretzels, carrot sticks, or cookies.

Cognitive Development Choices

- Invite the children to paint with fat/wide brushes and skinny/narrow paintbrushes. "What kind of lines can you make with each type of paintbrush?" "Which paintbrush is easier to paint with?" "Which paintbrush covers more space?"

- Invite the children to build wide and narrow roads with blocks. Provide cars for the roads. "Which roads are easier to travel?"

- Encourage the children to paint on a regular sheet of paper and then on a sheet of cardboard. "Which picture is on skinny/thin paper and which is on fat paper?"

- Provide funnels, cups, strainers, colanders, and squeeze bottles in the water play table. Encourage the children to create wide spouts of water and skinny spouts of water using the water play materials.

- Take a walk outdoors in search of fat and skinny, and narrow and wide things.

- Provide photos of animals and have the children sort them into categories of fat and skinny.

- Make a Fishing Game and let the children catch fat and skinny fish. Attach a piece of yarn to a coat hanger tube and tie a round magnet (available at hardware stores) to the other end of the yarn. Cut fish into fat and skinny sizes and laminate them. Attach a paper clip to the nose of each fish. Place the fish on the floor and encourage the little fishermen to catch the fish by touching the magnet to the paper clip on the nose of the fish. After all the fish are caught, ask the children to sort their "catch" by fat and skinny fish.

- Problem-solving suggestion: Encourage the children to play a xylophone. Point out the wide keys at one end of the board and the narrow keys at the opposite end of the board. "Which keys make a high sound?" "Which keys make a low sound?" Can they play one high sound and one low sound to make a pattern?

REFLECTION ON THE DAY

Ask the children to tell you something they have learned about fat and skinny and wide and narrow. Ask the "not yet talkers" to show you something that is fat and skinny and wide and narrow.

Day and Night

WORDS TO PRACTICE

dark	night	sun
day	nighttime	
daytime	play	
light	sleep	
moon	stars	

GETTING STARTED

- Ask the children what they did last night. Ask them how what they did last night is different from what they are doing right now. Ask questions to find out what the children know about the differences in *day* and *night*. Talk about the sun, the moon, and the stars and when you see each of these things.

- Tell the children that today they will be learning about the opposites *day* and *night*.

- Read your favorite book about day and night to the children or select a book from the Story Circle Suggestions below to check out of the library and read.

STORY CIRCLE SUGGESTIONS

- *Night and Day* by Ellen Weiss
- *Wake Up and Goodnight* by Charlotte Zolotow
- *What the Sun Sees, What the Moon Sees* by Nancy Tafuri

PREPARATION FOR "DAY AND NIGHT" ACTIVITIES AND EXPERIENCES

- Gather daytime and nighttime pictures.
- Gather peaches, cheese, and hot chocolate ingredients.
- Cut out construction paper moons and suns.
- Cut a moon, sun, and star out of poster board.
- Make Moon and Sun Puzzles (see p. 268).

Language Enrichment Choices*

▦ Show the children pictures of day and night activities. Discuss some things that they do in the daytime and some things that they do at night.

▦ Use the words *day* and *night* in a sentence. For example, "I play during the *day* and sleep at *night*."

▦ Teach the children the American Sign Language signs for *day* and *night* (Appendix p. 431, 435).

Physical Development Choices

▦ Take the children outside to chase their shadows. When you go inside, encourage the children to dance between a light source and a wall to create an indoor shadow. Explain to older toddlers that nighttime shadows are created by indoor light and daytime shadows are most often created by the sunlight.

▦ Invite the children to do a daytime dance and a nighttime dance. Encourage them to dance with yellow streamers to some lively daytime march music, and then dance with white streamers to some lullaby music.

Social and Emotional Development Choices

▦ Sing "Mister Sun" and "Mister Moon" with the children. Ask older toddlers what things are different in the songs. They will, of course, point out the moon and the sun.

Mister Sun
Oh, Mister Sun, Sun, Mister Golden Sun
Won't you please shine down on me?
Oh, Mister Sun, Sun, Mister Golden Sun
Hiding behind that tree.
These little children are asking you
To please come out so we can play with you.
Oh, Mister Sun, Sun, Mister Golden Sun,
Won't you please shine down on me?

* Toddlers and twos present a wide range of developmental needs, abilities, and interests. For each learning area, select among the following activity and experience choices that are appropriate for the children in your care.

Mister Moon
Oh, Mister Moon, Moon, bright and shiny Moon
Won't you please shine down on me?
Oh, Mister Moon, Moon, bright and shiny Moon,
Won't you please set me fancy free?
I'd like to linger but I've got to run,
Mama's callin' "Baby get your homework done!"
O Mister Moon, Moon, bright and shiny Moon,
Won't you please shine down on me?
Talk about your shine on, please shine down on me.

▦ Talk with the children about when they take their baths. "Do you bathe at night or in the morning?" "Who helps you with your bath?" "Do you have toys you play with in the tub?" Recite the poem, "After My Bath" to the children.

After My Bath
After my bath I try, try, try,
To rub with a towel till I'm dry, dry, dry.
Hands to dry, and fingers and toes,
And two wet legs and a shiny nose.
Just think how much less time it'd take
If I were a dog and could shake, shake, shake!

▦ Serve a Sunshine Salad with a nighttime cup of hot chocolate for snack time. To make the Sunshine Salad, give each child ½ of a peach and encourage them to place thin carrots sticks around the peach to create "sunrays."

Cognitive Development Choices

▦ Invite the children to paint a picture of something that they like to do during the day on one side of their paper and something they like to do at night on the other side of their paper. Ask the children to describe their work.

▦ Invite the children to make a starry night and sunny day picture. Give them a sheet of black construction paper. Encourage them to glue "stars" (rock salt) and a "moon" (a white construction paper circle) to the paper to create a starry night picture. Give the children a piece of light blue construction paper. Encourage them to glue a yellow "sun" (a yellow construction paper circle) and some "clouds" (cotton balls) to make a daytime picture.

▦ Provide large wiggle eyes. Encourage the children to take turns tossing the eyes into a box. "Are there more nighttime sleepy eyes (eyes facing down) or more daytime wakeful eyes (eyes facing up)?" Show older twos how to match the wakeful and sleepy eyes one-to-one.

Safety Warning: Make sure that the little ones do not put the wiggle eyes in their mouths as they can present a choking hazard.

- Show the children an alarm clock. Describe its purpose. Set the alarm and let the children hear it ring. Set the alarm again and hide the clock. When it rings, encourage the children to find it.

- Cover half a table with blue bulletin board paper (shiny side up) and the other half of the table with black bulletin board paper (shiny side up). Spray shaving cream on top of the paper. Invite the children to make clouds in the day and night sky. You can add a small amount of black tempera paint to the shaving cream on the night side of the table to make the clouds light gray if you would like. Point out to the children that clouds are present day and night.

- Encourage the children to sort pictures according to daytime and nighttime.

- Problem-solving suggestions:
  1. Cut out a moon, a sun, and a star from poster board. Show older twos how to roll the cutouts across the floor. Ask the children which of the cutouts won't roll.
  2. Give the children Moon and Sun Puzzles to work. Cut out a moon from white poster board and a sun from yellow poster board. Laminate each cutout and then cut them into three or four puzzle pieces.

REFLECTION ON THE DAY

Ask the children to tell you something that they learned about day and night. Encourage the "not yet talkers" to show you a daytime picture and a nighttime picture.

Hard and Soft

WORDS TO PRACTICE

hard	opposites	softest
harder	soft	
hardest	softer	

GETTING STARTED

- Ask the children to touch their teeth and then their tongue. Ask them which one is hard and which one is soft. Ask more questions to find out what the children know about *hard* and *soft*.
- Tell the children that today they will be learning more about the opposites *hard* and *soft*.
- Read your favorite book about opposites to the children or select a book from the Story Circle Suggestions below to check out of the library and read.

STORY CIRCLE SUGGESTIONS

- *Hard and Soft (Animal Opposites)* by Rod Theodorou
- *Pat the Bunny* by Dorothy Kunhardt

PREPARATION FOR "HARD AND SOFT" ACTIVITIES AND EXPERIENCES

- Gather pairs of hard and soft items such as a hard sole and soft sole shoe, a chair cushion and a chair bottom, a soft purse and a hard purse, a peanut and peanut butter, and so on.
- Make Paper Bag Blocks (see p. 272), if not already made.
- Get hard and soft snacks.
- Gather homemade rhythm band instruments (e.g., crumpled paper, blocks, spoons, boxes, and so on).
- Make Feely Box (see p. 272), if not already made.

Sing a Song of Opposites

Language Enrichment Choices*

- Show the children some pairs of soft and hard things that you have collected. For example, a hard sole and soft sole shoe, a chair cushion and a chair bottom, a soft purse and a hard purse, a peanut and peanut butter, an apple and applesauce, and so on. If you can't gather pairs of things, just show some soft and hard objects. Explain that *hard* and *soft* are opposites.

- Sing "Sing a Song of Opposites" to the tune of "Mary Had a Little Lamb" using the hard and soft items you have shown the children. You can sing other verses about other pairs of opposites you have already introduced.

  Sing a Song of Opposites
  This is hard and this is soft,
  This is hard; this is soft.
  This is hard and this is soft,
  Sing along with me.

- Use *hard* and *soft* in a sentence. For example, "A block is *hard*, but a feather is *soft*."

- Teach the children the American Sign Language signs for *hard* and *soft* (Appendix p. 433, 438).

Physical Development Choices

- Invite the children to play with hard and soft balls such as Nerf balls and Ping-Pong balls. "Which balls are more fun to bounce?"

- Encourage the children to ride their riding toys on the hard sidewalk and the soft grass. "Which surface is easier to ride on?"

- Invite the children to play hard and soft homemade rhythm band instruments. You can use spoons, crumpled paper, blocks, boxes, and squeeze toys. "Which toys make a loud noise?"

Social and Emotional Development Choices

- Talk with the children about hard and soft areas of their bodies. Compare toenails to the underside of the toes and fingernails to the underside of the fingers. Feel cheeks and lips and teeth. "Which area is hard?" Ask them to knock on their head. "Is it hard?"

* Toddlers and twos present a wide range of developmental needs, abilities, and interests. For each learning area, select among the following activity and experience choices that are appropriate for the children in your care.

■ If available, read soft and hard books to the children.

■ Serve a snack of hard and soft treats such as bread/muffin, carrot sticks, bananas, pretzels, and apple wedges. Boil an egg and then let the children help peel it and sample the soft inside.

■ Sing "There Once Were Three Brown Bears" to the tune of "Twinkle, Twinkle, Little Star." Discuss the mama bear's and papa bear's beds. Point out the other opposites in the song: *hot* and *cold*, and *high* and *low*.

> **There Once Were Three Brown Bears** by Pam Schiller and Thomas Moore
> *There once were three brown bears,*
> *Mother, Father, Baby Bear.*
> *Mother's food was way too cold.*
> *Father's food was way too hot.*
> *Baby's food was all gone.*
> *Someone ate it, so he cried.*
>
> *There once were three brown bears,*
> *Mother, Father, Baby Bear.*
> *Mother's chair was way too low.*
> *Father's chair was way to high.*
> *Baby's chair was just so right,*
> *But when she sat-she broke it.*
>
> *There once were three brown bears,*
> *Mother, Father, Baby Bear.*
> *Mother's bed was way too soft.*
> *Father's bed was way too hard.*
> *Baby's bed was occupied.*
> *Someone strange was sleeping there.*
>
> *"Come here quickly," Baby cried.*
> *"Someone's sleeping in my bed!"*
> *"Who are you?" asked Baby Bear.*
> *"Who are you?" asked Goldilocks.*
> *"You better run," said Baby Bear.*
> *"I will!" said Goldilocks.*

Cognitive Development Choices

■ Invite the children to build with a combination of hard and soft blocks. You can make Paper Bag Blocks by stuffing lunch sacks three-quarters full of wadded newspaper and then squaring off and taping down the opening of the bag. "Which blocks make more noise when they fall?"

■ Invite the children to drop hard and soft items such as a cotton ball, a button, a piece of fabric, and a bead into a tin pan. "Which ones make a noise?"

■ Give the children your collection of hard and soft items and encourage them to sort the objects into hard and soft categories.

■ Give the children hard-sole and soft-sole shoes to explore. "Which ones make more noise when you walk across the floor?" "Which ones are more comfortable?"

■ Invite the children to make paint prints on drawing paper with soft sponges and hard cookie cutters. "Which item is easier to use?"

■ Problem-solving suggestion: Place hard and soft items inside a Feely Box. Invite the children to stick their hands into the box and tell you if an item is hard or soft before removing it. To make a Feely Box, cut a 2" to 3" hole in the lids of a shoebox and tape the lids to the bottom of the box.

REFLECTION ON THE DAY

Ask the children what they have learned about hard and soft today. Invite the "not yet talkers" to show you something that is hard and something that is soft.

Fast and Slow

WORDS TO PRACTICE

fast	quick	slower
faster	quickly	slowes
fastest	slow	slc

GETTING STARTED

- Give the children a fan and encourage them to fan themselves slowly and then ask them to fan themselves quickly. Point out that fast and slow are opposites. Ask the children questions to find out what they know about the words *fast* and *slow*.
- Tell the children that today they will be learning more about the opposites *fast* and *slow*.
- Read your favorite book about opposites to the children or select a book from the Story Circle Suggestions below to check out of the library and read.

STORY CIRCLE SUGGESTIONS

- *Fast and Slow* by Alvin Granowsky
- *Pooh Goes Fast and Slow* by A.A. Milne & Margaret Milnes
- *The Tortoise and the Hare* (many versions available)

PREPARATION FOR "FAST AND SLOW" ACTIVITIES AND EXPERIENCES

- Make a folded fan for each child.
- Make "The Tortoise and the Hare" puppet story (Appendix p. 571-572).
- Make Fast and Slow Observation Bottles and Weighted Cans (see p. 275-276).

Language Enrichment Choices*

- Sing "Mary Had a Little Lamb" in a normal tempo and then in a slower tempo. Sing it again in a fast tempo. Discuss the different speed in which you sang the song. Remind the children that fast and slow are opposites.

* Toddlers and twos present a wide range of developmental needs, abilities, and interests. For each learning area, select among the following activity and experience choices that are appropriate for the children in your care.

▪ Sing "Sing a Song of Opposites" to the tune of "Mary Had a Little Lamb" using pictures of things that move fast and things that move slowly, such as a rabbit and a turtle, a racer and a stroller, and a runner and a walker. Add other verses using pairs of opposites that the children have studied.

Sing a Song of Opposites
This is fast and this is slow,
This is fast; this is slow.
This is fast and this is slow,
Sing along with me.

▪ Use the words *fast* and *slow* in a sentence. For example, "I like riding my bike *fast* better than I like riding it *slowly*."

▪ Present "The Tortoise and the Hare" flannel board story (Appendix p. 571-572). Discuss the movements of the animals. Ask a volunteer to demonstrate the movements of each animal.

▪ Teach the children the American Sign Language signs for *fast* and *slow* (Appendix p. 432, 437). Review other signs.

Physical Development Choices

▪ Sing "Head, Shoulders, Knees, and Toes" slowly and then quickly. Touch body parts as they are mentioned in the song. "Is it more difficult to do the song fast or slow?"

Head, Shoulders, Knees, and Toes
Head, shoulders, knees, and toes,
Knees and toes.
Head, shoulders, knees, and toes,
Knees and toes.
And eyes and ears and mouth and nose.
Head, shoulders, knees, and toes,
Knees and toes!

▪ Show the children how to take baby steps and giant steps. Ask them to walk across the room taking baby steps and then giant steps. Which steps enabled them to move more slowly and which steps allowed them to move more quickly?

■ Encourage the children to pass a beanbag around a circle starting slowly and building speed until they are passing the beanbag quickly. "Is it more difficult to pass the beanbag quickly or slowly?"

Social and Emotional Development Choices

■ Sing "Drink, Drink, Drink Your Milk" to the tune of "Row, Row, Row Your Boat." Discuss the benefits of drinking and eating slowly.

> **Drink, Drink, Drink Your Milk** by Pam Schiller
> *Drink, drink, drink your milk*
> *A little at a time.*
> *Drink it slow, drink it fast,*
> *Drink it to this rhyme.*
>
> *Chew, chew, chew your food*
> *A little at a time*
> *Chew it slow, chew it good,*
> *Chew it to this rhyme.*

■ Teach the children "Slowly, Slowly." Talk about moving slow and fast. Ask the children to show you how they move quickly and how they move slowly.

> **Slowly, Slowly**
> *Slowly, slowly, very slowly* (walk finger up arm slowly)
> *Creeps the garden snail.*
> *Slowly, slowly, very slowly*
> *Up the wooden rail.*
>
> *Quickly, quickly, very quickly* (run fingers up arm)
> *Runs the little mouse.*
> *Quickly, quickly, very quickly*
> *Round about the house.*

Cognitive Development Choices

■ Give the children Fast and Slow Observation Bottles. Fill a half-liter bottle with white corn syrup. Fill a second half-liter bottle ¾ full of water and ¼ full of white corn syrup. Drop a button or a marble into each bottle. When both buttons (or marbles)

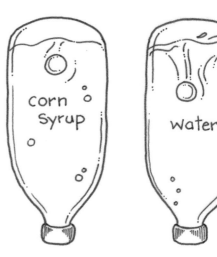

have settled to the bottom of the bottles, turn the bottles upside down and watch the buttons race. "In which bottle does the button drop faster?" "Which bottle holds the button that drops slowly?"

- Invite the children to color to fast and slow music. "Which is more fun?"

- Provide photos of animals and encourage the children to sort the photos according to how the animals move—fast or slow.

- Encourage the children to play with the tortoise and the hare stick puppets. Ask them if they remember which one is fast and which is slow.

- Problem-solving suggestion: Prepare Weighted Cans. Fill one-pound coffee cans with sand or blocks. Place a different amount of sand or blocks into each can so that they each have a different weight. Provide an inclined plank and invite the children to roll the cans down the plank. "Which cans roll more quickly? Why?" You can also ask the children to roll the cans on the floor to test which cans roll more quickly.

REFLECTION ON THE DAY

Ask the children to tell you something that they learned about fast and slow today. Ask the "not yet talkers" to show you something that moves fast and something that moves slowly.

Thick and Thin

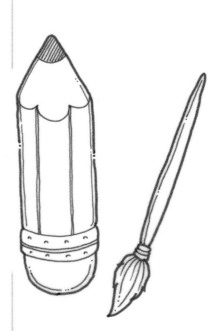

WORDS TO PRACTICE

narrow	thicker	thinner
opposites	thickest	thinnest
thick	thin	wide

GETTING STARTED

▪ Gather the children into a circle. Pass around two small, thick blankets and two small, thin blankets (or two pieces of thick fabric and two pieces of thin fabric) for the children to feel. Point out that one is *thick* and one is *thin*. Tell the children that *thick* and *thin* are opposites. Ask questions to find out what the children know about the words *thick* and *thin*. Ask them to show you thick and thin things in the room.

▪ Tell the children that today they will be learning more about the opposites *thick* and *thin*.

▪ Read your favorite book about opposites to the children or select a book from the Story Circle Suggestions below to check out of the library and read.

STORY CIRCLE SUGGESTIONS

▪ *Exactly the Opposite* by Tana Hoban
▪ *Sam and the Tigers* by Julius Lester

PREPARATION FOR "THICK AND THIN" ACTIVITIES AND EXPERIENCES

▪ Collect pairs of thick and thin items.

▪ Gather milk, vanilla, sugar, small and large zipper-closure bags, ice, and rock salt for the Baggie Ice Cream (see p. 279) and chocolate and caramel toppings.

▪ Make Paper Bag Blocks (see p. 279) and the Drop Slot Can (see p. 280) and chips.

Language Enrichment Choices*

▦ Show the children several pairs of items that are thick and thin such as a piece of cardboard, a cookie, a book, and a piece of fabric. Explain that thick and thin are opposites.

▦ Sing "Sing a Song of Opposites" to the tune of Mary Had a Little Lamb," using the pairs of thick and thin items you collected as props for the song. Add other verses for other pairs of opposites the children have learned.

> **Sing a Song of Opposites**
> *This is thick and this is thin,*
> *This is thick; this is thin,*
> *This is thick and this is thin,*
> *Sing along with me.*

▦ Use the words *thick* and *thin* in a sentence. For example, "I like a *thick* layer of peanut butter on my sandwich and a *thin* layer of jelly."

▦ Teach the children the American Sign Language signs for *thick* and *thin* (Appendix p. 439). Review the signs for wide and narrow.

Physical Development Choices

▦ Encourage the children to walk and then crawl on a thick and thin line of masking tape. "Which one is easier to walk on?"

▦ Invite the children to pretend they are walking through a big rain puddle. Then encourage them to pretend the puddle is full of caramel sauce. How would their ability to walk change? Encourage them to pretend to walk through other thick and thin substances such as syrup and apple juice.

▦ Encourage the children to tear thick paper (poster board, index cards, and wallpaper scraps) and thin paper (tissue, drawing) into pieces. "Which one is easier to tear?"

Social and Emotional Development Choices

▦ Serve thick cookies, such as double-stuffed sandwich cookies, and thin cookies, such as graham crackers, for snack.

* Toddlers and twos present a wide range of developmental needs, abilities, and interests. For each learning area, select among the following activity and experience choices that are appropriate for the children in your care.

- Invite the children to drink their milk or juice through thick straws and thin straws (coffee stirrers).

- Help the children make Baggie Ice Cream. For each child, place $\frac{1}{2}$ cup of milk, 1 tablespoon of sugar, and $\frac{1}{4}$ teaspoon of vanilla into a small zipper-closure bag and seal it. Place the bag and 3 tablespoons of rock salt into a large zipper-closure bag with ice cubes. Encourage the children to shake the bag. Be prepared to help the younger ones shake. Discuss the ingredients in the ice cream mixture. "Are they thick or thin?" "After the ice cream has frozen, is it thick or thin?" Invite the children to eat their ice cream with chocolate and caramel sauces on top. "Are the sauces thick or thin?"

Cognitive Development Choices

- Encourage the children to paint with thick and thin paint. "Which paint is runny?" "Which paint do you like best?" Provide thick and thin brushes to use with the paint.

- Encourage the children to sort the pairs of thick and thin items you collected.

- Give the children thick and thin dress-up clothes such as sweaters, coats, mittens, silk scarves, and nightgowns to explore.

- Show the children how to roll thick and thin playdough snakes. "Which one looks more like a real snake?"

- Encourage the children to build with thick and thin blocks. Make thick and thin Paper Bag Blocks. Fill paper lunch sacks $\frac{3}{4}$ full with crumpled newspaper to make thick blocks or $\frac{1}{4}$ full to make thin blocks. Square off the top and tape down the mouth of the bags.

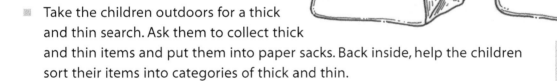

- Take the children outdoors for a thick and thin search. Ask them to collect thick and thin items and put them into paper sacks. Back inside, help the children sort their items into categories of thick and thin.

■ Problem-solving suggestion: Encourage the children to insert thick and thin poker chips into the Drop Slot Can. To make the can, cut a 1 ½" slot into the lid of an empty coffee can. Cut a second slot the same length but make it ½" wide. Replace the lid. Provide individual poker chips as thin chips and glue three poker chips together to make fat chips. Challenge the children to sort the chips into thick and thin piles, and then check their sorting by poking the chips through the correct slot in the can.

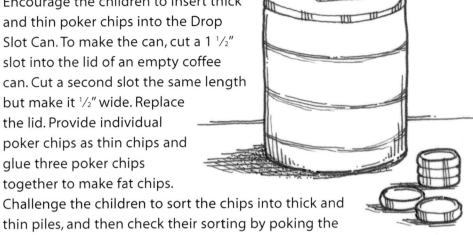

REFLECTION ON THE DAY

Ask the children to show you something that is thick and something that is thin.

Loud and Soft

WORDS TO PRACTICE

loud	soft	volume
music	voices	

GETTING STARTED

- Sing "Itsy Bitsy Spider" in a tiny, soft voice, and then sing it again in a big, loud voice.
- Tell the children that today they will be learning about the opposites *loud* and *soft*.
- Read your favorite book about opposites to the children or select a book from the Story Circle Suggestions below to check out of the library and read.

STORY CIRCLE SUGGESTIONS

- *Barnyard Banter* by Denise Fleming
- *It's Too Noisy!* by Joanna Cole

PREPARATION FOR "LOUD AND SOFT" ACTIVITIES AND EXPERIENCES

- Collect items that make sound at two volumes.
- Make "The Three Billy Goats Gruff" flannel board story, if not already made (Appendix p. 561-567).
- Make Sound Canisters and Sound Shakers (see p. 284).
- Make Sound Cards (Appendix p. 467-468) and a cassette tape of matching sounds.

Language Enrichment Choices*

- Provide some items that make noises at two volumes such as an alarm clock, a rhythm band instrument, a radio, cassette player and tape, and so on. Make each item produce a soft sound and then a loud sound. With the alarm clock, ask the children to first listen to the ticking and then the alarm sounding. Discuss *loud* and *soft* and that they are opposites. Explain that the words *loud* and *soft* refer to volume.

* Toddlers and twos present a wide range of developmental needs, abilities, and interests. For each learning area, select among the following activity and experience choices that are appropriate for the children in your care.

- Sing "Sing a Song of Opposites" to the tune of "Mary Had a Little Lamb," using the items you have collected as props. Add verses about other opposites you have introduced.

   Sing a Song of Opposites
   This is soft, and this is loud,
   This is soft; this is loud,
   This is soft, and this is loud,
   Sing along with me.

- Use the words *loud* and *soft* in a sentence. For example, "The rain was making a *soft* sound on the rooftop until it started raining hard. Then the sound got very *loud*."

- Tell the flannel board story of "The Three Billy Goats Gruff" (Appendix p. 561-567). Discuss the voices of each of the goats and the troll. "Who had a loud, gruff voice?" "Who had a soft voice?" "Who had a medium-size voice?"

- Teach the children the American Sign Language signs for *loud* and *soft* (Appendix p. 435, 438).

Physical Development Choices

- Invite the children to play rhythm band instruments. Encourage them to play the instruments softly and then loudly. "Which way do the instruments sound the best?"

- Play Loud and Soft Hide and Seek. Select one child to be IT. Ask IT to close her eyes. Hide a beanbag. Tell IT that you will sing a song. When she is close to the beanbag, you will sing loudly. When she is moving away from where the beanbag is hidden, you will sing softly. Play the game several times. Sing a simple song that the children can sing with you such as "Mary Had a Little Lamb."

- Take the children outdoors and encourage them to run and yell. Discuss the volume of their "outdoor voices."

Social and Emotional Development Choices

- Ask older twos to discuss loud and soft sounds they hear around their homes.

"Do some loud sounds frighten you?" "Are you afraid of the vacuum cleaner?" "Thunder?" Read "My Noisy House." "Which sounds are loud?" Which sounds are soft? Which sounds can be both?"

My Noisy House
My house is always noisy
Sound stirs all around.
We're hustling, bustling, on the move.
We're making lots of sound.

Telephone rings,
Doorbell buzzes,
Someone's knocking,
Toilet flushes.

Television blares,
And the radio too.
Vacuum roars,
What can I do?

My house is always noisy,
And busy as can be.
We're never ever quiet here,
We're loud and nois-eeeeee!

▤ Discuss taking care of our ears. Talk about how to wash them during a bath and how to protect them from loud noises. Show the children how to place cotton in their ears to lower the volume of sound. You can sing, "This Is the Way We Wash Our Face" to the tune of "The Mulberry Bush" with the children to help reinforce washing their ears.

This Is the Way We Wash Our Face
This is the way we wash our face,
Scrub our cheeks,
Scrub our ears.
This is the way we wash our face,
Until we're squeaky clean.

▤ Serve loud- and soft-sounding snacks. Try pretzels for louder sounds and bananas for softer sounds. Call the children's attention to the sound of the snacks as they chew them.

Cognitive Development Choices

- Give the children objects that make soft sounds (such as cotton balls, pompoms, and feathers) and objects that are loud (such as blocks, beads, and jar lids) to drop into a metal bucket or tray. Encourage the children to sort the items according to whether they make loud or soft sounds.
  Safety Warning: Supervise closely so the children do not put small items into their mouths.

- Give the children Sound Canisters to explore. Place pennies, washers, buttons, toothpicks, tissue paper balls, and paperclips inside of film canisters (or pill canisters). Glue the lids on. Encourage the children to shake the Sound Canisters and decide if the sounds they hear are loud or soft.

- Record sounds on a cassette tape and then ask the children to match the sounds to Sound Cards (Appendix p. 467-468).

- Encourage the children to build towers and then knock them down. Ask them to try this on a floor with a hard surface and then on carpet. "On which surface do the blocks make the loudest sound?"

- Encourage the children to explore the rhythm band instruments. Discuss the various sounds they make. "Which sounds are loud? Which sounds are soft?"

- Take the children on a walk outdoors to listen for soft and loud sounds.

- Make Sound Shakers. Fill a half-liter, clear soda bottle about $\frac{1}{4}$ full with water. Fill a second half-liter bottle about $\frac{1}{4}$ full with white corn syrup. Glue and tape on the lids securely. Encourage the children to shake the bottles. "What sounds do you hear?" "Which bottle makes the loudest sound?"

- Problem-solving suggestion: Fill squirt bottles with water. Encourage the children to squirt the bottles on a piece of thick paper and then on a cookie sheet. Which target produces the loudest sound? If possible, adjust the spray of the bottle. Can the children determine that a mist will be softer than a direct spray?

REFLECTION ON THE DAY
Ask the children to make a loud and a soft sound for you.

Light and Heavy

WORDS TO PRACTICE

heavier	light	oppos.
heaviest	lighter	weight
heavy	lightest	

GETTING STARTED

- Put a heavy object into one plastic egg and a light o~~b~~ into another egg to make Weighted Eggs. For example, pla~~ce~~ magnet inside one egg to make it heavy and a paper clip or cotton ball inside the other egg to make it light. Tape the eggs closed. Encourage the children to examine both eggs to determine which egg is the heavy egg and which egg is the light egg. Ask questions to find out what the children know about *heavy* and *light* things. Explain that the words *heavy* and *light* refer to weight and are opposites.

- Tell the children that today they will be learning more about the opposites *heavy* and *light*.

- Read your favorite book about opposites to the children or select a book from the Story Circle Suggestions below to check out of the library and read.

STORY CIRCLE SUGGESTIONS

- *Elephant, Elephant: A Book of Opposites* by Francisco Pittau
- *Heavy and Light (Animal Opposites)* by Rod Theodorou

PREPARATION FOR "LIGHT AND HEAVY" ACTIVITIES AND EXPERIENCES

- Ask families in advance for the birth weight of their children (Appendix p. 440).
- Gather light and heavy objects (e.g., brick, thick book, feather, handkerchief, and so on).
- Make Weighted Eggs above and Weighted Cans (see p. 288).
- Make "The Great Big Pumpkin" flannel board story (Appendix p. 492-494).

- Gather five-pound and one-pound bags of sugar and wrap them in tissue paper.
- Obtain a pulley, rope, and bucket (optional).

Language Enrichment Choices*

- Show the children the heavy and light objects that you have collected. Discuss each of the objects and pass them around so that the children can feel their weight.

- Sing "Sing a Song of Opposites" to the tune of "Mary Had a Little Lamb" using the item you have collected as props. Add other verses for other opposites you have introduced.

   Sing a Song of Opposites
   This is light and this is heavy,
   This is light; this is heavy,
   This is light and this is heavy,
   Sing along with me.

- Use the words *heavy* and *light* in a sentence. For example, "My juice cup is *heavy* before I drink my juice, but when I finish drinking my juice the cup is *light*."

- Present "The Great Big Pumpkin" flannel board story (Appendix p. 492-494) to the children. "Was the pumpkin heavy or light?" "How do you know?"

- Teach the children the American Sign Language signs for *heavy* and *light* (Appendix p. 433-434). Review other signs.

Physical Development Choices

- Fill two zipper-closure plastic bags with sand. Place a small amount of sand into one bag to create a light bag of sand. Fill the second bag with sand to create a heavier bag of sand. Glue or tape the bags securely closed. During outdoor play, invite the children to toss each bag. "Which bag is easier to toss?" "Which bag goes the greatest distance?" "Which bag is heavy?" "Which bag is light?"

- Play a modified version "One Elephant" with the children. Ask the children to join hands as new elephants join the line. Discuss the heavy elephant on the light spider web. Do they think the web could hold the weight of the great big elephant?

* Toddlers and twos present a wide range of developmental needs, abilities, and interests. For each learning area, select among the following activity and experience choices that are appropriate for the children in your care.

- If a seesaw is available, use it to show heavy and light. Children begin to get a good sense of heavy and light when they feel their own weight being adjusted on a seesaw.

Social and Emotional Development Choices

- Weigh and record the weight of each of the children. Talk with them about how much heavier they are now than when they were born. To demonstrate their weight at birth, wrap up a five-pound bag of sugar and four one-pound bags of sugar. Hand each child the right combination to equal his birth weight (rounded off).

- Provide heavy and light objects such as a clean Clorox bottle filled with sand, a bag of feathers, a scarf, and a box filled with some blocks. Encourage the children to move them from one area to another. Discuss the difficulty of moving the heavier objects. If available, encourage the children to use wagons to pull heavier objects. Point out how the wagon makes pulling a heavy load easier.

- Talk with the children about not picking up things that are too heavy. Explain that lifting heavy objects can hurt their back and stomach.

Cognitive Development Choices

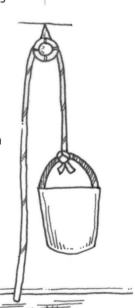

- Add more eggs to the Weighted Eggs and ask the children to sort the eggs by those that are heavy and those that are light. Talk with the children as they sort. Encourage them to hold two light eggs at the same time. "Are the two light eggs heavy when held together?"

- If available, attach a pulley to the ceiling and then run a rope through it. Attach a bucket to one end of the rope. Show the children how to make the bucket go up by pulling the rope through the pulley. Give the children some objects that are heavy such as a brick and a thick book. Show them how the pulley makes lifting the objects easier. "Does it make the object feel lighter?"
  Safety Warning: Do not let children play with the pulley unattended. If a child lets go of the rope, it can fall and hit that child or another child.

- Give the children photos of animals and ask them to decide it the animal is heavy or light. Ask them to explain their answer. "Have you seen this animal before?"

287

■ Provide a balance scale and encourage the children to try putting light and heavy objects on the scale. Can they make it balance? Show the children how to test the item in their hand to decide if it is heavy or light. Explain that this makes it easier to tell which object will help them balance the scale.

■ Provide a tub of water and some cups, plastic jars or pails, and funnels. Ask the children how many cups of water they can put into the jar before it is heavy.

■ Problem-solving suggestion: Make Weighted Cans by filling one pound coffee cans with sand or blocks. Place a different amount of sand or blocks into each can so that they are each a different weight. Make some heavy and some light. Give the children Weighted Cans and let them explore rolling the cans across the floor and down a ramp. "Which cans roll faster across the floor and which cans roll faster down the ramp?"

REFLECTION ON THE DAY

Ask the children to show you something that is light and something that is heavy.

Nursery Rhymes

Humpty Dumpty

WORDS TO PRACTICE

egg	spill
hard-boiled	wall
king's men	white
on	yoke
raw	

GETTING STARTED

- Teach the children "Humpty Dumpty," including the new verse (Appendix p. 589-591). Use the flannel board patterns to illustrate the rhyme as you say it. "Has anyone heard this rhyme before?" Encourage children to say the words "Humpty Dumpty." They will like the funny sounding words.
- Tell the children that today they will be learning more about "Humpty Dumpty."
- Read your favorite book of nursery rhymes to the children or select a book from the Story Circle Suggestions below to check out of the library and read.

STORY CIRCLE SUGGESTIONS

- *Animal Crackers* by Jane Dyer
- *Humpty Dumpty* by Daniel Kirk

PREPARATION FOR "HUMPTY DUMPTY" ACTIVITIES AND EXPERIENCES

- Make the "Humpty Dumpty" flannel board story (Appendix p. 589-591).
- Make the Humpty Dumpty Puzzles and Puppets (see p. 294).
- Make the Weighted Eggs (see p. 294).
- Get eggs and hard boil a few.

Language Enrichment Choices*

▦ Sing the "Humpty Dumpty" verse of the "Nursery Rhyme Rap" to the tune of "Ninety-Nine Bottles of Pop on the Wall."

Humpty Dumpty Sat on a Wall
Humpty Dumpty sat on a wall,
Humpty Dumpty had a great fall.
All the king's horses and all the king's men
Couldn't put Humpty together again.

Chorus
Oh, A B C D E F G...H I J K L...M N O P...Q R S...T U V W X Y Z!

▦ Read the listening poem, "Humpty's New Ears." Encourage the children to touch their ears when they hear the word "ear." Point out that we use our ears for listening.

Humpty's New Ears by Pam Schiller
Humpty Dumpty sat on a wall,
Humpty Dumpty had a great fall.
All the king's horses and all the king's men
Couldn't put Humpty together again.

Humpty Dumpty started to cry,
Humpty said, "Oh, please, won't you try?"
His friend, Jack Horner, knew what to do.
He fixed Humpty Dumpty with his glue.

When Humpty Dumpty saw himself new,
He no longer felt all sad and blue.
He looked in the mirror and said with glee,
"Let's glue some ears to the side of me."

A pair of ears will look real nice,
Like they do on elephants and mice.
One on the left, and one on the right,
Humpty with ears—what a sight!

Jack made two ears, and then with his glue
He carefully attached ear one and ear two.
Humpty looked in the mirror and said with glee,
"I'm a good-looking egg, don't you agree?"

* Toddlers and twos present a wide range of developmental needs, abilities, and interests. For each learning area, select among the following activity and experience choices that are appropriate for the children in your care.

■ Discuss the vocabulary in the rhyme. Review the positional words *on* and *out*.

■ Play with the rhyming words in the rhyme. Say *wall* and *fall*, *hill* and *spill*, and *glue* and *new*. Encourage the children to say some of the rhyming words with you.

■ Invite the children to use the flannel board pieces to practice saying the rhyme. To help the children learn it, say a line and then encourage them to fill in rhyming words or the last word of all the sentences.

■ Review or teach the American Sign Language signs for *ears* (Appendix p. 431).

Physical Development Choices

■ Teach the children how to do Humpty Dumpty Rolls. Ask them to draw their legs and arms up to make themselves into a ball and then try rolling around on the floor.

■ Invite the children to play Egg Rolls. Make a masking tape start and finish line, about 8' apart on the floor. Show the children how to roll a plastic egg across the floor by gently nudging it with their toes. Remind them that in this game it is not speed that counts—it is getting the egg from the start to the finish line.

■ Teach the children "The Grand Old Duke of York." Discuss how the Duke's men march. Ask the children if they think the Duke's men could have fixed Humpty Dumpty if they tried harder.

> **The Grand Old Duke of York**
> *The grand old Duke of York* (salute)
> *He had ten thousand men.* (hold up ten fingers)
> *He marched them up to the top of the hill,* (point up)
> *And he marched them down again.* (point down)
> *And when they're up, they're up.* (stand tall)
> *And when they're down, they're down.* (squat)
> *But when they're only halfway up,* (stoop down)
> *They're neither up nor down.* (open arms and shrug)

■ Play "Humpty Dumpty Dumpty" from *I Am Special* CD/Tape by Thomas Moore. Teach the children to do the dance.

Social and Emotional Development Choices

▪ Examine a raw egg and then a hard-boiled egg with the children. Discuss the differences in the eggs' consistency. Point out the white and the yoke of the egg. Slice the hard-boiled egg, and after examining it, encourage the children to taste it.
Safety Warning: Check for allergies before serving any food to children. Also, be sure to wash hands thoroughly after handling raw eggs.

▪ Teach the children the chant/song "The Baby Chicks." Discuss how both human mothers and animal mothers take care of their babies. Try the actions that go with the chant/song with older toddlers. Explain to the children that chickens lay eggs.

The Baby Chicks
Baby chicks say, "Peep, peep, peep,"
As they wake from sleep, sleep, sleep. (rub eyes)

Baby chicks say, "Peep, peep, peep,"
And hear the birds go "cheep, cheep, cheep." (repeat "cheep, cheep, cheep")

Baby chicks say, "Peep, peep, peep,"
As they leap, leap, leap. (jump up and down)

Baby chicks say, "Peep, peep, peep,"
Mama says it's time for sleep, sleep, sleep. (lay head in hands)

Cognitive Development Choices

▪ Encourage the children to build a wall with blocks. Provide stuffed animals to set on the wall. "What happens when they fall?"

▪ Give the children colored plastic eggs. Take them all apart and encourage the children to put them back together by matching the colors.

▪ Make Humpty Dumpty Puppets. Use the flannel board pattern of Humpty Dumpty (Appendix p. 589-591) to make several puppets. Photocopy the patterns, color them, cut them out, laminate them, and glue them to tongue depressors. Encourage the children to play with the puppets.

■ Place items of varying weights inside plastic eggs to create Weighted Eggs. Encourage the children to explore rolling the eggs. "Which roll the easiest?" "Which eggs are difficult to roll?" You can also have the children arrange the eggs according to weight. If you make two of each egg, the children can match the eggs that are the same weight. Be sure to use items that vary greatly in weight.

■ Display pictures of eggs. Discuss where eggs come from.

■ Use the shells of the eggs that you used to make hard-boiled eggs to make an eggshell collage. Invite the children to glue the shells onto a piece of paper. Encourage children to explore the eggshells with their hands. "Are the eggshells heavy or light? Soft or hard?"

■ Problem-solving suggestion: Invite the children to put Humpty Dumpty Puzzles together. Cut out a large oval shape from poster board and draw a face and clothes on it, or photocopy and enlarge the Humpty Dumpty flannel board pattern (Appendix p. 589-591). Color, laminate, and cut into simple puzzle pieces (three or four pieces).

REFLECTION ON THE DAY
Invite the children to say the "Humpty Dumpty" rhyme with you. If they can't say the rhyme, ask them to tell you what the rhyme is about.

Little Miss Muffet

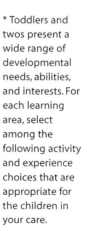

WORDS TO PRACTICE

curds and whey	on
down	tuffet

GETTING STARTED

- Teach the children "Miss Muffet," including the new verse (Appendix p. 597-599). Use the flannel board patterns to illustrate the rhyme as you say it. "Has anyone heard this rhyme before?"
- Tell the children that today they will be learning more about "Miss Muffet."
- Read your favorite book of nursery rhymes to the children or select a book from the Story Circle Suggestions below to check out of the library and read.

STORY CIRCLE SUGGESTIONS

- *Animal Crackers* by Jane Dyer
- *Little Miss Muffet* by Lucy Cousins

PREPARATION FOR "MISS MUFFET" ACTIVITIES AND EXPERIENCES

- Make the "Miss Muffet" flannel board story (Appendix p. 597-599).
- Gather the curds and whey (cottage cheese).
- Make a pipe-cleaner spider.

Language Enrichment Choices*

- Sing the "Miss Muffet" verse of the "Nursery Rhyme Rap" to the tune of "Ninety-Nine Bottles of Pop on the Wall." If you have already taught "Humpty Dumpty," sing that verse too.

    Little Miss Muffet sat on her tuffet
    Eating her curds and whey.
    Along came a spider and sat down beside her
    And frightened Miss Muffet away!

* Toddlers and twos present a wide range of developmental needs, abilities, and interests. For each learning area, select among the following activity and experience choices that are appropriate for the children in your care.

Chorus:
Oh, A B C D E F G...H I J K L...M N O P...Q R S...T U V W X Y Z!

- Read the "Miss Muffet" listening poem. Encourage the children to move their fingers like spiders when they hear the word "spider."

    Miss Muffet (second verse by Pam Schiller)
    Little Miss Muffet sat on her tuffet
    Eating her curds and whey.
    Along came a spider and sat down beside her
    And frightened Miss Muffet away!

    Miss Muffet felt silly to have run away,
    From that little, bitty, tiny spider.
    So she took a deep breath, picked up her whey,
    Said "hi" to the spider and sat down beside her.

- Discuss the vocabulary in the rhyme. Review the positional words *on* and *down*.

- Play with the rhyming words in the rhyme. Say *Muffet* and *tuffet*, *whey* and *away*, and *beside her* and *spider*. Encourage the children to say some of the rhyming words with you.

- Invite the children to use the flannel board pieces to practice saying the rhyme. To help the children learn it, say a line and then encourage them to fill in rhyming words or the last word of all the sentences.

- Review or teach the American Sign Language signs for *on* and *down* (Appendix p. 431, 436).

Physical Development Choices

- Invite the children to walk like a spider by walking on their hands and feet, keeping their legs bent. If the children are able to walk like this, you may want to encourage them to race. Show the older toddlers how to do a group spider walk. Have four children stand back-to-back in a circle, hook elbows for support, and then attempt to walk using eight legs.

- Encourage the children to dance their fingers like slow-moving spiders, fast spiders, tired spiders, happy spiders, and graceful spiders.

Social and Emotional Development Choices

- Serve some curds and whey (cottage cheese) to the children. If desired, you can make your own curds and whey using the following recipe. Point out why they call it curds and whey in the rhyme. Discuss the texture of the curds and whey. "How does it taste?" You may want to provide fruit with this snack to make it tastier.

    Miss Muffet's Curds and Whey (Cottage Cheese)
    1 quart milk
    2 tablespoons vinegar
    Salt
    Sour cream (optional)
    Fruit

    Heat milk until bubbles begin to form (adults only). Remove from heat and stir in vinegar. Continue to stir while mixtures cools and curds form. Hold a strainer over a glass bowl and pour the mixture through to separate the curds from the liquid (whey). Gently press the curds with a wooden spoon to further squeeze whey. Add salt to taste and a little sour cream for smoothness. Serve with fresh fruit.

- Sing "Itsy Bitsy Spider" with the children. "How is this spider different from the one in the "Little Miss Muffet" rhyme?" (He didn't scare anyone.)

    Itsy Bitsy Spider

The itsy bitsy spider	*Up came the sun*
Went up the waterspout.	*And dried up all the rain.*
Down came the rain	*And the itsy bitsy spider*
And washed the spider out.	*Went up the spout again.*

- Discuss things that frighten children. Some children are afraid of the dark and shadows. Others are afraid of thunder, costumes, or animals. Fears are often something that just take time to overcome, but try to reassure children when you can.

Cognitive Development Choices

- Encourage the children to make paper plate spiders. Give each child a paper plate and eight legs cut from black construction paper and folded accordion-style. Show them how to glue the legs onto their plate. Encourage children to name their spiders.

▓ Provide pictures of spiders and spider webs for the children to look at. Ask the children to show you the spider's legs. Count the legs with the children.

▓ Invite children to paint a spider web by dipping a golf ball into white tempera paint and then putting it into a shallow box lined with a piece of black drawing paper. Show the little ones how to roll the ball back and forth to create a painted web effect.

▓ Show the children how to make spider shadow puppets by dancing their fingers like spiders in front of a light source.

▓ Give the children some pillows to make a tuffet on which to sit. Closely supervise this activity to make sure that the children don't topple off their tuffets.

▓ Give the children spoons, bowls, and pompoms. Encourage the children to spoon the "curds and whey" (pompoms) into the bowl.

▓ Problem-solving suggestion: Make a spider by twisting four pipe cleaners together at the center to make eight legs. Hide the spider in a place a spider might be found, such as under a shelf or cushion or in a cabinet. Encourage the little ones to go on a spider hunt. Provide clues—your clues will help the hunters become aware of the habits of spiders.

REFLECTION ON THE DAY
Invite the children to say the "Miss Muffet" rhyme with you. If they can't say the rhyme, ask them to tell you what the rhyme is about.

Jack and Jill

WORDS TO PRACTICE

caper	hill	trot
crown	nob	tumbling
fetch	pail	

GETTING STARTED

- Teach the children "Jack and Jill" (see next page). Use the flannel board patterns (Appendix p. 592-594) to illustrate the rhyme as you say it. "Has anyone heard this rhyme before?" "Does anyone have the same name as the boy and girl in the rhyme?"
- Tell the children that today they will be learning more about "Jack and Jill."
- Read your favorite book of nursery rhymes to the children or select a book from the Story Circle Suggestions below to check out of the library and read.

STORY CIRCLE SUGGESTIONS

- *Animal Crackers* by Jane Dyer
- *Jack and Jill and Other Nursery Rhymes* by Lucy Cousins

PREPARATION FOR "JACK AND JILL" ACTIVITIES AND EXPERIENCES

- Make the "Jack and Jill" flannel board story (Appendix p. 592-594).
- Make the Jack and Jill Puppets (see p. 301).

Language Enrichment Choices*

- Sing the "Jack and Jill" verse of the "Nursery Rhyme Rap" to the tune of "Ninety-Nine Bottles of Pop on the Wall." If you have already taught "Humpty Dumpty" and "Miss Muffet," sing those verses too.

* Toddlers and twos present a wide range of developmental needs, abilities, and interests. For each learning area, select among the following activity and experience choices that are appropriate for the children in your care.

Jack and Jill

Jack and Jill went up the hill
To fetch a pail of water.
Jack fell down and broke his crown,
And Jill came tumbling after.

Chorus:
Oh, A B C D E F G...H I J K L...M N O P...Q R S...T U V W X Y Z!

▪ Read the "Jack and Jill" listening poem. Have the children touch their heads when they hear the word "Jack."

Jack and Jill

Jack and Jill went up the hill	*Up Jack got and home did trot*
To fetch a pail of water.	*As fast as he could caper.*
Jack fell down and broke his crown,	*Went to bed and plastered his head*
And Jill came tumbling after.	*With vinegar and brown paper.*

▪ Discuss the vocabulary in the rhyme. Review the positional words *up* and *down*. Show the children a pail, if available.

▪ Play with the rhyming words in the rhyme. Say *Jill* and *hill*, *caper* and *paper*, *down* and *crown*, *bed* and *head*, and *got* and *trot*. Encourage the children to say some of the rhyming words with you.

▪ Invite the children to use the flannel board pieces to practice saying the rhyme. To help the children learn it, say a line and then encourage them to fill in rhyming words or the last word of all the sentences.

▪ Review or teach the American Sign Language signs for *up* and *down* (Appendix p. 431, 439).

Physical Development Choices

▪ Provide a pail of water and paintbrushes. Encourage the children to paint the fence or the wall of the building outdoors. Tell the children that the pail is similar to the one Jack and Jill were going up the hill to get (fetch).

▪ Show the children how to do somersaults and forward rolls. If there is a hill close by, show it to the children. If it is safe, let them roll down the hill.

Social and Emotional Development Choices

▨ Discuss getting hurt and how we care for our hurts. Talk about the bandage that Jack's mother put on Jack's head. Provide Band-Aids for the children to put on a sore spot.

▨ Sing "Two Little Blackbirds" with the children. "What things do this song and the "Jack and Jill" rhyme have in common?"

> **Two Little Blackbirds**
> *Two little blackbirds* (hold up index finger of each hand)
> *Sitting on a hill.*
> *One named Jack.* (hold right hand/finger forward)
> *One named Jill.* (hold left hand/finger forward)
> *Fly away, Jack.* (wiggle right finger and place behind your back)
> *Fly away, Jill.* (wiggle left finger and place behind your back)
> *Come back, Jack.* (bring right hand back)
> *Come back, Jill.* (bring left hand back)

Cognitive Development Choices

▨ Give the children pails and encourage them to pick up small blocks and put them into their pails. "Can two children carry a pail together like Jack and Jill were going to do?"

▨ Provide a tub of water and water play items such as sponges, funnels, basters, and cups. Encourage the children to play in the water.

▨ Make Jack and Jill Puppets for the children to play with. Photocopy Jack and Jill from the flannel board patterns (Appendix p. 592-594). Color them, cut them out, laminate them, and glue them to tongue depressors.

▨ Give the children dolls and bandages and let them bandage their dolls' "broken crowns."

▨ Problem-solving suggestion: Give the children a pail of water and some items to sort into sink or float categories. Talk about the items and what might make them sink or what might make them float.

REFLECTION ON THE DAY
Invite the children to say the "Jack and Jill" rhyme with you. If they can't say it, ask them to tell you what the rhyme is about.

Little Boy Blue

WORDS TO PRACTICE

corn	horn
haystack	meadow

GETTING STARTED

- Teach the children "Little Boy Blue." Use the flannel board patterns to illustrate the rhyme as you say it. "Has anyone heard this rhyme before?" "Why do they call the boy 'little boy blue'?"

  ### Little Boy Blue
  Little Boy Blue, come blow your horn,
  The sheep's in the meadow the cow's in the corn.
  Where is the boy who looks after the sheep?
  He's under the haystack, fast asleep!

- Tell the children that today they will be learning more about "Little Boy Blue."
- Read your favorite book of nursery rhymes to the children or select a book from the Story Circle Suggestions below to check out of the library and read.

STORY CIRCLE SUGGESTIONS

- *Animal Crackers* by Jane Dyer
- *Little Boy Blue: And Other Rhymes* by Iona Opie

PREPARATION FOR "LITTLE BOY BLUE" ACTIVITIES AND EXPERIENCES

- Make the "Little Boy Blue" flannel board rhyme (Appendix p. 595-596).
- Make Ground Cover and Sheep and Cow Puppets (see p. 305).
- Get whipping cream and let it set until it reaches room temperature.
- Get popcorn.

Language Enrichment Choices*

▪ Sing the "Little Boy Blue" verse of the "Nursery Rhyme Rap" to the tune of "Ninety-Nine Bottles of Pop on the Wall." If you have already taught "Humpty Dumpty," "Miss Muffet," and "Jack and Jill," add those verses.

Little Boy Blue
Little Boy Blue, come blow your horn,
The sheep's in the meadow the cow's in the corn.
Where is the boy who looks after the sheep?
He's under the haystack, fast asleep!

Chorus:
Oh, A B C D E F G...H I J K L...M N O P...Q R S...T U V W X Y Z!

▪ Read the "Little Boy Blue" listening story. Invite the children to blow their "horns" (fists placed to the mouth) when they hear the word "horn."

Little Boy Blue (second verse by Pam Schiller)
Little Boy Blue, come blow your horn,
The sheep's in the meadow, the cow's in the corn.
Where is the boy who looks after the sheep?
He's under the haystack fast asleep!

Little Boy Blue, awake! Awake!
The sheep await the sound of your horn.
No time to sleep, no nap to take.
Little Boy Blue, will you blow that horn?

▪ Teach the children the vocabulary in the rhyme. Review the positional words *in* and *under*. Show the children a horn, if available.

▪ Play with the rhyming words. Say *horn* and *corn* and *asleep* and *sheep*. Encourage the children to say the rhyming words with you.

▪ Encourage the children to use the flannel board pieces to practice saying the rhyme. To help the children learn it, say a line and then encourage them to fill in rhyming words or the last word of all the sentences.

▪ Review or teach the American Sign Language signs for *in, under*, and *blue* (Appendix p. 430, 434, 439).

* Toddlers and twos present a wide range of developmental needs, abilities, and interests. For each learning area, select among the following activity and experience choices that are appropriate for the children in your care.

Physical Development Choices

- Play The Farmer in the Dell. Choose one child to be the Farmer. The other children walk in a circle around the Farmer. Sing the song together. You can change the words "cat" and "dog" to "cow" and "sheep" if desired.

   The Farmer in the Dell
   The farmer in the dell, the farmer in the dell.
   Heigh-ho the derry-o, the farmer in the dell.

   The farmer takes a wife/husband/friend. (Farmer brings a second child into the circle)
   The farmer takes a wife/husband/friend.
   Heigh-ho the derry-o, the farmer takes a wife/husband/friend.
   The wife/husband/friend takes a child... (Wife chooses a third child to join in the circle)
   The child takes a dog...
   The dog takes a cat...
   The cat takes a rat...
   The rat takes the cheese...

   The cheese stands alone... (Everyone except Cheese leaves the center of the circle)

- Invite the children to dance creatively with blue streamers.

Social and Emotional Development Choices

- Sing "Old MacDonald Had a Farm" with the children. Tell the children that farmers look after sheep just like Little Boy Blue does in the rhyme.

   Old MacDonald Had a Farm
   Old MacDonald had a farm,
   E-I-E-I-O
   And on this farm she had a cow,
   E-I-E-I-O
   With a moo, moo here,
   And a moo, moo there,
   Here a moo, there a moo,
   Everywhere a moo, moo.
   Old MacDonald had a farm,
   E-I-E-I-O!

Additional verses:
   Sheep—baa, baa
   Pig—oink, oink
   Cat—meow, meow
   Dog—bow-wow
   Horse—neigh, neigh

▪ Invite the children to help make butter. Place two tablespoons of whipping cream in a plastic baby food jar and shake, shake, shake until it turns to butter. Spread the butter on crackers and enjoy. Explain that cream comes from cows. You can also serve the butter on popcorn.

Cognitive Development Choices

▪ Give the children toy farm animals and farm props to play with. Make a Ground Cover by spray painting (adult only) earth-tone colors (such as greens, gray, and browns) onto a section of an old sheet. Make a barn by covering a cardboard box with red paper and a silo by covering an oatmeal container. You can use Fun Foam to create roofs for the barn and the silo. Encourage the children to place the sheep in the "meadow."

▪ Give the children empty toilet paper tubes to use for horns. Show them how to "toot" their horns. Make sure that they do not "toot" their horn near another child's ear.

▪ Encourage the children to paint with different shades of blue paint. "Which shade of blue do you like best?"

▪ Fill a tub with hay (dried grass). Hide small toys or small plastic animals in the hay and encourage the children to find them. Talk about how hay is used on a farm.

▪ Make Sheep and Cow Puppets by photocopying the sheep and the cow in the flannel board patterns (appendix p. 595-596). Color them, laminate them, and glue them to tongue depressors. Encourage the children to play with the puppets.

- Pop popcorn and serve it to the children. Tell the children that corn is grown on a farm and that in the rhyme, "Little Boy Blue," the cow was eating the corn. You may want to serve the butter the children made on their popcorn.

- Give the children some large wiggle eyes. Ask them to drop the eyes into a box. Tell the children that eyes facing upward are "wakeful eyes" and eyes facing down are "sleepy eyes." Ask them which kind of eyes Little Boy Blue had.
  Safety Warning: Make sure that the children do not put the eyes in their mouths as they present a choking hazard.

- Problem-solving suggestion: Place some hay (dried grass) in a shallow tub. Provide a bucket and a small shovel and encourage the children to remove the hay from the tub and deliver it to an empty tub several feet away. For older children, you can provide a second method for picking up the hay such as a dustpan and whisk broom.

REFLECTION ON THE DAY
Invite the children to say the "Little Boy Blue" rhyme with you. If they can't say the rhyme, ask them to tell you what the rhyme is about.

The Cat and the Fiddle

WORDS TO PRACTICE

cat	dog	spoon
cow	fiddle	
dish	moon	

GETTING STARTED

- Teach the children "The Cat and the Fiddle" (see next page). Use the flannel board patterns (Appendix p. 548-586) to illustrate the rhyme as you say it. "Has anyone heard this rhyme before?"
- Tell the children that today they will be learning more about "The Cat and the Fiddle.
- Read your favorite book of nursery rhymes to the children or select a book from the Story Circle Suggestions below to check out of the library and read.

STORY CIRCLE SUGGESTIONS

- *Animal Crackers* by Jane Dyer
- *Hey Diddle Diddle* by Jeanette Winter
- *Hey Diddle Diddle* by Kin Eagle

PREPARATION FOR "THE CAT AND THE FIDDLE" ACTIVITIES AND EXPERIENCES

- Make the "The Cat and the Fiddle" flannel board rhyme (Appendix p. 584-586).
- Cut out poster board moons for the children to jump over.
- Make Moon Rollers and Moon Puzzles (see p. 309).

Language Enrichment Choices*

- Sing the "The Cat and the Fiddle" verse of the "Nursery Rhyme Rap" to the tune of "Ninety-Nine Bottles of Pop on the Wall." If you have already taught "Humpty Dumpty," "Miss Muffet," "Jack and Jill," and "Little Boy Blue," add some of those verses.

* Toddlers and twos present a wide range of developmental needs, abilities, and interests. For each learning area, select among the following activity and experience choices that are appropriate for the children in your care.

The Cat and the Fiddle
Hey, diddle diddle, the cat and the fiddle,
The cow jumped over the moon.
The little dog laughed to see such sport,
And the dish ran away with the spoon!

Chorus:
Oh, A B C D E F G...H I J K L...M N O P...Q R S...T U V W X Y Z!

- Read the following "The Cat and the Fiddle" listening story. Have the children pretend to play a fiddle when they hear the word "fiddle."

    The Cat and the Fiddle (first verse, traditional (see above);
    second verse by Pam Schiller)
    Hey diddle diddle the dog got the fiddle
    And he played a jubilant tune.
    The cow and the cat danced to the fiddle
    And so did the dish and the spoon.

- Discuss the vocabulary in the rhyme. Review the positional word *over*. Show the children a fiddle, a dish, and a spoon.

- Play with the rhyming words. Say *diddle* and *fiddle* and *moon* and *spoon* a few times. Encourage the children to say the rhyming words with you.

- Invite the children to use the flannel board pieces to practice saying the rhyme. To help the children learn it, say a line and then encourage them to fill in rhyming words or the last word of all the sentences.

- Review or teach the American Sign Language sign for *over* (Appendix p. 436).

Physical Development Choices

- Cut out a large round moon from construction paper or use a white paper plate to represent the moon. Place the moon on the floor and invite the children to jump over it. "Can a cow really jump over the moon?"

- Invite the children to dance to fiddle music. A good example is "Turkey in the Straw," which is usually played with a fiddle. Appalachian music almost always includes a fiddle.

Social and Emotional Development Choices

▓ Encourage the children to help set the table at snack or lunchtime. Discuss the plates and the utensils on the table. "Which of the items on the table ran off together in the 'The Cat and the Fiddle'?"

▓ Teach the children the rhyme "I See the Moon." Discuss the moon, such as its location and shape.

> **I See the Moon**
> *I see the moon,*
> *The moon sees me.*
> *I love the moon,*
> *The moon loves me.*

Cognitive Development Choices

▓ Invite the children to play with Moon Rollers. Cut out moons from white poster board or use paper plates to represent moons. Invite the children to roll the moons across the floor. Read *Goodnight Moon* by Margaret Wise to the children.

▓ Provide play dishes and encourage the children to set the table. Encourage the children to name each dish. "How are bowls and plates different?"

▓ Encourage the children to pretend to be dogs. Ask them to get down on all fours and bark. Teach them some tricks, such as how to shake, lie down, and roll over.

▓ Encourage the children to pretend to be cats. Ask them to get down on all fours and meow. Show them how to stretch and how to stalk.

▓ Problem-solving suggestion: Make Moon Puzzles by cutting out a moon from white poster board, laminating it, and then cutting it into simple puzzle pieces (three or four pieces). Encourage the children to work the puzzles.

REFLECTION ON THE DAY
Invite the children to say the "The Cat and the Fiddle" rhyme with you. If they can't say the rhyme, ask them to tell you what the rhyme is about.

The Mouse and the Clock

WORDS TO PRACTICE

clock	down	one
dock	mouse	up

GETTING READY

- Teach the children "The Mouse and the Clock" (see next page). Use the flannel board patterns to illustrate the rhyme as you say it. "Has anyone heard this rhyme before?"
- Tell the children that today they will be learning more about "The Mouse and the Clock."
- Read your favorite book of nursery rhymes to the children or select a book from the Story Circle Suggestions below to check out of the library and read.

STORY CIRCLE SUGGESTIONS

- *Animal Crackers* by Jane Dyer
- *The Completed Hickory Dickory Dock* by Jim Aylesworth
- *Hickory Dickory Dock* by Patricia Sechi Johnson

* Toddlers and twos present a wide range of developmental needs, abilities, and interests. For each learning area, select among the following activity and experience choices that are appropriate for the children in your care.

PREPARATION FOR "THE MOUSE AND THE CLOCK" ACTIVITIES AND EXPERIENCES

- Make the "The Mouse and the Clock" flannel board rhyme (Appendix p. 600), Magnetic Mouse and Clock and Mice Puppets (see p. 313).
- Draw the large clock on butcher paper.
- Gather clocks, cheese, and crackers.

Language Enrichment Choices*

- Sing the "The Mouse and the Clock" verse of the "Nursery Rhyme Rap" to the tune of "Ninety-Nine Bottles of Pop on the Wall." If you have already taught other nursery rhymes, add some of those verses, too.

The Mouse and the Clock
Hickory dickory dock!
The mouse ran up the clock.
The clock struck one,
The mouse ran down!
Hickory dickory dock!

Chorus:
Oh, A B C D E F G...H I J K L...M N O P...Q R S... T U V W X Y Z!

- Read the following listening story, "Hickory Dickory Dock." Encourage the children to clap their hands when they hear the words, "hickory," "dickory," and "dock." The children will clap three times—once on hickory, once on dickory, and once on dock.

The Mouse and the Clock (second verse by Pam Schiller)

Hickory dickory dock!   *Hickory dickory dock!*
The mouse ran up the clock.   *The cat is by the clock.*
The clock struck one,   *Mouse saw the cat,*
The mouse ran down!   *And mouse did scat,*
Hickory dickory dock!   *Hickory, dickory, dock!*

- Discuss the vocabulary in the rhyme. Review the positional words *up* and *down*. Show the children a clock. If possible, show more than one kind of clock.

- Play with the rhyming words in the rhyme. Say *hickory* and *dickory*, *dock* and *clock*, and *one* and *run* a few times. Encourage the children to say the rhyming word pairs with you.

- Invite the children to use the flannel board pieces to practice saying the rhyme. To help the children learn it, say a line and then encourage them to fill in rhyming words or the last word of all the sentences.

- Review or teach the American Sign Language signs for *up* and *down* (Appendix p. 431, 439).

Physical Development Choices

- Draw a large, simple grandfather clock on butcher paper. You can copy the clock in the flannel board patterns (appendix page 600). Encourage the children to crawl up and down the clock like little mice.

- Play "Old Gray Cat" with the children.

Old Gray Cat
The old gray cat is sleeping, sleeping, sleeping.
The old gray cat is sleeping in the house.
(one child is Cat and curls up, pretending to sleep)

The little mice are creeping, creeping, creeping.
The little mice are creeping through the house.
(other children are Mice creeping around sleeping Cat)

The old gray cat is waking, waking, waking.
The old gray cat is waking through the house.
(Cat slowly sits up and stretches)

The old gray cat is chasing, chasing, chasing.
The old gray cat is chasing through the house.
(Cat chases Mice)

All the mice are squealing, squealing, squealing.
All the mice are squealing through the house.
(Mice squeal; when Cat catches a Mouse, that Mouse becomes the Cat)

Social and Emotional Development Choices

- Do "'Round the House" with the children. Point out the similarities and differences in "The Mouse and the Clock" and this rhyme. Both rhymes have a mouse, which goes up something. Discuss the things that are different in the rhymes. The mouse goes up a clock in one rhyme and stairs in the other.

Round the House
'Round the house (use index finger to trace a circle on the child's open palm)
'Round the house
Goes the little mousie.
Up the stairs (walk index finger and middle finger up the child's arm)
Up the stairs
In his little housie. (tickle the child under his chin)

- Serve a snack of crackers and a couple of different kinds of cheeses. Call the snack Mice Treats. Point out that mice love to eat cheese.

- Sing "Three White Mice" to the tune of "Three Blind Mice."

Three White Mice
(used with permission by Barbara Drolshagen and JoAnn Rajchel, Greendale, WI)
Three white mice, three white mice,
See how they dance, see how they dance.
They danced and danced for the farmer's wife,
Who played for them on a silver fife.
Did you ever see such a sight in your life
As three white mice!

Cognitive Development Choices

- Make a Magnetic Mouse and Clock. Photocopy the flannel board pattern of the clock and the mouse (Appendix p. 600). Color them, cut them out, and laminate them. Glue the clock to the bottom of a shallow box, such as a stationery box. Glue a piece of magnetic strip to the mouse. Show the children how to run the mouse up the clock by using a magnet under the box.

- Invite the children to make mice fingerprints. Provide fingerpaint and show the children how to dip their fingers into the paint and then press them on a piece of paper. Add some eyes and a tail for them so that their fingerprints will look like little mice. With the children, count the number of mice each child makes.

- Discuss famous mice such as Mighty Mouse, Mickey Mouse, and Jerry (in Tom and Jerry).

- Provide Mice Puppets for the children to play with. To make the puppets, paint 6" paper plates using gray tempera paint. After the plates dry, glue construction paper ears, whiskers, and wiggle eyes on the mouse face. Draw a nose and mouth on the face with a marker. Attach the faces to tongue depressor. Encourage the children to name their puppets.

- Prepare an inclined plank and encourage the children to run stuffed mice, plastic mice, or the Mice Puppets up and down the plank.

- Problem-solving suggestion: Hide a ticking clock and invite the children to find it. How do they know where to look?

REFLECTION ON THE DAY
See if anyone can say "The Mouse and the Clock" with you. If they can't say the rhyme, ask them to tell you what the rhyme is about.

Three Little Kittens

WORDS TO PRACTICE

dear	mittens	purr
kittens	naughty	

GETTING READY

- Teach the children "Three Little Kittens" (Appendix p. 603-606). Use the flannel board patterns to illustrate the rhyme as you say it. "Has anyone heard this rhyme before?" "Has anyone ever lost anything?"
- Tell the children that today they will be learning more about "Three Little Kittens."
- Read your favorite book of nursery rhymes to the children or select a book from the Story Circle Suggestions below to check out of the library and read.

STORY CIRCLE SUGGESTIONS

- *Animal Crackers* by Jane Dyer
- *The Mitten* by Jan Brett
- *Three Little Kittens* by Lorianne Siomades
- *Three Little Kittens* by Paul Galdone

PREPARATION FOR "THREE LITTLE KITTENS" ACTIVITIES AND EXPERIENCES

- Make the "Three Little Kittens" flannel board rhyme (Appendix p. 603-606).
- Make the Three Little Kittens Puppets (see p. 316).
- Gather ingredients for Cherry Pies (see p. 316).
- Cut out mittens from contact paper and construction paper.

Language Enrichment Choices*

- Sing "The Three Little Kittens" with the children. Encourage the children to act out the rhyme as you sing it.

* Toddlers and twos present a wide range of developmental needs, abilities, and interests. For each learning area, select among the following activity and experience choices that are appropriate for the children in your care.

- Discuss the new words in the rhyme such as *naughty, purr,* and in some parts of the country, *mittens.*

- Play with the rhyming words in the rhyme. Say *mittens* and *kittens, dear* and *fear,* and *dear* and *here.* Encourage the children to say the rhyming words with you.

- Invite the children to use the flannel board pieces to practice saying the rhyme. To help the children learn it, say a line and then encourage them to fill in rhyming words or the last word of all the sentences.

- Review or teach the American Sign Language sign for *little* (Appendix p. 434).

Physical Development Choices

- Play Copycat. Show the children how to stretch like a cat, slink like a cat, wash their faces like a cat, and pounce like a cat. Encourage them to copy each of the movements as you make them.

- Play "Old Gray Cat." You be the cat and let the children be the mice.

   Old Gray Cat
   The old gray cat is sleeping, sleeping, sleeping.
   The old gray cat is sleeping in the house.
   (one child is Cat and curls up, pretending to sleep)

   The little mice are creeping, creeping, creeping.
   The little mice are creeping through the house.
   (other children are Mice creeping around sleeping Cat)

   The old gray cat is waking, waking, waking.
   The old gray cat is waking through the house.
   (Cat slowly sits up and stretches)

   The old gray cat is chasing, chasing, chasing.
   The old gray cat is chasing through the house.
   (Cat chases Mice)

   All the mice are squealing, squealing, squealing.
   All the mice are squealing through the house.
   (Mice squeal; when Cat catches a Mouse, that Mouse becomes the Cat)

Social and Emotional Development Choices

- Discuss things that children do at home that might make their mommy or daddy unhappy. For example, not picking up their toys or not doing something they are told to do. Point out how important it is that children listen to their mommies and daddies.

- Make Cherry Pies with the children. Show them how to put a vanilla wafer in the bottom of a cupcake wrapper, add a couple of tablespoons of cherry pie filling, and then a dab of whipped cream on top. "How do the pies taste?" "What color is the filling?"

Cognitive Development Choices

- Provide playdough, pie tins, and rolling pins. Invite the children to roll out the playdough to make "pie crusts."

- Make Three Little Kitten Stick Puppets using the flannel board patterns (Appendix p. 603-606). Photocopy the kittens, color them, cut them out, laminate them, and attach them to tongue depressors. Invite the children to play with the puppets. Encourage the children to count the kittens.

- Provide pictures of kittens and cats for the children to look at. Point out the whiskers, paws, tails, and other features.

- Cut out mittens from contact paper and stick them to the tabletop. Spray the tabletop with shaving cream and invite the children to find the mittens in the "snow."

- Problem-solving suggestions:
  1. Give the children mittens to match. "How do you know which mittens go together?"
  2. Hide a mitten and invite the children to find it. Give clues. Do the children follow the clues?

REFLECTION ON THE DAY

Ask the children to say the "Three Little Kittens" rhyme with you. If they can't say the rhyme, ask them to tell you what the rhyme is about.

Hush-a-Bye

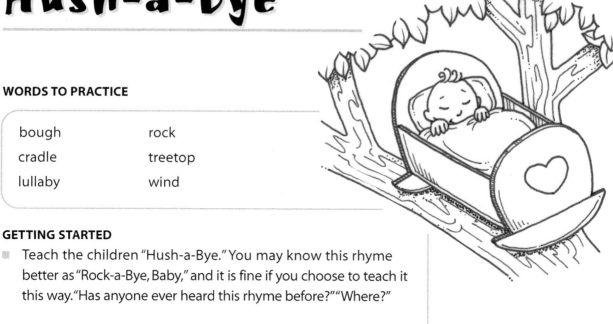

WORDS TO PRACTICE

bough	rock
cradle	treetop
lullaby	wind

GETTING STARTED

- Teach the children "Hush-a-Bye." You may know this rhyme better as "Rock-a-Bye, Baby," and it is fine if you choose to teach it this way. "Has anyone ever heard this rhyme before?" "Where?"

Hush-a-Bye
Hush-a-bye, baby, on the treetop!
When the wind blows the cradle will rock;
When the bough breaks the cradle will fall;
Down will come baby, cradle and all.

- Tell the children that today they will be learning more about "Hush-a-Bye."
- Read your favorite book of nursery rhymes to the children or select a book from the Story Circle Suggestions below to check out of the library and read.

STORY CIRCLE SUGGESTIONS

- *Hush Little Baby* by Sylvia Long
- *Rock-a-Bye Baby* by Heather Collins

PREPARATION FOR "HUSH-A-BYE" ACTIVITIES AND EXPERIENCES

- Collect baby pictures of the children in advance. Make Baggie Books (see p. 319).
- Gather bread, margarine, and cheese.
- Ask families to donate old baby rattles they are no longer using.

Language Enrichment Choices*

- Sing "Hush-a-Bye" ("Rock-a-Bye Baby") with the children. Point out that this rhyme is often used as a lullaby.

- Discuss the unusual words in the rhyme such as *bough, cradle,* and *hush-a-bye.*

- Play with the rhyming words in the rhyme. Say *top* and *rock* and *fall* and *all.* Encourage the children to say the rhyming words with you.

- Teach the children the American Sign Language sign for *baby* (Appendix p. 430).

Physical Development Choices

- Invite the children to have a crawling race. Place a masking tape start and finish line on the floor. Encourage the children to get down on all fours and crawl like a baby from the start to the finish line. Who makes it across the finish line first?

- Invite the children to shake baby rattles to some upbeat music. "Who usually plays with rattles?"

Social and Emotional Development Choices

- Play lullaby music for the children at naptime. Discuss the soft sound of the music. Remind the children that "Hush-a-Bye" is often used as a lullaby.

- Rock each of the children today. Sing "Hush-a-Bye" or "Rock-a-Bye, Baby" as you rock.

- Make Goodnight Baby Snacks. Give each child 1½ slices of bread and a piece of cheese. Help the children spread a small amount of butter or margarine on their full slice of bread. Provide a gingerbread person cookie cutter. Help the children cut out a gingerbread person from the cheese and then place it on the full slice of bread. Cover the bottom of the gingerbread person with the half slice of bread and toast. Eat and enjoy.

* Toddlers and twos present a wide range of developmental needs, abilities, and interests. For each learning area, select among the following activity and experience choices that are appropriate for the children in your care.

Cognitive Development Choices

▓ Give the children dolls and encourage them to rock the babies. Encourage them to sing.

▓ Photocopy the baby photos that the children brought in and place them in a Baggie Book. To make a Baggie Book, gather enough zipper-closure plastic bags to hold the photos of all the children. Two photos will go back to back inside each bag. Staple the determined number of bags together at the bottom of the bags. Cover the staples with vinyl tape. Place the books in the library area for the children to enjoy. Discuss the various photos and encourage them to guess who is who.

▓ Use the outlines provided (Appendix p. 444) to create Baby Item Stencils. Tape each stencil on drawing paper and encourage the children to paint over the stencils. When the stencils are removed, the outline of the baby item will be revealed.

▓ Problem-solving suggestion: Give the children a box of baby items such as rattles, bottles, pacifiers, baby jars, squeeze toys, and so forth. Provide duplicates of each item. Ask the children to match the items. Encourage older children to sort the items by how they are used. "Which items are used to take care of a baby?" "Which items are used to entertain a baby?"

REFLECTION ON THE DAY
Ask the children to say the "Hush-a-Bye" rhyme to you. If they can't say it, ask them to tell you what the rhyme is about.

FIVE TOES

WORDS TO PRACTICE

five	roast beef
market	toes
piggy	

GETTING STARTED

■ Teach the children "Five Toes." Ask the children to take off their shoes and wiggle their toes as you say the rhyme. Use the flannel board patterns (Appendix p. 587-588) to illustrate the rhyme as you say it. If you know this rhyme as "This Little Piggy" teach it that way.

Five Toes

This little piggy went to market, (wiggle big toe)
This little piggy stayed home, (wiggle second toe)
This little piggy had roast beef, (wiggle middle toe)
This little piggy had none, (wiggle fourth toe)
And this little piggy cried,
"Wee-wee-wee!" all the way home. (wiggle little toe)

■ Tell the children that today they will be learning more about "Five Toes."
■ Read your favorite book of nursery rhymes to the children or select a book from the Story Circle Suggestions below to check out of the library and read.

STORY CIRCLE SUGGESTIONS

■ *This Little Piggy* by Ann Shufflebotham
■ *This Little Piggy* by Heather Collins
■ *This Little Piggy* by Jane K. Manning

PREPARATION FOR "FIVE TOES" ACTIVITIES AND EXPERIENCES

■ Make the "Five Toes" flannel board rhyme (Appendix p. 587-588) and "The Three Little Pigs" flannel board story, if not already made (Appendix p. 568-570).

- Make the Glove Puppet, if not already made (Appendix p. 568-570).
- Make the "Five Toes" Puppets (Appendix p. 587-588).
- Gather ingredients for Pigs in a Blanket (see p. 322).

Language Enrichment Choices*

- Present the Glove Puppet version of "Five Toes" (Appendix p. 453). Use the same patterns that you used for the flannel board story. Photocopy them, color them, cut them out, laminate them, and glue a piece of Velcro on the back of each piece. Say the rhyme using the glove puppet.

- Present the "The Three Little Pigs" flannel board story (Appendix p. 568-570).

- Discuss the possible new words in the rhyme such as *market, none,* and *roast beef.*

- Sing the song, "Down by the Bay" using all pig verses. For example, sing, "Did you ever see a pig that is big, big, big?" "Did you ever see a pig eating a fig, fig, fig?" or "Did you ever see a pig wearing a wig, wig, wig?"

   Down by the Bay
   Down by the bay where the watermelons grow,
   Back to my home I dare not go,
   For if I do my mother will say,
   "Did you ever see a pig dancing the jig?"
   Down by the bay.

- Invite the children to use the "Five Toes" flannel board pieces to practice saying the rhyme. To help the children learn it, say a line and then encourage them to fill in rhyming words or the last word of all the sentences.

- Review the American Sign Language signs for *feet* and *toes* (see Appendix p. 432, 439).

Physical Development Choices

- Teach the children to do a "Pig Jig" to some frolicking music. Any jumping and kicking moves will do.

- Play Snort. Have the children stand perfectly still until they hear a pig "snort." Then they can dance, run, and play. When they hear a second snort, they have to stop and stand still again. Continue playing until the "little piglets" get tired of the game.

* Toddlers and twos present a wide range of developmental needs, abilities, and interests. For each learning area, select among the following activity and experience choices that are appropriate for the children in your care.

Social and Emotional Development Choices

▪ Say "Terrific Toes" for the children. Talk with each child about the things she can do with her toes.

Terrific Toes
I have such terrific toes
I take them with me wherever I goes.
I have such fantastic feet.
No matter what, they still smell sweet.
Toes and feet and feet and toes.
There's nothing else as fine as those.

▪ Invite the children to make Pigs in a Blanket. Give each child a refrigerator biscuit and a pre-cooked small sausage link. Help the children wrap the biscuit around the sausage. Cook in a toaster oven for four minutes on each side. **Safety Warning:** Supervise closely at all time. Check for allergies or food preferences before serving any food to children. Cut the Pigs in a Blanket into small pieces before serving.

Cognitive Development Choices

▪ Provide toy farm animals and props and encourage the children to build a farm. "Where do pigs live on the farm?" "What do they eat?"

▪ Display pictures of pigs. Talk with the children about pigs. "What color are they?" "What sounds do they make?" "Where are their snouts?"

▪ Help the children think of some famous pigs such as Porky, the Three Little Pigs, Piglet, and Wilbur.

▪ Encourage the children to build a home out of blocks for "the pig that stayed home." Will their house look like one of the Three Little Pig's houses?

▪ Provide pink tempera paint and encourage the children to paint a pig. Talk with the children about their painting.

▪ Make a Pig Snout for each child. Attach a piece of elastic string to a small paper cup. Encourage the children to paint their snouts with pink tempera paint. Draw two round circles on the bottom of each "snout" or cut two small holes into the bottom of each cup for nostrils.

▨ This is a messy activity but worth the mess. Ask the children to remove their shoes and then step into a shallow tub of tempera paint. Help them out of the paint and onto a 10′ strip of butcher paper. Hold their hands while they walk the length of the paper leaving a trail of footprints behind. Have a tub of soapy water and a towel available at the end of the walk. Label one of each child's footprints with her name. Point out the toe part of the footprints.

▨ Ask the children to remove their shoes and socks. Challenge them to pick up a spool or a handkerchief with their "little piggies" (toes). "Is it more difficult than using your fingers?"

▨ Problem-solving suggestion: Encourage the children to brainstorm reasons the last little pig was crying. All answers are acceptable, since we don't really know why he cried all the way home.

REFLECTION ON THE DAY
Invite the children to say the "Five Toes" rhyme with you. If they can't say the rhyme, ask them to tell you or show you what the rhyme is about.

One, Two, Buckle My Shoe

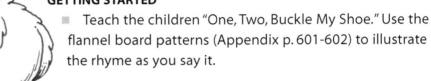

WORDS TO PRACTICE

buckle	straight
hen	
sticks	

GETTING STARTED

▩ Teach the children "One, Two, Buckle My Shoe." Use the flannel board patterns (Appendix p. 601-602) to illustrate the rhyme as you say it.

One, Two, Buckle My Shoe

One, two, buckle my shoe.
Three, four, shut the door.
Five, six, pick up sticks.
Seven, eight, lay them straight.
Nine, ten, a big fat hen.

▩ Tell the children that today they will be learning more about "One, Two, Buckle My Shoe."

▩ Read your favorite book of nursery rhymes to the children or select a book from the Story Circle Suggestions below to check out of the library and read.

STORY CIRCLE SUGGESTIONS

▩ *Big Fat Hen* by Keith Baker
▩ *One, Two, Buckle My Shoe* by Heather Collins

PREPARATION FOR "ONE, TWO, BUCKLE MY SHOE" ACTIVITIES AND EXPERIENCES

▩ Make the "One, Two, Buckle My Shoe" flannel board rhyme (Appendix p. 601-602).
▩ Make Mystery Pictures Folders (see p. 326).
▩ Collect shoes that buckle and cardboard boxes.

Language Enrichment Choices*

▨ Invite the children to march around the room as you recite "One, Two, Buckle My Shoe." Repeat the rhyme three or four times. Each time you say, "big fat hen," stop quickly.

▨ Discuss the possible new words in the rhyme such as *buckle, straight*, and *hen*. The children are probably familiar with the word *chicken*, but they may not know the word *hen*.

▨ Invite the children to use the flannel board pieces to practice saying the rhyme. To help the children learn it, say a line and then encourage them to fill in rhyming words or the last word of all the sentences.

▨ Review the American Sign Language sign for *fat* (see Appendix p. 432).

Physical Development Choices

▨ Invite the children to act out "Little Chicks." Talk about the mother hen taking care of her babies.

Little Chicks
Little chicks say, "Peep, peep, peep,"
As they wake from sleep, sleep, sleep. (rub eyes)
Little chicks say, "Peep, peep, peep,"
And hear the birds go "cheep, cheep, cheep." (repeat "cheep, cheep, cheep")
Little chicks say, "Peep, peep, peep,"
We are hungry, "Peep, peep, peep." (rub belly)
Mama feeds them and then she says,
"Now it's time to sleep, sleep, sleep." (lay head in hands)

▨ Play Hide and Seek with the children. Count to 10 before uncovering your eyes and starting the hunt.

Social and Emotional Development Choices

▨ Talk with each child about the many ways his clothing fastens. Remind the children that buckles can hold their shoes in place but are also found on belts and overalls.

* Toddlers and twos present a wide range of developmental needs, abilities, and interests. For each learning area, select among the following activity and experience choices that are appropriate for the children in your care.

- Discuss opening and shutting doors. Show the children how to carefully open and shut the classroom door. Discuss opening and closing doors gently, and not slamming doors. Point out the safety issues related to opening and closing doors. For example, explain that when they open a door, they must open it slowly and be careful not to open it into someone who may be on the other side of the door. They must also be careful not to close their fingers in the door. Look around the classroom for other kinds of doors, such as those on cabinets.

Cognitive Development Choices

- Provide buckets or pails and tongue depressors. Invite the children to spill the "sticks" (tongue depressors) and then pick them up and put them in the bucket. Encourage them to say the lines of the rhyme, "Five, six, pick up sticks, seven, eight, lay them straight" as they play with the sticks.

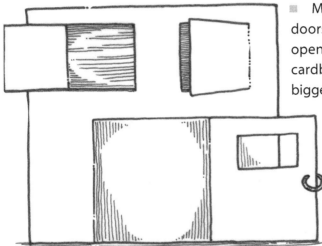

- Make cardboard houses out of small boxes. Cut doors into each house and show the children how to open and shut the doors. If you have access to a large cardboard box, (e.g., a large refrigerator box), make a bigger house that children can actually play inside.

- Provide dress-up clothes for the children to explore. Discuss the many ways that the clothing items fasten.

- Provide a variety of shoes that buckle. Invite the children to practice buckling the shoes. Encourage them to say, "One, two, buckle my shoe" as they work with the buckles.

- Provide pictures of hens for the children to look at. "Is the hen fat?" "What color is she?"

- Invite the children to explore Mystery Pictures Folders. Glue pictures to the inside of file folders. Cut small flaps (doors) into the outside of the folders. Encourage the children to open the doors, one at a time, and identify the pictures inside the door. You should be able to include four or five pictures in each folder.

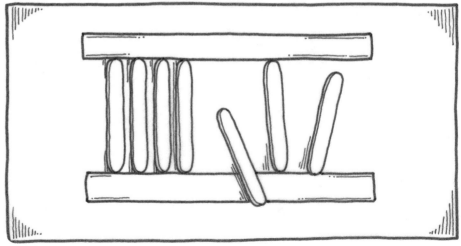

- Invite the children to paint using a feather as a brush. Encourage the children to talk about their paintings.

- Problem-solving suggestion: Place two 12" strips of masking tape on a tabletop, one over the other, with a distance between them that is equal to the length of a Popsicle stick. Give the children a handful of Popsicle sticks and help them lay the sticks out straight, using the masking tape strips as a guide. Encourage them to say, "Seven, eight, lay them straight" as they work.

REFLECTION ON THE DAY

Ask the children to say the "One, Two, Buckle My Shoe" rhyme with you. If they can't say the rhyme, ask them to tell you what the rhyme is about.

Favorite Songs

ITSY BITSY SPIDER

TWINKLE, TWINKLE LITTLE STAR

IF YOU'RE HAPPY AND YOU KNOW IT

OLD MACDONALD HAD A FARM

THE WHEELS ON THE BUS

Itsy Bitsy Spider

WORDS TO PRACTICE

down	spider	up
rain	sun	waterspout

GETTING STARTED

- Sing "Itsy Bitsy Spider" with the children. Tell the children that today they will learn more about the song. "Who has seen a spider?" "Where did you see it?" "What was it doing?"

   Itsy Bitsy Spider
   The itsy bitsy spider
   Went up the waterspout.
   Down came the rain
   And washed the spider out.
   Up came the sun
   And dried up all the rain.
   And the itsy bitsy spider
   Went up the spout again.

- Read your favorite book about this song or another children's song to the children or select a book from the Story Circle Suggestions below to check out of the library and read.

STORY CIRCLE SUGGESTIONS

- *Itsy Bitsy Spider* retold by Pam Schiller
- *The Itsy Bitsy Spider* by Iza Trapani
- *The Itsy Bitsy Spider* by Rosemary Wells

PREPARATION FOR "ITSY BITSY SPIDER" ACTIVITIES AND EXPERIENCES

- Make the "Miss Muffet" flannel board rhyme (Appendix p. 597-599), if not already made.
- Make Pipe Cleaner Spiders (see p. 332).

Language Enrichment Choices*

- Sing the "Itsy Bitsy Spider." Discuss the vocabulary in the song—*up, down, itsy, bitsy, spider, waterspout, rain,* and *sun.* Take a walk outdoors to look for a *waterspout* (gutter). If none are available outdoors, show the children the waterspout on a sink.

- Ask older toddlers where they think the spider was going. Ask them if this spider could be the same spider that is in the "Miss Muffet" nursery rhyme. Encourage them to explain their thinking.

- Teach the children the American Sign Language sign for *spider* (Appendix p. 438). Review the signs for *up, down, sun,* and *rain.*

Physical Development Choices

- Show the children how to use their fingers as a spider. Encourage them to dance their fingers like a happy spider, a mad spider, a frightened spider, and a funny spider.

- Show the children how to walk like four-legged spiders by placing their hands on the floor and keeping their legs straight to walk on all fours. Play some music and let the children do some "spider dancing."

- Show older twos how to do the spider walk. Stand four children back-to-back in a circle. Ask them to hook their elbows for support and then attempt to walk using eight legs. You decide on the direction.

Social and Emotional Development Choices

- Discuss the lesson in the song, which is determination. You might explain to the children that the harder they try to do something that may be difficult, the better they will become at doing it.

- Present the "Miss Muffet" flannel board rhyme (Appendix p. 597-599) to the children. Ask the children if they think that the spider was afraid of Miss Muffet. Remind them that Miss Muffet is much bigger than the spider. Ask the children what they think the spider might have said to Miss Muffet to frighten her.

- Sing the song, changing the description of the spider. Match the sound of your voice to the description of the spider. For example, you can sing about the "very happy spider," "big enormous spider," "silly-nilly spider," and the "very timid spider."

* Toddlers and twos present a wide range of developmental needs, abilities, and interests. For each learning area, select among the following activity and experience choices that are appropriate for the children in your care.

Cognitive Development Choices

▨ Provide a light source and show the children how to wiggle their fingers to make a shadow spider on the wall. Make the spider go up and then down.

▨ Make Pipe Cleaner Spiders and give them to the children to play with. Cut pipe cleaners in half and then twist four pipe cleaners together at their center to create an eight-legged spider. Attach a piece of elastic thread to make a dancing spider puppet.

▨ Place a teaspoon of black tempera paint on a piece of construction paper. Give the children straws and encourage them to blow on the paint to create a spider.
Safety Warning: Make sure the children blow OUT, not in. Cut a small slit or hole near the blowing end of the straw to prevent the children from sucking paint into their mouths.

▨ Take a walk outdoors to look for spiders and spider webs. Remind the children not to touch any creatures outdoors. "Where should we look for spiders?"

▨ Display a real spider in a jar, if possible. Provide a magnifying glass so the children can get a closer look at it. Be sure to let the spider go at the end of the day.

▨ Provide photographs of spiders and spider webs. Discuss the photos with the children. "How many legs does a spider have?" "What color are they?" "Are the webs pretty?"

▨ Take a spray bottle of water and a Pipe Cleaner Spider outdoors. Place the spider on a table or on the sidewalk. Show the children how to move the spider by spraying it with a stream of water. Let each child have a try.

REFLECTION ON THE DAY

Ask the children to tell you what the song is about. Ask the "not yet talkers" to do the hand motions to the song as you sing it.

Twinkle, Twinkle Little Star

WORDS TO PRACTICE	above	star
	diamond	twinkle
	sky	up

world

GETTING STARTED

▨ Sing "Twinkle, Twinkle Little Star" with the children. Tell the children that today they will learn more about this song. "Where can you see stars?" "When can you see stars?" "Where are the stars during the daytime?"

Twinkle, Twinkle Little Star
Twinkle, twinkle, little star,
How I wonder what you are!
Up above the world so high,
Like a diamond in the sky.
Twinkle, twinkle, little star,
How I wonder what you are!

▨ Read your favorite book about this song or another children's song to the children or select a book from the Story Circle Suggestions below to check out of the library and read.

STORY CIRCLE SUGGESTIONS

▨ *Twinkle, Twinkle, Little Star* by Heather Collins
▨ *Twinkle, Twinkle, Little Star* by Iza Trapani
▨ *Twinkle, Twinkle, Little Star: A Traditional Lullaby* by Jane Taylor

PREPARATION FOR "TWINKLE, TWINKLE LITTLE STAR" ACTIVITIES AND EXPERIENCES

- Prepare gelatin in advance.
- Make the "Twinkle, Twinkle Little Star" Song Cards (Appendix p. 611-612).
- Cut out large poster board stars and felt stars and moon.
- Cut out Fun Foam Stars, sponge stars, and white construction paper stars.
- Make Star Puzzles (see p. 336).
- Get rock salt and stick-on stars and dots.

Language Enrichment Choices*

- Sing "Twinkle, Twinkle, Little Star" using the "Twinkle, Twinkle, Little Star" Song Cards (Appendix p. 611-612) to illustrate the song. Discuss the vocabulary in the song—*up, above, high, diamond, world,* and *sky.*

- Change the words of the song to reflect different-sized stars, such as a teeny star and a great big star. Sing the song in a voice that is appropriate for the size of the star. For example, sing about the "teeny star" in a tiny, quiet voice.

- Ask older toddlers about the stars they see at night. "What do they look like?" "Where are they located?"

- Teach the children the American Sign Language sign for *star* (Appendix p. 438). Review the signs for *up, in,* and *above.*

Physical Development Choices

- Invite the children to do Star Jumping. Cut out large stars from poster board, cover them with clear contact paper, and tape them to the floor. Encourage the children to jump from star to star.

- Challenge the children to Catch a Star. Cut out stars from Fun Foam. Cut them large, but small enough for the children to handle. Toss a star to the children and see if they can catch it.

- Invite the children to toss the Fun Foam stars into a box or basket.

- Hide construction paper stars around the room and encourage the children to go on a Star Search. Hide the stars so part of each star is visible to the children.

* Toddlers and twos present a wide range of developmental needs, abilities, and interests. For each learning area, select among the following activity and experience choices that are appropriate for the children in your care.

Social and Emotional Development Choices

- Teach the children "Star Light, Star Bright." Give older children a white construction paper star and ask them to make a wish. Write their wishes on their stars and post the stars on the classroom door.

  Star Light, Star Bright
  Star light, star bright,
  First star I've seen tonight.
  I wish I may, I wish I might,
  Have this wish, I wish tonight.

- Make Star-Shaped Gelatin Jigglers. Mix flavored gelatin with half the amount of water suggested on the box. Pour onto a cookie sheet and refrigerate. Help the children cut it into star shapes using a star-shaped cookie cutter.

Cognitive Development Choices

- Cut out stars and a moon from white felt and encourage the children to create a starry night sky on the flannel board. "Which is bigger: a star or the moon?"

- Give each child a piece of black or blue construction paper, a white construction paper moon, and some rock salt to use as stars. Encourage them to glue the moon and the stars (rock salt) to their construction paper to make a nighttime sky. **Caution:** Supervise closely so children do not eat the rock salt.

- Challenge older twos to use large tweezers to pick up rock salt "stars." Show them how to transfer the stars from a black piece of felt to a bowl. Tell them they are collecting stars. **Caution:** Supervise closely so children do not eat the rock salt.

- Display pictures of night skies. Encourage the children to point out the stars and the moon. "What else is in the sky?" (clouds)

- Provide star-shaped cookie cutters and encourage the children to cut out stars from playdough.

- Cut sponges into star shapes and invite the children to sponge paint white stars on blue construction paper. Attach clothespins to the sponges to make them easier to manipulate. Do the stars on their paintings look like the stars they see in the sky?

■ Provide stick-on stars and let the children stick the stars to a piece of paper. Provide a white stick-on dot for the moon.

■ Problem-solving suggestions:
1. Give the children Star Puzzles to put together. Cut out large stars from poster board. Laminate them and cut them into three or four puzzle pieces.
2. Give the children the "Twinkle, Twinkle Little Star" Song Cards (Appendix p. 611-612) and invite them to arrange the cards in an order that reflects the words of the song. Encourage them to sing the song while they work.

REFLECTION ON THE DAY

Ask the children to tell you what the song is about. Encourage the "not yet talkers" to do the hand motions to the song as you sing it.

If You're Happy and You Know It

WORDS TO PRACTICE

clap

happy

stomp

GETTING STARTED

▦ Sing "If You're Happy and You Know It" with the children. Tell the children that today they will learn more about this song. "What does it mean when you clap your hands?"

> **If You're Happy and You Know It**
> *If you're happy and you know it, clap your hands.*
>   (clap hands twice)
> *If you're happy and you know it, clap your hands.* (repeat)
> *If you're happy and you know it then your face will
>   surely show it.* (point to face)
> *If you're happy and you know it, clap your hands.*
>   (clap hands twice)

Additional verses:
> *Stomp your feet* (stomp feet twice)
> *Shout hurray!* (raise hand)

▦ Read your favorite book about this song or another children's song to the children or select a book from the Story Circle Suggestions below to check out of the library and read.

STORY CIRCLE SUGGESTIONS

▦ *Daisy Says If You're Happy and You Know It* by Jane Simmons

▦ *If You're Happy and You Know It* by David Carter

▦ *If You're Happy and You Know It* by Penny Dann

PREPARATION FOR "IF YOU'RE HAPPY AND YOU KNOW IT" ACTIVITIES AND EXPERIENCES

▨ Prepare the "What Makes Me Laugh?" flannel board rhyme (Appendix p. 576-578).

▨ Make the Pin the Mouth on the Happy Face Game (see p. 339), Make Happy/Sad Face Puppets (see p. 341), and Happy Face Puzzles (see p. 342).

▨ Gather English muffins, pizza sauce, olives, mushrooms, pepperoni, and cheese for Happy Face Pizzas (see p. 341).

Language Enrichment Choices*

▨ Sing "If You're Happy and You Know It," changing the requested actions in the song. For example, "If you're happy and you know it, point to a friend,""…point to the door," or "…point to something red."

▨ Discuss the vocabulary in the song. Ask the children to show you their happy faces. Ask them to show you their hands and feet. "What other things can you do with your hands and feet?"

▨ Present the "What Makes Me Laugh?" flannel board rhyme (Appendix p. 576-578). Follow up on the last line of the rhyme, which is "What makes you laugh?"

▨ Teach or review the American Sign Language signs for *happy*, *hands*, and *feet* (Appendix p. 432-433).

Physical Development Choices

▨ Teach the children one of the following "I Clap My Hands" action rhymes. Suit the actions to the words. Demonstrate various ways to clap your hands for different reasons. For example, clapping your hands when you are happy, when you want someone's attention, and when you are applauding someone's effort.

I Clap My Hands (Version 1)
I clap my hands to make a sound—
Clap, clap, clap!
I tap my toe to make a sound—
Tap, tap, tap!

I open my mouth to say a word—
Talk, talk, talk!
I pick up my foot to take a step—
Walk, walk, walk!

* Toddlers and twos present a wide range of developmental needs, abilities, and interests. For each learning area, select among the following activity and experience choices that are appropriate for the children in your care.

I Clap My Hands (Version 2)
I clap my hands, I touch my feet,
I jump up from the ground.
I clap my hands, I touch my feet,
And turn myself around.

▪ Teach the children "Five Little Fingers." Ask them to show you how their fingers move when they are happy. If they need help, give them some ideas like dancing your fingers, hopping your fingers up and down and wiggling your fingers.

Five Little Fingers
One little finger standing on its own. (hold up index finger)
Two little fingers, now they're not alone. (hold up middle finger)
Three little fingers happy as can be. (hold up ring finger)
Four little fingers go walking down the street. (hold up all fingers)
Five little fingers—this one is a thumb. (hold up four fingers and thumb)
Wave bye-bye 'cause now we are done. (wave bye-bye)

▪ Play Pin the Mouth on the Happy Face. Draw a happy face without the mouth on a piece of yellow poster board or construction paper and laminate. Cut out a red semi-circle mouth (smiling mouth) from red construction paper. Loop a piece of masking tape, sticky side out, and attach it to the back of the mouth. Challenge the children to close their eyes and try to stick the mouth in the correct spot on the happy face. Landing in the wrong spot should result in giggles!

▪ Invite the children to play rhythm band instruments while they sing, "If You're Happy and You Know It." Encourage them to shake their instruments with enthusiasm at the points in the song that they would have clapped their hands. Replace the words in the song "clap your hands" with "make some noise."

▪ Invite the children to do a happy dance with streamers to some happy music. Mention that upbeat music makes us feel happy.

Social and Emotional Development Choices

■ Sing "I Have Something in My Pocket" with the children. Discuss the fact that we smile when we are happy. Explain to the children that when we smile, people can tell we are happy just by looking at our faces.

I Have Something in My Pocket
I have something in my pocket,
It belongs across my face.
I keep it very close at hand
In a most convenient place.

I bet you could not guess it,
If you guessed a long, long while.
So I'll take it out and put it on,
It's a great, big, happy SMILE!

■ Talk with the children about how the people they love and people in their families make them happy. "What things do you do with your families that make you feel happy?" Share the poem below with them.

Mommy and me dance and sing.
Daddy and me laugh and play.
Mommy, Daddy and me
Dance and sing,
Laugh and play,
Kiss and hug
A zillion times a day!
　　　　　—by Pam Schiller

■ Sit each child in front of an unbreakable mirror and encourage her to look at the features on her face. Say the poem, "I Look in the Mirror" to them as the two of you look at your faces. Suit actions to the rhyme.

I Look in the Mirror by Pam Schiller
I look in the mirror and what do I see?
I see a funny face looking at me.
A scrunched-up nose, twisted mouth, squinty eyes,
And two fuzzy eyebrows—what a surprise!
I look in the mirror and what do I do?
I giggle and laugh at the sight of me.

▪ Describe some things that make you laugh. Ask the children about things that make them laugh. Read the rhyme, "You Make Me Laugh" below. Tell the children that laughing is good for them. It keeps them healthy and it helps them do a better job of remembering things they learn.

> **You Make Me Laugh** by Pam Schiller
> *You make me laugh!*
> *You stick out your tongue—I jump with joy.*
> *You make a funny face—I can barely contain myself.*
> *You play a game with me—I wiggle and giggle.*
> *You wear a goofy hat—I'm in awesome wonder.*
> *We make silly faces in the mirror—I shake with delight.*
> *You talk to me—I babble and coo and smile.*
> *You tickle me—I laugh out loud.*
> *You give me a hug—I smile from the inside out.*
> *You make me laugh!*

▪ Invite the children to make Happy Face Pizzas. Give each child half of an English muffin. Invite them to spread pizza sauce on the muffin with a pastry brush and then create a face using olives for eyes, a mushroom for a nose, and slice of pepperoni cut into a smile (quarter-moon shape) for a mouth. Sprinkle with cheese and toast in a toaster oven at 375° for 10 minutes (adult only). **Safety Warning:** Always check for allergies before serving food.

▪ Sing "If You're Happy and You Know It," changing the emotions expressed. For example, "If you're sad and you know it say, 'boohoo'" and "If you're surprised and you know it say, 'Oh, my!'"

Cognitive Development Choices

▪ Invite the children to play Tummy Ticklers. Ask them to lie on the floor on their backs with their heads on someone else's tummy. Do something silly to make the children start laughing. "What is making your head jiggle?" This activity should cause contagious laughter.

▪ Make Happy/Sad Face Puppets for the children. Cut out circles from yellow construction paper. Draw happy faces on some and sad faces on the others, and laminate them. Glue a happy face and a sad face back to back on a tongue depressor. Encourage older children to think of a reason the puppet might be happy and why it might be sad.

- Place fingerpaint directly on a tabletop. Show the children how to use their fingers to draw a happy face in the paint. Show them how to cover their hands with paint and make a handprint on a piece of paper.

- Encourage the children to look through books and magazines for pictures of people with happy faces. "What do they think might have made this person happy?" "How can you tell when a person is happy?"

- Teach the children a clapping pattern such as clap, clap, pause, clap or clap, pause, clap, pause.

- Cut out facial features and a round face from felt. Encourage the children to make faces on the flannel board. Be sure to use several shades of skin tone for the face itself and a variety of eye colors for the eyes.

- Problem-solving suggestion: Make a Happy Face Puzzle and encourage the children to put it together. Draw a Happy Face on a piece of poster board, laminate it, and cut it into three or four puzzle pieces.

REFLECTION ON THE DAY
Ask the children to tell you what the song is about. Ask the "not yet talkers" to do the hand motions to the song as you sing it.

Old MacDonald Had a Farm

WORDS TO PRACTICE

cat	hen
cow	horse
dog	pig
duck	rooster
farm	sheep

GETTING STARTED

Sing "Old MacDonald Had a Farm" with the children. Tell the children that today they will be learning more about Old MacDonald and his farm. "Has anyone ever been to a farm?" "Has anyone ever seen a cow?" "Where?"

Old MacDonald Had a Farm

Old MacDonald had a farm
E-I-E-I-O
And on this farm she had a cow
E-I-E-I-O
With a moo, moo here,
And a moo, moo there,
Here a moo, there a moo,
Everywhere a moo, moo.
Old MacDonald had a farm
E-I-E-I-O!

Additional verses:
  Pig—oink, oink
  Cat—meow, meow
  Dog—bow-wow
  Horse—neigh, neigh
  Duck—quack, quack
  Rooster—cock-a-doodle-do
  Hen—cluck, cluck

- Read your favorite book about this song, another children's song, or a farm to the children or select a book from the Story Circle Suggestions below to check out of the library and read.

STORY CIRCLE SUGGESTIONS
- *Barnyard Banter* by Denise Fleming
- *Old MacDonald Had a Farm* by Carol Jones
- *Old MacDonald Had a Farm* by David A. Carter
- *Old MacDonald Had a Farm* by Penny Dann

PREPARATION FOR "OLD MACDONALD HAD A FARM" ACTIVITIES AND EXPERIENCES
- Make the "Old MacDonald Had a Farm" Song Cards (Appendix p. 607-610) and "The Little Red Hen" flannel board story (Appendix p. 518-522).
- Make a cassette recording of animals sounds.
- Gather pictures of baby animals and their mothers.
- Cut out animal shapes from poster board.
- Make Farm Animal Puzzles (see p. 346).

Language Enrichment Choices*

- Sing "Old MacDonald Had a Farm" using the "Old MacDonald Had a Farm" Song Cards (Appendix. p. 607-610) to illustrate the song as you sing it.

- Ask the children if any of them have been on a farm. Show them a picture of a farm. Discuss the animals and the purpose of the farm.

- Present the "Little Red Hen" flannel board story (Appendix p. 518-522)."Which animals appear both in 'Old MacDonald's Farm' and the story of 'The Little Red Hen'?"

- Teach the children the American Sign Language sign for *farm* (Appendix p. 432). Review the signs for any animals that the children have learned.

Physical Development Choices

- Play "The Farmer in the Dell" with the children. Choose one child to be the Farmer. The other children walk in a circle around the Farmer. Sing the song together.

The Farmer in the Dell
The farmer in the dell, the farmer in the dell.
Heigh-ho the derry-o, the farmer in the dell.

* Toddlers and twos present a wide range of developmental needs, abilities, and interests. For each learning area, select among the following activity and experience choices that are appropriate for the children in your care.

The farmer takes a wife/husband/friend. (Farmer brings a second child into
  the circle)
The farmer takes a wife/husband/friend.
Heigh-ho the derry-o,
The farmer takes a wife/husband/friend.

The wife/husband/friend takes a child… (Wife chooses a third child to join in
  the circle)
The child takes a dog…
The dog takes a cat…
The cat takes a rat…
The rat takes the cheese…

The cheese stands alone… (Everyone except Cheese leaves the center of
  the circle)

▨ Show the children how to move like different farm animals. They can stretch
like cats, roll over like dogs, waddle like ducks, and roll on their backs like pigs.

Social and Emotional Development Choices

▨ Show the children pictures of baby animals and their mothers. Talk about how
mother animals take care of their babies.

▨ Act out "Baby Chicks" with the children.

Baby Chicks
Baby chicks say, "Peep, peep, peep,"
As they wake from sleep, sleep, sleep. (rub eyes)
Baby chicks say, "Peep, peep, peep,"
And hear the birds go "cheep, cheep, cheep." (repeat "cheep, cheep, cheep")
Baby chicks say, "Peep, peep, peep,"
We are hungry, "Peep, peep, peep." (rub belly)
Mama feeds them and then she says,
"Now it's time to sleep, sleep, sleep."
  (lay head in hands)

345

- Sing "Five Little Ducks" with the children. "Where do ducks live on the farm?" "What do ducks do all day?" "Where might the ducks have been hiding when their mother/father couldn't find them?"

  Five Little Ducks
  Five little ducks went out one day,
  Over the hills and far away.
  Papa duck called with a "Quack, quack, quack."
  Four little ducks came swimming back.

  Repeat, losing one more duck each time until only one duck is left. For that verse, Mama duck calls and it ends with "five little ducks came swimming back."

Cognitive Development Choices

- Provide a tub of dried grass (hay). Hide plastic farm animals in the hay and encourage the children to find them. Name the animals as the children find them. Ask older children to name the animals as they find them.

- Provide playdough and animal cookie cutters. Encourage the children to cut out some farm animals. Encourage them to name the animal as they cut it out.

- Build a farm with blocks. Provide plastic animals for the farm. Encourage the children to play with the farm and animals. Talk with the children about where the animals live.

- Make Farm Animal Puzzles by making photocopies of the animals in the "Old MacDonald Had a Farm" Song Cards (Appendix p. 607-610). Color them, laminate them, and cut them into simple puzzles.

- Invite the children to arrange the "Old MacDonald Had a Farm" Song Cards as they sing the song.

- Problem-solving suggestion: Give the children a recording of animal sounds and the illustrations from the "Old MacDonald Had a Farm" Song Cards. Encourage them to match each animal to the sound it makes. "Which animal sound do you like best?"

REFLECTION ON THE DAY
Ask the children to tell you what the song is about. Ask the "not yet talkers" to point to each farm animal as you name it.

The Wheels on the Bus

WORDS TO PRACTICE

bus	round
driver	town
horn	wheels
money	windshield wipers

GETTING STARTED

- Sing "The Wheels on the Bus" with the children. Tell the children that today they will be learning more of the song.

   The Wheels on the Bus
   The wheels on the bus go round and round, (move hands in circular motion)
   Round and round, round and round.
   The wheels on the bus go round and round,
   All around the town. (extend arms up and out)

   Additional Verses
   The wipers on the bus go swish, swish, swish. (sway hands back and forth)
   The baby on the bus goes, "Wah, wah, wah." (rub eyes)
   People on the bus go up and down. (stand up, sit down)
   The horn on the bus goes beep, beep, beep. (pretend to beep horn)
   The money on the bus goes clink, clink, clink. (drop change in)
   The driver on the bus says, "Move on back." (hitchhiking movement)

- Read your favorite book about this song or another children's song to the children or select a book from the Story Circle Suggestions below to check out of the library and read.

STORY CIRCLE SUGGESTIONS
- *The Wheels on the Bus* by Maryann Kovalski
- *The Wheels on the Bus* by Paul O. Zelinsly
- *The Wheels on the Bus* by Raffi

PREPARATION FOR "THE WHEELS ON THE BUS" ACTIVITIES AND EXPERIENCES
- Make "The Wheels on the Bus" Song Cards (Appendix p. 613-615).
- Locate a bus driver's hat.

Language Enrichment Choices*

- Sing "The Wheels on the Bus" using "The Wheels on the Bus" Song Cards (Appendix p. 613-615) to illustrate the song as you sing. Discuss words in the song that may be new to the children such as *bus, wheels, horn, money*, and *driver*.

- Ask the children about their experience with buses. "Has anyone been on a bus?" Talk with the children about how they travel to school. Tell them that older children often go to school on a bus and that many people travel to their jobs on a bus. Show the children pictures of buses.

- Teach the children the American Sign Language sign for *wheels* (Appendix p. 439). Review the signs for *on* and *round*.

Physical Development Choices

- Give the older twos "wheels" (Styrofoam plates) to roll. For younger children, roll the "wheels" and let them catch them. Point out that the wheels go round and round as they roll.

- Sing "My Little Red Wagon" with the children. "How does the ride in the wagon resemble the ride on the bus?" Sing the verse of the song about the people going up and down.

    My Little Red Wagon
    Bumping up and down in my little red wagon,
    Bumping up and down in my little red wagon,
    Bumping up and down in my little red wagon
    Won't you be my darlin'?

* Toddlers and twos present a wide range of developmental needs, abilities, and interests. For each learning area, select among the following activity and experience choices that are appropriate for the children in your care.

Social and Emotional Development Choices

▧ Sing the verse of the song about the babies going, "Wah, wah, wah." Help the children think of ways they can calm a crying baby. Give them dolls to pretend with. Provide blankets, pacifiers, bottles, and baby squeeze toys. Show them how to rock the baby and how to hum the baby a lullaby.

▧ Remind the children that buses provide a means of travel for people to get from one place to another. Talk with the children about how they travel from one place to another—on their feet. Teach them the song, "Walk, Walk, Walk Your Feet" to the tune of "Row, Row, Row Your Boat."

> **Walk, Walk, Walk Your Feet**
> *Walk, walk, walk your feet*
> *Everywhere you go.*
> *Walk 'em fast, walk 'em slow*
> *Walk them heel to toe.*

Cognitive Development Choices

▧ Give the children small cars, trucks, and buses to play with. Help them use blocks to build a town and some roads for their vehicles to travel. Encourage them to name the vehicles as they use them.

▧ Provide small cars and tempera paint. Pour tempera paint into a shallow tray (meat trays work well). Encourage the children to roll the cars in the paint and then on a piece of paper to create tire tracks.

▧ If there is a bus on the premises or close by, take the children on a tour of the bus or at least outside to get a closer look at the bus.

▧ If available, provide a bus driver's hat (or captain's hat) so the children can pretend to be the bus driver. Ask them to sing the verse of the song about the bus driver saying, "Move on back."

▧ Provide a squeeze horn and encourage the children to try it out. Can they make it beep by squeezing it and stepping on it? Encourage the children to sing the verse of the song about the horns going beep, beep, beep.

- On the playground give the children squeegees to play with. Provide a spray bottle of water and let them wipe the water away with the wipers (squeegees). Encourage the children to sing the verse of the song about the wipers going swish, swish, swish.

- Give the children large washers to represent money to drop into a jar. "Does it make a clinking sound?" Invite the children to toss the washers into a tin pail or dish. "What sound does it make?" "What sound do you hear when you drop the money (washers) on a carpet square?" Encourage the children to sing the verse of the song about the money going clink, clink, clink.
  Safety Warning: Supervise closely so children do not put the washers in their mouths.

- Provide spools and tempera paint. Encourage the children to use the spools to make painted wheels on their paper. "What shape are the wheels?"

- Encourage the children to roll spools across the floor. Point out that the spools are going round and round just like wheels.

- Problem-solving suggestion: Invite the children to place "The Wheels on the Bus" Song Cards (Appendix p. 613-615) in an order that represents the verses of the song. Encourage them to sing the song as they arrange the cards.

REFLECTION ON THE DAY
Ask the children to tell you what the song is about. Ask the "not yet talkers" to do the hand motions to the song as you sing it.

Favorite Stories

Goldilocks and the Three Bears

WORDS TO PRACTICE

baby	mama	papa
bears	manners	small
large	medium	

GETTING STARTED

- Present "Goldilocks and the Three Bears" magnetic story (Appendix p. 485-491). Use a cookie sheet for a background. Ask questions about the story. "Where were the bears when Goldilocks came to their house?" "Which bear had a big voice and a big bed?"

- Tell the children that today they will learn more about the story, "Goldilocks and the Three Bears."

- Read your favorite version of this story to the children or select a book from the Story Circle Suggestions below to check out of the library and read.

STORY CIRCLE SUGGESTIONS

- *Goldilocks and the Three Bears* by Jan Brett
- *Goldilocks and the Three Bears* by Valeri Gorbachev
- *Three Bears* by Paul Galdone

PREPARATION FOR "THE THREE BEARS" ACTIVITIES AND EXPERIENCES

- Make "The Three Bears" magnetic story (Appendix p. 485-491).
- Make the Walk-On Nursery Rhyme path (on the next page).

Language Enrichment Choices*

- Discuss the words *small, medium,* and *large* as they are used in the story. Use the magnetic story (Appendix p. 485-491) to sort the beds, porridge bowls, and chairs that belong to each bear.

* Toddlers and twos present a wide range of developmental needs, abilities, and interests. For each learning area, select among the following activity and experience choices that are appropriate for the children in your care.

- Discuss the size of the children's eating utensils and the size of the utensils that their parents use. Have a child-size and adult-size plate, cup, fork, and spoon available for comparison. "Which size plates, cups, and utensils do you prefer?" "Why?"

- Teach or review the American Sign Language signs for *small* and *large* (Appendix p. 434, 437).

Physical Development Choices

- Prepare a Walk-On Nursery Rhyme path and invite the children to walk it to the following chant, "Goldilocks, Goldilocks." To make the path, cut a piece of butcher paper 15' long. Draw the following items on the paper in this sequence: a pair of feet (trace shoes), a spiral arrow, a pair of walking feet, grass, a pair of walking feet, a door, a pair of walking feet, a bowl, a pair of walking feet, a chair, a pair of walking feet, a bed, a pair of walking feet, and finally, a pair of walking feet going off the end of the paper. Laminate for durability.

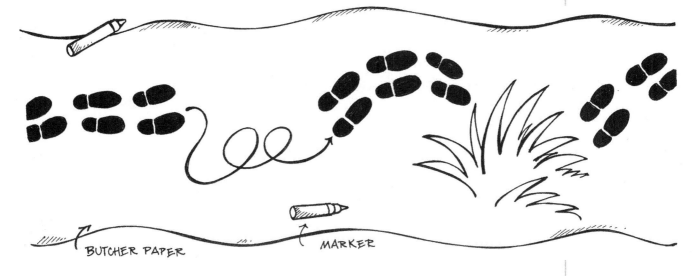

BUTCHER PAPER   MARKER

Goldilocks, Goldilocks
Goldilocks, Goldilocks, turn around. (turn around)
Goldilocks, Goldilocks, touch the ground. (touch the ground)
Goldilocks, Goldilocks, knock on the door. (knock with hand)
Goldilocks, Goldilocks, eat some porridge. (pretend to eat porridge)
Goldilocks, Goldilocks, have a seat. (squat)
Goldilocks, Goldilocks, go to sleep. (put head on folded hands)
Goldilocks, Goldilocks, run, run, run. (run off paper and back to beginning)

- Say the "Teddy Bear, Teddy Bear" chant (on the next page). "How is it similar to the 'Goldilocks, Goldilocks' chant?" Suit the actions to the words.

Teddy Bear, Teddy Bear

Teddy bear, teddy bear, turn around.
Teddy bear, teddy bear, touch the ground.
Teddy bear, teddy bear, touch your shoe.
Teddy bear, teddy bear, say, "How-di-do."
Teddy bear, teddy bear, go up the stairs.
Teddy bear, teddy bear, say your prayers.
Teddy bear, teddy bear, turn out the light.
Teddy bear, teddy bear, say good night.

Social and Emotional Development Choices

- Sing "Once There Were Three Brown Bears" to the tune of "Twinkle, Twinkle, Little Star." Point out the temperature of each bear's porridge, the sizes of each bear's chair, and the feel of each bear's bed.

Once There Were Three Brown Bears

There once were three brown bears,
Mother, Father, Baby Bear.
Mother's food was way too cold.
Father's food was way too hot.
Baby's food was all gone.
Someone ate it, so he cried.

There once were three brown bears,
Mother, Father, Baby Bear.
Mother's chair was way too low.
Father's chair was way too high.
Baby's chair was just so right,
But when she sat, she broke it.

There once were three brown bears,
Mother, Father, Baby Bear.
Mother's bed was way too soft.
Father's bed was way too hard.
Baby's bed was occupied.
Someone strange was sleeping there.

"Come here quickly," Baby cried.
"Someone's sleeping in my bed!"
"Who are you?" asked Baby Bear.
"Who are you?" asked Goldilocks.
"You better run," said Baby Bear.
"I will!" said Goldilocks.

- Discuss manners. Explain to the children that manners are the rules that tell us how we should behave. Talk about not going into someone's home uninvited. Remind the children that Goldilocks didn't use her manners. Discuss the use of "please" and "thank you." Teach the children the following rhyme, "Thank You."

Thank You

My hands say thank you
With a clap, clap, clap.
My feet say thank you
With a tap, tap, tap.

Clap, clap, clap.
Tap, tap, tap.
I turn around,
Touch the ground,
And with a bow,
I say, "Thank you" now.

- Invite the children to sample some porridge (oatmeal). Discuss its temperature and its texture.
  Safety Warning: Always check for allergies before serving food to children.

Cognitive Development Choices

- Provide sponges cut into bear shapes and brown tempera paint. Encourage the children to make a sponge painting of bears. Attach clothespins to the sponges to make them easier to manipulate. Talk with the children as they paint.

- Show the children either a bear from the story or a stuffed bear. Ask them to show you the bear's nose and then their own nose, the bear's feet and then their own feet, and the bear's ears and then their own ears.

- Give the children a large and a small chair to sit in. Ask them which is more comfortable for them. If a medium-size chair is available, use it too. "Which chair do you like best?"

- Provide stuffed bears for the children to play with. Ask them to describe the texture of the bears.

- Encourage the children to arrange large, medium, and small spoons from largest to smallest. How do they know which spoon is the largest?

- Problem-solving suggestion: Give the children the magnetic story (Appendix p. 485-491) to play with. Help them organize the props in the story. Talk with them about the characters and the items that belong to each bear. "How do you know which item belongs to each bear?"

REFLECTION ON THE DAY
Ask the children to tell you what happens in the story. Ask younger toddlers to show you the papa bear, the mama bear, and the baby bear.

The Three Little Pigs

WORDS TO PRACTICE

bricks	huff	sticks
ears	pig	straw
feet	puff	tail
houses	snout	wolf

GETTING STARTED

- Present "The Three Little Pigs" flannel board story (Appendix p. 568-570) to the children. Ask questions about the story. "Why were the pigs building houses?" "Who tried to get inside the houses?" "Who huffed and puffed?"
- Tell the children that today the will learn more about the story, "The Three Little Pigs."
- Read your favorite version of this story to the children or select a book from the Story Circle Suggestions below to check out of the library and read.

STORY CIRCLE SUGGESTIONS

- *The Three Little Pigs* by Margot Zemach
- *The Three Little Pigs* by Paul Galdone
- *The Three Little Pigs: Board Book* by Peter Stevenson

PREPARATION FOR "THE THREE LITTLE PIGS" ACTIVITIES AND EXPERIENCES

- Make the "The Three Little Pigs" flannel board story (Appendix p. 568-570).
- Find photos of real pigs.
- Make Pig Tails (on the next page) and Pig Snouts (see p. 358-359).
- Gather biscuits and sausages for Pigs in a Blanket (see p. 358).

Language Enrichment Choices*

- Present the following musical version of the "Three Little Pigs" (on the next page). Use the flannel board patterns

Favorite Stories • Favorite Stories

(Appendix p. 568-570) to help illustrate the song as you sing it. Sing the story to the tune of "The Farmer in the Dell."

The Three Little Pigs

There once were three pigs,	*Each pig built a house,*
There once were three pigs,	*Each pig built a house,*
Heigh-ho the merrio,	*Heigh-ho the merrio,*
There once were three pigs.	*Each pig built a house.*

Additional verses:
The first one's made of straw…
The second one's made of sticks…
The third one's made of bricks…
The wolf came a-puffing…
The houses go a-flying…
The brick house stands alone…
The pigs are safe at last…

- Discuss the houses of each little pig. Show the children examples of straw (dried grass), sticks (twigs), and brick. Let the children hold each type of building material. "Which one is the heaviest?" "Which one is the lightest?"

- Show the children pictures of real pigs. Discuss the parts of the pig—snout, ears, tail, and feet. Ask the children to show you their snouts (nose), ears, and feet.

- Teach the children the American Sign Language sign for *pig* (Appendix p. 436). Review other signs for animals that the children have learned.

Physical Development Choices

- Play chase on the playground with the children. The teacher is the wolf and the children are the pigs. Say, "Here comes the big bad wolf."

- Teach the children how to do a Pig Jig. Play some Irish music and encourage the children to kick up their feet and do a jig. Say the words "pig jig" several times. The children will enjoy the rhyming word sounds.

- Invite the children to toss Pig Tails into a pail. Make Pig Tails by dragging 12" strips of pink paper "ribbon" across one blade of a pair of scissors to curl them. Talk with the children about the curly tails as they play with them.

Social and Emotional Development Choices

▣ Help the children make Pigs in a Blanket. Give them a sausage and a refrigerator biscuit. Show them how to wrap the sausage in the biscuit. Bake in a toaster oven at 375° for four minutes. Turn after four minutes. Talk about each step as the children make the tasty snacks.
Safety Warning: Supervise closely. Always check for allergies before serving food to children.

▣ Ask the children to remove their shoes and do "This Little Piggy." Ask them why they think their toes are called "piggies."

> **This Little Piggy**
> *This little piggy went to market,* (wiggle big toe)
> *This little piggy stayed home,* (wiggle second toe)
> *This little piggy had roast beef,* (wiggle middle toe)
> *This little piggy had none,* (wiggle fourth toe)
> *And this little piggy cried,*
> *"Wee-wee-wee!" all the way home.* (wiggle little toe)

Cognitive Development Choices

▣ Invite the children to build houses for the pigs using blocks. Talk about the size of their houses. "What size door do you need?" "Where will the pigs sleep?"

▣ Encourage the children to make a collage using straw (dried grass), sticks (twigs), or bricks (pebbles or broken flooring tiles). Ask the children to describe the textures of each of the collage materials. Help them think of ways to describe each item.

▣ Give the children the flannel board pieces to play with. Sit with them while they play and help them match one pig to one house. Say, "There is one pig for each house and one house for each pig." This is a good beginning activity for one-to-one correspondence.

▣ Invite the children to paint with pink tempera paint in honor of pigs. Talk with them about other things that are pink.

▣ Make Pig Snouts for the children to wear. Paint small paper cups pink. When the cups are dry, draw nostrils on the bottom using a black marker. Attach elastic string to the cup so that it will stay on the child's face. Punch a couple of small holes in the nostrils so that it will be easier for the child to breathe. Ask the children to put on their snouts and look at themselves in the mirror. "What do you think?" "Do you look like pigs?"

■ Problem-solving suggestion: Ask the children to huff and puff to blow bubbles through a wand. "Is it better to huff and puff or to blow gently?"

REFLECTION ON THE DAY
Ask the children to tell you something that they learned about The Three Pigs. Encourage younger children to show you which house the wolf couldn't blow down. Display the flannel board pieces for them to look at.

The Three Billy Goats Gruff

WORDS TO PRACTICE

billy goats	meadow
bridge	sisters
brothers	troll
family	

GETTING STARTED

■ Present "The Three Billy Goats Gruff" flannel board/shadow puppet story (Appendix p. 561-567) to the children. Ask questions about the story. "Where were the goats going?" "What made the troll come out from under the bridge?"

■ Tell the children that today they will be learning more about the story, "The Three Billy Goats Gruff."

■ Read your favorite version of this story to the children or select a book from the Story Circle Suggestions below to check out of the library and read.

STORY CIRCLE SUGGESTIONS

■ *The Three Billy Goats Gruff* by Paul Galdone
■ *The Three Billy Goats Gruff* by Stephen Carpenter
■ *The Three Billy Goats Gruff: A Norwegian Folktale* by Susan Blair

PREPARATION FOR "THE THREE BILLY GOATS GRUFF" ACTIVITIES AND EXPERIENCES

■ Make the "The Three Billy Goats Gruff" flannel board/shadow puppet story (Appendix p. 561-567).
■ Locate cardboard boxes.
■ Get oatmeal.

Language Enrichment Choices*

■ Encourage older toddlers and twos to become the characters in the story and re-enact it. As the teacher tells

* Toddlers and twos present a wide range of developmental needs, abilities, and interests. For each learning area, select among the following activity and experience choices that are appropriate for the children in your care.

the story, the "goats" pass over the bridge one at a time. Make sure the goats and the audience say, "Trip, trap, trip, trap" with each crossing. The teacher will probably have to handle the dialogue for most of the actors.

- After the "play," discuss the size of each goat. Ask the children if they have brothers or sisters. "Are they younger or older?"

- Teach the children the American Sign Language signs for *brother* and *sister* (Appendix p. 431, 437).

Physical Development Choices

- Encourage the children to walk or march around the room saying, "Trip, trap, trip, trap." Show them how to take big steps, little steps, and medium-size steps. Show them how to take heavy steps and light steps. Use a variety of adjectives to describe the steps.

- Make a bridge out of sturdy blocks or draw one on a piece of butcher paper. Ask the children to stand on the bridge and march to the rhythm of the following chant, "Who Is Traipsing on My Bridge?" When they come to the last line, have them run off the bridge and hide.

  Who Is Traipsing on My Bridge? by Pam Schiller
  Who is traipsing on my bridge?
  Trip, trap, trip, trap! Get off my bridge!
  No one should be traipsing there.
  Get off! Get off! Don't you dare!

Social and Emotional Development Choices

- Talk about brothers and sisters. "What do you like to do with your brother or sister?" Explain that brothers and/or sisters are part of the child's family. Say the action rhyme, "Family Fun."

  Family Fun
  Sister plays the violin, (pretend to play instruments)
  Bother plays the flute.
  Little (child's name) plays the horn,
  Toot, toot, toot, toot, toot!

- Problem-solving suggestion: Talk with older children about ways that the goats might have been able to make friends with the troll. "Could they have asked him to play?" "What about inviting him to go to the meadow with them?"

- Sing "Mary Had a Little Goat" with the children. Point out the differences between a goat and a lamb. Show the children photographs, if available.

  Mary Had a Little Goat,
  Mary had a little goat,
  Little goat, little goat.
  Mary had a little goat;
  Its hair was white as snow.

Cognitive Development Choices

- Provide a light source and encourage the children to stand between the light source and the wall and use their bodies to create shadow trolls. Help the children describe the shadows that they make. If you have presented "The Three Billy Goats Gruff" as a shadow story, the children can use the shadow puppets to retell the story.

- Give the children drums or upside-down boxes. Invite them to beat the drums as they chant, "Trip, trap, trip, trap." Beat the drums softly to represent the small goat walking across the bridge, a little harder for the medium goat, and very hard for the big billy goat. "What makes the steps of each goat different?"

- Make a bridge by cutting an arch into either side of a medium-sized cardboard box. Give the children copies of the troll from the flannel board patterns (Appendix p. 564-565) and encourage them to place the troll *under* the bridge, *over* the bridge, *beside* the bridge, *on top* of the bridge, and so forth.

- Explain that goats eat oats. Show the children some raw oats (oatmeal). Cook oatmeal and encourage the children to sample some Goat Oats. "How do the oats taste?" "What texture are the oats?" "Do you like the oatmeal?"
  Safety Warning: Always check for allergies before serving food to children.

- Problem-solving suggestions:
  1. Encourage older children to make up new sounds the goats might make crossing the bridge such as "sludge, drudge," or "clipity clap."
  2. Invite the children to arrange the goats from large to small. After the children have arranged the goats from large to small, ask them to reverse the order. Use the goats from the flannel board or shadow story you have made.

REFLECTION ON THE DAY
Ask the children to tell you what the story is about. Show the younger children the three goats from the story and ask them to point to the big goat.

The Gingerbread Man

WORDS TO PRACTICE

fox

gingerbread man

GETTING STARTED

- Present "The Gingerbread Man" flannel board story (Appendix p. 479-484) to the children. Ask the children questions about the story. "Who was chasing the gingerbread man?" "Why do you think the gingerbread man was running?"
- Tell the children that today they will be learning more about the story, "The Gingerbread Man."
- Read your favorite version of this story to the children or select a book from the Story Circle Suggestions below to check out of the library and read.

STORY CIRCLE SUGGESTIONS

- *The Gingerbread Man* by Karen Schmidt
- *Gingerbread Man* by Pam Adams

PREPARATION FOR "THE GINGERBREAD MAN" ACTIVITIES AND EXPERIENCES

- Make the "The Gingerbread Man" flannel board story (Appendix p. 479-484).
- Cut gingerbread men out of sponges and construction paper.
- Get gingerbread cake mix.
- Make an "oven" using a shoebox.
- Make Gingerbread Man Puzzles (see p. 366).

Language Enrichment Choices*

- Read the story-poem, "The Gingerbread Baby," (on the next page) to retell the story in another form. Use the same flannel board characters with this version.

* Toddlers and twos present a wide range of developmental needs, abilities, and interests. For each learning area, select among the following activity and experience choices that are appropriate for the children in your care.

The Gingerbread Baby by Pam Schiller
There once was a baby made out of bread
With beautiful skin of brownish-red
And a warm cookie sheet for his bed.

He jumped from that bed one sunny day
Decided he wanted to run away.
He ran away from the nice old woman.
He ran and ran from the kind old man,
From the dog and the cat he ran, ran, ran.
A sly old fox soon caused him to stop
Invited him on his nose to hop.
Before the baby could think it funny
He ended up in the fox's tummy.

Alternate ending for older children:
A sly old fox soon caused him to stop,
Invited him on his nose to hop.
Now, if you know how this story goes,
You know not to hop on a fox's nose.

- Ask the children to demonstrate how the gingerbread man ran. "Do his legs bend?" "How can he run if his legs don't bend?" Have an older child demonstrate.

- Teach the American Sign Language sign for *run* (Appendix p. 437). Review the signs for *legs, knees*, and *feet* (Appendix p. 432, 434).

Physical Development Choices

- Say "Gingerbread Runaways" with the children. Hold up fingers as each gingerbread man speaks and dance all five men away at the end of the rhyme.

Gingerbread Runaways
Five sleepy men made of gingerbread
Awoke one morning on a cookie sheet bed.
"Hey!" said One, "Let's go play."
"No," said Two, "Let's run away!"
"Shhh," said Three, "Someone will hear."
"Phooey," said Four, "There's no one near."
"Come on," said Five, as he jumped to the floor,
And the five little men danced out the door.

- Play Catch Me If You Can with the children. Ask them to say, "Catch me if you can," and run from you. When you tag a child, give her a hug and send her running again.

Social and Emotional Development Choices

- Use the directions of the gingerbread cake box to make gingerbread with the children. Bake it in a toaster oven so that they can watch the bread as it cooks and enjoy the aroma. Discuss the aroma of the bread as it cooks.

- Problem-solving suggestion: Say "There Once Was a Man" with the children. Encourage the children to guess the answer (the fox).

   There Once Was a Man by Pam Schiller
   There once was a man made out of bread
   Who awoke one day on a cookie sheet bed (rub eyes as if waking up)
   He ran away from the little old lady, (walk index finger and middle finger
      on palm of opposite hand.)
   He ran away from the little old man, (repeat)
   He ran away from the animals three, (repeat)
   And he even ran away from me. (point to self)

   He escaped the hands of the little old woman, (clap hand and hold up
      palms facing outward)
   And escaped the hands of the little old man. (repeat)
   He escaped the hands of the animals three, (repeat)
   But he didn't escape me! (shake index finger side to side)

   Do you know who I am?

Cognitive Development Choices

- Provide playdough and gingerbread man cookie cutters. Invite the children to cut out gingerbread men from the playdough. Ask the children to show you the gingerbread man's legs and feet.

- Cut sponges into gingerbread man shapes. Provide brown paint and paper and encourage the children to make a gingerbread man picture. After the paint is dry, provide materials for the children to use to decorate their gingerbread men, such as rickrack, lace, feathers, and so forth.

- Make an "oven" out of a cardboard box or shoebox. Cut out gingerbread men from brown construction paper. Provide a large Styrofoam meat tray to use for a cookie sheet. Invite the children to put the men in the oven and take them out of the oven.

- Provide tempera paint and gingerbread cookie cutters. Pour the paint into a shallow bowl or a large Styrofoam meat tray. Encourage the children to dip the cookie cutters into the paint to make gingerbread outlines on their art paper.

- Tape brown construction paper gingerbread men all over the room in odd places, such as on the ceiling, on the windowpane, under the table, on an easel, under the children's lunch plates, and so forth. Encourage the children to spend the day looking for gingerbread men. When someone finds a gingerbread man, take it down, write her name on it, and put it away. At the end of the day, count the gingerbread men that each child found to see who found the most.

- Problem-solving suggestion: Cut out a gingerbread man shape from brown construction paper or poster board to make Gingerbread Man Puzzles. Laminate the shapes and cut them into simple puzzles. Young toddlers may only be able to put together two pieces while older toddlers may be able to put together three or four pieces. Make a variety of difficulty levels to match the ability levels of the children.

REFLECTION ON THE DAY
Ask the children to tell you about the story. Invite the younger children to point to a gingerbread man.

The Little Red Hen

WORDS TO PRACTICE

cottage	harvest	thresh
grain	mill	weeds
grind	miller	wheat

GETTING STARTED

▨ Show the children "The Little Red Hen" flannel board patterns (Appendix p. 518-522).

▨ Tell the children that today they will be learning more about the story, "The Little Red Hen."

▨ Read your favorite version of this story to the children or select a book from the Story Circle Suggestions below to check out of the library and read. Ask questions about the story. "Why do you think the animals wouldn't help the hen?" "What happened when the animals wanted to eat some of the hen's bread?"

STORY CIRCLE SUGGESTIONS

▨ *The Little Red Hen* by Byron Barton

▨ *The Little Red Hen* by Paul Galdone

PREPARATION FOR "THE LITTLE RED HEN" ACTIVITIES AND EXPERIENCES

▨ Make "The Little Red Hen" flannel board story (Appendix p. 518-522).

▨ Make the Little Red Hen Puzzles (see p. 370).

▨ Get bread, jam, and butter.

Language Enrichment Choices*

▨ Tell the story, "The Little Red Hen" again using the flannel board patterns (Appendix p. 518-522). Assign one child to be the cat, another to be the dog, and a third to be the goose. When you get to the parts of the story where each of these

* Toddlers and twos present a wide range of developmental needs, abilities, and interests. For each learning area, select among the following activity and experience choices that are appropriate for the children in your care.

animals says, "Not I," point to the child who is speaking for that animal and let him fill in the dialogue. If none of the children speak well enough to handle the dialogue, simply tell the story again.

- Talk about some of the new and unusual words in the story. Show the children what a grain of wheat looks like. Talk about grinding. Demonstrate grinding with a pestle and mortar. Explain that harvest time means that the wheat is ready to be cut down.

- Review the American Sign Language sign for *red* (Appendix p. 437).

Physical Development Choices

- Do "Tiny Seed" with the children. Explain that the grain of wheat that the little red hen found was a seed.

   Tiny Seed
   Tiny seed planted just right, (children tuck themselves into a ball)
   Not a breath of air, not a ray of light.
   Rain falls slowly to and fro,
   And now the seed begins to grow. (children begin to unfold)
   Slowly reaching for the light,
   With all its energy, all its might.
   The little seed's work is almost done,
   To grow up tall and face the sun. (children stand up tall with arms stretched out)

- Invite the children to do the "Little Chicks" action rhyme. "What do the chicks eat?"

   Little Chicks
   Little chicks say, "Peep, peep, peep,"
   As they wake from sleep, sleep, sleep. (rub eyes)
   Little chicks say, "Peep, peep, peep,"
   And hear the birds go "cheep, cheep, cheep." (repeat "cheep, cheep, cheep")
   Little chicks say, "Peep, peep, peep,"
   We are hungry, "Peep, peep, peep." (rub belly)
   Mama feeds them and then she says,
   "Now it's time to sleep, sleep, sleep." (lay head in hands)

- Encourage the children to march around the room saying, "Not I."

- Give the children some hen food (kernels of corn), a pastry brush, a bowl, and a scoop. Show them how to use the pastry brush to sweep the corn into the scoop and then dump it into the bowl.
  Safety Warning: Supervise closely so children do not put the kernels of corn in their mouths.

Social and Emotional Development Choices

- Talk with the children about sharing. Read "I'm a Family Helper" to them. "What things do you do at home to help your family?"

> **I'm a Family Helper** by Pam Schiller
> *I set the table every night,*
> *I learned to do it right.*
> *One place for mom, one for me,*
> *And Daddy's place makes three.*
>
> *I pick my toys up every day,*
> *I put everything away.*
> *My cars, my blocks, my books*
> *All go into their nooks.*
>
> *A family helper is what I am*
> *You can be one, too.*
> *Mommy say's I'm quite a ham*
> *When it comes to jobs I do.*

- Serve wheat bread with butter and jam. Explain that this is the kind of bread the little red hen made. "What does the bread taste like?" What kind of jam do the children choose for their bread?

- Ask older children to help think of ways the hen might have gotten the animals to help so she didn't have to do all the work herself. "Could she have promised them some bread in the beginning?" "Could she have told them she really needed their help?"

Cognitive Development Choices

- Give the children playdough, rolling pins, and baking tins. Encourage them to pretend to make some bread. "Who likes bread?" "What do you eat on your bread?"

- Place a hen feather on the edge of the table and invite the children to blow it off the other side of the table. "Is it easy to move with your breath or is it hard?"

- Encourage the children to paint with red tempera paint in honor of the little red hen. Talk with them about other red things. Older children can paint with feathers.

- Plant rye grass seeds in small containers. Ask questions. "What do you think will happen to the seeds?" "What will we need to do to take care of the seeds?"

- Give the children the flannel board pieces (Appendix p. 518-522) and encourage them to tell the story. Talk them through the events of the story. Encourage them to use the repetitive line in the story: "Not I."

- Encourage the children to use blocks to build a cottage for the Little Red Hen. Remind them that she does a lot of baking. Therefore, she will need a kitchen in her cottage. "What else will she need?"

- Problem-solving suggestion: Make Little Red Hen Puzzles. Make photocopies of the little red hen from the patterns (Appendix p. 522). Color them, laminate them, and cut them into puzzle pieces. Make several different difficulty levels by cutting a couple of the puzzles into two pieces, and others into four or five pieces. To help identify which pieces go to the same puzzle, place a color dot on the backs of pieces that belong together.

REFLECTION ON THE DAY

Ask the children to tell you what happens in the story of the "Little Red Hen."

Seasons

FALL

WINTER

SPRING

SUMMER

Fall

WORDS TO PRACTICE

acorns	jackets	squirrels
autumn	leaves	sweaters
fall	rake	
geese	season	

GETTING STARTED

- Show the children some pictures that depict fall. Discuss the colors of the leaves, the clothing people are wearing, and the activities that are occurring. Read the poem, "Fall" to the children. Discuss the signs of fall described in the poem.

  Fall by Pam Schiller
  Fall is here,
  Frost is in the air.
  Chill is on my cheeks,
  Static in my hair.

  Colorful leaves fall like rain.
  Sun and clouds play hide and seek.
  The wind blows across the grass.
  Apples are ripe and at their peak.

  I help at home to rake the leaves.
  We put them in a sack.
  We sweep the roof and clean the eaves.
  Before we finish…the leaves are back.

  Fall is in the air,
  Static in my hair.
  Leaves on the lawn,
  And autumn frost at dawn.

- Tell the children that today they will be learning more about *fall*.

▨ Read your favorite book about fall to the children or select a book from the Story Circle Suggestions below to check out of the library and read.

STORY CIRCLE SUGGESTIONS
▨ *Fall* by Maria Rius
▨ *Fall Leaves Fall* by Zoe Hall

PREPARATION FOR "FALL" ACTIVITIES AND EXPERIENCES
▨ Make the Magnetic Dress-Me Dolls for Fall (Appendix p. 455-466) and "The Great Big Pumpkin" flannel board story (Appendix p. 492-494).
▨ Gather some fall leaves.
▨ Make Fall Observation Bottles and Leaf Puzzles (see p. 376).
▨ Gather fall dress-up clothing.
▨ Get ingredients for Applesauce (see p. 375).

Language Enrichment Choices*

▨ Sing "This Is the Way We Dress for Fall" to the tune of "The Mulberry Bush." Discuss each clothing item. Point out the items that the children are wearing

> **This Is the Way We Dress for Fall** by Pam Schiller
> *This is the way we dress for fall*
> *Dress for fall, dress for fall.*
> *This is the way we dress for fall*
> *September of the year.*

Additional verses:
> *We wear our long-sleeved shirts today…September of the year.*
> *We wear our sweaters to keep us warm…September of the year.*
> *We wear our shoes that cover our toes…September of the year.*

▨ Show the children the Magnetic Dress-Me Dolls for Fall (Appendix p. 455-466). Discuss the articles of fall clothing as you place them on the dolls.

▨ Present "The Great Big Pumpkin" flannel board story (Appendix p. 492-494). Tell the children that pumpkins are a fall food. Ask older children what they think about when they see pumpkins. Remind them of Jack-O-Lanterns on Halloween and pumpkin pies on Thanksgiving.

▨ Teach the children the American Sign Language sign for *fall* (Appendix p. 432).

* Toddlers and twos present a wide range of developmental needs, abilities, and interests. For each learning area, select among the following activity and experience choices that are appropriate for the children in your care.

Physical Development Choices

- Invite the children to dance like fall leaves, waving streamers in fall colors.

- Sing the song, "This Is the Way We Rake the Leaves" to the tune of "The Mulberry Bush." Suit the actions to the words. Discuss falling leaves. Show examples, if available. If you do not live in a part of the country where fall changes are noticeable, try to find some pictures of fall leaves covering the ground.

    This Is the Way We Rake the Leaves by Pam Schiller
    This is the way we rake the leaves
    Rake the leaves, rake the leaves.
    This is the way we rake the leaves
    Day after day in the fall.

    This is the way we bag the leaves
    Bag the leaves, bag the leaves.
    This is the way we bag the leaves
    Day after day in the fall.

    Additional verses:
    This is the way we toss the leaves…Day after day in the fall.
    This is the way we play in the leaves…Day after day in the fall.

- Do the following action rhyme, "Autumn Leaves", with the children. After you finish the rhyme, talk about the different ways that the leaves fell to the ground.

    Autumn Leaves by Pam Schiller
    Autumn leaves are falling, falling, falling. (move from standing position to squatting)
    Autumn leaves are spinning, spinning, spinning. (stand and turn)
    Autumn leaves are floating, floating, floating. (sway side to side)
    Autumn leaves are turning, turning, turning. (turn slowly)
    Autumn leaves are dancing, dancing, dancing. (stand on toes, sway forward and back)
    Autumn leaves are blowing, blowing, blowing. (take several steps forward)
    Autumn leaves are falling, falling, falling. (squat)
    Autumn leaves are sleeping, sleeping, sleeping. (place hands together on side of head)

- Say "Little Red Apple" (on the next page) with the children. "Has anyone ever picked an apple?" "Where do apples come from?"

Little Red Apple
A little red apple grew high in a tree. (point up)
I looked up at it. (shade eyes and look up)
It looked down at me. (shade eyes and look down)
"Come down, please," I called. (use hand to motion downward)
And that little red apple fell right on my head. (tap the top of your head)

▨ Sing "Gray Squirrel." Discuss what animals do in the fall. For example, squirrels gather nuts and acorns, birds fly south, bears prepare to hibernate, and so on. Show photos of these animals, if available.

Gray Squirrel
Gray squirrel, gray squirrel, (stand with hands on bent knees)
Swish your bushy tail. (wiggle your behind)
Gray squirrel, gray squirrel, (stand with hands on bent knees)
Swish your bushy tail. (wiggle your behind)
Wrinkle up your funny nose, (wrinkle nose)
Hold an acorn in your toes. (pinch index and thumb fingers together)
Gray squirrel, gray squirrel, (stand with hands on bent knees)
Swish your busy tail. (wiggle your behind)

▨ Give the children a box of acorns or large nuts and an unbreakable container with a wide opening. Encourage the children to put the acorns through the mouth of the bottle.
Safety Warning: Acorns can be a choking hazard. Supervise this activity closely.

Social and Emotional Development Choices

▨ Discuss fall foods such as apples, nuts, and pumpkins. Show examples of any fall foods that you have available or show some photos of fall foods. Encourage the children to tell you or show you the foods they like.

▨ Make Homemade Applesauce with the children. Peel, core, and cut up six apples and put them into a large saucepan. Add $\frac{1}{2}$ cup of water, 1 teaspoon of lemon juice, and $\frac{1}{4}$ cup of sugar. Cook until tender. Add a pinch of cinnamon. Press through a colander and serve.

▨ Discuss dressing warmly when the weather begins to turn chilly. Invite the children to dress the Magnetic Dress-Me Dolls for Fall (Appendix p. 455-466). As they dress the dolls, talk with them about similar types of clothing they have at home. "How are these clothes different from winter clothes?" "Summer clothes?"

Cognitive Development Choices

◾ Provide a tub of fall leaves for the children to play with. Provide a second tub of dried leaves and encourage the children to crumble the leaves.

◾ Give the children a large leaf and a magnifying glass to examine it. Talk to the children about what they see." Can you find the veins in the leaf?" "What do the edges look like?"

◾ Give the children fall dress-up clothes to explore. As they try on different outfits, discuss the texture and weight of the clothing item.

◾ Provide tempera paint in fall colors and encourage the children to paint a fall picture. Ask older toddlers to describe their paintings to you.

◾ Go on a nature walk to find fall things. Make a list of some of the things you might see on your walk. When you return, check off the things you saw.

◾ Collect fall leaves. Place a leaf or two under a piece of drawing and show the children how to rub over the leaves with a crayon. Talk about the leaves. Look at the rough (or smooth) edges. Point out the veins in the leaves. "What colors are the rubbings?"

◾ Make Fall Observation Bottles. Place fall items such as acorns, berries, and leaves inside a clean, clear, half-liter soda bottle. Glue on the lids securely. Encourage the children to look closely at the items inside. Ask them to name the things they see in the bottle.

◾ Problem-solving suggestions: Give the children Leaf Puzzles to put together. Cut large fall leaves out of red, yellow, and brown construction paper. Laminate them and cut them into puzzle pieces.

REFLECTION ON THE DAY
Ask the children to tell you something that they learned about fall. Ask the younger children to show you a fall leaf.

Winter

WORDS TO PRACTICE

boots	gloves	snow
chilly	hats	snowflakes
coats	season	winter

GETTING STARTED

- Show the children some pictures that depict winter. Discuss the cold weather, the clothing people are wearing, and the activities that people are doing. Sing "Winter Is Coming" to the tune of "The Muffin Man." Discuss the signs of winter described in the song.

  Winter Is Coming by Pam Schiller
  Can you feel the wind blow cold?
  The wind blow cold?
  The wind blow cold?
  Can you feel the wind blow cold?
  Winter's coming soon.

  Other verses:
  Can you see the darker skies?
  Can you hear the cold wind blow?
  Can you see the trees all bare?
  Can you button up your coat?
  Can you put your mittens on?

- Tell the children that today they will be learning more about *winter*.
- Read your favorite book about winter to the children or select a book from the Story Circle Suggestions below to check out of the library and read.

STORY CIRCLE SUGGESTIONS

- *Flannel Kisses* by Linda Crotta Brennan
- *Frozen Noses* by Jan Carr
- *The Snowy Day* by Ezra Jack Keats
- *Winter* by Maria Riuz

PREPARATION FOR "WINTER" ACTIVITIES AND EXPERIENCES

- Make the Magnetic Dress-Me Dolls for Winter (Appendix p. 460-461) and the "Frosty the Snowman" flannel board story (Appendix p. 475-478).
- Make Winter Observation Bottles (see p. 381).
- Gather winter dress-up clothing.
- Get ingredients for hot chocolate.

Language Enrichment Choices*

- Sing "This Is the Way We Dress for Winter" to the tune of "The Mulberry Bush." Discuss each clothing item mentioned in the song. Point out the winter items that the children are wearing.

  This Is the Way We Dress for Winter by Pam Schiller
  This is the way we dress for winter,
  Dress for winter, dress for winter.
  This is the way we dress for winter
  Because it's cold outside.
  We'll wear snow pants and jackets today…because it's cold outside.
  We'll wear warm socks and boots today…because it's cold outside.
  We'll wear our scarves and mittens today…because it's cold outside.

- Show the children the Magnetic Dress-Me Dolls for Winter (Appendix p. 460-461). Name the articles of winter clothing as you place them on the dolls.

- Sing "Caps, Mittens, Shoes, and Socks" to the tune of "Head, Shoulders, Knees, and Toes." Ask the children to point to the part of the body where the clothing item is worn.

  Caps, Mittens, Shoes, and Socks
  Caps, mittens, shoes, and socks,
  Shoes and socks.
  Caps, mittens, shoes, and socks,
  Shoes and socks.
  And pants and belt, and shirt and tie
  Go together wet or dry
  Wet or dry!

* Toddlers and twos present a wide range of developmental needs, abilities, and interests. For each learning area, select among the following activity and experience choices that are appropriate for the children in your care.

378

- Recite the poem "Jack Frost" to the children. Explain that Jack Frost is a nickname for winter.

     Jack Frost
     Jack Frost bites your noses.
     He chills your cheeks and freezes your toes.
     He comes every year when winter is here
     And stays until spring is near.

- Teach the children the American Sign Language sign for *winter* (Appendix p. 440).

Physical Development Choices

- Invite the children to dance creatively with white streamers to imitate snowflakes in the air.

- Do the following action rhyme, "Dancing Snowflakes" with the children. After you have finished the rhyme, talk about all the ways that snowflakes fall to the ground.

     Dancing Snowflakes
     Snowflakes are falling, falling, falling. (move from standing position to squatting)
     Snowflakes are spinning, spinning, spinning. (stand and turn)
     Snowflakes are floating, floating, floating. (sway side to side)
     Snowflakes are turning, turning, turning. (turn slowly)

     Snowflakes are dancing, dancing, dancing. (stand on toes, sway forward and back)
     Snowflakes are blowing, blowing, blowing. (take several steps forward)
     Snowflakes are falling, falling, falling. (squat)
     Snowflakes are sleeping, sleeping, sleeping. (place hands together on side of head)

- Say "Five Little Snowmen" (on the next page) with the children. Discuss making snowmen during the winter. "Has anyone ever made a snowman?" Show any photos of snowmen you may have.

Five Little Snowmen

Five little snowmen happy and gay, (hold up five fingers and move one for
   each snowman)
The first one said, "What a nice day!"
The second one said, "We'll cry no tears,"
The third one said, "We'll stay for years."
The fourth one said, "But what happens in May?"
The fifth one said, "Look, we're melting away!" (hold hands out like saying
   all gone)

Social and Emotional Development Choices

- Talk about the foods that are associated with winter, such as hot chocolate
  and soup. Show examples of any foods that you have available or show some
  photos of winter foods. Serve hot chocolate for snack. Recite the "Hot
  Chocolate Rhyme" below as the children drink their winter drink.
  Safety Warning: Always check for allergies before serving food to children.

  Hot Chocolate

  A cup of warm milk, blow, blow, blow, (pretend to blow)
  A teaspoon of chocolate, stir, stir, stir, (pretend to stir)
  Marshmallows on top, one, two, three, (hold up fingers, one, two, three)
  A perfect winter treat for me. (rub tummy)

- Discuss dressing warmly when the weather begins to turn chilly. Invite the
  children to dress the Magnetic Dress-Me Dolls for Winter (Appendix p. 460-
  461). As they dress the dolls, talk with them about similar types of clothing
  they have at home. "How are these clothes different from fall clothes?"

- Sing or say "The Snowflake Song" with the children. "Has anyone ever seen
  snowflakes?" "What color are they?" "Are they cold?"

  The Snowflake Song

  If all of the snowflakes (wiggle fingers in the air)
  Were candy bars and milk shakes, (tap index finger in palm)
  Oh, what a snow it would be. (wiggle fingers in the air)
  I'd stand outside with my mouth open wide. (open mouth as if catching
     snowflakes)
  Ah-ah-ah-ah-ah-ah-ah-ah.
  If all of the snowflakes (wiggle fingers in the air)
  Were candy bars and milk shakes, (tap index finger in palm)
  Oh, what a snow it would be. (wiggle fingers in the air)

SEASONS

Cognitive Development Choices

▣ Invite the children to use the flannel board pieces to practice saying the rhyme "Frosty the Snowman" (Appendix p. 475-478). Help them learn it by saying a line, and then letting the children fill in rhyming words or the last word of all sentences.

▣ Wet a glass and put it in the freezer. Give the children a magnifying glass to examine the ice crystals on the glass. If you are using this activity on a cold day, you may find ice crystals on the windows or on outdoor equipment.

▣ Give the children winter dress-up clothes to explore. As they try on different outfits, discuss the texture and weight of each clothing item.

▣ Provide white tempera paint and blue paper and encourage the children to paint a winter picture. Ask older toddlers to describe their paintings to you.

▣ Go on a nature walk to find winter things. Make a list of some of the things you might see on your walk. When you return, check off the things you saw.

▣ Make Winter Observation Bottles. Place winter nature items such as berries, moss, and twigs inside a clean, clear, half-liter soda bottle. Glue the lid on securely. Make a second bottle filled with white glitter and water. Glue the lid on securely. Encourage the children to look closely at the items inside both bottles and help them name the things they see inside the bottles.

▣ Hide a mitten and encourage the children to find it. Give them clues as they search.

▣ Problem-solving suggestions:
  1. Show toddlers how to put their coats on by laying it on the floor in front of them, putting their arms in the sleeves, and pulling the coat overhead.
  2. Give the children felt pieces to use to construct a snowman on the flannel board. Include white felt circles, cutouts for facial features, and cutouts for clothing such as a hat, boots, and scarf. Encourage the children to build a snowman.

REFLECTION ON THE DAY
Ask the children to tell you something that they learned about winter. Invite the children to point to an article of winter clothing.

381

Spring

WORDS TO PRACTICE

birds	rain	spring
flowers	season	
insects	seeds	

GETTING STARTED

▨ Show the children some pictures that depict spring such as flowers, green trees, insects, and birds. Discuss the flowers, the clothing people are wearing, and the activities that are occurring. Sing "Spring Is Here" to the tune of "The Mulberry Bush." Discuss the signs of spring described in the song along with other signs of spring, such as insects and rain.

Spring Is Here by Pam Schiller
All the grass is turning green,
Turning green, turning green,
All the grass is turning green,
Spring is here!

Additional verses:
All the flowers are growing tall…
All the birds are building nests…
All the trees are budding now…

▨ Tell the children that today they will be learning more about *spring.*

▨ Read your favorite book about spring to the children or select a book from the Story Circle Suggestions below to check out of the library and read.

STORY CIRCLE SUGGESTIONS

▨ *Listen to the Rain* by Bill Martin, Jr.
▨ *Spring Song* by Barbara Seuling
▨ *When Will It Be Spring?* by Catherine Walters

PREPARATION FOR "SPRING" ACTIVITIES AND EXPERIENCES

- Make the Magnetic Dress-Me Dolls for Spring (Appendix p. 462-463) and "Ms. Bumblebee Gathers Honey" puppet story (Appendix p. 535-537).
- Gather some spring flowers.
- Make Spring Observation Bottles (see p. 387).
- Gather spring dress-up clothing.
- Get ingredients for Ants on a Log (see p. 386).
- Get fruits and vegetables or photographs of fruits and vegetables.

Language Enrichment Choices*

- Sing "This Is the Way We Dress for Spring" to the tune of "The Mulberry Bush." Discuss each clothing item mentioned in the song. Point out the spring items that the children are wearing.

> **This Is the Way We Dress for Spring** by Pam Schiller
> *This is the way we dress for spring,*
> *Dress for spring, dress for spring.*
> *This is the way we dress for spring*
> *When the flowers begin to bloom.*

> Additional verses:
> *We'll wear a raincoat in case it rains…when the flowers begin to bloom.*
> *We'll wear rain boots to splash in puddles…when the flowers begin to bloom.*
> *We'll bring our kites to fly in the wind…when the flowers begin to bloom.*

- Show the children the Magnetic Dress-Me Dolls for Spring (Appendix p. 462-463). Discuss the articles of spring clothing as you place them on the dolls.

- Sing "Itsy Bitsy Spider." Remind the children that rain is a big part of spring.

> **Itsy Bitsy Spider**
> *The itsy bitsy spider*
> *Went up the waterspout.*
> *Down came the rain*
> *And washed the spider out.*
> *Up came the sun*
> *And dried up all the rain.*
> *And the itsy bitsy spider*
> *Went up the spout again.*

* Toddlers and twos present a wide range of developmental needs, abilities, and interests. For each learning area, select among the following activity and experience choices that are appropriate for the children in your care.

■ Present the "Ms. Bumblebee Gathers Honey" puppet story (Appendix p. 535-537) to the children, using the puppets to act out the story. Ask the children if they have noticed more insects outdoors. Explain that spring is the time of year when we see lots of insects. For older children, explain that the insects are attracted to the flowers. Sing "Baby Bumblebee" with the children.

Baby Bumblebee
I caught myself a baby bumblebee.
Won't my mommy be so proud of me!
I caught myself a baby bumblebee.
Ouch! He stung me!
I'm talking to my baby bumblebee.
Won't my mommy be so proud of me!
I'm talking to my baby bumblebee.
"Oh," he said, "I'm sorry."
I let go of my baby bumblebee.
Won't my mommy be so proud of me!
I let go of my baby bumblebee.
Look he's happy to be free!

■ Teach the children the American Sign Language sign for *spring* (Appendix p. 438).

Physical Development Choices

■ Invite the children to dance like spring rain as they wave blue streamers. Encourage them to dance like a soft rain and then to dance like a hard rain.

■ Sing "The Raindrop Song." Again, the children that a large amount of rain accompanies spring in most parts of the country.

The Raindrop Song
If all of the raindrops (wiggle fingers in the air)
Were lemon drops and gumdrops (tap one index finger against palm of other hand)
Oh, what a rain it would be. (wiggle fingers in the air)
I'd stand outside with my mouth open wide.
Ah-ah-ah-ah-ah-ah-ah-ah-ah-ah! (stand, looking up with mouth open)
If all of the raindrops (wiggle fingers in the air)
Were lemon drops and gumdrops (tap one index finger against palm of other hand)
Oh, what a rain it would be. (wiggle fingers in the air)

■ Do the action rhyme, "Tiny Seed" with the children. When you finish the rhyme, talk about how seeds are often planted in the spring. Tell the children that it takes both sun and rain to help the seeds grow.

Tiny Seed
Tiny seed planted just right, (children tuck themselves into a ball)
Not a breath of air, not a ray of light.
Rain falls slowly to and fro,
And now the seed begins to grow. (children begin to unfold)
Slowly reaching for the light,
With all its energy, all its might.
The little seed's work is almost done,
To grow up tall and face the sun. (children stand up tall with arms
    stretched out)

■ Encourage the children to march and sing "The Ants Go Marching." Remind them that ants are a part of spring.

The Ants Go Marching
The ants go marching one by one
Hurrah, hurrah.
The ants go marching one by one
Hurrah, hurrah.
The ants go marching one by one,
The little one stops to suck his thumb.
And they all go marching down
Into the ground
To get out
Of the rain.
BOOM! BOOM! BOOM! BOOM!

Additional verses:
Two... tie her shoe...
Three... climb a tree...
Four... shut the door...
Five... take a dive...

Social and Emotional Development Choices
■ Talk about the foods that are associated with spring, such as fresh fruits and vegetables. Show the children real fruits and vegetables or photos of fruits and vegetables. Ask the children to tell or show you foods they like. Tell them which ones you like.

■ Serve Ants on a Log for snack. Provide logs (celery sticks with peanut butter spread in the groove) and let the children place the ants (raisins) on the log. "Have you ever seen real ants on a real log?" "What about ants in the park?"

Safety Warning: Always check for allergies before serving food to children.

■ Sing "Birdie, Birdie, Where Is Your Nest?" Discuss what animals do in the spring. For example, birds build nests, chicks are hatched, and so on. Show photos of baby animals, if available. "What other things do birds do in the spring?"

Birdie, Birdie, Where Is Your Nest?
Birdie, birdie, where is your nest?
Birdie, birdie, where is your nest?
Birdie, birdie, where is your nest?
In the tree that I love best.

■ Discuss dressing cooler when the weather begins to turn warm. Invite the children to dress the Magnetic Dress-Me Dolls for Spring (Appendix p. 462-463). As the children dress the dolls, talk with them about similar types of clothing they have at home. "How are these clothes different from winter clothes?" "Summer clothes?"

Cognitive Development Choices

■ Get a tub of dried or silk flowers for the children to play with. Teach them the refrain, "Spring showers bring May flowers."

■ Give the children a live flower and a magnifying glass to examine it. Talk to the children about what they see. "Do you see any bugs?" "What do the edges of the flowers look like?"

■ Give the children spring dress-up clothes to explore. As they try on different outfits, discuss the texture and weight of the clothing item.

■ Provide bright colors of tempera paint and encourage the children to paint a spring picture. Ask older children to describe their paintings to you.

■ Go on a nature walk to find spring things. Make a list of some of the things you might see on your walk. When you return, check off the things you saw. While on the walk, look for spring clouds.

■ Place rubber ducks in a tub of water. Point out that ducks are often seen in the springtime. Invite the children to play with the duck. Teach them the song "Little Ducky Duddle."

Little Ducky Duddle
Little Ducky Duddle went wading in a puddle,
Went wading in a puddle quite small.
"Quack, quack!"
Said he, "It doesn't matter
How much I splash and splatter.
I'm only a ducky after all.
Quack, quack!"

■ Invite the children to make Butterfly Blottos. Fold a piece of construction paper in half and then re-open it. Place a small amount of tempera paint in the middle where the fold is. Fold the paper and encourage the children to rub their hands over the paper to spread the paint inside. When the paper is opened, the print inside should look like a butterfly.

■ Make Spring Observation Bottles. Place spring items such as flowers, grass, and seeds inside clean, clear, half-liter soda bottles. Glue the lids on securely. Encourage the children to look closely at the items inside. Help the children name the items that they see.

■ Problem-solving suggestions: Make Flower Puzzles for the children to work. Cut out flowers from construction paper. Laminate and cut them into puzzle pieces. Cut some puzzles into two or three pieces and others into four or five pieces in order to provide for a range of ability levels. Place color dots on the backs of each puzzle to help identify which puzzle pieces go together.

REFLECTION ON THE DAY
Ask the children to tell you something that they learned about spring. Ask the younger children to show you a spring flower.

Summer

WORDS TO PRACTICE

beach	season	water
ocean	summer	
picnic	sunshine	

GETTING STARTED

■ Show the children some pictures that depict summer. Discuss the sunny weather, the clothing people are wearing, and the activities that are occurring. Sing "Summer Is Coming" to the tune of "Are You Sleeping?"

Summer Is Coming by Pam Schiller
Summer is coming,
Summer is coming
Yes, it is!
Yes, it is!
Fun is in the air.
Sunshine here and there.
Summer's here.
Summer's here.

■ Tell the children that today they will be learning more about *summer*.

■ Read your favorite book about summer to the children or select a book from the Story Circle Suggestions below to check out of the library and read.

STORY CIRCLE SUGGESTIONS

■ *Sally Goes to the Beach* by Stephen Huneck
■ *The Very Hungry Caterpillar* by Eric Carle
■ *What Can You Do in the Sun?* by Anna Grossnickle Hines

PREPARATION FOR "SUMMER" ACTIVITIES AND EXPERIENCES

■ Make the Magnetic Dress-Me Dolls for Summer (Appendix p. 455-457).

- Make Wave Machines, Summer Observation Bottles, and Sunshine Puzzles (see p. 392).
- Gather summer dress-up clothing and sunglasses.
- Get ingredients for Baggie Ice Cream (see p. 390).

Language Enrichment Choices*

- Sing "This Is the Way We Dress for Summer" to the tune of "The Mulberry Bush." Discuss each clothing item. Point out the items that the children are wearing.

> **This Is the Way We Dress for Summer** by Pam Schiller
> *This is the way we dress for summer,*
> *Dress for summer, dress for summer.*
> *This is the way we dress for summer*
> *When we go out to play.*

> Additional verses:
> *This is the way we put on our shorts... When we go out to play.*
> *This is the way we put on our sunscreen... When we go out to play.*
> *This is the way we put on our sandals... When we go out to play.*
> *This is the way we wear sunglasses... When we go out to play.*

- Show the children the Magnetic Dress-Me Dolls for Summer (Appendix p. 455-457). Name the articles of summer clothing as you place them on the dolls.

- Teach the children the American Sign Language sign for *summer* (Appendix p. 438).

Physical Development Choices

- Invite the children to participate in the following action rhyme, "Going for a Swim." Suit the actions to the words. Ask the children if they have been to the beach. Ask about any experiences they have had related to swimming.

> **Going for a Swim** by Pam Schiller
> *I love to swim. I love to swim. I love to swim.*
> *When we are going to the beach I wake up early,*
> *I wash my goggles.*
> *I blow up my float.*
> *I fold my beach towel.*

* Toddlers and twos present a wide range of developmental needs, abilities, and interests. For each learning area, select among the following activity and experience choices that are appropriate for the children in your care.

I put on my sandals.
I put on my swimsuit.
I eat my breakfast.
I know I will need lots of energy for a day at the beach.
Then I help to pack the car.
We will need our cooler, our picnic basket, and our beach chairs.
Then we are off to the beach.
When we arrive, I hop out of the car.
I help find a place on the beach.
It is hard to walk in the sand.
I stop and listen to the wind on the ocean.
Then I rub on my sunscreen.
Now I can head to the water.
I love the ocean.
I love to swim. I love to swim. I love to swim.
Don't you?

■ Show the children how to play Shadow Tag. The children try to step on someone's shadow. "Can you catch your own shadow?"

■ Blow bubbles and invite the children to catch them. Describe the way the bubbles float on the summer air.

Social and Emotional Development Choices

■ Talk about the foods that are associated with summer, such as ice cream, watermelon, corn on the cob, and lemonade. Show examples of any foods that you have available or show some photos of summer foods.

■ Make Baggie Ice Cream with the children. For one serving, pour ½ cup of milk, 1 tablespoon of sugar, and ¼ teaspoon of vanilla into a small zipper-closure plastic bag and seal. Place the small bag, with rock salt, inside a large zipper-closure plastic bag and seal. Shake the bag for approximately 10 minutes. Let the children help. "Why is ice cream so tasty on a hot day?" Teach the children "I Scream for Ice Cream."

I Scream for Ice Cream
You scream, I scream,
We all scream for ice cream!

- Discuss dressing in clothing that is not too warm. Invite the children to dress the Magnetic Dress-Me Dolls for Summer (Appendix p. 455-457). Talk with them as they dress the dolls about similar types of clothing they have at home. "How are these clothes different from winter clothes?" "Spring clothes?"

- Talk with the children about wearing sunscreen during the summer. Show them how to put sunscreen on their arms and legs, if appropriate.

- Sing "Down by the Bay" below with the children. Talk about summertime things in the song, such as watermelons, sunburn, and the bay itself.

> **Down by the Bay**
> *Down by the bay where the watermelons grow*
> *Back to my home I dare not go.*
> *For if I do my mother will say,*
> *"Did you ever see a pig dancing the jig?"*
> *Down by the bay.*

Additional verses:
> *"Did you ever see a whale with a polka dot tail?"*
> *"Did you ever see a bear combing his hair?"*

Cognitive Development Choices

- Fill a tub with sand for the children to play with. Provide funnels, shovels, cups, and pails. "Has anyone ever been to the beach?" "What is the sand like at the beach?"
  Safety Warning: Supervise closely so children do not get sand in their eyes or mouth.

- Give the children some sand and a magnifying glass to examine it. Talk with the children about what they see. "What does the sand look like up close?"

- Give the children summer dress-up clothes to explore. Be sure to include sun hats. As they try on different outfits, discuss the texture and weight of the clothing item. Provide a small suitcase and encourage the children to pack clothes for a vacation trip. "Where would you like to go?"

- Provide tempera paint in summer colors and encourage the children to paint a summer picture. Ask older toddlers to describe their paintings to you.

- Go on a nature walk to find summer things. Make a list of some of the things you might see on your walk. When you return, check off the things you did see.

- Provide a variety of sunglasses and a mirror. Encourage the children to take a look at themselves in the different glasses. Ask them how things look when looking through the sunglasses.

- Give the children Wave Machines to enjoy. Fill clear plastic bottles ¼ full with mineral oil or clear vegetable oil. Finish filling with denatured alcohol and a few drops of blue or green food coloring. Glue the lids on securely and invite the children to rotate the bottle to create waves. Individual wave machines can be made using 20-ounce bottles.

- Make Summer Observation Bottles. Fill a half-liter clear soda bottle with sand, plastic fish, and blue water (water with blue food coloring). Glue on the lid securely. Fill a second bottle with leaves, plastic fish, and dried flowers. Glue on the lid securely. Encourage the children to observe the things in the bottles closely. What things can they name?

- Problem-solving suggestions: Give the children Sunshine Puzzles to put together. Cut out large circles from yellow construction paper or poster board. Laminate them and cut them into puzzle pieces. Create a variety of difficulty levels by cutting some puzzles into two or three pieces and others into four or five pieces. Use same color stick-on dots on the backs of pieces of puzzles that go together.

REFLECTION ON THE DAY
Ask the children to tell you something that they learned about summer.

Celebrations

HALLOWEEN

THANKSGIVING

CHRISTMAS

HANUKKAH

VALENTINE'S DAY

MOTHER'S DAY

FATHER'S DAY

EVERYBODY'S BIRTHDAY

Halloween

WORDS TO PRACTICE

candy	mask	scary
costumes	October	spooky
Halloween	pumpkin	trick or treat

GETTING STARTED

- Show the children several Halloween masks. Be sensitive to children who may be frightened by masks. Ask them what time of year they see people wearing masks. If no one responds, remind them that it is Halloween. Ask questions to find out what the children know about *Halloween*.
- Tell the children that today they will be learning more about *Halloween*.
- Read your favorite book about Halloween to the children or select a book from the Story Circle Suggestions below to check out of the library and read.

STORY CIRCLE SUGGESTIONS

- *A Costume for Bear* by Kiki Thorpe
- *Apples and Pumpkins* by Anne F. Rockwell
- *Today Is Halloween* by P.K. Hallinan

PREPARATION FOR "HALLOWEEN" ACTIVITIES AND EXPERIENCES

- Make "The Strange Visitor" prop story (Appendix p. 559-560).
- Find a pumpkin.
- Make the Magnetic Dress-Me Dolls for Halloween (Appendix p. 464-466).
- Gather Halloween costumes and masks.
- Gather props for "Perky Pumpkin's Open House" (Appendix p. 549).
- Obtain a large appliance box and paint it.
- Make felt jack-o-lanterns.
- Make Jack-O-Lantern Puzzles (see p. 399).

Language Enrichment Choices*

▪ Show the children the Magnetic Dress-Me Dolls for Halloween (Appendix p. 464-466). Put costumes on each doll. Invite the children to tell you about the costumes.

▪ Present "The Strange Visitor" prop story (Appendix p. 559-560). Ask the children if they think the story might have happened on Halloween night.

▪ Present the "Perky Pumpkin's Open House" prop story (Appendix p. 549). Talk about real pumpkins. "What do you think is inside of a real pumpkin?"

▪ Encourage the children to touch a real pumpkin. Discuss the way it feels. Let them try to lift it. "Is it heavy?" "Does it roll?" Carve the pumpkin with the children. Let them see what is inside. Encourage them to touch the meat of the pumpkin. "What does it feel like?" Describe facial features as you create them. Toast the seeds for snack.
Safety Warning: Have other adults with you to help supervise this activity. Check for any allergies before serving seeds and make sure the children chew the seeds well before swallowing.

▪ Teach the children the American Sign Language sign for *Halloween* (Appendix p. 433).

Physical Development Choices

▪ Say the following "Trick or Treat" rhyme with the children. Ask them to move as directed by the words in the rhyme.

> **Trick or Treat**
> *Trick or treat touch your feet.* (touch your feet)
> *Trick or treat have a seat.* (sit down)
> *Trick or treat smile real sweet.* (big smile)
> *Trick or treat keep the beat.* (clap six times)
>
> Repeat

▪ Play Pumpkin Roll. Ask the children to sit in a circle with their legs stretched out in front of them. Then ask them to spread their legs so that their feet are touching the feet of the children on either side of them. Give them a ball. Pretend that the ball is a pumpkin. Roll it to one of the children. Make sure all the children have a turn to catch and roll the ball. If desired, use a small pumpkin for the ball.

* Toddlers and twos present a wide range of developmental needs, abilities, and interests. For each learning area, select among the following activity and experience choices that are appropriate for the children in your care.

■ Draw a jack-o-lantern on a piece of orange poster board or bulletin board paper. Lay it on the floor and give the children beanbags to toss on it. Ask them to say which facial feature they are trying to hit before tossing the beanbag. After a child tosses the beanbag, ask her to describe where it landed.

■ Play Hopping Through the Pumpkin Patch. Cut out small pumpkins from orange construction paper and tape them in a path on the floor. Invite the little ones to hop through the "pumpkin patch."

■ Invite older children to participate in the following action story, "Candy Land Journey."

> **Candy Land Journey** by Pam Schiller
> *Let's go on a trip. Who wants to go to Candy Land?* (raise hand) *OK! Let's go!* (sweep arm in forward motion)
> *It's just a short trip from here. First, we walk.* (walk in place about 10 steps)
> *Now we need to get on a plane and fly.* (put arms out to fly for a few seconds) *Look! We're here!* (put arms down and take a few steps)
> *Wow! Here is a sidewalk made of Peppermint Disks. Let's hop on them and see where they go.* (jump from disk to disk about five times) *Be careful not to fall off.*
> *What do we have here? It looks like a river made of caramel. Let's try to walk across* (walk as if stepping in something gooey)
> *That was fun! Who likes caramel?* (raise hands) *Let's taste some.* (stop and scoop up some caramel and pretend to taste it). *Yummm!*
> *Hey, look at the Lemon Drop tree.* (point) *Let's pick some Lemon Drops.* (pretend to pick Lemon Drops) *Let's taste one.* (pretend to chew/crunch)
> *Let's go over there into the forest.* (take a few steps) *Here are some Licorice Laces. Let's play jump rope.* (pretend to jump rope)
> *It's time to go now. Let's head back to the plane. We have to cross the Caramel River again* (cross river) *and hop across the Peppermint Disks.* (jump from disk to disk)
> *Oh! Look at those great lollipops growing like flowers in a garden. Let's pick one to take home.* (pick a lollipop)
> *OK. Let's fly.* (fly)
> *Now let's walk back to our classroom.* (walk)
> *We're home! Who had a good time?* (raise hand) *Me, too. I love Candy Land!*

Social and Emotional Development Choices

■ Sing "Jack-O-Lantern" to the tune of "Clementine" with the children. Use the pumpkin head from "The Strange Visitor" flannel board story or one of the pumpkin puppets as a visual.

Jack-O-Lantern

Jack-o-lantern, Jack-o-lantern,
You are such a funny sight.
As you sit there in my window
Looking out into the night.

You were once a yellow pumpkin
Growing on a sturdy vine.
Now you are my Jack-o-lantern.
Let your candlelight shine.

■ Say "Five Waiting Pumpkins." Point out that pumpkins grow in a pumpkin patch on a vine. You may also want to point out that each of the pumpkins is saying goodbye in a different language.

Five Waiting Pumpkins

Five little pumpkins growing on a vine,
First one said, "It's time to shine!"
Second one said, "I love the fall"
Third one said, "I'm round as a ball."
Fourth one said, "I want to be a pie."
Fifth one said, "Let's say good-bye."
"Good-bye!" said one.
"Adios!" said two.
"Au revoir!" said three.
"Ciao!" said four.
"Aloha!" said five.
And five little pumpkins were picked that day!

■ Say "Five Little Pumpkins" (on the next page). Talk about the pumpkins being frightened. "What scared them?"

Five Little Pumpkins

Five little pumpkins sitting on a gate. (hold up five fingers)
First one said, "It's getting late." (wiggle first finger)
Second one said, "There's witches in the air." (wiggle second finger)
Third one said, "We don't care." (wiggle third finger)
Fourth one said, "Let's run, let's run." (wiggle fourth finger)
Fifth one said, "Oh, it's just Halloween fun." (wiggle fifth finger)
But "whooo" went the wind and out went the light, (hold hands to sides of
  your mouth and blow)
And five little pumpkins rolled out of sight. (roll hand over hand)

▨ Provide several different masks for the children to try on. Be sure to have an
unbreakable mirror handy. Discuss the character each mask represents. Use
descriptive words. "Are they scary?" Some children may be frightened by
masks and costumes. Attempt to help them see that the masks are like
pictures that they hold in front of their faces. They are not real.

Cognitive Development Choices

▨ Hide small toys in a bucket or box of hay (dried grass). Encourage the children
to find them. Ask the children to name the toys when they are found.

▨ Make a house out of a large appliance box. Encourage the children to take
turns being the person who lives in the house and the "trick or treater." Ask
the children which role they like best. Reinforce *in* and *out* and *open* and *shut*.

▨ Provide costumes for the children to dress up in. Ask older children to
describe their outfits. Be sure to provide an unbreakable mirror.

▨ Give the children the Magnetic Dress-Me Dolls for Halloween (Appendix p.
464-466). Encourage them to dress the dolls in the various costumes. "Which
costume do you like best? Why?"

▨ Give the children felt jack-o-lanterns to arrange on the flannel board. Make
them with different faces and in different sizes. You may want to make
matching pairs of pumpkins and invite the older children to match the pairs.

▨ Give the children orange playdough and Halloween cookie cutters. What
shapes do they cut out? Ask them to describe the shapes.

▨ Give the children orange and black tempera paint and encourage them to
paint a Halloween picture. Encourage them to describe their picture to you.

■ Problem-solving suggestion: Make Jack-O-Lantern Puzzles. Cut out large pumpkins from orange construction paper or poster board. Make a pattern for facial features. Draw an outline of the facial features on the pumpkins and then use the patterns to cut facial features out of black construction paper. Laminate the pumpkins and the facial features. Encourage the children to place the features in the correct places on the pumpkins.

REFLECTION ON THE DAY

Ask the children to tell you something about Halloween. Ask younger children to show you something that is a symbol of Halloween.

Thanksgiving

WORDS TO PRACTICE

dinner	Native Americans	pumpkins
family	November	thankful
feathers	pilgrims	Thanksgiving
friends	pumpkin pie	turkey

GETTING STARTED

▨ Sing "Five Fat Turkeys Are We" with the children.

Five Fat Turkeys Are We
Five fat turkeys are we.
We spent the night in a tree.
When the cook came around,
We couldn't be found,
And that's why we're here you see—gobble, gobble!

Oh, five fat turkeys are we.
We spent the night in a tree.
It sure does pay
On Thanksgiving Day
To sleep in the tallest tree—gobble, gobble!

▨ Tell the children that today they will be learning more about *Thanksgiving.*

▨ Read your favorite book about Thanksgiving to the children or select a book from the Story Circle Suggestions below to check out of the library and read.

STORY CIRCLE SUGGESTIONS

▨ *Franklin's Thanksgiving* by Sharon Jennings and Brenda Clark
▨ *Over the River and Through the Wood* by Lynne Cravath (Illustrator)
▨ *The Best Thanksgiving Ever!* by Nancy Inteli
▨ *Today Is Thanksgiving* by P.K. Hallinan

- *We're Thankful* by Angelo C. Santomero and Jennifer Brackenbury

PREPARATION FOR "THANKSGIVING" ACTIVITIES AND EXPERIENCES
- Get pumpkin cupcake holders, vanilla wafers, pumpkin pie filling, and whipped cream for miniature pumpkin pies.

Language Enrichment Choices*

- Ask questions to find out what the children know about Thanksgiving. Who knows what is eaten on Thanksgiving? What is their favorite Thanksgiving food? Discuss the holiday. Explain that Thanksgiving provides an opportunity to celebrate our families and friends. Families and friends get together and eat a meal that is traditionally turkey, dressing, and pumpkin pie. Show pictures of Thanksgiving foods.

- Teach the children the American Sign Language sign for *thank you* (Appendix p. 439).

Physical Development Choices

- Show the children how to bobble their heads and walk like a turkey. Encourage them to walk like a turkey. Say the "Mighty Fine Turkey" rhyme as the children imitate turkeys.

  Mighty Fine Turkey
  I'm a mighty fine turkey
  And I sing a fine song—gobble, gobble, gobble.
  I strut around the barnyard all day long—
  My head goes—bobble, bobble, bobble.
  On Thanksgiving Day
  I run away with a—waddle, waddle, waddle.
  So on the day after
  My head will still—bobble, bobble, bobble.

- Teach the children the fingerplay, "Our Turkey Is a Big Fat Bird," on the following page. Ask a volunteer to show you how a turkey walks and to make a sound like a turkey.

* Toddlers and twos present a wide range of developmental needs, abilities, and interests. For each learning area, select among the following activity and experience choices that are appropriate for the children in your care.

Our Turkey Is a Big Fat Bird

Our turkey is a big fat bird. (hold hands out to indicate large)
He gobbles when he talks. (move hand, thumb to fingers, like talking)
Our turkey is a big fat bird. (hold hands out to indicate large)
He waddles when he walks. (wiggle hand side to side)
Our turkey is a big fat bird. (hold hands out to indicate large)
He spreads his tail this way. (spread fingers on hand like a fan)
On Thanksgiving Day our fat bird (hold hands out to indicate large)
Lifts his wings and flies away. (flap arms to fly)

Social and Emotional Development Choices

- Say "Five Waiting Pumpkins" with the children. Suit the actions to the words. Point out that pumpkin pies are made with the inside meat of the pumpkin. Tell the children that each pumpkin is saying goodbye in a different language.

Five Waiting Pumpkins

Five little pumpkins growing on a vine,
First one said, "It's time to shine!"
Second one said, "I love the fall"
Third one said, "I'm round as a ball."
Fourth one said, "I want to be a pie."
Fifth one said, "Let's say good-bye."
"Good-bye!" said one.
"Adios!" said two.
"Au revoir!" said three.
"Ciao!" said four.
"Aloha!" said five.
And five little pumpkins were picked that day!

- Make miniature pumpkin pies with the children. Give each child a vanilla wafer and a cupcake holder. Ask them to place their cookies inside the cupcake holders. Encourage the children to place two large spoonfuls of pumpkin pie filling on top of their cookies. Bake in a toaster oven at 375° for 15 minutes. Remove from oven and let cool. Top with whipped cream and serve. Call attention to the wonderful spicy aroma while the pies are cooking. **Safety Warning:** Supervise closely; always check for food allergies before serving food to children.

- Invite another class to join you for lunch or snack. Have each group contribute something to the lunch or snack. Discuss sharing. Point out how nice it is to enjoy the company of others.

- Say the following fingerplay, "Five Little Pumpkins" with the children. Ask the children to put one finger up for each pumpkin and then fold all their fingers down when the pumpkins bow their heads.

  Five Little Pumpkins
  Five little pumpkins on Thanksgiving Day,
  The first one said, "I'll have cake if I may."
  The second one said, "I'll have turkey roasted."
  The third one said, "I'll have chestnuts toasted."
  The fourth one said, "I'll have pumpkin pie."
  The fifth one said, "Oh, cranberries I spy."
  But before they had any turkey and dressing,
  They all bowed their heads for a Thanksgiving blessing.

Cognitive Development Choices

- Cover each child's hand with fingerpaint and press it on a piece of construction paper to make a handprint. Show them how to make the handprint into a turkey by adding an eye and a wattle to the thumbprint, and two legs and feet just under the palm. Let the children draw scenery around their turkey, if desired.

- Invite the children to paint with a turkey feather. "How is painting with the feather different than painting with a brush?" Encourage them to name their turkey.

- Give the children pots and pans to play with. Add dishes and invite the older children to pretend to fix a Thanksgiving dinner. What food do they prepare?

- Lay a feather on the table and invite the children to blow it off. Ask them to think of other ways they can get the feather to move besides blowing it with their mouths.

- Invite the children to draw pictures of their families. Scribbles are fine. Label each person as the children direct. Discuss family members. "What things do you do with your families?" "Who is the tallest member of the family?" "Who is the shortest?"

REFLECTION ON THE DAY
Ask the children to tell you something they have learned about Thanksgiving. Ask the "not yet talkers" to show you something that represents Thanksgiving.

Christmas

WORDS TO PRACTICE

Christmas	present	tree
elves	Santa	
holiday	stocking	

GETTING STARTED

- Sing "We Wish You a Merry Christmas" with the children. Sing only as much of the song as the children are interested in. Young children may have enough with one verse. Ask questions to find out what the children know about *Christmas*.

  We Wish You a Merry Christmas
  We wish you a Merry Christmas,
  We wish you a Merry Christmas,
  We wish you a Merry Christmas,
  And a Happy New Year.

  Now bring us some figgy pudding,
  Now bring us some figgy pudding,
  Now bring us some figgy pudding,
  And a cup of good cheer.

  We won't go until we get some,
  We won't go until we get some,
  We won't go until we get some,
  So bring it right now.

  We wish you a Merry Christmas,
  We wish you a Merry Christmas,
  We wish you a Merry Christmas,
  And a Happy New Year.

- Tell the children that today they will be learning more about *Christmas*.

- Read your favorite book about Christmas to the children or select a book from the Story Circle Suggestions below to check out of the library and read.

STORY CIRCLE SUGGESTIONS

- *Christmas in the Big Woods* by Laura Ingalls Wilder
- *Mouse's First Christmas* by Lauren Thompson
- *The Night Before Christmas* by Clement Moore
- *We Wish You a Merry Christmas* by Tracey Campbell Pearson

PREPARATION FOR "CHRISTMAS" ACTIVITIES AND EXPERIENCES

- Make the "What's in the Box?" flannel board story (Appendix p. 579-583).
- Gather Christmas items.
- Make Bell Ringers and Bell Balls (on the next page).
- Get roll of sugar cookie dough, icing, and decorative items.
- Cut sponges into Christmas symbol shapes.
- Make Scented Playdough (see p. 407).
- Cut out construction paper trees for the children and a second set in graduated sizes.
- Wrap presents and place items that produce sound (e.g., bells and buttons) inside.

Language Enrichment Choices*

- Sing "Santa Claus Is Coming to Town" with the children. Discuss Santa's clothing. Ask questions. "What color boots does Santa wear?" "What color is his suit?" "How does he get from house to house?"

Santa Claus Is Coming to Town

Oh! You better watch out,
You better not cry,
You better not pout,
I'm telling you why:
Santa Claus is coming to town!

He's making a list,
Checking it twice,
Gonna find out who's naughty or nice.
Santa Claus is coming to town!

He sees you when you're sleeping,
He knows when you're awake.
He knows if you've been bad or good,
So be good for goodness sake!

Oh! You better watch out,
You better not cry,
You better not pout,
I'm telling you why:
Santa Claus is coming to town!

* Toddlers and twos present a wide range of developmental needs, abilities, and interests. For each learning area, select among the following activity and experience choices that are appropriate for the children in your care.

- Show the children some symbols of Christmas such as Santa Claus, Christmas trees, gifts, Christmas and carolers, stars, and sparkling lights. Introduce the items or pictures of the items. Ask questions to find out what the children know about each item.

- Present "What's in the Box?" flannel board story (Appendix p. 579-583). Change the present in the story to represent a Christmas present. You may want to make the wrapping paper look like Christmas paper. Discuss the item in the box. "What would you like it to be?" "What would you like to unwrap on Christmas?"

- Teach the children the American Sign Language sign for *Merry Christmas* (Appendix p. 435).

Physical Development Choices

- Make Bell Ringers by filling clean, empty potato chip cans with jingle bells and taping them closed securely. Invite the children to play the Bell Ringers as they sing "Jingle Bells."

  Jingle Bells
  Jingle bells! Jingle bells!
  Jingle all the way.
  Oh, what fun it is to ride in a one-horse, open sleigh, Hey!
  Jingle bells! Jingle bells!
  Jingle all the way.
  Oh, what fun it is to ride in a one-horse, open sleigh.

- Invite the children to roll or bounce Bell Balls, or drop them into a box. To make Bell Balls, cut four or five Ping-Pong balls in half or partially in half and put two or three jingle bells inside of each. Use masking tape or duct tape to put the Ping-Pong balls back together.

Social and Emotional Development Choices

- Bake Sugar Cookies using a pre-mixed cookie dough. Provide Christmas cookie cutters so the children can cut out their favorite shape. Bake them in a toaster oven in the classroom so the children can watch as they bake and smell their wonderful aroma at the same time. Provide icing and decorations for the children to use to decorate their special cookie. Discuss the shapes of the cookie cutters and the texture of the icings and decorations.
  Safety Warning: Supervise closely. Always check for allergies before serving food to children.

Teach the children "Rudolph the Red-Nosed Reindeer." Ask the children how they think Rudolph felt when the other reindeer laughed at him and called him names. "Why did the other reindeer laugh at Rudolph?" "What color nose do the other reindeer have?" Remind the children that being different can be a good thing.

Rudolph the Red-Nosed Reindeer
Rudolph the red-nosed reindeer
Had a very shiny nose.
And if you ever saw it,
You would even say it glows.
All of the other reindeer
Used to laugh and call him names;
They never let poor Rudolph
Join in any reindeer games.

Then one foggy Christmas night,
Santa came to say:
"Rudolph with your nose so bright,
Won't you guide my sleigh tonight?"
Then how the reindeer loved him
As they shouted out with glee,
"Rudolph the Red-Nosed Reindeer,
You'll go down in history!"

Cognitive Development Choices

Encourage the children to use Christmas cookie cutters to cut playdough Christmas cookies. Ask the children to describe the playdough shapes.

Cut sponges into Christmas symbols such as bells, trees, and stars. Invite the children to make a Christmas sponge painting. Attach clothespins to the sponges to make them easier to manipulate. Let them help you label the items in their pictures.

Provide Scented Playdough. Add peppermint extract to your favorite recipe for playdough. Discuss the scent of the dough as the children play with it. Ask questions. "What does the playdough smell like?" "Do you like the smell?" "What else smells like this?"

■ Give the children presents to shake and rattle. Place some interesting sounding items such as buttons, washers, and gravel inside boxes. Wrap the boxes in Christmas paper. Encourage the children to arrange the boxes by size and then to shake the boxes and describe the sound of the items inside.

■ Cut out tree shapes from green construction paper. Give the children the trees and stick-on dots (about 1" big) in a variety of colors. Encourage them to decorate their tree with stick-on dots and stars.

■ Problem-solving suggestion: Cut construction paper trees in graduated sizes. Ask the children to help arrange the trees from smallest to largest.

REFLECTION ON THE DAY
Ask the children to tell you something they have learned about Christmas. Ask the "not yet talkers" to show you something that represents Christmas.

Hanukkah

WORDS TO PRACTICE

candles	holiday	traditions
dreidel	latkes	
Hanukah	menorah	

GETTING STARTED

▨ Sing "Hanukkah's Here" to the tune of "Are You Sleeping?" For younger children you may want to sing only one verse.

Hanukkah's Here
Hanukkah's here,
Hanukkah's here,
Memories dear,
Time to cheer.
Happy children singing,
Merry bells are ringing,
Hanukkah,
Hanukkah.

Hanukkah's here,
Hanukkah's here,
Memories dear,
Time to cheer.
Candles burning brightly,
Dreidels spinning lightly,
Hanukkah,
Hanukkah.

▨ Tell the children that Hanukkah is a Jewish holiday that is celebrated every year. Tell them that today they will learn more about *Hanukkah*.

▨ Read your favorite book about Hanukkah to the children or select a book from the Story Circle Suggestions on the next page to check out of the library and read.

STORY CIRCLE SUGGESTIONS

- *Latkes and Applesauce: A Hanukkah Story* by Fran Manushkin
- *My First Chanukah* by Tomie dePaola
- *My First Hanukkah Board Book*

PREPARATION FOR "HANUKKAH" ACTIVITIES AND EXPERIENCES

- Make the "What's in the Box?" flannel board story (Appendix p. 579-583).
- Cut out felt candles.
- Make toilet paper and paper towel tube candles.
- Get applesauce and ingredients for latkes if you are going to make them (see next page).
- Locate menorah and dreidel.
- Wrap presents and place items that produce sound (e.g., bells and buttons) inside.

Language Enrichment Choices*

- Show the children a menorah and a dreidel or pictures of each. Children this age won't understand all the significance of the story of Hanukkah. Just explain that these items are symbols of the holiday. Focus on vocabulary.

- Present the "What's in the Box?" flannel board story (Appendix p. 579-583). Discuss the presents that children get during the Hanukkah season. It is usually eight gifts, one for each of the eight days the candles are burned.

- Teach the children the American Sign Language sign for *Happy Hanukkah* (Appendix p. 433).

Physical Development Choices

- Play "My Dreidel" and invite the children to turn and spin it like a top. If you do not have the music to "My Dreidel" you can sing the song or just play another piece of music.

My Dreidel

I have a little dreidel,
I made it out of clay;
And when it's dry and ready,
Then dreidel I shall play.

It has a lovely body,
With legs so short and thin;
And when it is all tired.
It drops and then I win.

Oh dreidel, dreidel, dreidel,
I made it out of clay;
Oh dreidel, dreidel, dreidel,
Now dreidel I shall play.

* Toddlers and twos present a wide range of developmental needs, abilities, and interests. For each learning area, select among the following activity and experience choices that are appropriate for the children in your care.

■ Encourage the children to dance with orange streamers (candles burning).

Social and Emotional Development Choices

■ Serve the children latkes for snacks. If desired, make them using the following recipe:

Mix 1 grated onion, 1 teaspoon salt, 1 egg, and 6 grated potatoes in a bowl. Add 3 tablespoons flour and ½ teaspoon baking powder to the mixture. Drop by the spoonfuls into a frying pan. Brown on both sides. Cool and serve with applesauce. Describe the latkes to the children and explain that latkes are a traditional Hanukkah treat.

Safety Warning: Always check for allergies before serving food to children.

■ Sing "My Dreidel" (see previous page) with the children. If available, show them a dreidel and spin it while you sing.

■ Say "Eight Candles" to the children. Use it as a fingerplay—ask the children to hold up one finger for each candle.

> **Eight Candles**
> *Eight little candles in a row,*
> *Gaily colored, all aglow.*
> *Scarlet, purple, green, white, blue*
> *Pink and yellow, orange too.*
> *The menorah, shining bright,*
> *Hold a rainbow Hanukkah night.*

Cognitive Development Choices

■ Give the children wrapped packages to shake. Place items inside that create a sound when they are shaken, such as jingle bells, pieces of gravel, washers, buttons, and so forth. Discuss the sounds that each package makes and invite the children to guess what is inside.

■ Provide some toddler spinning tops for the children to play with. Talk about the tops as they spin. "How do they stay up?" "How fast are they spinning?"

■ Make felt candles and encourage the children to arrange them on a flannel board. Point out the candlestick and its flame. Count the candles. "Who can arrange them in a row?"

■ Provide clay. Encourage the children to work freely with the clay. Remind them that the song ("My Driedel") says the dreidel is made from clay. Working with clay is a different experience than working with playdough. Talk with the children about the texture and the coolness of the clay. Ask the children to describe the feel of the clay.

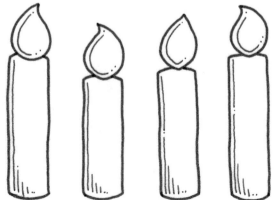

■ Problem-solving suggestion: Make candles by covering toilet and paper towel tubes in construction paper and adding an orange construction paper flame. Encourage the children to stand the candles on the table. For older children, you may want to cut the paper towel tubes to lengths that will allow them to arrange the candles like a menorah.

REFLECTION ON THE DAY
Ask the children to tell you something they have learned about Hanukkah.

Valentine's Day

WORDS TO PRACTICE

cards	heart
decorations	love
family	sweethearts
friends	Valentines

GETTING STARTED

- Make a trail of hearts from the doorway to the area where you hold circle time. Encourage the children to follow them into the room. Ask the children if they know why the hearts are on the floor. Show them some valentines. Pass them around for the children to look at. Explain that Valentine's Day is a day set aside to let our friends and family know how much we love them.
- Tell the children that today they will be learning more about *Valentine's Day*.
- Read your favorite book about Valentine's Day to the children or select a book from the Story Circle Suggestions below to check out of the library and read.

STORY CIRCLE SUGGESTIONS

- *A Book of Hugs* by Dave Ross
- *Counting Kisses* by Karen Katz
- *The Day It Rained Hearts* by Felicia Bond

PREPARATION FOR "VALENTINE'S DAY" ACTIVITIES AND EXPERIENCES

- Gather Valentines.
- Make the "Valerie Valentine" flannel board story (Appendix p. 573-575).
- Make the Leap of Hearts Game (on the next page) and Broken Heart Puzzles (see p. 416).
- Cut out felt heart, sponge hearts, and construction paper hearts.
- Fill the candy boxes with sound-producing items.

▪ Cut out paper hearts to make a trail from the doorway to the circle area of the room.

Language Enrichment Choices*

▪ Say "Five Pink Valentines" with the children. Count off the valentines as you say the rhyme. Discuss giving valentines to friends. Discuss the colors, shapes, and sizes of valentines.

> **Five Pink Valentines** by Pam Schiller
> *Five pink valentines from the card store,*
> *I gave one to [Sam], now there are four.*
> *Four pink valentines, pretty ones to see.*
> *I gave one to [Maddie], now there are three.*
> *Three pink valentines, pink through and through,*
> *I gave one to [Austin], now there are two.*
> *Two pink valentines having lots of fun,*
> *I gave one to [Gabrielle], now there is one.*
> *One pink valentine, my story is almost done,*
> *I gave it to you, now there are none.*

▪ Present the "Valerie Valentine" flannel board story (Appendix p. 573-575). "What did Valerie do to get someone to notice her?"

▪ Teach the children the American Sign Language sign for *I love you* (Appendix p. 434).

Physical Development Choices

* Toddlers and twos present a wide range of developmental needs, abilities, and interests. For each learning area, select among the following activity and experience choices that are appropriate for the children in your care.

▪ Cut out large hearts from red poster board or vinyl to create a Leap of Hearts Game. Place them on the floor and invite the children to leap (or hop, or walk, or move in any way) from heart to heart. Talk about the word "leap." It will probably be a new word for most children.

▪ Cut out a heart from red felt. Cut a small hole in the center of it and slip it over a service bell. Invite the children to toss beanbags at the heart and try to ring the bell.

Social and Emotional Development Choices

▦ Help the children make valentines for their families. Provide cut-out hearts, doilies, lace, markers, paint, tissue paper, and so on. Give each child a large heart and encourage her to glue the decorative collage items on it. Turn it over and paste a copy of the verse below ("You're My Valentine"). The children can sign their card with a handprint. Coat the child's hand with fingerpaint and then help her press it on the back of her card. Be sure to date it—some day families may look back and wish they could remember the year the card was made. Talk with children about the tradition of giving cards to their friends and people they love on Valentine's Day. Discuss the items used to decorate the cards.

▦ Sing "You're My Valentine" to the tune of "Jingle Bells" with the children.

> **You're My Valentine**
> *Valentine,*
> *Valentine,*
> *You're my Valentine.*
> *'Cause I like you, oh, so much,*
> *Sweet Valentine of mine.*

▦ Serve heart-shaped cookies and let the children ice and decorate them. Talk about the cookies as the children work. "What color icing are you using?" "What kind of decorations are you using?"

Cognitive Development Choices

▦ Give the children playdough and heart-shaped cookie cutters. Invite them to cut out Valentine hearts.

▦ Fill heart-shaped candy boxes with items that will make a noise when shaken, such as buttons, washers, paper clips, and so forth. Seal the boxes securely. Encourage the children to shake the boxes. "What sounds do you hear?" "Which boxes make a loud sound?" "Which boxes make a soft sound?"

▦ Hide construction paper hearts all around the room. Be sure part of the heart is visible to the children. Encourage them to be on the lookout for hearts all day. As the children find the hearts, collect them and print the finder's name on the heart. At the end of the day, count the hearts to see who found the most.

■ Give the children four hearts cut in graduated sizes. Help them arrange the hearts from largest to smallest.

■ Cut sponges into heart shapes and let the children play with the hearts in a tub of water.

■ Give the children empty candy boxes to play with. They can fill them or stack them inside of each other. Talk with them about the shape of the boxes. Encourage them to run their fingers around the perimeter of the boxes.

■ Problem-solving suggestion: Give the children Broken Heart Puzzles to put together. Cut three or four construction paper hearts into two-part puzzles pieces. Invite the children to put the broken hearts back together. You can make all the hearts the same color to make this activity more difficult, or you can make the hearts different colors to make it easier.

REFLECTION ON THE DAY
Ask the children to tell you something they have learned about Valentine's Day. Ask the "not yet talkers" to show you a heart.

Mother's Day

WORDS TO PRACTICE

family	mommy
grandmother	mother
mama	

GETTING STARTED

- Invite the children to bring in photos of their moms and show them to the class. Encourage them to talk about their mommies. Ask questions about what their mommies are doing in the picture. "What does your mommy like to do?" Be sensitive to the fact that many children may not have a mother who plays an active role in their lives. Explain that Mother's Day is a special day set aside to make mommies feel special by showing them how much we love them and appreciate them.

- Tell them that today they will be learning more about *mommies*.

- Read your favorite book about mothers or families to the children or select a book from the Story Circle Suggestions below to check out of the library and read.

STORY CIRCLE SUGGESTIONS

- *Flower Garden* by Eve Bunting
- *I Love My Mommy Because—* by Laurel Porter-Gaylord
- *I Love You, Stinky Face* by Lisa McCourt
- *In Grandmother's Arms* by Jayne C. Shelton
- *Love You Forever* by Sheila McGraw
- *Mama, Do You Love Me?* by Barbara Joosee
- *Mother's Day Mice* by Eve Bunting
- *Over the Moon: An Adoption Tale* by Karen Katz
- *Tell Me Again About the Night I Was Born* by Jamie Lee Curtis

PREPARATION FOR "MOTHER'S DAY" ACTIVITIES AND EXPERIENCES

- In advance, ask families to send in a photo of the child's mother. Encourage the children who do not have access to their mothers to bring in photos of someone special to them (Appendix p. 441).
- Make the "Three Little Kittens" flannel board rhyme (Appendix p. 603-606), if not already made.
- Cut sponges into heart and flower shapes.
- Find pictures of animals and their babies.

Language Enrichment Choices*

- Read "My Mommy" to the children. Ask the children to think of things they enjoy doing with their mommies. Make some suggestions for those children who are not talking, such as reading a book, playing, laughing, eating, and getting dressed.

   My Mommy
   I love to sit in Mommy's lap
   I feel all safe and sound.
   I give my mom a hug and kiss
   Before she puts me down.

- Discuss the many different things that children call their mothers. Encourage the children to tell you what name they call their mother.

- Present the "Three Little Kittens" flannel board rhyme (Appendix p. 603-606) to the children. Talk to them about how children are supposed to mind their mommies. Point out that the kittens got in trouble because they disobeyed their mother, and how happy the mother cat was when the kittens found their mittens.

- Teach the children the American Sign Language sign for *mother* (Appendix p. 435).

Physical Development Choices

- Sing and act out "The Baby Chicks." Discuss all the things the mother chick does to take care of her babies.

* Toddlers and twos present a wide range of developmental needs, abilities, and interests. For each learning area, select among the following activity and experience choices that are appropriate for the children in your care.

The Baby Chicks
Baby chicks say, "Peep, peep, peep,"
As they wake from sleep, sleep, sleep. (rub eyes)
Baby chicks say, "Peep, peep, peep,"
And hear the birds go "cheep, cheep, cheep." (repeat "cheep, cheep, cheep")
Baby chicks say, "Peep, peep, peep,"
We are hungry, "Peep, peep, peep." (rub belly)
Mama feeds them and then she says,
"Now it's time to sleep, sleep, sleep." (lay head in hands)

■ Sing "One Little Duck" with the children. It is a slightly different version of "Five Little Ducks" and is sung to the same tune. Discuss the mother watching out for her ducklings. "Has anyone been to feed the ducks with your mother?"

One Little Duck
One little duck went out to play (hold up one finger)
Down by the pond on a fine spring day. (make hitchhiking sign over shoulder)
Another one said, "That's fun to do!" (shake head yes)
He joined in and that made two. (hold up two fingers)

Two little ducks went out to play (repeat using correct number of fingers)
Down by the pond on a fine spring day.
Another one said, "Hey wait for me!"
He joined in and that made three.

Three little ducks went out to play (repeat using correct number of fingers)
Down by the pond on a fine spring day.
Another one peeked 'round the old bar door,
He joined in and that made four.

Four little ducks went out to play (repeat using correct number of fingers)
Down by the pond on a fine spring day.
Another one saw them dip and dive,
He joined in and that made five.

Five little ducks went out to play (hold up five fingers)
Down by the pond on a fine spring day. (hitchhiking sign)
The mother duck wished they all would come back. (hands on cheeks)
She called them home with a quack, quack, quack. (hands around mouth as if calling and then clap three times)

Social and Emotional Development Choices

▪ Talk about all the nice things mommies or special friends do for their children. For example, they prepare food for them, play with them, provide clothing for them, rock them, read to them, and so forth. Provide a baby doll and a few props so that the children can pretend to be a mommy taking care of and playing with little ones.

▪ Sing "Over in the Meadow" with the children. Discuss baby animals and their mothers. Explain that mother animals take care of their babies like human mothers do.

Over in the Meadow
Over in the meadow, in the sand, in the sun,
Lived an old mother frog and her little froggie one.
"Croak!" said the mother; "I croak!" said the one,
So they croaked and they croaked in the sand, in the sun.

Over in the meadow, in the stream so blue,
Lived an old mother fish and her little fishies two.
"Swim!" said the mother; "We swim!" said the two.
So they swam and they swam in the stream so blue.

Over in the meadow, on a branch of the tree,
Lived an old mother bird and her little birdies three.
"Sing!" said the mother; "We sing!" said the three,
And they sang and they sang on a branch of the tree.

Cognitive Development Choices

▪ Ask the children to draw a picture for their mothers. Encourage talkers to describe their picture. With permission, transcribe their description on the back of their work.

▪ Make Mother's Day cards. Fold a piece of construction paper in half. Provide flower- and heart-shaped sponges and paint and encourage the children to sponge paint flowers and hearts on the front of their cards. Attach clothespins to the sponges to make them easier to manipulate. Photocopy the poem below to go inside. Coat each child's hand with fingerpaint and help the children "sign" their cards with a handprint.

I Love You, Mommy
I love you, mommy,
I love you true.
Happy Mother's Day, Mommy,
From me to you!

■ Provide mommy dress-up clothes for the children to explore. Be sure to include female accessories such as jewelry, purses, and hats. Encourage children to look at themselves in a mirror. "Do you think you look like mommies?"

■ Encourage the children to look through magazines for pictures of mommies and children. As they find pictures, ask them questions about what the mommies and the children in the pictures are doing. "How do you know mommies and babies belong together?"

■ Problem-solving suggestion: Provide photographs of baby animals and their mothers. Encourage the children to find a mommy for each baby.

REFLECTION ON THE DAY
Ask the children to tell you something they have learned about mothers.

Father's Day

WORDS TO PRACTICE

daddy	grandfather
family	papa
father	

GETTING STARTED

- Invite the children to show the photos that they have brought in of their daddies. Ask questions about what their daddy is doing in the picture. "What does your daddy like to do?" Be sensitive to the fact that many children may not have a father who plays an active role in their lives. Explain that Father's Day is a special day set aside to make daddies feel special by showing them how much we love them and appreciate them.

- Tell them that today they will learning more about *daddies*.

- Read your favorite book about fathers or families to the children or select a book from the Story Circle Suggestions below to check out of the library and read.

STORY CIRCLE SUGGESTIONS

- *Baseball, Football, Daddy, and Me* by David Friend
- *I Love My Daddy Because—* by Laurel Porter-Gaylord
- *A Perfect Father's Day* by Eve Bunting
- *The Secret Father's Day Present* by Andrew Clements

PREPARATION FOR "FATHER'S DAY" ACTIVITIES AND EXPERIENCES

- In advance, ask families to send in a photo of the child's father. Encourage the children who do not have access to their fathers to bring in a photo of someone special to them (Appendix p. 441).

- Make the "My Father Picks Oranges" flannel board story (Appendix p. 538-541).

- Cut sponges into bat and ball shapes.

- Find pictures of animals and their parents.

Language Enrichment Choices*

- Read "My Daddy" to the children. Ask the children to think of things they enjoy doing with their daddies or someone special to them.

  My Daddy by Pam Schiller
  I love to feel my daddy's arms
  When he lifts me from the ground.
  I give my dad a hug and kiss
  Before he puts me down.

- Discuss the many different things that children call their daddies. Let the children each tell you what they call their daddy.

- Teach the children the American Sign Language sign for *father* (Appendix p. 432).

Physical Development Choices

- Play "Daddy-O."

  Daddy-O
  Daddy-O, Daddy-O, 'round we go, (walk in a circle)
  Daddy-O, Daddy-O, let's go slow. (walk slowly and speak the line slowly)
  Daddy-O, Daddy-O, touch your toe, (stop and touch toes)
  Daddy-O, Daddy-O, can you blow? (blow)
  Daddy-O, Daddy-O, up we go, (stand on tiptoes)
  Daddy-O, Daddy-O, say hello! (say or sign "hello")

Social and Emotional Development Choices

- Talk about all the nice things daddies or special friends do for their children. Discuss how daddies play with them, provide clothing for them, rock them, read to them, and so forth. Provide a baby doll and a few props so that the children can pretend to be a daddy taking care of and playing with little ones.

- For older children, present the "My Father Picks Oranges" flannel board story (Appendix p. 538-541). Discuss the work that fathers do. Help the children find something beneficial in each job discussed.

* Toddlers and twos present a wide range of developmental needs, abilities, and interests. For each learning area, select among the following activity and experience choices that are appropriate for the children in your care.

Cognitive Development Choices

- Have the children draw a picture just for daddy or a special friend. Encourage talkers to describe their picture. With permission, transcribe their description on the back of their work.

- Make Father's Day cards. Fold a piece of construction paper in half. Provide flower- and heart-shaped sponges and paint and encourage the children to sponge paint flowers and hearts on the front of their cards. Attach clothespins to the sponges to make them easier to manipulate. Photocopy the poem below to go inside. Coat each child's hand with fingerpaint and help the children "sign" their cards with a handprint.

    I Love You, Daddy
    I love you, daddy,
    I love you true.
    Happy Father's Day, Daddy
    From me to you!

- Provide daddy dress-up clothes for the children to explore. Be sure to include male accessories such as billfolds, baseball hats, and ties. Try to provide a variety of work clothes because the children are often most familiar with daddies in uniforms of some kind. Talk with the children as they dress. Discuss the different items of clothing. "Where are they worn?" "Which pieces of clothing look like things you see your daddies wear?" Be sure to include a mirror.

- Invite the children to look through magazines for pictures of fathers and children. Ask questions about the pictures they find. "What is the father in the picture doing?" "What are the children doing?"

- Problem-solving suggestion: Provide photographs of baby animals and their fathers. Encourage the children to find a daddy for each baby. "How do you know that daddies and babies go together?"

REFLECTION ON THE DAY
Ask the children to tell you something they learned about fathers today.

Everybody's Birthday

WORDS TO PRACTICE

birth	cake	presents
birthday	celebration	
candles	growing	

GETTING STARTED

▧ Sing "Happy Birthday to Us." Tell the children that birthdays are intended to celebrate the special day on which each person is born. Usually people have different birthdays, but sometimes people we know are born on the same day we were born.

Happy Birthday to Us
Happy Birthday to us.
Happy Birthday to us.
Happy Birthday to everyone,
Happy Birthday to us.

▧ Tell the children that today they are going to celebrate everyone's *birthday* at the same time.

▧ Read your favorite book about celebrations to the children or select a book from the Story Circle Suggestions below to check out of the library and read.

STORY CIRCLE SUGGESTIONS

▧ *Birthday Monsters!* by Sandra Boynton
▧ *Carl's Birthday* by Alexandra Day
▧ *Happy Birthday to You* by Dr. Seuss
▧ *It's My Birthday* by Helen Oxenbury

PREPARATION FOR "EVERYBODY'S BIRTHDAY" ACTIVITIES AND EXPERIENCES

▧ Make the "What's in the Box?" (Appendix p. 579-583) and "Miguel's Birthday" (Appendix p. 532-533) flannel board stories.

- Get cupcakes, icing, decorations, and birthday candles.
- Cut out cakes and candles from felt.
- Make plastic rings.

Language Enrichment Choices*

- Talk about birthdays. "Which children in the group were born in the same month?" "Who is one?" "Who is two?" "Who is three?" Read "When I Was One" to the children.

  When I Was One
  When I was one I was so small, (hold up one finger)
  I could not speak a word at all. (shake head)
  When I was two, I learned to talk. (hold up two fingers)
  I learned to sing, I learned to walk. (point to mouth and feet)
  When I am three, I'll learn and grow, (hold up two fingers)
  There's no telling what I'll know. (point to head)

- Teach the children "Feliz Cumpleanos" ("Happy Birthday" in Spanish) below.

  Cumpleaños a tí   **Cumpleaños Feliz**
  ¡Feliz Cumpleaños a tí   *¡Cumpleaños Feliz*
  ¡Feliz Cumpleaños a tí   Or   *¡Cumpleaños Feliz*
  ¡Que la pases muy bien!   *¡Cumpleaños Cumpleaños*
  ¡Feliz Cumpleaños a tí.   *¡Cumpleaños Feliz*

- Present the "What's in the Box?" flannel board story (Appendix p. 579-583). Let the children guess what's in the box as you tell the story. Talk about birthday presents and the excitement of waiting to unwrap them. Stress descriptive words.

- Teach the children the American Sign Language sign for *Happy Birthday* (Appendix p. 433).

Physical Development Choices

- Play the traditional birthday party game Drop the Clothespin in the Bottle. Provide a large-mouth bottle (jar) and some clothespins. Encourage the children to try to hold the clothespins waist high and then drop them into the bottle.

- Invite the children to participate in "Let's Pretend to Bake a Cake" (on the next page). Encourage the children to copy your actions. "Has anyone helped someone make a real cake?"

* Toddlers and twos present a wide range of developmental needs, abilities, and interests. For each learning area, select among the following activity and experience choices that are appropriate for the children in your care.

426

Let's Pretend to Bake a Cake by Pam Schiller
*Who wants to bake a cake? I need all the bakers to come sit by me. Let's see. We
    need a mixer, two bowls, measuring cups and spoons, and a cake pan.* (pretend
    to take items out of shelves and drawers) *Now I think we are ready.*
First we put our butter and sugar in our bowl. (place both into bowl) *Now
    we need the mixer.* (run it over bowl as you make a humming noise)
    That looks nice and smooth. Let's add the eggs. (count and crack four
    eggs into bowl) *Let's mix again.* (run mixer and hum) *This looks good.*
Now we need to add the flour. (measure two cups full and dump into bowl)
    Just one more ingredient—a teaspoon of vanilla. (measure in a teaspoon
    of vanilla) *A final mix* (mix) *and we are ready to pour our batter into our
    cake pan.* (pour) *Now it's time to put our cake in the oven.* (open oven door
    as you make a squeaking sound, slide the cake in and close the door.)
Now our cake is baking. (tap fingers to act like you are waiting) *I can't wait!
    Who can smell it cooking?* (sniff) *That smells good! OK! Let's take our cake
    out of the oven.* (take the cake out and smell it) *Who wants some cake?*

- Say the fingerplay, "Birthday Candles" with the children. "How many candles
will be on your next birthday cake?"

Birthday Candles
Birthday candles one—two—three (hold up fingers on the count)
Birthday candles just for me! (point to self)
Last year two—next year four, (hold up two fingers on left hand and four
fingers on right)
Birthday candles I want more! (hold up 10 fingers)

Social and Emotional Development Choices

- Provide cupcakes, icing, and decorations. Let the children help ice and
decorate their cupcakes. Discuss the colors of the icing and the decorations.
Discuss the locations children choose to place their decorations.

- Present the "Miguel's Birthday" flannel board story (Appendix p. 532-533).
"What things do you do to celebrate your birthday?" Remind them that
everyone has a birthday. It is a special day for celebrating their birth.

Cognitive Development Choices

■ Give the children cake shapes and candles cut from different colors of felt. Encourage them to make a birthday cake on the flannel board. "What does a pink cake taste like? A brown cake? A white cake?"

■ Give the children wrapped boxes with a variety of items inside to shake. Wrap up cotton balls, paperclips, washers, magazines, and so forth. Ask the children questions as they play with the boxes. "Which boxes are large?" "Which ones are small?" "Which ones are heavy?" "Which ones are lighter?" "Which ones make a big noise?" "Which ones make a softer noise?"

■ Provide birthday party props such as hat, plates, cups, and streamers. Invite the children to play birthday party. As the children play, name the items they are playing with and discuss how each item is used for the birthday party.

■ Give the children playdough to make birthday cakes and real birthday candles to decorate them. "How may candles would you have on your cake?"

■ Problem-solving suggestion: Place a birthday party hat in the middle of the floor and give the children plastic rings (cut out the centers of large plastic coffee can lids) to toss at the hat. Can any of the children get their ring around the hat? Try standing closer and then further away. "Which is easier?" Talk about where the rings land in relationship to the hat.

REFLECTION ON THE DAY
Encourage the children to tell you something they learned about birthdays today.

Appendix

American Sign Language

American Sign Language Signs

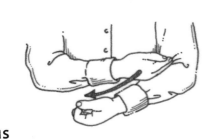

ARMS

BACKWARD (BACKPEDALING)

BIG

BLACK

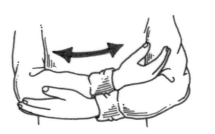

BABY

BLUE

BACK

BOTTOM

BROTHER

DAY

CHIN

DOWN

CIRCLE

EAR

CLOUDS

ELBOW

COLD

EYE

431

American Sign Language

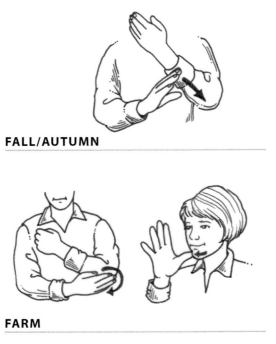

FALL/AUTUMN

FEET

FARM

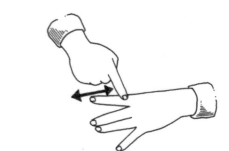

FINGER

FAST

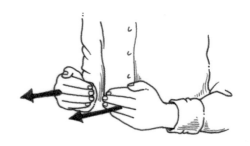

FIRST

FAT

FORWARD

FATHER

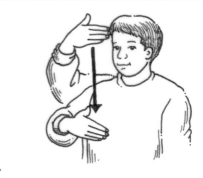

FRONT

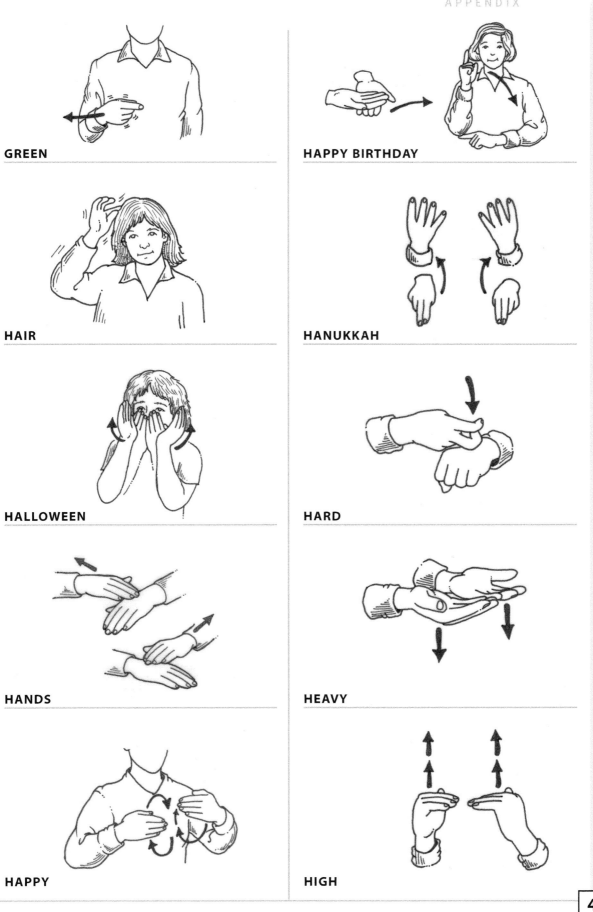

GREEN

HAPPY BIRTHDAY

HAIR

HANUKKAH

HALLOWEEN

HARD

HANDS

HEAVY

HAPPY

HIGH

433

American Sign Language

HOT

LARGE

HUG

LAST

I LOVE YOU

LEG

IN/INSIDE

LIGHT

KNEE

LITTLE

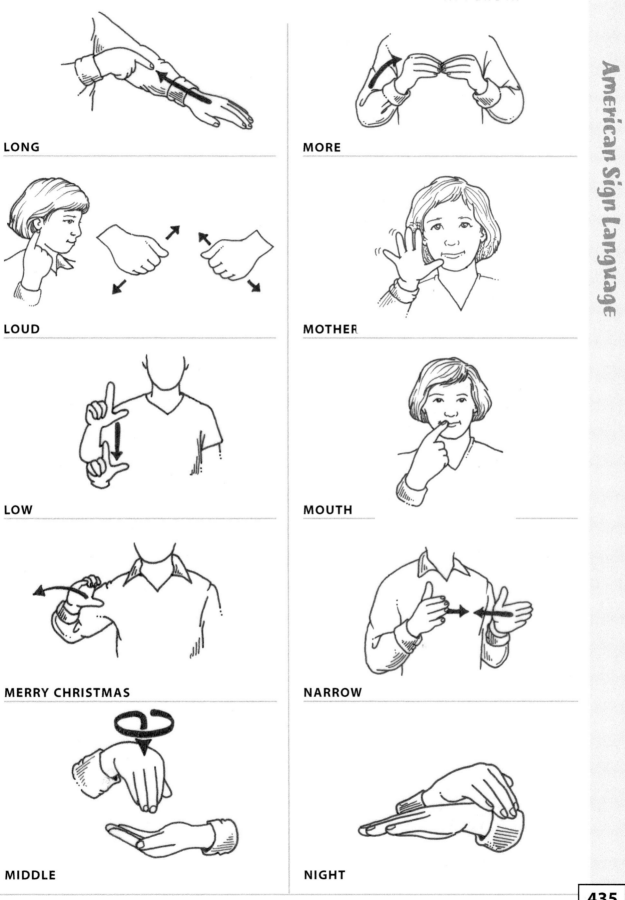

LONG

MORE

LOUD

MOTHER

LOW

MOUTH

MERRY CHRISTMAS

NARROW

MIDDLE

NIGHT

American Sign Language

NEXT

NOSE

OFF

ON

ORANGE

OUT/OUTSIDE

OVER/ABOVE

PIG

PURPLE

RAIN

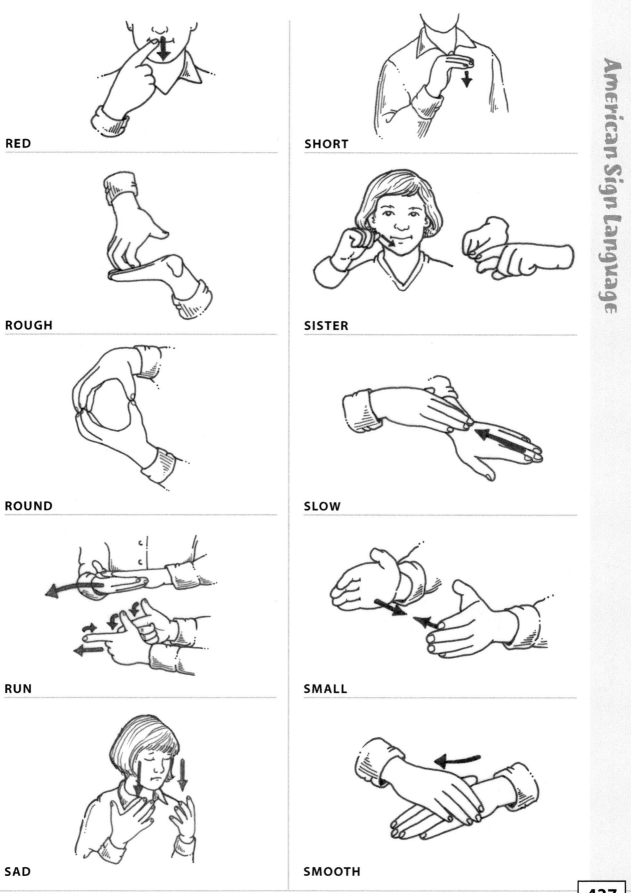

RED

SHORT

ROUGH

SISTER

ROUND

SLOW

RUN

SMALL

SAD

SMOOTH

American Sign Language

American Sign Language

SOFT

STOP

SPIDER

STRIPES

SPRING

SUMMER

SQUARE

SUNNY

STAR

TALL

THANK YOU

UNDER/BELOW

THICK

UP

THIN/SKINNY

WHEELS

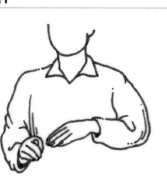

TOES

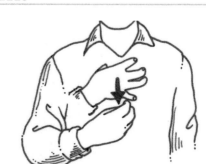

WHITE

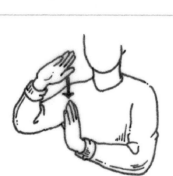

TOP

WIDE

439

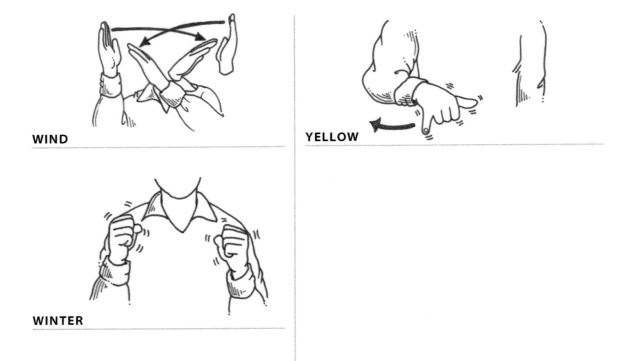

WIND

YELLOW

WINTER

REQUEST FOR BIRTH WEIGHT AND LENGTH

Dear Family,

We are learning about opposites at school. Soon we will be discussing heavy and light and tall and short. To help children see the differences in each of these pairs of opposites, we will be making comparisons of current weight and birth weight and in current height and birth length. Will you please let us know your child's birth information (length and weight)?

Thank you.

Sincerely,

REQUEST FOR TOOTHBRUSH

Dear Family,

We are learning about our mouth, teeth, and tongue. One of our activities will involve learning how to brush our teeth. We are requesting that each family bring in a toothbrush for their child that can be kept in the classroom. Your children will brush their teeth daily after lunch and will use the tooth brushing routine to learn other concepts such as up and down and first, next, and last.

Thank you.

Sincerely,

Family Letters

REQUEST FOR PHOTOGRAPHS (CHILD AND FAMILY)

Dear Family,

We will be doing several activities during the year that will require having a photograph of the children and their families. Please bring in a photograph of your child and his or her mother and father or guardian. We will make photocopies of the photographs and return them unharmed. Thank you for your help.

Sincerely,

Family Letters

Family Letters

REQUEST FOR THROW-AWAY ITEMS

Dear Family,

We often use throw-away materials for our classroom activities. Will you help us collect the following items?

buttons
egg cartons
fabric scraps
felt
half-liter soda bottles
heart-shaped boxes
lace
lunch-size sacks
newspapers
paper grocery sacks
potato chip cans
rickrack
small boxes with lids
square tissue boxes
Styrofoam meat trays
toilet paper and paper towel tubes
washers

Thank you for your contributions.

Sincerely,

COLOR SCHEDULE

Dear Family,

We will be studying colors for the next several days. We would like the children to dress in the color of the day. Here is the order in which we will introduce each color:

Red
Yellow
Blue
Green
Purple
Orange
Black
White

You can dress your child completely in the color of the day or you can let him or her wear one article of clothing that is the color of the day. Either way is great. Thank you for your support.

Sincerely,

Baby Item Stencils

Directions: Trace the baby item outlines below onto poster board to make stencils. The stencils can be used to trace or rub. They also can be used to create outlines if you place them on a piece of paper and then spray paint over them.

Dog and Bone Game

Directions: Photocopy the dog and bones below and on the next page. Color them, cut them out, and laminate them. Use a matte knife to cut around the dog's mouth so he can hold the bone. If desired, color the collar and stick a matching colored dot on the bone for matching.

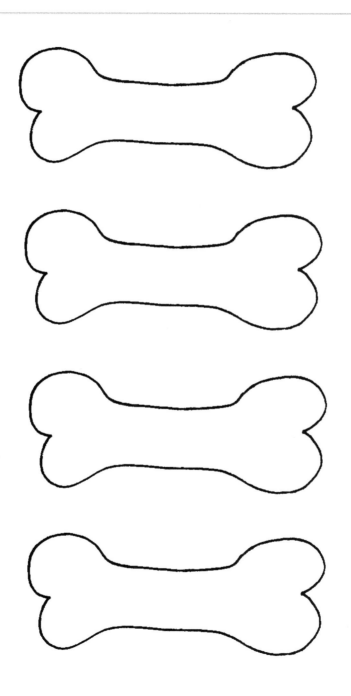

Dog and Bone Game

Finger Puppets

Directions: Photocopy the finger puppets below and on next page. Color them, cut them out, and laminate them. Cut out the holes for the legs on each puppet.

Finger Puppets

Glove Puppets

Directions: Photocopy the patterns on pages 449-454 to make a glove puppet to accompany the rhymes and stories of The Three Little Pigs, p. 356; Five Toes, p. 320; and Five Little Pumpkins p. 398. Color the patterns, cut them out, and laminate them. Attach a piece of Velcro to the back of each pumpkin and each snowman, and then attach a matching piece of Velcro to the fingers of a work glove. Make sure to attach the Velcro to the fingers that face the children when the back of your hand is facing you.

Glove Puppets

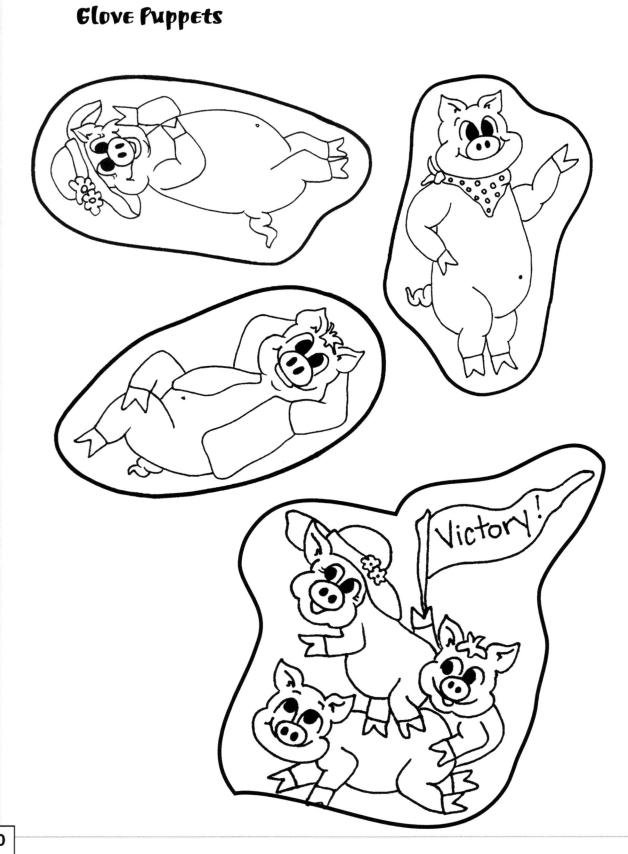

Glove Puppets

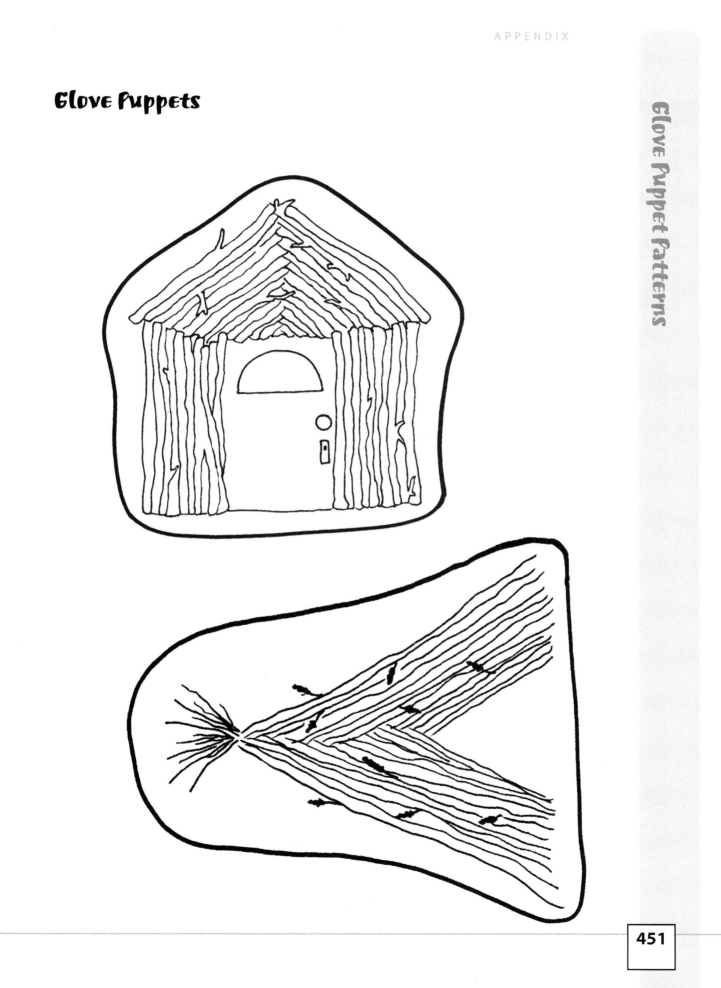

Glove Puppets

Glove Puppets

Glove Puppets

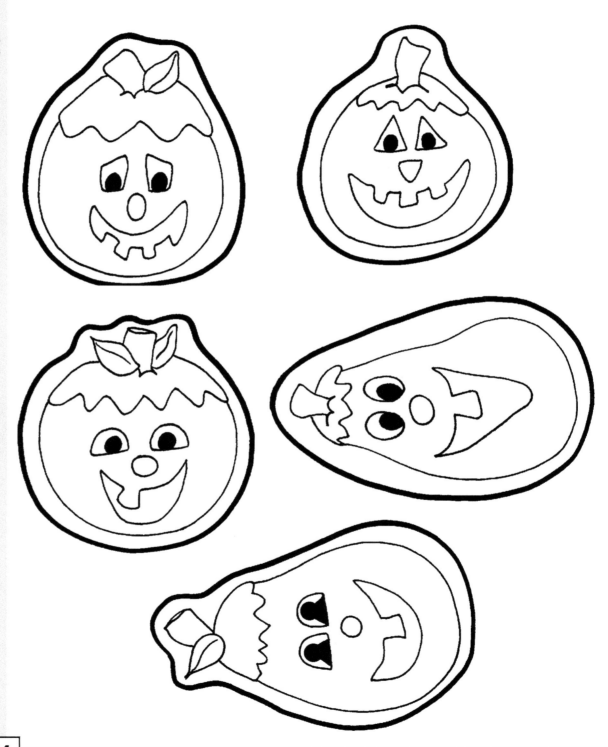

Magnetic Dress-Me Dolls (clothing for fall, winter, spring, summer, and Halloween)

Directions: Photocopy the patterns on pages 455-466. Color them, cut them out, and laminate them. Glue a strip of magnetic tape to the back of the dolls and their clothes. Provide a cookie tray for a workspace.

Magnetic Dress-Me Dolls (clothing for fall, winter, spring, summer, and Halloween)

Magnetic Dress-Me Dolls (clothing for fall, winter, spring, summer, and Halloween)

Magnetic Dress-Me Dolls (clothing for fall, winter, spring, summer, and Halloween)

Magnetic Dress-Me Dolls (clothing for fall, winter, spring, summer, and Halloween)

Magnetic Dress-Me Dolls (clothing for fall, winter, spring, summer, and Halloween)

Magnetic Dress-Me Dolls (clothing for fall, winter, spring, summer, and Halloween)

Magnetic Dress-Me Dolls (clothing for fall, winter, spring, summer, and Halloween)

Magnetic Dress-Me Dolls (clothing for fall, winter, spring, summer, and Halloween)

Magnetic Dress-Me Dolls (clothing for fall, winter, spring, summer, and Halloween)

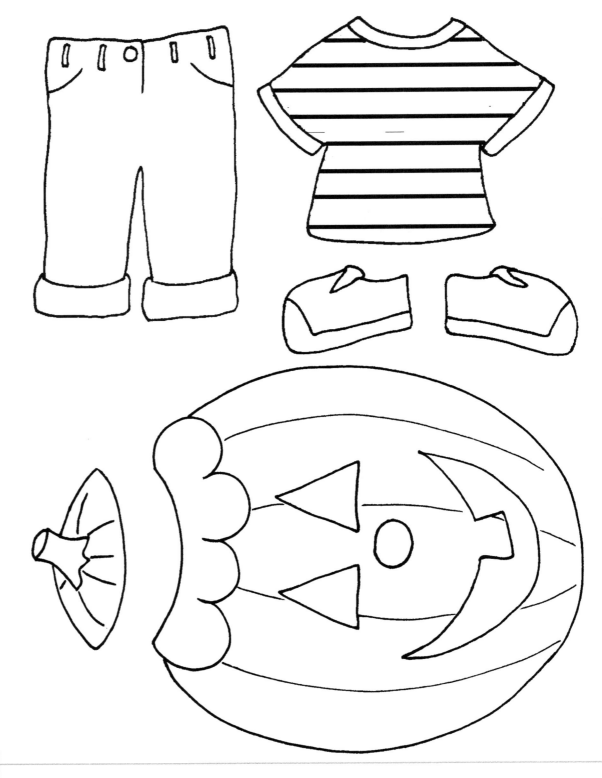

Magnetic Dress-Me Dolls (clothing for fall, winter, spring, summer, and Halloween)

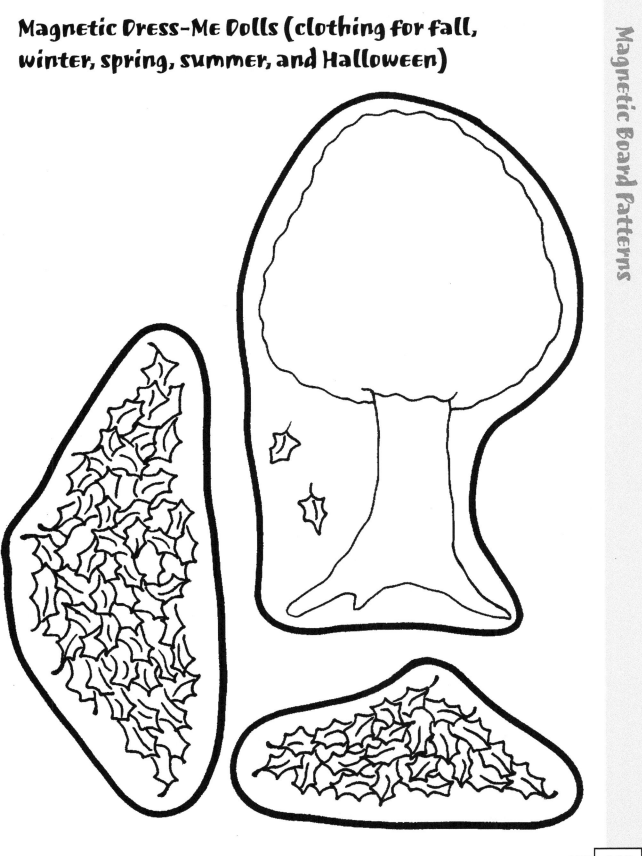

Magnetic Dress-Me Dolls (clothing for fall, winter, spring, summer, and Halloween)

Sound Cards

Directions: Photocopy the patterns on p. 467-468. Color them, cut them out, and laminate them. Record the sound of each item on a cassette tape. Children will listen to the tape and pick the sound card that matches the sound they hear.

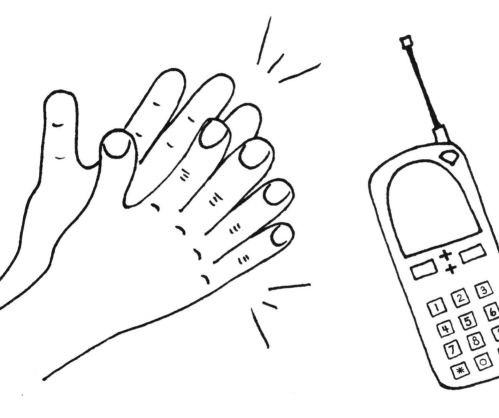

Sound Cards

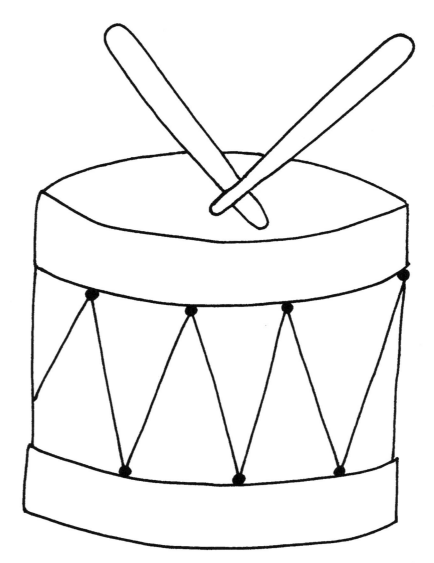

Stick the Tail on the Bunny Game

Directions: Photocopy and, if desired, enlarge the pattern of the bunny below. Color it and laminate it. Provide a cotton ball for a tail.

Top, Middle, and Bottom Monster Puzzles

Directions: Make multiple photocopies of the three patterns on pages 470-472. Color them, laminate them, and cut them into the three designated parts.

Top, Middle, and Bottom Monster Puzzles

Top, Middle, and Bottom Monster Puzzles

Two-Sided Teddy Bear Puppet

Directions: Photocopy the bear front and back patterns below. Color them, cut them out, and laminate them. Glue the bear front to back on a tongue depressor to create a puppet with a front and a back.

Weather Wheel

Directions: Photocopy the pattern on below, color it, cut it out, and glue it to a piece of poster board. Laminate and use a brad to attach the pointer.

Frosty the Snowman (Flannel Board Story)

Directions: Photocopy the story patterns on pages 476-478. Use a fine-point permanent marker to trace the patterns onto pelon. Color them with crayons and cut them out.

Frosty the Snowman was a jolly happy soul,
With a corncob pipe and a button nose and two eyes made out of coal.
Frosty the snowman is a fairy tale they say:
He was made of snow but the children know how he came to life one day.
There must have been some magic in that old silk hat they found.
For when they placed it on his head, he began to dance around.
Oh, Frosty the snowman was alive as he could be,
And the children say he could laugh and play just the same as you and me.

Frosty the Snowman knew the sun was hot that day,
So he said, "Let's run and we'll have some fun now before I melt away."
Down to the village with a broomstick in his hand,
Running here and there all around the square, sayin', "Catch me if you can."
He led them down the streets of town right to the traffic cop.
And he only paused a moment when he heard him holler, "Stop!"
For Frosty the snowman had to hurry on his way.
So he waved goodbye, sayin', "Don't you cry; I'll be back again someday."

Thumpety, thump thump, thumpety thump thump,
Look at Frosty go;
Thumpety thump thump, thumpety thump thump,
Over the hills of snow.

Frosty the Snowman (Flannel Board Story)

Frosty the Snowman (Flannel Board Story)

Frosty the Snowman (Flannel Board Story)

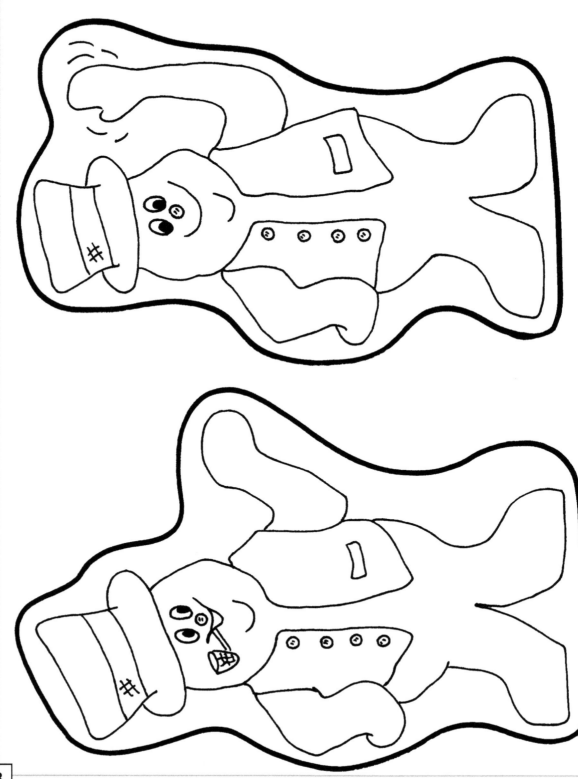

The Gingerbread Man (Flannel Board Story)

Directions: Photocopy the patterns on pages 481-484. Use a black, fine-point permanent marker to trace them onto pelon. Color them and cut them out.

Once upon a time, a little old woman and a little old man lived in a little old house in a little old village.

One day the little old woman decided to make a gingerbread man. She cut him out of dough and put him in the oven to bake. After a while, the little old woman said to herself, "That gingerbread man must be ready by now." She went to the oven door and opened it. Up jumped the gingerbread man, and away he ran.

As he ran he shouted, "Run, run as fast as you can. You can't catch me. I'm the gingerbread man!"

The little old woman ran after the gingerbread man, but she couldn't catch him.

He ran past the little old man who was working in the garden. "Stop, stop!" called the little old man.

But the gingerbread man just called back, "Run, run as fast as you can. You can't catch me. I'm the gingerbread man."

The little old man joined the little old woman and ran as fast as he could after the gingerbread man, but he couldn't catch him.

The gingerbread man ran past a dog. "Stop, stop!" said the dog.

But the gingerbread man just called back, "Run, run as fast as you can. You can't catch me. I'm the gingerbread man."

The dog joined the little old woman and the little old man and ran as fast as he could after the gingerbread man, but he couldn't catch him.

The gingerbread man ran past a cat. "Stop, stop!" said the cat.

But the gingerbread man just called back, "Run, run as fast as you can. You can't catch me. I'm the gingerbread man."

The cat joined the little old woman and the little old man and the dog, but she couldn't catch the gingerbread man.

Soon the gingerbread man came to a fox lying by the side of a river, and he shouted.

"Run, run, as fast as you can. You can't catch me. I'm the gingerbread man! I ran away from the little old woman, the little old man, the dog, and the cat, and I can run away from you, I can."

But the sly old fox just laughed and said, "If you don't get across this river quickly, you will surely get caught. If you hop on my tail I will carry you across."

The gingerbread man saw that he had no time to lose, so he quickly hopped onto the fox's tail.

"Oh!" said the fox. "The water is getting deeper. Climb on my back so you won't get wet."

And the gingerbread man did.

"Oh!" said the fox. "The water is getting deeper. Climb on my head so you won't get wet."

And the gingerbread man did.

"Oh!" said the fox. "The water is getting deeper. Climb on my nose so you won't get wet."

And the gingerbread man did.

Then the fox tossed the gingerbread man into his mouth. And that was the end of the gingerbread man!

The Gingerbread Man (Flannel Board Story)

The Gingerbread Man (Flannel Board Story)

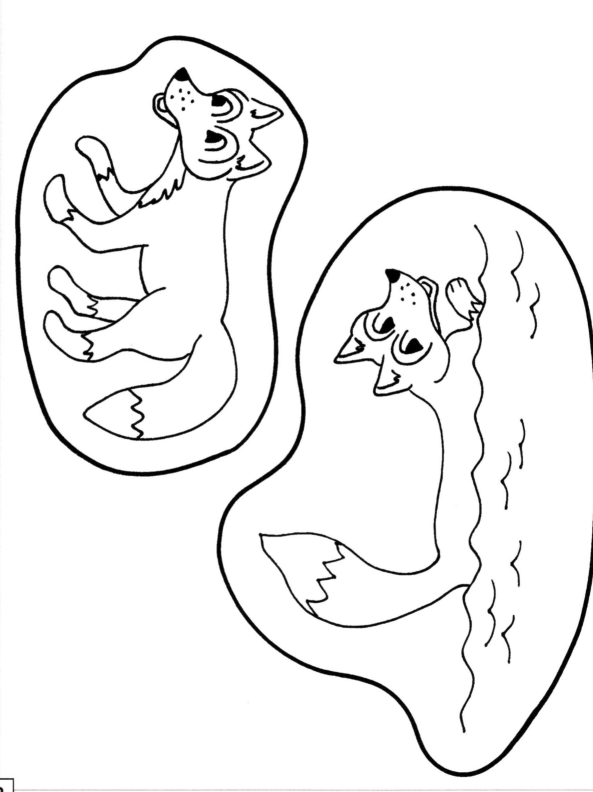

The Gingerbread Man (Flannel Board Story)

The Gingerbread Man (Flannel Board Story)

Goldilocks and the Three Bears (Magnetic Story)

Directions: Photocopy the patterns on pages 486-491. Color them, cut them out, and laminate them. Glue a piece of magnetic tape to the back of each pattern. Use a cookie sheet or magnetic board to display.

Once upon a time there were three bears. There was a mama bear, a papa bear, and a little bear. They all lived in the forest. One day the bears went out for a walk to visit a sick friend.

While they were gone a little girl named Goldilocks was walking in the woods. Finding that she had lost her way, she walked till she came to a small cottage. Upon entering the house she saw three bowls of porridge sitting on a table. She was very hungry. She tasted the porridge in the large bowl. It was too hot. So she tried the porridge in the middle-size bowl. It was too cold. She tried the porridge in the small bowl. It was just right. Goldilocks ate it all up.

After eating she went over to the three chairs sitting before a fireplace. She found the biggest chair to be too hard! The middle-size chair was too soft! She sat in the third chair because it seemed just right. As she sat in the chair it wobbled, rattled, and fell apart.

By now the little girl was very tired and so she went into the other room and found three beds. The first was very hard. The second bed was too soft. But the third bed was just right! She fell asleep right away.

Meanwhile the bears came home from their walk. Finding an empty bowl on the table made Mama Bear and Papa Bear scratch their heads. At the same time the little bear found his chair in pieces on the floor. He was very upset and started crying.

Hearing the noise, the little girl came down to find out what was wrong. When she saw the bears she was very surprised and a little frightened! She explained that she was lost and that she was sorry she ate the porridge and broke the chair. The bears were kind bears. They told Goldilocks she was forgiven. Mama Bear packed Goldilocks a basket of cookies and Papa Bear and Baby Bear helped her find her way to the path back home.

Goldilocks and the Three Bears
(Magnetic Story)

Goldilocks and the Three Bears
(Magnetic Story)

Goldilocks and the Three Bears
(Magnetic Story)

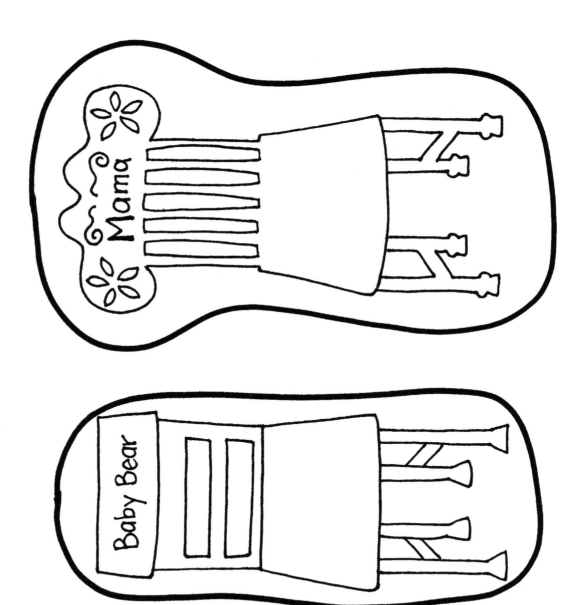

Goldilocks and the Three Bears
(Magnetic Story)

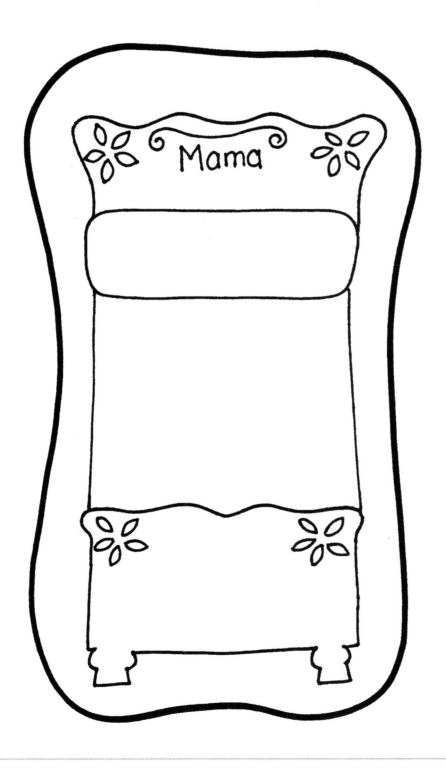

Goldilocks and the Three Bears
(Magnetic Story)

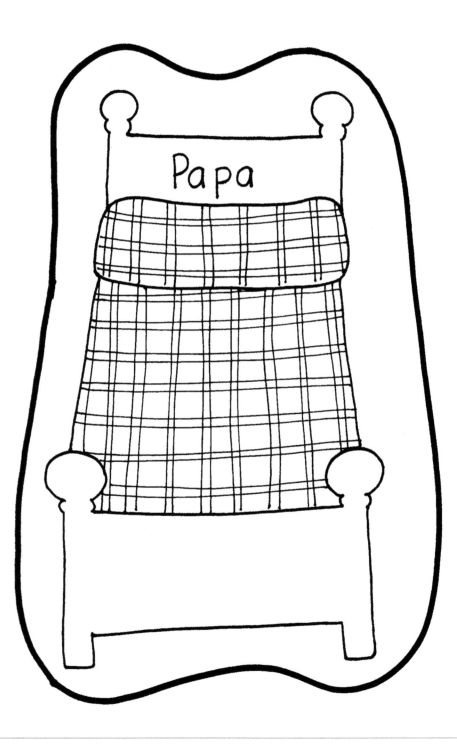

Goldilocks and the Three Bears
(Magnetic Story)

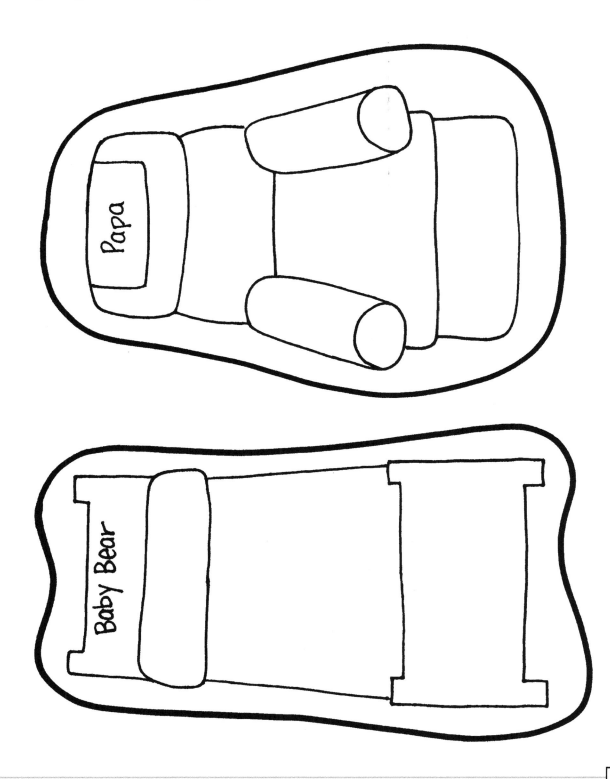

The Great Big Pumpkin (Flannel Board Story)

BY PAM SCHILLER

Directions: Photocopy the patterns on pages 493-494. Use a fine-point permanent marker to trace the patterns onto pelon. Color them with crayons and cut them out.

One day Little Bear was out looking for honey. She was very hungry. But she couldn't find a single thing to eat.

Just as she was about to give up, she spied a very funny something. It was big, very big, and round, very round, and orange, very orange. Little Bear had never seen anything quite like it. She went to get a closer look.

"I'm going to take you home to my Mama," she said. Little Bear tried to roll the big, round, orange something. It didn't move. She tried again. It didn't move.

Just then Skunk came along. "Hey, what's that?"

"I don't know," said Little Bear. "I want to take it home to my Mama, but I can't move it."

"Let me help," said Skunk.

Little Bear and Skunk pushed and pushed. The big, round, orange thing didn't move.

Just then Squirrel came along. "Hey, what's that?"

"We don't know," said Little Bear. "I want to take it home to my Mama, but we can't move it."

"Let me help," said Squirrel.

Little Bear and Skunk and Squirrel pushed and pushed and pushed. The big, round, orange thing didn't move.

Just then Mouse came along. "Hey, what's that?"

"I don't know," said Little Bear. "I want to take it home to my Mama, but we can't move it."

"Let me help," said Mouse.

Little Bear and Skunk and Squirrel and Mouse pushed and pushed and pushed and pushed.

Slowly, the big, round, orange thing started to move. Then it started to roll. It rolled and rolled and rolled all the way to Little Bear's den. Little Bear's Mama came out to see what was going on. "Where did you find this lovely, big, round, orange pumpkin?" she asked.

The four friends looked at each other and said, "PUMPKIN?"

The Great Big Pumpkin (Flannel Board Story)

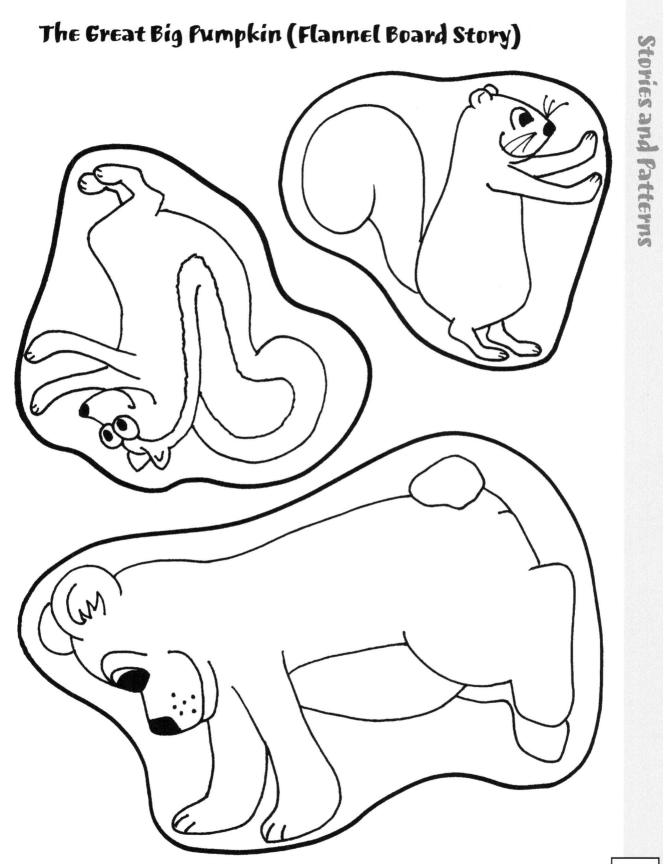

The Great Big Pumpkin (Flannel Board Story)

The Great Big Turnip (Flannel Board Story)

Directions: Photocopy the patterns on pages 496-497. Use a fine-point permanent marker to trace them onto pelon. Color them with crayons and cut them out.

Once upon a time an old man planted a turnip. The turnip grew and grew. At last it was ready to be pulled.

The old man tugged at the turnip. He pulled and he tugged. He tugged and he pulled. But the turnip would not come out of the ground.

The old man called the old woman. The old man tugged at the turnip. The old woman tugged at the old man. They pulled and they tugged. They tugged and they pulled. But the turnip would not come out of the ground.

The old woman called the dog.

The old man tugged at the turnip. The old woman tugged at the old man. The dog tugged at the old woman. They pulled and they tugged. They tugged and they pulled. But the turnip would not come out of the ground.

The dog called the pig.

The old man tugged at the turnip. The old woman tugged at the old man. The dog tugged at the old woman. The pig tugged at the dog. They pulled and they tugged. They tugged and they pulled. But the turnip would not come out of the ground.

The pig called the cat.

The old man tugged at the turnip. The old woman tugged at the old man. The dog tugged at the old woman. The pig tugged at the dog. The cat pulled at the pig. They pulled and they tugged. They tugged and they pulled. But the turnip would not come out of the ground.

The cat called the mouse.

The old man tugged at the turnip. The old woman tugged at the old man. The dog tugged at the old woman. The pig tugged at the dog. The cat pulled at the pig. The mouse tugged at the cat. They pulled and they tugged. They tugged and they pulled—oh, how they pulled! Oh, how they tugged! And the turnip came out of the ground.

The Great Big Turnip (Flannel Board Story)

The Great Big Turnip (Flannel Board Story)

Use the dog pattern on page 481, the pig pattern on page 453, and the cat pattern on page 481.

Henny-Penny (Flannel Board Story or Magnetic Story)

Directions: Photocopy the patterns on pages 500-501. To make a flannel board story, use a black, fine-point permanent marker to trace the patterns onto pelon. Color them with crayons and cut them out. To make a magnetic story, color the patterns, cut them out, laminate them, and glue a piece of magnetic tape to the back of each character. Use a cookie sheet as a background on which to tell the story.

Once upon a time there was a little hen named Henny-Penny. She lived in a barnyard with her friends, Cocky-Locky, Ducky-Lucky, Turkey-Lurkey, and Goosey-Loosey. Everyday the farmer's wife would scatter seeds and grain for Henny-Penny and her friends to eat.

One day while Henny-Penny was peck, peck, pecking the seeds and grains the farmer's wife had scattered, something hit her right on top of her head. "What was that?" asked Henny-Penny. She looked up at the sky and seeing nothing but sky she began to cluck loudly.

"Something just hit me on the head. The sky is falling. I must go quickly and tell the king."

So off Henny-Penny went walking as fast as she could. Soon she met Cocky-Locky.

"Where are you going?" asked Cocky-Locky.

Without even looking back, Henny-Penny answered, "The sky is falling! I'm off to tell the king."

Cocky-Locky looked up at the sky. He said, "The sky looks fine to me."

"A piece of the sky fell right on my head," said Henny-Penny.

"Oh, my!" said Cocky-Locky, and he joined Henny-Penny on her journey.

So on Henny-Penny and Cocky-Locky went walking as fast as they could. Soon they met Ducky-Lucky.

"Where are you going?" asked Ducky-Lucky.

Without even looking back, Henny-Penny answered, "The sky is falling! We're off to tell the king."

Ducky-Lucky looked up at the sky. She said, "The sky looks fine to me."

"A piece of the sky fell right on my head," said Henny-Penny.

"Oh, my!" said Ducky-Lucky, and she joined Henny-Penny and Cocky-Locky on their journey.

So on Henny-Penny, Cocky-Locky, and Ducky-Lucky went walking as fast as they could. Soon they met Turkey-Lurkey.

"Where are you going?" asked Turkey-Lurkey.

Without even looking back, Henny-Penny answered, "The sky is falling! We're off to tell the king."

Turkey-Lurkey looked up at the sky. He said, "The sky looks fine to me."

"A piece of the sky fell right on my head," said Henny-Penny.

"Oh, my!" said Turkey-Lurkey, and he joined Henny-Penny, Cocky-Locky, and Ducky-Lucky on their journey.

So on Henny-Penny, Cocky-Locky, Ducky-Lucky, and Turkey-Lurkey went walking as fast as they could. Soon they met Goosey-Loosey.

"Where are you going?" asked Goosey-Loosey.

Without even looking back, Henny-Penny answered, "The sky is falling! We're off to tell the king."

Goosey-Loosey looked up at the sky. She said, "The sky looks fine to me."

"A piece of the sky fell right on my head," said Henny-Penny.

"Oh, my!" said Goosey-Loosey and she joined Henny-Penny, Cocky-Locky, Ducky-Lucky, and Turkey-Lurkey on their journey. Soon the five friends met Foxy-Loxy. "Where are you going?" asked Foxy-Loxy.

"The sky is falling. We're off to tell the king," the five answered together.

"May I show you the way?" asked Foxy-Loxy.

The five friends suddenly realized that they did not know where the king lived. So they said, "Oh, thank you Foxy-Loxy."

Foxy-Loxy took Henny-Penny, Cocky-Locky, Ducky-Lucky, Turkey-Lurkey, and Goosey-Loosey straight to his den and they were never seen again. Do you know what happened to them?

Henny-Penny (Flannel Board Story or Magnetic Story)

Henny-Penny (Flannel Board Story or Magnetic Story)

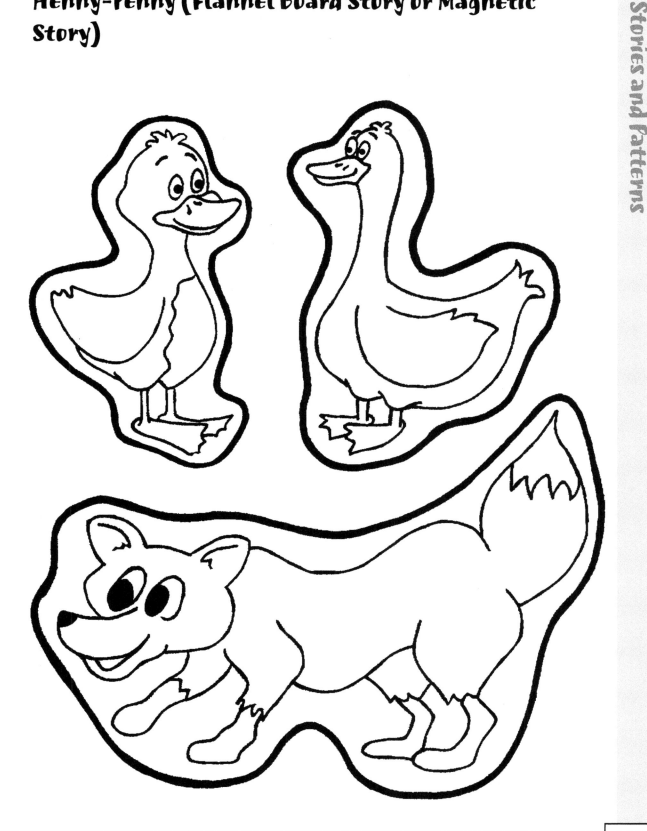

The Lion and the Mouse (Flannel Board Story)

Directions: Photocopy the story patterns on pages 503-504. Use a fine-point permanent marker to trace the patterns onto pelon. Color them with crayons and cut them out.

A lion was awakened from sleep by a mouse running over his face. Rising up angrily, he caught the mouse by his tail and was about to kill him, when the mouse very pitifully said, "If you would only spare my life, I would surely repay your kindness someday."

The lion roared with laughter. "How could a small little creature like you ever repay a mighty lion?" The lion roared another laugh and let the mouse go. He settled back down to finish his nap. "Thank you mighty lion. You won't be sorry."

It happened shortly thereafter that the mighty lion was trapped by hunters. The hunters caught him in a net made of ropes. The lion roared in anguish.

The little mouse was not far away. He recognized the lion's roar and he came quickly and gnawed the ropes away to free the lion. The lion was very grateful and quite surprised to see the mouse. He was even more surprised that such a small creature was able to save his life.

The mouse said, "You ridiculed the idea that I might ever be able to help you or repay you. I hope you know now that it is possible for even a small mouse to help a mighty lion." The lion and the mouse were friends from that moment on.

The Lion and the Mouse (Flannel Board Story)

The Lion and the Mouse (Flannel Board Story)

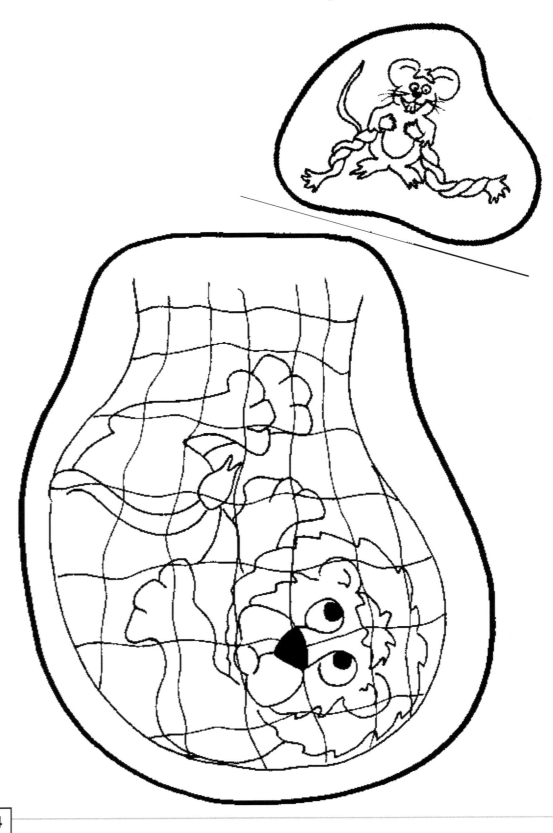

The Lion's Haircut (Puppet Story)

BY PAM SCHILLER

Directions: Photocopy the lion face on p. 506. Color, cut it out, and laminate (optional). Glue it to the center of a 10" Styrofoam plate. Punch small holes all around the edges of the plate. Cut several 8" pieces of yarn. Tie a knot in one end of the yarn. Use a crochet hook to pull the other end of the yarn through the holes in the plate, leaving only an inch of yarn exposed on the face side of the puppet. Glue the lion face to a tongue depressor, if desired. Pull the yarn through the plate during the story. You will need to replace the yarn each time you use the puppet.

Leo was a lively baby lion. He loved to frolic and graze in the green grass. He loved to chase butterflies. He loved to splash in the water of the nearby pond. But most of all he loved to look at his reflection in the pond and see how big he was growing.

Leo wanted to be just like his dad. He would look at his paws and then search for his dad's paw prints close by to compare to his own. He would look at his nose and ears and try to remember how much bigger his dad's looked when they were wrestling in the grass. He would look for his mane and simply sigh in sadness because he could tell, without any measuring or remembering, that it was nothing like his dad's. Leo would ask his mom, "When will my mane grow?" His mom would give him a lick and simply say, "In its own good time."

All through the spring, Leo watched his mane. It didn't grow an inch. All through the summer, Leo watched his mane. It grew only a little (pull mane through plate a little).

All through the fall, Leo watched his mane. It grew only a little more (pull mane through plate a little). All through the winter, Leo watched his mane. It grew only a little more (pull mane through plate a little).

Then when spring came again, something happened. Leo's mane began to grow (pull mane). And it grew and it grew and it grew until he had a full mane just like his dad's (pull until the mane is very long). Leo was so happy he felt like a million dollars, or in lion talk, a million butterflies.

Leo frolicked in the green grass. He chased butterflies. He splashed in the pond. He stopped to take a look at his lovely, long mane and when the water had calmed down and he could see himself, he shrieked. His mane was a tangled and matted mess.

He ran home to his mom in tears. His mom gave him a lick and simply said, "It's time for a haircut." She took out a pair of scissors and began to snip (cut mane to approximately two inches). When she was through the tangles were gone and Leo still had a beautiful mane. It was just the right size for a lively little lion.

The Lion's Haircut (Puppet Story)

Little Ants (Flannel Board Story)

Directions: Photocopy the story patterns on p. 507-510. Use a black, fine-point permanent marker to trace them onto a piece of pelon. Color them with crayons and cut them out.

Little Ants (Flannel Board Story)

Little Ants (Flannel Board Story)

Little Ants (Flannel Board Story)

Little Engine Ninety-Nine (Puppet Story)

BY PAM SCHILLER

Directions: Photocopy the patterns on pages 512-517. Color them, cut them out, and laminate them. Attach them to tongue depressors to create stick puppets.

Even before the last coat of the shiny black paint on his smokestack was dry, Little Engine Ninety-Nine knew what kind of a train he wanted to be.

He didn't want to pull tank cars full of chemicals. He didn't want to pull cars full of passengers. He didn't want to pull heavy equipment. He wanted to be a circus train. He wanted to pull cars full of elephants, giraffes, bears, and lions. He loved animals. He had been dreaming of being a circus train ever since the mechanics were tightening the first bolts on his wheels. Little Engine Ninety-Nine was getting tired of waiting.

Just when he was sure he could wait no longer, a man in striped coveralls came aboard. The man started the engine and Little Engine Ninety-Nine was overwhelmed with joy. He began to move forward slowly. Then he picked up speed. Then he was breezing along the tracks. Wow! He loved the way the wind felt on his face.

After a while, the man pulled back on the controls and stopped the engine. He got out and switched the tracks. When the man returned, he started the engine again. This time, Little Engine Ninety-Nine felt himself being pulled forward and then backward, then forward and then backward 'til CLINK! He was attached to some cars in back of him. Little Engine Ninety-Nine held his breath and looked back. The elephants, lions, giraffes, and bears that he had dreamed of hauling were not there. There was something even better. Do you know what it was?

Children—lots of happy, singing, laughing children.

Little Engine Ninety-Nine was thrilled.

Little Engine Ninety-Nine was a working engine. And he was an even better kind of engine than the kind of engine he dreamed he would be. He moved happily forward along the track with the breeze splashing in his face and the happy children behind him.

Toot-toot!

Little Engine Ninety-Nine (Puppet Story)

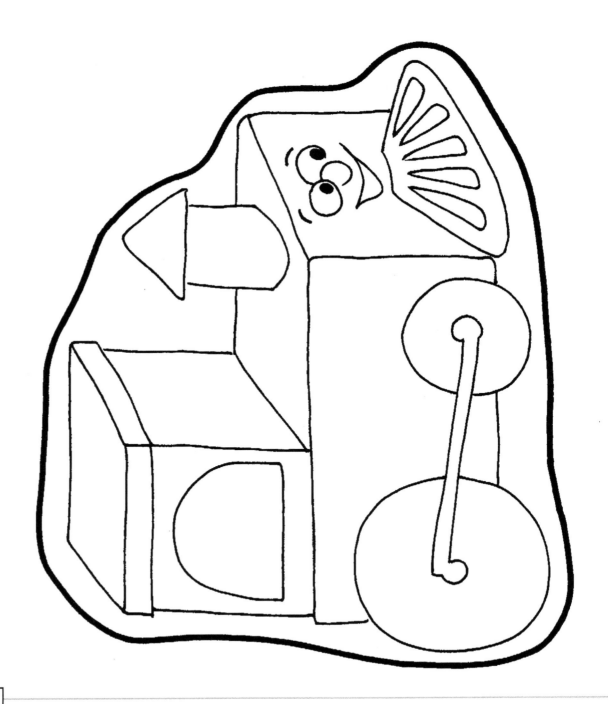

Little Engine Ninety-Nine (Puppet Story)

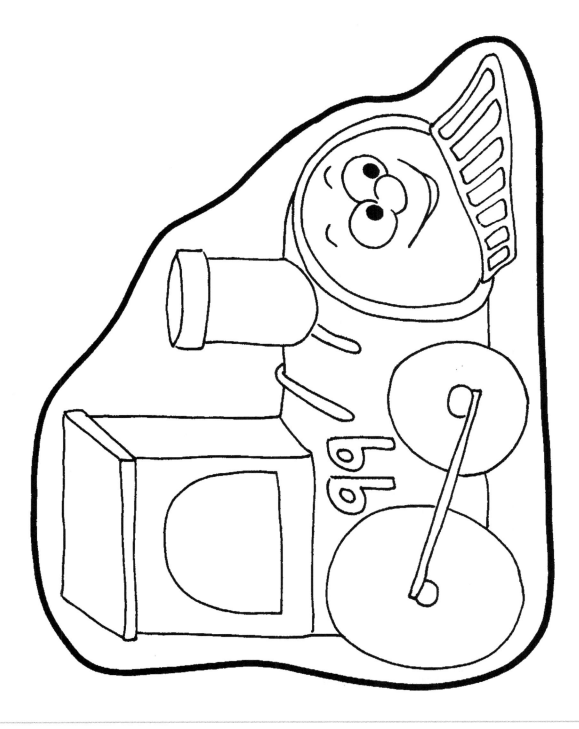

Little Engine Ninety-Nine (Puppet Story)

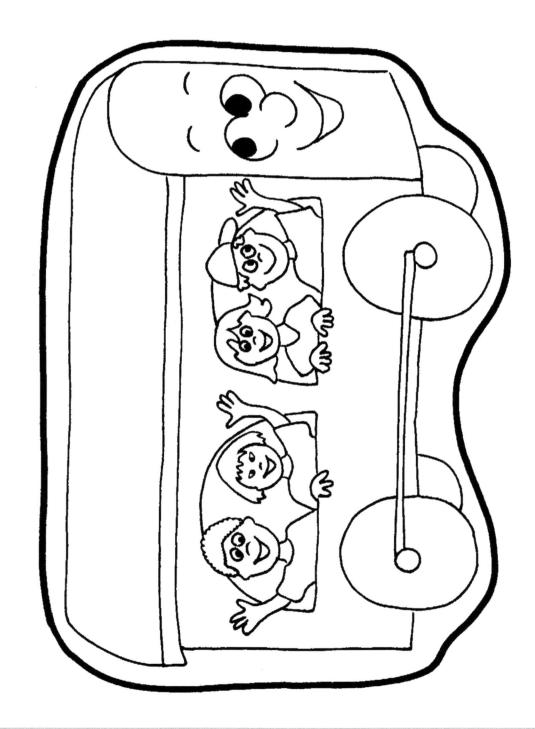

Little Engine Ninety-Nine (Puppet Story)

Little Engine Ninety-Nine (Puppet Story)

Little Engine Ninety-Nine (Puppet Story)

The Little Red Hen (Flannel Board Story)

Directions: Photocopy the patterns on pages 520-522. Use a fine-point permanent marker to trace them onto pelon. Color them and cut them out.

Once upon a time there was a Little Red Hen who shared her tiny cottage with a pig, a cat, and a dog. The pig was lazy. She played inthe mud all day long.

The cat was vain. She brushed her fur, straightened her whiskers, and polished her claws all day long. The dog was sleepy. He napped on the front porch all day long.

The little Red Hen did all the work. She cooked, she cleaned, and she took out the trash. She mowed, she raked, and she did all the shopping.

One day on her way to market, the Little Red Hen found a few grains of wheat. She put them in her pocket. When she got home she asked her friends, "Who will plant these grains of wheat?"

"Not I," said the pig.

"Not I," said the cat.

"Not I," said the dog.

"Then I will plant them myself," said the Little Red Hen. And she did.

All summer long she cared for the wheat. She made sure that it got enough water,

And she hoed the weeds out carefully between each row.

And when the wheat was finally ready to harvest, the Little Red Hen asked her friends, "Who will help me thresh this wheat?"

"Not I," said the pig.

"Not I," said the cat.

"Not I," said the dog.

"Then I will cut and thresh it myself," said the Little Red Hen. And she did!

When the wheat had been cut and threshed, the Little Red Hen scooped the wheat into a wheelbarrow and said, "This wheat must be ground into flour. Who will help me take it to the mill?"

"Not I," said the pig.

"Not I," said the cat.

"Not I," said the dog.

"Then I will do it myself," said the Little Red Hen. And she did.

The miller ground the wheat into flour and put it into a bag for the Little Red Hen. Then all by herself, she pushed the bag home in the wheelbarrow.

One cool morning a few weeks later, the Little Red Hen got up early and said, "Today is a perfect day to bake some bread. Who will help me bake it?"

"Not I," said the pig.

"Not I," said the cat.

"Not I," said the dog.

"Then I will bake the bread myself," said the Little Red Hen. And she did.

She mixed the flour with milk and eggs and butter and salt. She kneaded the dough. She shaped the dough into a nice plump loaf. Then she put the loaf in the oven and watched it as it baked. The smell of the bread soon filled the air.

The pig stopped playing. The cat stopped brushing, and the dog woke up. One by one they came into the kitchen.

When the Little Red Hen took the bread from the oven she said, "Who will help me eat this bread?"

"I will," said the pig.

"I will," said the cat.

"I will," said the dog.

"You will?" said the Little Red Hen. "Who planted the wheat and took care of it? Who cut the wheat and threshed it? Who took the wheat to the mill? Who baked the bread? I did it all by myself. Now I am going to eat it all by myself." And she did.

The Little Red Hen (Flannel Board Story)

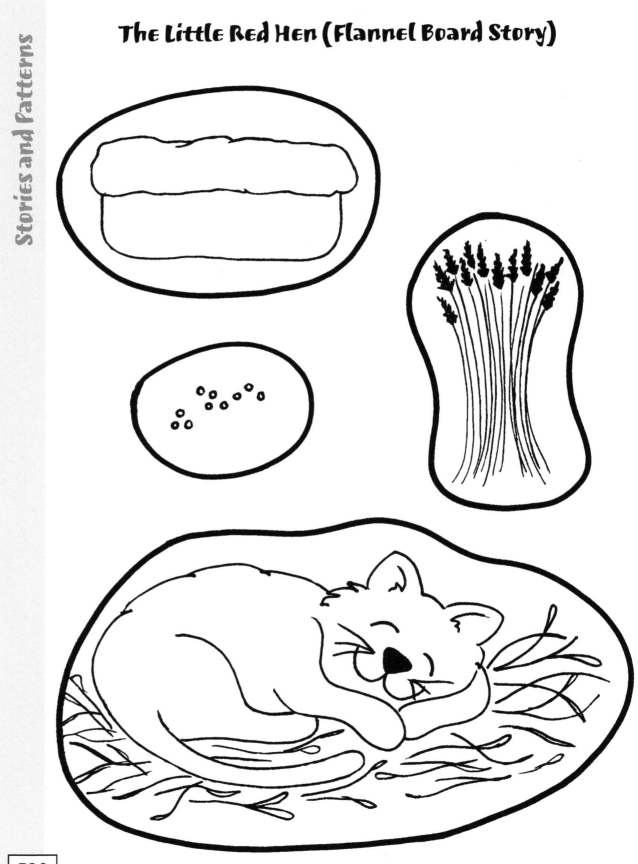

The Little Red Hen (Flannel Board Story)

The Little Red Hen (Flannel Board Story)

Little Red Riding Hood (Flannel Board Story)

Directions: Photocopy the patterns on pages 525-528. Use a fine-point permanent marker to trace the patterns onto pelon. Color them with crayons and cut them out.

It was a beautiful sunny day. The birds were singing, and the butterflies were darting here and there, collecting nectar from the flowers. Little Red Riding Hood skipped happily through the forest on her way to her grandmother's house. Suddenly in her pathway appeared a huge gray wolf. "Where are you going?" asked the wolf.

"To my grandmother's house," said Little Red Riding Hood. "I am taking her a basket of goodies."

"Where does your grandmother live?" asked the wolf.

"Up the path beside the stream," answered Little Red Riding Hood.

"Be careful," whispered the wolf. "The forest is full of surprises." Then off he ran. The wolf was thinking that Little Red Riding Hood and her grandmother would make a very tasty dinner. He knew a shortcut through the forest. He was sure he could be at grandmother's cottage before Little Red Riding Hood.

When the wolf arrived at the cottage, he knocked on the door. But no one answered. He knocked again. No answer. He opened the door and walked right in. No one was home.

The wolf grabbed grandmother's gown and hopped in her bed. He was hoping to fool Little Red Riding Hood. Soon there was a knock at the door. "Come in," said the wolf, pretending to be Little Red Riding Hood's grandmother.

Little Red Riding Hood walked into the cottage. It was dark inside. She walked all the way to her grandmother's bed before she realized how terrible her grandmother looked.

"Grandmother," she said, "you look terrible."

"I know, dear. I've been ill," said the wolf.

"Grandmother, what big eyes you have," said Little Red Riding Hood.

"All the better to see you with, my dear," whispered the wolf.

"Grandmother, what a black nose you have," said Little Red Riding Hood.

"All the better to smell you with, my dear," answered the sneaky wolf.

"Grandmother, what big teeth you have," she said.

"All the better to eat you with," said the wolf as he jumped from the bed.

Little Red Riding Hood screamed and ran for the door. The wolf tried to chase after her, but he was all tangled up in grandmother's gown. When Little Red Riding Hood opened the door, in ran grandmother with a broom in her hand. She hit the wolf hard on the nose. He yelped. She smacked him again as he jumped across the floor trying to untangle himself. When he was free, he ran for the door. Grandmother whacked him on the backside and swept him right out the door. The wolf ran so far away he was never seen again.

Little Red Riding Hood hugged her grandmother. "Grandmother, I am so glad you came home. Where were you?"

"I was out in the barn sweeping the floor. I heard you scream."

Little Red Riding Hood told her grandmother about meeting the wolf in the forest on the way to her house. Grandmother hugged her granddaughter, whom she loved more than anything, and then she asked, "Did you learn anything today?"

"Yes," said Red. "I learned not to talk to strangers."

"Good job!" said her grandmother.

Little Red Riding Hood (Flannel Board Story)

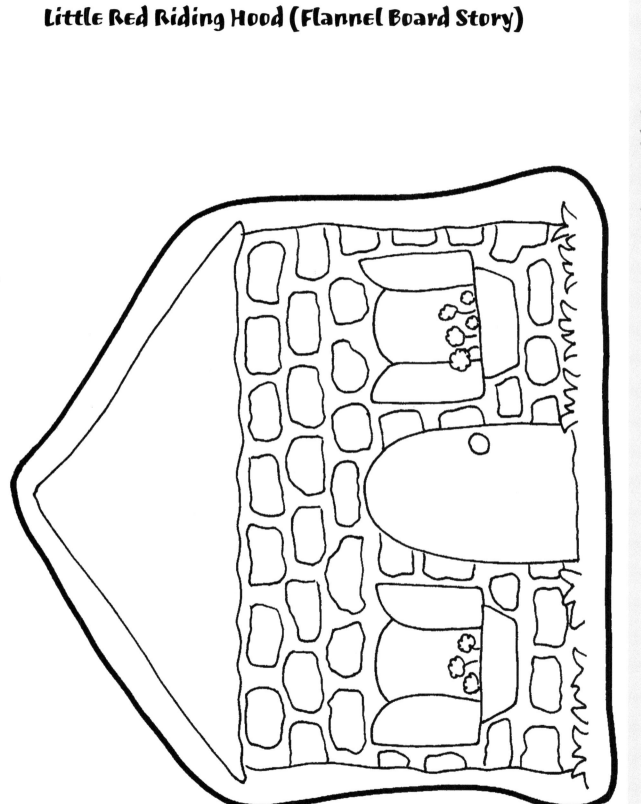

Little Red Riding Hood (Flannel Board Story)

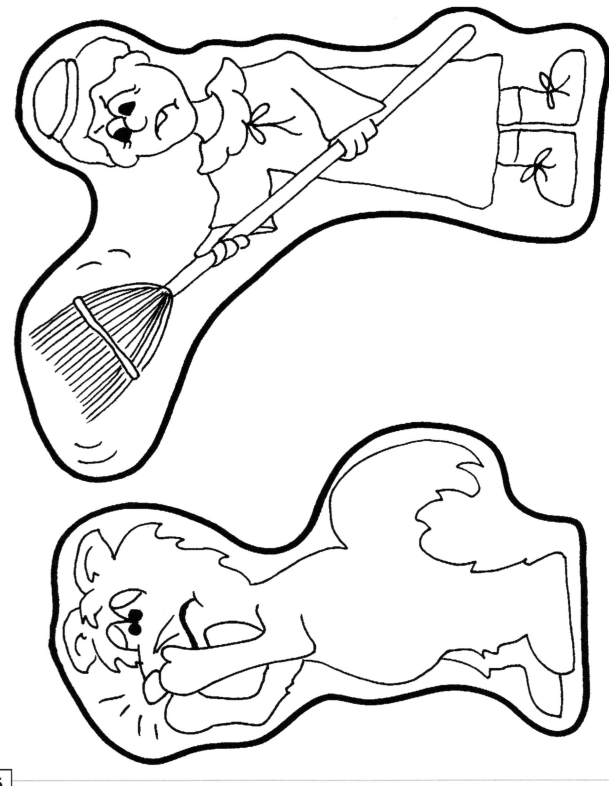

Little Red Riding Hood (Flannel Board Story)

Little Red Riding Hood (Flannel Board Story)

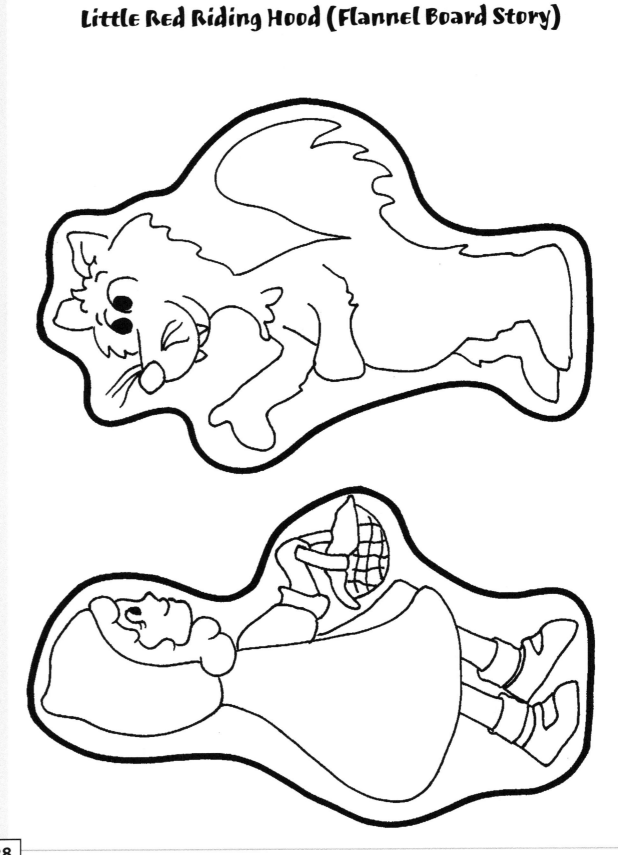

Madison's Day (Flannel Board Story)

BY PAM SCHILLER

Directions: Photocopy the story patterns on pages 530-531. Use a black fine-point permanent marker to trace them onto pelon. Color them with crayons and cut them out.

Let me tell you about my wonderful, terrific, super, great day! But first, I'll introduce you to my family. I'll start with my mom and dad. I have two brothers, Sam and Austin. Sam is the oldest. I have a sister, too. Her name is Gabrielle. Oh, I almost forgot—Madison, that's me. I'm four—almost five! I'm the youngest. Together we're the Markle family, and you'll never guess what happened to me on my wonderful, terrific, super, great day!

Yesterday our family went to the park. When everyone was all ready to go, Sam, Austin, and Gabrielle hurried downstairs and ran out the door. They were already getting into the van by the time I was at the door. "Wait for me!" I yelled as I ran. Last again! I am always last, I thought. Just once I would like to be first! Being the youngest and the littlest is hard. I try so hard to keep up with them. It's always the same old thing—I'm the last one Mom wakes up for school, the last one to get into the bathroom to brush my teeth, the last to get my food at the dinner table, and always, always the last to get in line for anything!

I went to bed that night wishing I could be first, first to do something—anything—just once! The very next morning, Mom came to wake me up. I took my good, old time getting downstairs, but when I got to the kitchen, guess what? I was the first one Mom had gotten out of bed! "Happy Birthday, Madison!" said Dad, smiling.

Wow! I forgot that today was my birthday! Sam, Austin, and Gabrielle came into the kitchen with big smiles and a birthday greeting. Mom had breakfast ready, and set a big plate of pancakes down right in front of me FIRST! After breakfast, I was the first one to brush my teeth, too. My whole day was like that— I got to do everything first! Wow! What a wonderful, terrific, super, great day! What a great birthday present!

Madison's Day (Flannel Board Story)

Madison's Day (Flannel Board Story)

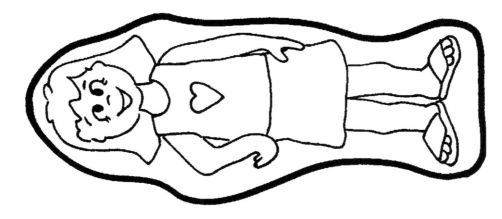

Miguel's Birthday (Flannel Board Story)

Directions: Photocopy the story patterns on p. 533. Use a fine-point permanent marker to trace them onto a piece of interfacing material. Color them and cut them out.

"Miguel?" Mom asked, "Would you like to help me put the candles on your birthday cake?" With a great, big smile, Miguel nodded yes. "Well, let's figure out how many candles we need to put on your cake."

Mom got a box of blue and white candles out of the cupboard. She took one candle out of the box and held it in her hand as she looked at Miguel. "When you were one, we put just one candle on your cake." Mom handed the candle to Miguel. He looked at the beautiful cake and carefully placed the candle on it. "One!" exclaimed Miguel.

"Then, when you were two, we put two candles on your birthday cake," said Mom. She handed one more candle to Miguel. He slowly placed it on the cake. "One, two. Now there are two candles on the cake."

"Now, you're three, and we need to add one more candle to your cake," said Mom. Miguel put the last candle on the cake. "One, two, three!" counted Miguel as he pointed to the candles. "I am three years old."

"That's right, Miguel," said Mom as she wrote the number three on the birthday cake with icing. "You're three years old today, Miguel. Happy Birthday!"

Miguel's Birthday (Flannel Board Story)

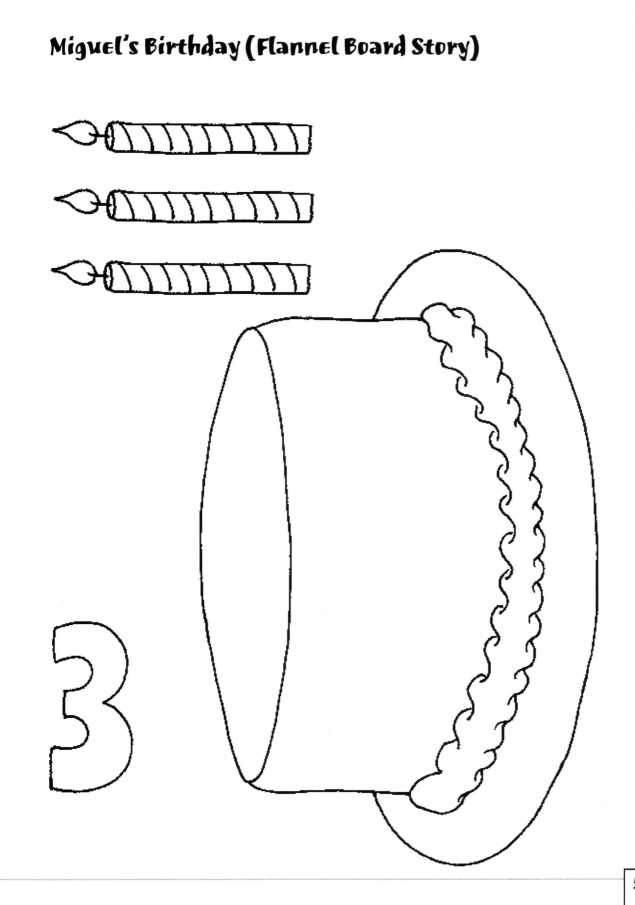

Mr. Wiggle and Mr. Waggle (Action Story)

This is Mr. Wiggle (hold up right hand, make a fist but keep the thumb pointing up—wiggle thumb) and this is Mr. Waggle (hold up left hand, make a fist but keep the thumb pointing up—wiggle thumb). Mr. Wiggle and Mr. Waggle live in houses on top of different hills and three hills apart (put thumbs inside fists).

One day, Mr. Wiggle decided to visit Mr. Waggle. He opened his door (open right fist), pop, stepped outside (raise thumb), pop, and closed his door (close fist), pop. Then he went down the hill and up the hill, and down the hill and up the hill, and down the hill and up the hill (move right hand up and down in a wave fashion to go with text).

When he reached Mr. Waggle's house, he knocked on the door—knock, knock, knock (tap right thumb against left fist). No one answered. So Mr. Wiggle went down the hill and up the hill, and down the hill and up the hill, and down the hill and up the hill to his house (use wave motion to follow text).

When he reached his house, Mr. Wiggle opened the door (open right fist), pop, went inside (place thumb in palm), pop, and closed the door (close fist), pop.

The next day, Mr. Waggle decided to visit Mr. Wiggle. He opened his door (open left fist), pop, stepped outside (raise thumb), pop, and closed his door (close fist), pop. Then he went down the hill and up the hill, and down the hill and up the hill, and down the hill and up the hill (move left hand up and down in a wave fashion to go with text).

When he reached Mr. Wiggle's house he knocked on the door—knock, knock, knock (tap left thumb against right fist). No one answered. So Mr. Waggle went down the hill and up the hill, and down the hill and up the hill, and down the hill and up the hill to his house (use wave motion to follow text). When he reached his house, Mr. Waggle opened the door (open left fist), pop, went inside (place thumb in palm), pop, and closed the door (close fist), pop.

The next day Mr. Wiggle (shake right fist) decided to visit Mr. Waggle, and Mr. Waggle (shake left fist) decided to visit Mr. Wiggle. So they opened their doors (open both fists), pop, stepped outside (raise thumbs), and closed their doors (close fists), pop. They each went down the hill and up the hill, and down the hill and up the hill (wave motion to follow text), and they met on top of the hill.

They talked and laughed and visited (wiggle thumbs) until the sun went down. Then they went down the hill and up the hill, and down the hill and up the hill, to their own homes (wave motion with both hands to text). They opened their doors (open fists), pop, went inside (tuck thumbs inside), pop, closed their doors (close fists), pop, and went to sleep (place your head on your hands).

Ms. Bumblebee Gathers Honey (Puppet Story)

BY PAM SCHILLER

Directions: Photocopy patterns on pages 536-537. Color them, cut them out, laminate them, and glue them to tongue depressors to create stick puppets. Move puppets as directed in the story.

Ms. Bumblebee spends her day gathering honey. Every morning she gets out of bed, walks to the edge of the beehive, and looks out at the beautiful spring flowers.

Most days she starts with the red flowers because red is her favorite color. She swoops down from the hive, circles around, and lands right on the biggest red flower she can find. (Hold the bee puppet in one hand and a red flower in the other. Move the bee slowly toward the flower, moving her in small circles as she approaches the flower.) She drinks nectar from the flower and then carries it back to the hive to make honey (move bee back to hive).

(continue to move bee as directed above)

Next Ms. Bumblebee tries the nectar of the blue flowers. Again she swoops from the hive and dances toward the flower. She drinks the nectar and then returns to the hive.

She continues to the yellow flowers, which are the queen bee's favorite flowers. She drinks the nectar and returns to the hive. A bee's work is very hard, but Ms. Bumblebee thinks it is also a lot of fun…and very tasty.

The last flowers Ms. Bumblebee visits are the orange zinnias. She likes them because they have lots of petals that make a big place for her to land. She takes a minute to look over the field of flowers (move puppet as if it is looking all around) before drinking and returning to the hive.

Ms. Bumblebee is tired. She is glad this is the last nectar for the day. Wait! What's this? Oh, it's that bear again. He wants to take the honey from the hive. Ms. Bumblebee is buzzing mad. She flies out and stings the bear right on the nose. The bear cries out, grabs his nose, and runs away. Ms. Bumblebee puts away her last bit of nectar and falls fast asleep.

Ms. Bumblebee Gathers Honey (Puppet Story)

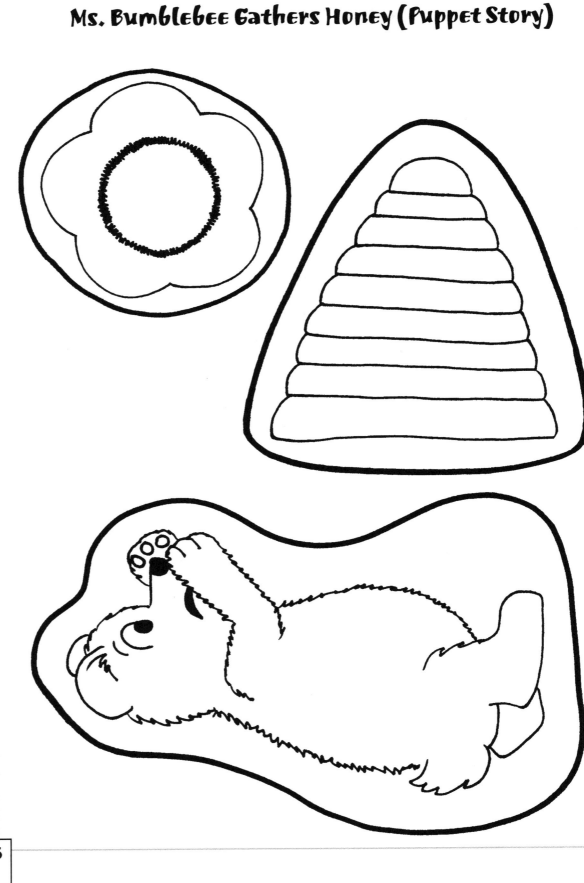

Ms. Bumblebee Gathers Honey (Puppet Story)

My Father Picks Oranges (Flannel Board Story)

BY PAM SCHILLER

Directions: Photocopy the patterns on pages 539-541. Use a fine-point permanent marker to trace them onto pelon. Color them and cut them out.

Everyday my father wakes very early. He dresses, eats his breakfast, kisses me good-bye while I am still tucked snugly in my bed, and walks out to the road to wait for the big truck to come and pick him up.

The truck takes him to the orange grove where he will pick oranges all day. He puts on his gloves, gathers a basket and a short ladder, and off he goes to the field of oranges.

My father picks each orange carefully. He examines it to be sure it is ripe enough and to be sure that no bugs have found the orange first. Then my father places the orange carefully in a basket.

The hot sun makes sweat trickle down my father's back, but still he carefully picks the oranges. His legs grow weary from standing on the ladder, but still he carefully picks the oranges.

At lunchtime, my father sits in the shade of a large tree and eats the lunch that my mother made for him. He laughs and jokes with the other orange pickers for a while, and then he returns to the grove to pick more oranges. At the end of the day, the man who owns the orange grove will count the baskets my father has picked, and he will say, "Very good, Jorge." My father will smile because he is happy to know that his oranges will soon go to the big store where people will buy them and take them home to their families.

When my father comes home, I jump into his arms. He smells of the sweet juice of the orange. He takes a gift from his pocket and hands it to me. It is an orange from the orange grove. My father says it is the juiciest orange he saw all day. When I eat the orange, I think of my father. I am happy to know that my father helps bring delicious oranges to people all over the country.

My Father Picks Oranges (Flannel Board Story)

My Father Picks Oranges (Flannel Board Story)

My Father Picks Oranges (Flannel Board Story)

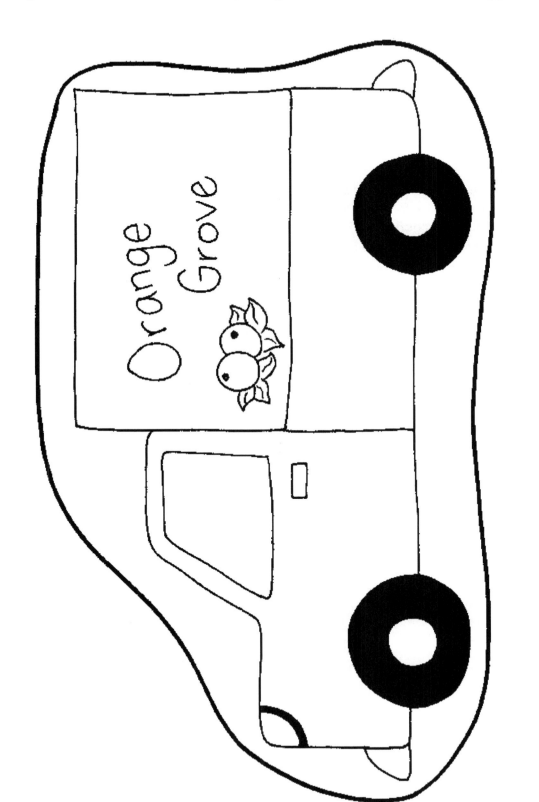

Orange Grove

My Little Red Wagon (Flannel Board Story)

BY PAM SCHILLER

Directions: Photocopy the patterns on pages 543-544. Use a fine-point permanent marker to trace them onto pelon. Color them with crayons and cut them out.

One day my Aunt Linda came to play with me. We took my red wagon and we started down the sidewalk. At the end of the block, we saw Mrs. Marotta working in her yard. She gave us a pretty plant. We put it in the wagon.

When we rolled past the empty lot, I saw something in the grass. A rock! We put it in the wagon.

Around the corner, the Bartkowiak's were having a yard sale. Aunt Linda bought a birdcage. We put it in the wagon. I bought a toy car. We put it in the wagon.

The wagon was getting crowded with the rock and the plant and the toy car and the birdcage, so we headed home. Just as we started up the driveway, my dog Comet came from out of nowhere and jumped in the wagon! What do you think happened?

The wagon tipped over and everything spilled out—the rock, the plant, the toy car, the birdcage, and Comet! What a mess! We picked everything up. Then Aunt Linda put ME in the wagon and took me home.

My Little Red Wagon (Flannel Board Story)

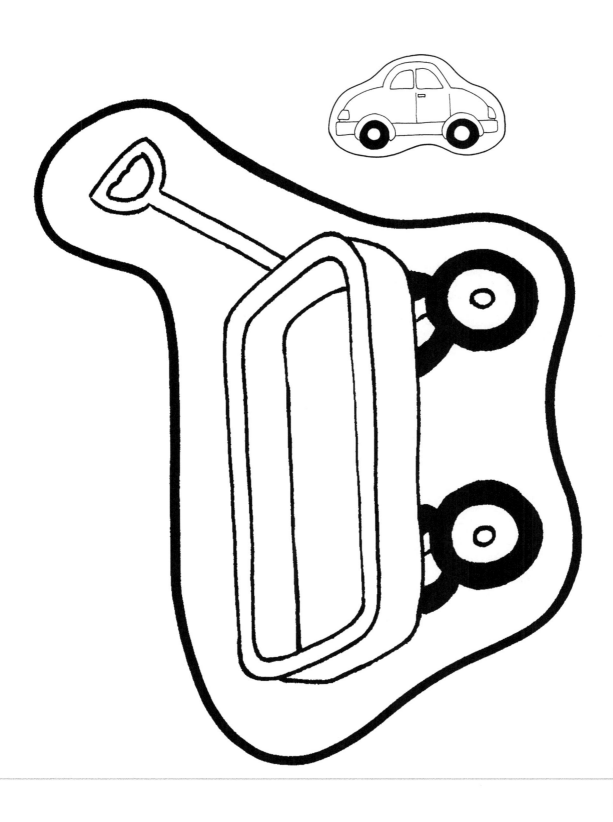

My Little Red Wagon (Flannel Board Story)

Peanut (Flannel Board Story)

BY PAM SCHILLER

Directions: Photocopy the story patterns on p. 546-548. Use a black, fine-point permanent marker to trace them onto a piece of interfacing material. Color them with crayons and cut them out.

Peanut was the happiest, teeniest, tiniest dog in the world. He lived on the fairgrounds and was the star attraction at the fair. Everyone loved Peanut, and every day, people would come from miles around just to see him. It was a good thing that so many people loved Peanut, because he didn't have any parents—at least none that he remembered.

Peanut had always lived at the fair. The pigs had raised him. One night in the middle of a huge thunderstorm, Peanut had wandered into the pigpen to get out of the rain. The pigs liked him right away. They fed him and kept him warm. When Jerry, the owner of the fair, saw Peanut in the pigpen the next morning, he was shocked. He picked Peanut up and looked at him closely. He said, "You're not a pig. You are, however, the teeniest, tiniest puppy I have ever seen. You will make a great addition to the fair. You will be my star attraction."

So every day after that, Jerry would put a small ruffled collar and a little clown hat on Peanut and gently place him under a teeny, tiny box. Then he would say, "Come one, come all, to see the teeniest, tiniest pup on the planet!" When Jerry lifted the box, everyone would gasp. They couldn't believe their eyes. No one had ever seen a puppy that small before.

Things went on like that for quite a while. One day, however, something awful happened. Peanut began to grow. He grew, and he grew, and he grew. Soon he was not the teeniest, tiniest puppy on the planet. He wasn't even close. He probably grew because he was so loved and well cared for now, but he was no longer the star attraction at the fair. No one wanted to come see an ordinary dog. Peanut was very sad. His little collar and hat wouldn't even fit on his foot. The little box that used to cover him wouldn't even hold his dinner.

Days passed, and Peanut continued to grow not only in size, but also in sadness. He knew he would have to leave the fair and find something else to do.

But then something else happened. Peanut kept on growing—and very quickly, too. He grew, and he grew, and he grew. He grew so large that he no longer fit in the pigpen. When Jerry saw how big Peanut had become, he laughed out loud. He said, "Peanut, you will be my star attraction again. Now you are the biggest dog on the entire planet."

He made Peanut a new collar and hat, and he built a new, very large box to cover him. Then he said, "Come one, come all, to see Peanut, the largest, grandest dog on the planet." People traveled from all around to see Peanut again. They couldn't believe their eyes. Under the box was the largest, grandest, happiest dog they had ever seen!

Peanut (Flannel Board Story)

Peanut (Flannel Board Story)

Perky Pumpkin's Open House (prop story)

Directions: Gather a 9" x 12" sheet of orange construction paper and a pair of scissors. Fold and cut as directed in the story.

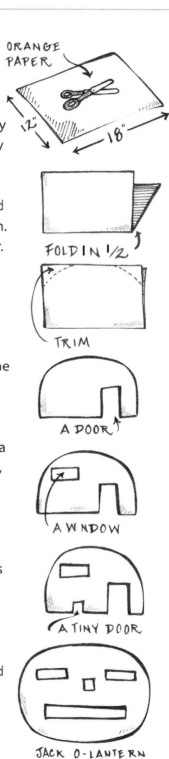

ORANGE PAPER

12" 18"

FOLD IN 1/2

TRIM

A DOOR

A WINDOW

A TINY DOOR

JACK O-LANTERN

Once upon a time there was a little man named Perky. Perky liked pumpkins so much that he even looked like a pumpkin. He was jolly and round. People called him Perky Pumpkin.

Perky's best friend was a cat named Kate. Everywhere that Perky went, Kate went too. They played together, they slept together, they went to school together—they did everything together.

Perky didn't live in a house. He lived in a field among the pumpkin vines. He had been thinking a lot about how nice it would be to have a nice, warm, snug, house that he could call his very own. He mentioned it to Kate and they decided to find a house together.

One crisp, fall morning they set out. In front of a school, they found a large piece of orange paper. "My favorite color," said Perky, "It's just what we need." Kate agreed.

With Kate's help, Perky tugged and pushed and pulled until he put the paper together like this: (fold paper in half)

With a pair of scissors, Perky carefully and slowly rounded off the corners, so the paper looked like this:

"Meow," said Kate. "Let's set it up and take a look at our work." And for a time, they just smiled in admiration.

But then Perky remembered he would need a door. He cut out a tall one, like this: "I think I'll add a window, too," he said. And he did, like this:

Perky was pleased with himself. But not Kate—she was curious to know where she would come in. "Meow...Meow." She grumbled.

Perky laughed. He quickly added another door—a teeny, tiny one that was just the right size for a rather thin cat. "This will always be open so you can come in and out as you like," Perky said. Kate purred her thanks.

On Halloween night, Perky and Kate invited all the Mother Goose and storybook friends to an open-house party. And when they opened the house to their friends, everyone was surprised and delighted, including Perky and Kate. For this is what they saw:

Just what Halloween needs—a nice round Jack-O-Lantern.

The Runaway Cookie Parade (Flannel Board Story)

BY PAM SCHILLER

Directions: Photocopy the patterns on pages 551-555. Use a fine-point permanent marker to trace them onto pelon. Color them with crayons and cut them out.

One day Ginny decided to bake some fancy cookies. She was in the mood to be creative.

She mixed up her batter and rolled it out on the table. Then she got out her favorite cookie cutters. She cut out a duck, a rabbit, a dog, a cat, and a teddy bear.

She baked the cookies until they were nice and brown. When the cookies were cool, Ginny was ready for the fun part—the decorating.

She made some icing and then she looked at each cookie with a creative eye.

She decided to make the duck purple with yellow dots. She thought the rabbit would look good with stripes. She made the dog with little spiral designs, the cat with small x designs, and the teddy bear with a plaid pattern.

When she had iced and decorated every cookie she stood back and sighed, "These are the pretties cookies in town."

Ginny placed the cookies in the cookie jar. She thought they were too pretty to eat.

What Ginny didn't know was that the ookie jar was magic. When the cookies were placed inside, they came to life. As soon as Ginny left the room, the cookies pushed off the cookie jar lid and danced right out of the jar.

They danced in a long line just like a parade. They danced onto the table, onto the chairs, onto the floor, and right out the door. Those beautiful cookies must be dancing still because they never returned to the cookie jar.

The Runaway Cookie Parade
(Flannel Board Story)

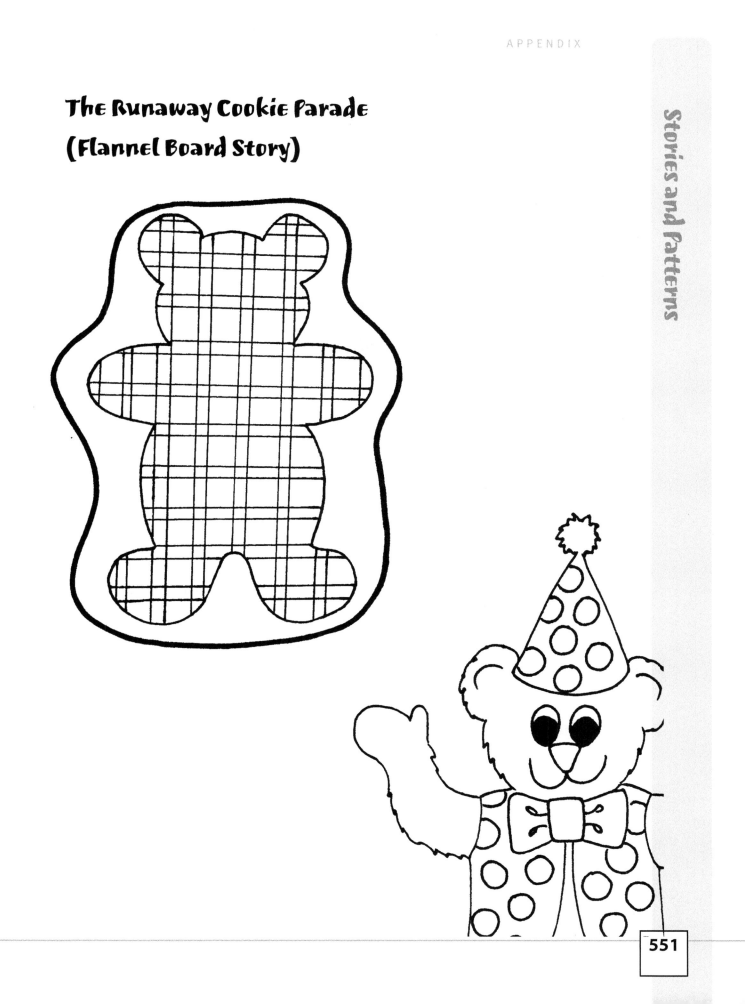

The Runaway Cookie Parade
(Flannel Board Story)

The Runaway Cookie Parade
(Flannel Board Story)

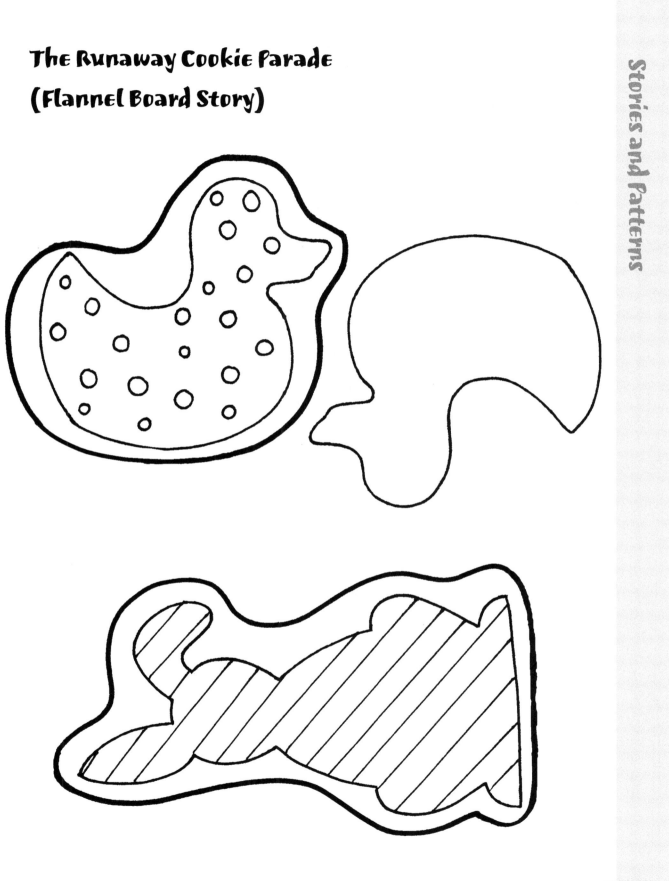

The Runaway Cookie Parade
(Flannel Board Story)

The Runaway Cookie Parade
(Flannel Board Story)

Stories and Patterns

Smart Cookie's Best Friend: Gabby Graham

(FLANNEL BOARD STORY) BY PAM SCHILLER

Directions: Photocopy the story patterns on pages 557-558. Use a fine-point permanent marker to trace the patterns onto pelon. Color them with crayons and cut them out.

Smart Cookie is a wonderful, round, perfect chocolate chip cookie. Gabby Graham is a fine, square, graham cracker. Smart Cookie and Gabby Graham are best friends. They can't wait to get to school each day so they can play together. Their favorite activity is building in the block center. The make roads and highways, barns and farms, tall skyscrapers and cozy cottages.

Smart Cookie always finds a square block that matches Gabby's graham cracker-shaped body and says with a laugh, "Hey, this block is the same shape you are." Gabby finds two half circle arches, puts them together, and says with a laugh, "Hey, these blocks are the same shape you are." Both cookies laugh.

Next to playing with the blocks, the cookies both love story time. They like all the Dr. Seuss stories but, of course, *If You Give a Mouse a Cookie* is their favorite story. Do you know why?

The cookies like drawing and painting. They love to play outdoors. They enjoy playing games with the other children and they both sing loudly during Morning Circle. The cookies love everything about school but there is no doubt that their favorite thing about school is the opportunity to spend time together. They are best friends. Do you have a best friend?

Smart Cookie's Best Friend: Gabby Graham

Smart Cookie's Best Friend: Gabby Graham

The Strange Visitor

Directions: Cut out two large shoes; two skinny, long legs; a pair of shorts; a shirt; two long, skinny arms; two large gloved hands; and a jack-o-lantern head (or happy face head) from construction paper or, even better, from Fun Foam. Lay each piece in front of you on the floor as it enters the old woman's cottage.

A little old woman lived all alone in a little old house in the woods.
One Halloween she sat in the chimney corner, and as she sat, she spun.
Still she sat and
Still she spun and
Still she wished for company.

Then she saw her door open a little way, and in came
A pair of broad, broad feet *(place the shoes on the floor in front of you)*
And sat down by the fireside.
"That is strange," thought the little old woman, but—
Still she sat and
Still she spun and
Still she wished for company.

Then in came
A pair of long, long legs *(place the pair of long skinny legs above the shoes)*
And sat down on the broad, broad feet.
"Now this is strange," thought the little old woman, but—
Still she sat and
Still she spun and
Still she wished for company.

Then in came
A wee, wee waist *(place the pair of shorts above the legs)*
And sat down on the long, long legs.
"Now this is strange," thought the little old woman, but—
Still she sat and
Still she spun and
Still she wished for company.

Then in came
A pair of broad, broad shoulders *(place the shirt above the shorts)*
And sat down on the wee, wee, waist.
"Now this is strange," thought the little old woman, but—
Still she sat and
Still she spun and
Still she wished for company.

Then in through the door came,
A pair of long, long arms, *(add the pair of long, skinny arms)*
And sat down on the broad, broad shoulders.
"Now that is strange," thought the little old woman, but—
Still she sat and
Still she spun and
Still she wished for company.

Then in came
A pair of fat, fat hands *(place the hands at the end of the arms)*
And sat down on the long, long arms.
"Now this is strange," thought the little old woman, but—
Still she sat and
Still she spun and
Still she wished for company.

Then in came
A round, round head *(place the big jack-o-lantern head on the shirt)*
And sat down on top of all
That sat by the fireside.

The little old woman stopped her spinning and asked,
"Where did you get such big, big feet?"
"By much tramping, by much tramping," said Somebody.

"Where did you get such long, long legs?"
"By much running, by much running," said Somebody.

"Where did you get such a wee, wee waist?"
"Nobody knows, nobody knows," said Somebody.

"Where did you get such long, long arms?"
"Swinging the scythe, swinging the scythe," said Somebody.

"Where did you get such fat, fat hands?"
"From threshing, from threshing," said Somebody.
"How did you get such a huge, huge head?"
"Of a pumpkin I made it," said Somebody.

Then said the little old woman, "What did you come for?"
"YOU!" *

* If you are concerned that the end of the story might frighten young children, change it. Simply add "to keep you company, to keep you company."

The Three Billy Goats Gruff (Flannel Board/Shadow Story)

Directions: Photocopy the patterns on pages 563-567. Use a fine-point permanent marker to trace them onto pelon. Color them and cut them out. To present this story as a shadow story, photocopy the patterns, color them, cut them out, laminate them, and attach them to a tongue depressor. Hold them between a light source and the wall to create shadows. Notice that these illustrations do not have a cut line around them like other flannel board patterns in this book. If you are using the illustrations to tell a flannel board story, you may want to draw a circle around them so that you do not have to cut around the details of the illustrations. If you are using the illustrations to tell a shadow story you will need the details so that the shadow images are recognizable.

Once upon a time there were three billy goats called Gruff. In the winter they lived in a barn in the valley. When spring came they longed to travel up to the mountains to eat the lush sweet grass.

On their way to the mountains, the three Billy Goats Gruff had to cross a rushing river. But there was only one bridge across it, made of wooden planks. And underneath the bridge there lived a terrible, ugly troll.

Nobody was allowed to cross the bridge without the troll's permission—and nobody ever got permission. He always ate them up.

The smallest Billy Goat Gruff was first to reach the bridge. Trippity-trop, trippity-trop went his little hooves as he trotted over the wooden planks. Ting-tang, ting-tang went the little bell round his neck.

"Who's that trotting over my bridge?" growled the troll from under the planks.

"Billy Goat Gruff," squeaked the smallest goat in his little voice. "I'm only going up to the mountain to eat the sweet spring grass."

"Oh, no, you're not!" said the troll. "I'm going to eat you for breakfast!"

"Oh no, please Mr. Troll," pleaded the goat. "I'm only the smallest Billy Goat Gruff. I'm much too tiny for you to eat, and I wouldn't taste very good. Why don't you wait for my brother, the second Billy Goat Gruff? He's much bigger than me and would be much more tasty."

The troll did not want to waste his time on a little goat if there was a bigger and better one to eat. "All right, you can cross my bridge," he grunted. "Go and get fatter on the mountain and I'll eat you on your way back!"

So the smallest Billy Goat Gruff skipped across to the other side.

The troll did not have to wait long for the second Billy Goat Gruff. Clip-clop, clip-clop went his hooves as he clattered over the wooden planks. Ding-dong, ding-dong went the bell around his neck.

"Who's that clattering across my bridge?" screamed the troll, suddenly appearing from under the planks.

"Billy Goat Gruff," said the second goat in his middle-sized voice. "I'm going up to the mountain to eat the lovely spring grass."

"Oh, no, you're not!" said the troll. "I'm going to eat you for breakfast."

"Oh, no, please," said the second goat. "I may be bigger than the first Billy Goat Gruff, but I'm much smaller than my brother, the third Billy Goat Gruff. Why don't you wait for him? He would be much more of a meal than me."

The troll was getting very hungry, but he did not want to waste his appetite on a middle-sized goat if there was an even bigger one to come. "All right, you can cross my bridge," he rumbled. "Go and get fatter on the mountain and I'll eat you on your way back!"

So the middle-sized Billy Goat Gruff scampered across to the other side.

The troll did not have to wait long for the third Billy Goat Gruff. Tromp-tramp, tromp-tramp went his hooves as he stomped across the wooden planks. Bong-bang, bong-bang went the big bell round his neck.

"Who's that stomping over my bridge?" roared the troll, resting his chin on his hands. "Billy Goat Gruff," said the third goat in a deep voice. "I'm going up to the mountain to eat the lush spring grass."

"Oh, no, you're not!" said the troll as he clambered up on to the bridge. "I'm going to eat you for breakfast!"

"That's what you think," said the biggest Billy Goat Gruff. Then he lowered his horns, galloped along the bridge, and butted the ugly troll. Up, up, up went the troll into the air, then down, down, down into the rushing river below. He disappeared below the swirling waters, and was never seen again.

"So much for his breakfast," thought the biggest Billy Goat Gruff. "Now what about mine!" And he walked in triumph over the bridge to join his two brothers on the mountain pastures. From then on anyone could cross the bridge whenever they liked—thanks to the three Billy Goats Gruff.

The Three Billy Goats Gruff (Flannel Board/Shadow Story)

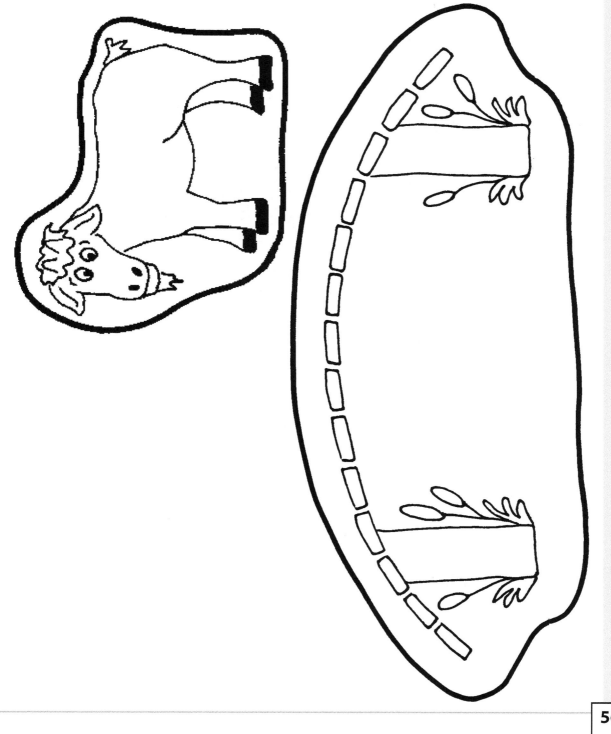

The Three Billy Goats Gruff (Flannel Board/Shadow Story)

The Three Billy Goats Gruff (Flannel Board/Shadow Story)

The Three Billy Goats Gruff (Flannel Board/Shadow Story)

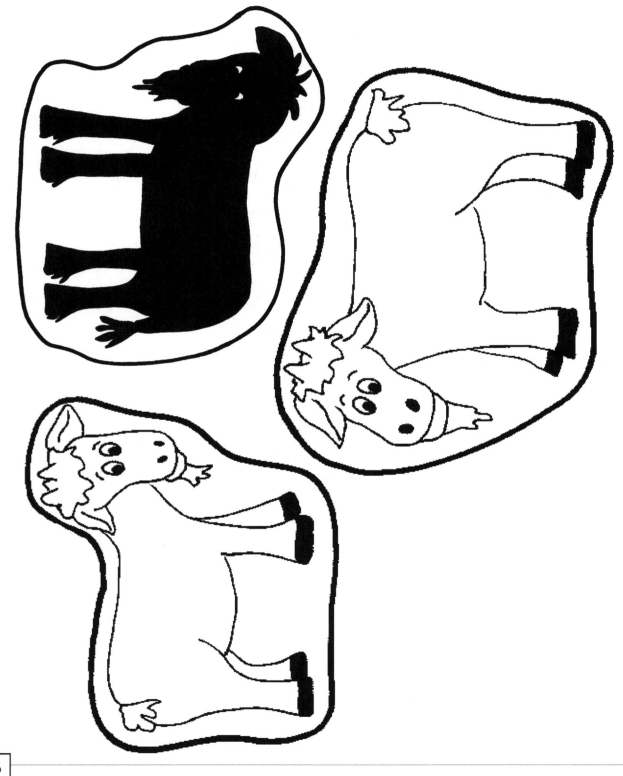

The Three Billy Goats Gruff (Flannel Board/Shadow Story)

The Three Little Pigs (Glove Puppet/Flannel Board Story)

Directions for the Glove Puppets: Photocopy the story patterns on pages 449-453. Color them, cut them out, laminate them, and glue a piece of Velcro on the back of each character. Glue the matching piece of Velcro to each finger of an old work glove.

Directions for the Flannel Board: Photocopy the patterns on page 570. Use a fine-point permanent marker to trace them onto pelon. Color them and cut them out.

Once upon a time, there were three little pigs who left their mother and father to find their places in the world.

All summer long, they roamed through the woods and over the plains, playing games and having fun. None were happier than the three little pigs, and they easily made friends with everyone. Wherever they went they were given a warm welcome, but as summer drew to a close, they realized that folk were returning to their usual jobs and preparing for winter.

Autumn came and it began to grow cold and rainy. The three little pigs decided they needed a real home. Sadly they knew that the fun was over now and they must set to work like the others, or they'd be left in the cold and rain with no roof over their heads.

They talked about what kind of home they would build. The first little pig said he'd build a house made from straw.

"It will only take a day," he said.

"It's too fragile," his brothers said. But the first pig didn't care. He was anxious to get back to playing.

Not quite so lazy, the second little pig went in search of planks of seasoned wood.

"Clunk! Clunk! Clunk!" It took him two days to nail them together.

The third little pig did not like the wooden house.

"That's not the way to build a house!" he said. "It takes time, patience, and hard work to build a house that is strong enough to stand up to the wind and rain and snow, and most of all, protect us from the wolf!"

The days went by, and the wisest little pig's house took shape, brick by brick. From time to time, his brothers visited him, saying with a chuckle, "Why are you working so hard? Why don't you come and play?"

"No" said the last little pig. He diligently continued his work.

Soon his work was done and just in time. One autumn day when no one expected it, along came the big bad wolf, scowling fiercely at the first pig's straw house.

"Little pig, little pig, let me in, let me in," ordered the wolf, his mouth watering.

"Not by the hair of my chinny, chin, chin!" replied the little pig in a tiny voice.

"Then I'll huff and I'll puff and I'll blow your house down!" growled the wolf angrily.

The wolf puffed out his chest, and he huffed and he puffed and he blew the first little pig's house of straw right down.

Excited by his own cleverness, the wolf did not notice that the little pig had slithered out from underneath the heap of straw and was dashing towards his brother's wooden house. When he realized that the little pig was escaping, the wolf grew wild with rage.

"Come back!" he roared, trying to catch the pig as he ran into the wooden house. The second little pig greeted his brother, shaking like a leaf.

"Open up! Open up! I only want to speak to you!" growled the hungry wolf.

"Go away," cried the two little pigs.

So the angry wolf puffed out his chest and he huffed and he puffed and he huffed and he puffed and he blew the wooden house clean away.

Luckily, the wisest little pig had been watching the scene from the window of his own brick house, and he quickly opened the door to his fleeing brothers. And not a moment too soon, for the wolf was already hammering furiously on the door. This time, the wolf wasted no time talking. He puffed out his chest and he huffed and he puffed and he blew and blew and blew, but the little brick house wouldn't budge. The wolf tried again. He puffed out his chest and he huffed and he puffed and he huffed and he puffed, but still the little house stood strong.

The three little pigs watched him and their fear began to fade. Quite exhausted by his efforts, the wolf decided to try one of his tricks. He scrambled up a nearby ladder, on to the roof to have a look at the chimney. However, the now wiser little pigs knew exactly what the wolf was up to.

"Quick! Light the fire! He is coming down the chimney."

The big bad wolf began to crawl down the chimney. It wasn't long before he felt something very hot on his tail. "Ouch!" he exclaimed. His tail was on fire. He jumped out of the chimney and tried to put the out the flames on his tail. Then he ran away as fast as he could.

The three happy little pigs, dancing round and round the yard, began to sing, "Tra-la-la! Tra-la-la! The big bad wolf will never come back...!" And he never did!

The Three Little Pigs (Glove Puppet/Flannel Board Story)

The Tortoise and the Hare (Puppet Story)

Directions: Photocopy the story patterns on this page and the next. Color them, cut them out, and laminate them. Glue them to a tongue depressor.

One day a hare was making fun of a tortoise. "You are a slowpoke," he said. "You couldn't run if you tried."

"Don't laugh at me," said the tortoise. "I bet that I could beat you in a race."

"Couldn't," replied the hare.

"Could," replied the tortoise.

"All right," said the hare. "I'll race you. But I'll win, even with my eyes shut."

They asked a passing fox to set them off.

"Ready, set, go!" said the fox.

The hare went off at a great pace. He got so far ahead, he decided he might as well stop for a rest. Soon he fell fast asleep.

The tortoise came plodding along, never stopping for a moment.

When the hare woke up, he ran as fast as he could to the finish line. But he was too late—the tortoise had already won the race!

The Tortoise and the Hare (Puppet Story)

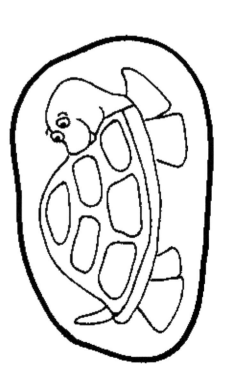

Valerie Valentine (Flannel Board Story)

BY PAM SCHILLER

Directions: Photocopy the patterns on pages 574-575. Use a fine-point permanent marker to trace them onto pelon. Color them and cut them out.

It was almost Valentine's Day. Valerie couldn't wait. She had been looking forward to finally being old enough to be a store valentine. Her brothers, Victor and Vance, had left home last year, and now it was her turn.

She wanted to look vibrant. She put on her Victorian lace trim. She thought it was her very best outfit.

She found a good spot on the shelf at Valerie's Card Shop. She put on her best smile and waited. The first day came and went and no one bought Valerie. She was very sad. She didn't want to sound vain but she really thought she looked better than any other card. Valerie decided to put on her black hat with the lace veil. That should do it.

The next day was the same. People came and went and never even picked her up. When the school van came loaded with children and no one even noticed her, she was devastated.

That night Valerie gathered a honeysuckle vine and wrapped it around her middle. Then she picked a vacant spot on the shelf where she would be right in view of the door. "Surely this will work," she thought.

But the next day was the same. When the store closed, Valerie started to cry. She was too sad to even think of another idea. Then suddenly she heard a voice beside her. It was Valentino, the Beanie Baby Bear. He said he knew a secret that would be just the right thing to make Valerie the most special Valentine on the shelf. He whispered it into her ear. Do you know what it was?

It was a special verse. Valerie wrote it right across her face with a violet crayon. It said;

> "Roses are red,
> Violets are blue,
> Sugar is sweet
> And so are you!"

And at last Valerie was victorious. She was the first valentine to be bought the next morning.

Valerie Valentine (Flannel Board Story)

Valerie Valentine (Flannel Board Story)

What Makes Me Laugh? (Flannel Board Rhyme)

BY PAM SCHILLER

Directions: Photocopy the patterns on pages 576-578. Use a fine-point permanent marker to trace them onto pelon. Color them and cut them out.

Bubbles in the air.
My fingers in your hair.
Silly songs we sing.
Balloons on a string.
Jack-in-the-box.
And spinning tops.
Tickles on my toes.
Kisses on my nose.

What makes you laugh?

What Makes Me Laugh? (Flannel Board Rhyme)

What Makes Me Laugh? (Flannel Board Rhyme)

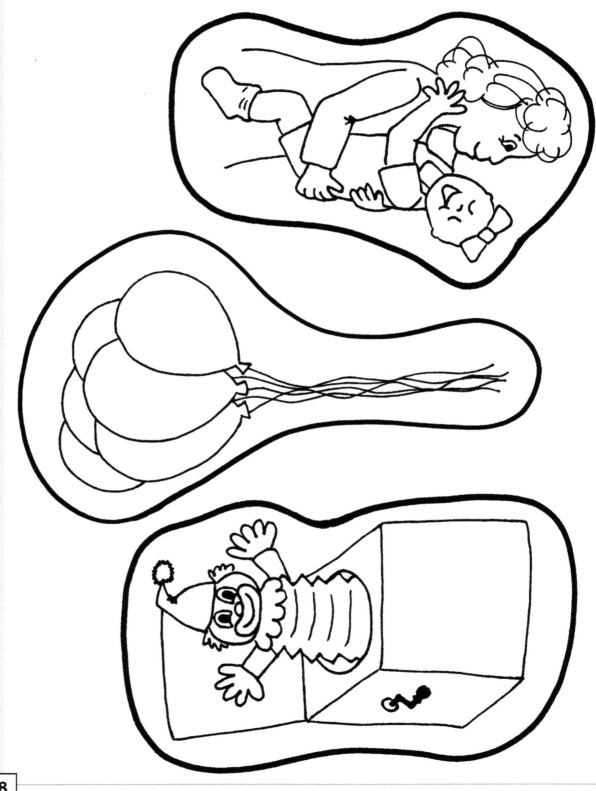

What's In the Box?

BY PAM SCHILLER (FLANNEL BOARD STORY)

Directions: Photocopy the patterns on pages 579-583. Use a black, fine-point permanent marker to trace them onto pelon. Color them with crayons and cut them out. Vary this story to represent the situation for which you are using it. For example, if using it with Hanukkah, call the present a Hanukkah present. If using it for Everybody's Birthday, call it a birthday present.

Look at this wonderful box. It's all wrapped up. It has pretty paper and a pretty bow. It's a present. I wonder what's inside. Do you wonder what's inside?

What do you think is in the box? Maybe it's a ball. Maybe it's a doll. Maybe it's a rattle for baby.

If we could pick up the box, we'd know if it was heavy or light. If we could shake the box, we might hear something inside. We'd know if the thing inside makes a hard sound or a soft sound. But we can't shake this box so we just have to guess.

Maybe it's a book. Maybe it's a toy car. Maybe it's a jack-in-the-box. Let's find out.

First we take off the bow. We'll put it right here. It's so pretty. Maybe we can use it again. Now let's take off the paper. If we are gentle and don't tear it, we can use the paper again, too.

OK! Are you ready to see what's inside? Look! It's a top!

And now it is out of the box!

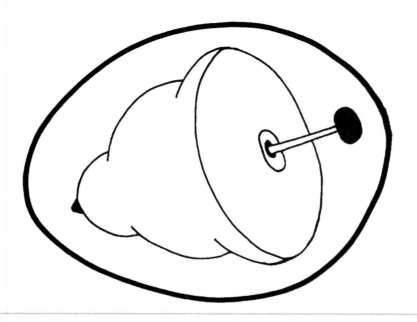

What's In the Box?

What's In the Box?

Jack in the Box

What's In the Box?

What's In the Box?

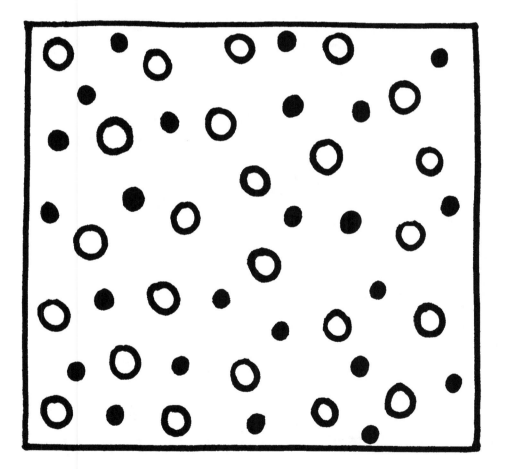

The Cat and the Fiddle

Directions: Photocopy the patterns on pages 584-586. Use a black sharpie pen to trace the patterns onto pelon. Color them with crayons and cut them out.

The Cat and the Fiddle

The Cat and the Fiddle

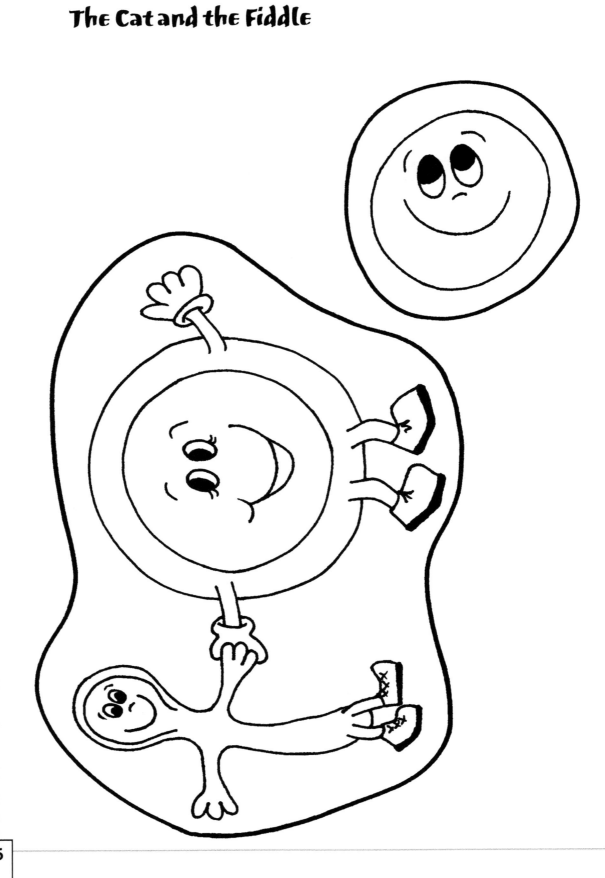

Five Toes

Directions: Photocopy the patterns on pages 587-588. Use a black sharpie pen to trace the patterns onto pelon. Color them with crayons and cut them out.

Five Toes

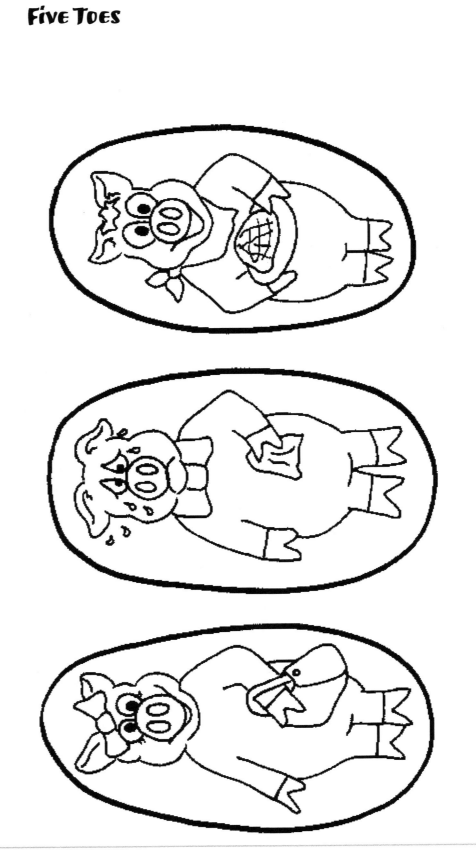

Humpty Dumpty

Directions: Photocopy the patterns on pages 589-591. Use a fine-point permanent marker to trace the patterns onto pelon. Color them with crayons and cut them out.

Humpty Dumpty sat on a wall.
Humpty Dumpty had a great fall.
All the king's horses and all the king's men
Couldn't put Humpty Dumpty together again.

NEW VERSE BY PAM SCHILLER:
Humpty Dumpty sat on a hill,
Humpty Dumpty had a great spill.
That genius, Jack Horner, pulled out his glue
Now Humpty Dumpty's as good as new!

Humpty Dumpty

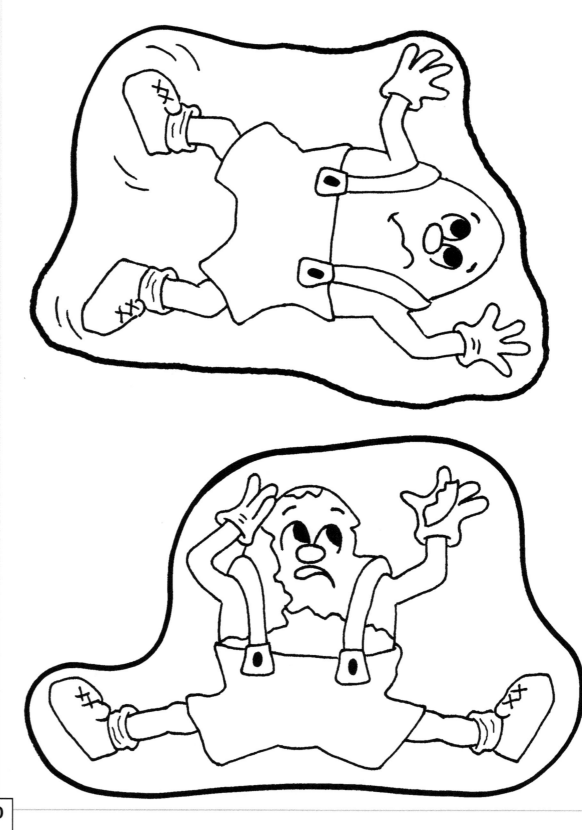

Humpty Dumpty

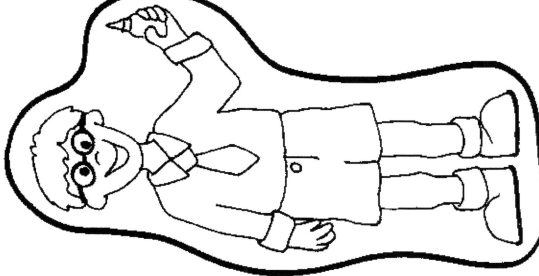

Jack and Jill

Directions: Photocopy the patterns on pages 592-594. Use a black sharpie pen to trace the patterns onto pelon. Color them with crayons and cut them out.

.

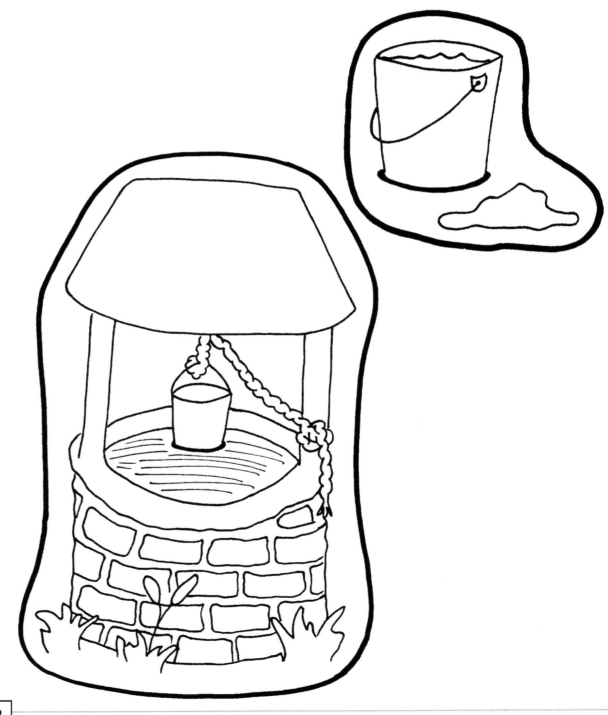

Jack and Jill

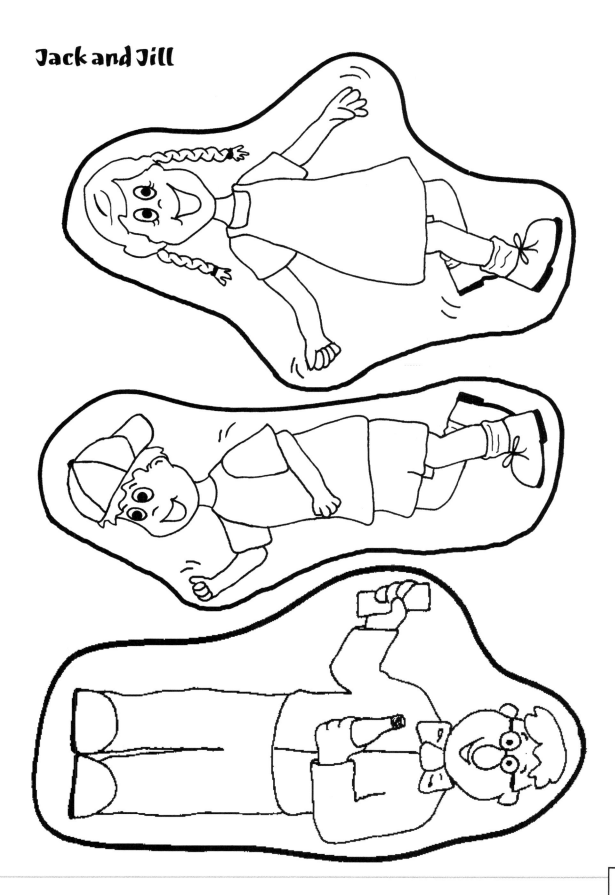

Jack and Jill

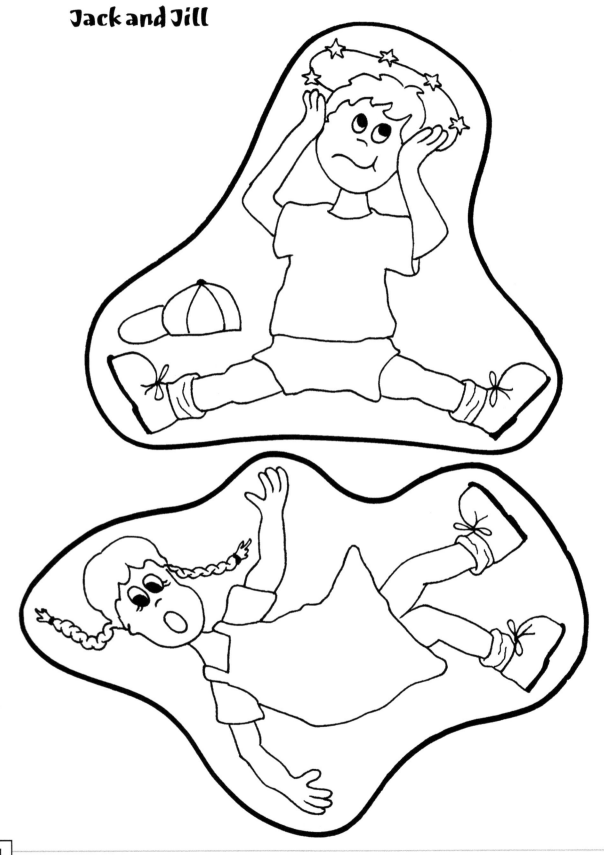

Little Boy Blue

Directions: Photocopy the patterns on pages 595-596. Use a black sharpie pen to trace the patterns onto pelon. Color them with crayons and cut them out.

Little Boy Blue, come blow your horn!
The sheep's in the meadow, the cow's in the corn.
Where's the little boy that looks after the sheep?
He's under a haystack, fast asleep!

Little Boy Blue

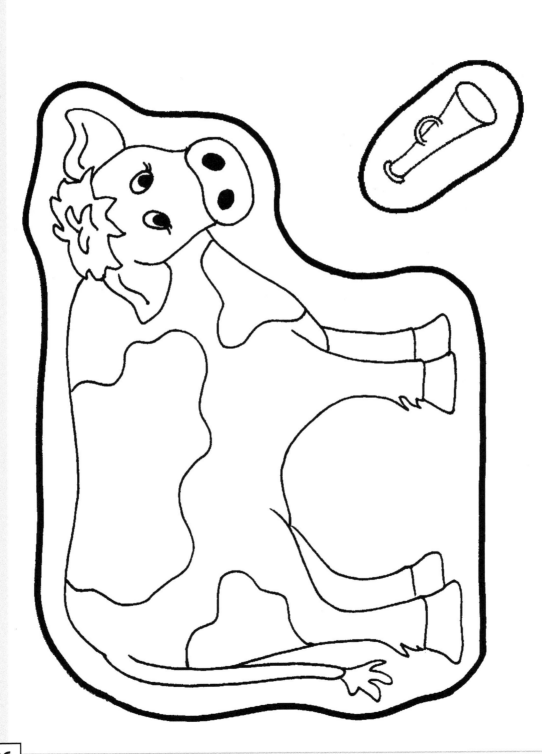

Miss Muffet

Directions: Photocopy the patterns on pages 597-599. Use a black sharpie pen to trace the patterns onto pelon. Color them with crayons and cut them out.

Little Miss Muffet sat on her tuffet
Eating her curds and whey.
Along came a spider
And sat down beside her
And frightened Miss Muffet away.

New verse by Pam Schiller:
Little Miss Muffet went back to her tuffet,
And said, "You gave me a scare!
I can see you are nice. I should have looked twice
So my breakfast with you I will share."

Miss Muffet

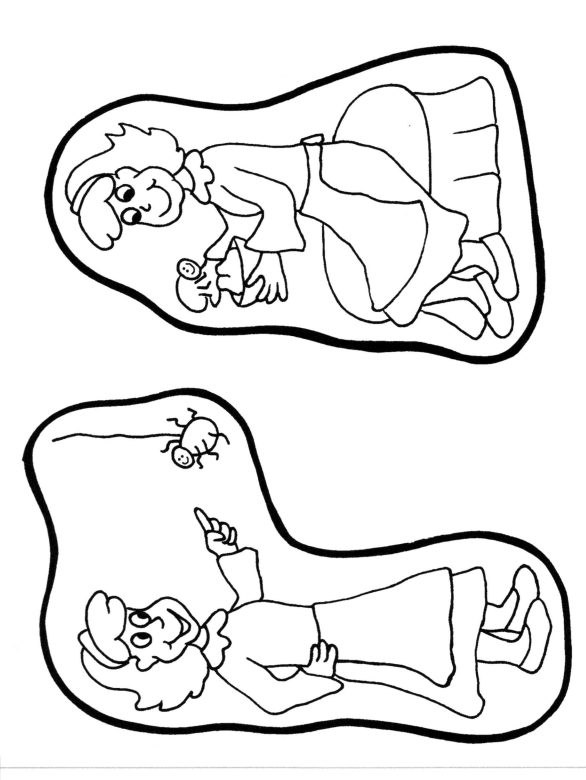

Miss Muffet

The Mouse and the Clock

Directions: Photocopy the patterns below. Use a black sharpie pen to trace the patterns onto pelon. Color them with crayons and cut them out.

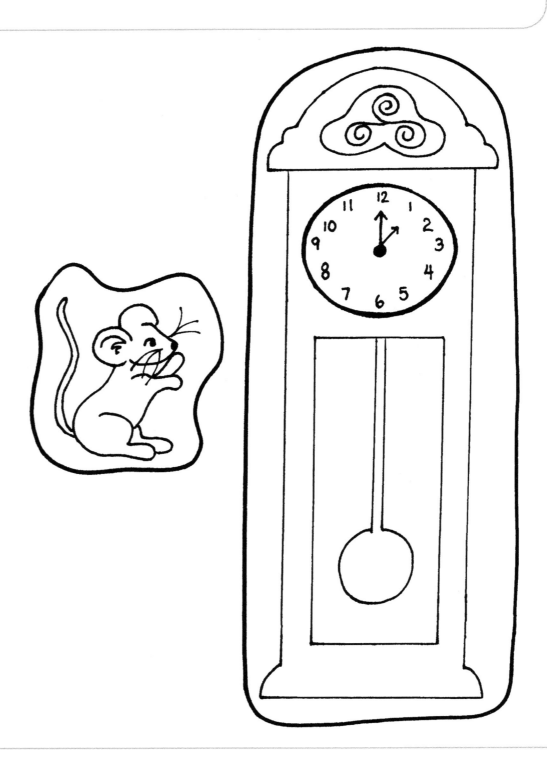

One, Two, Buckle My Shoe

Directions: Photocopy the patterns on pages 601-602. Use a black sharpie pen to trace the patterns onto pelon. Color them with crayons and cut them out.

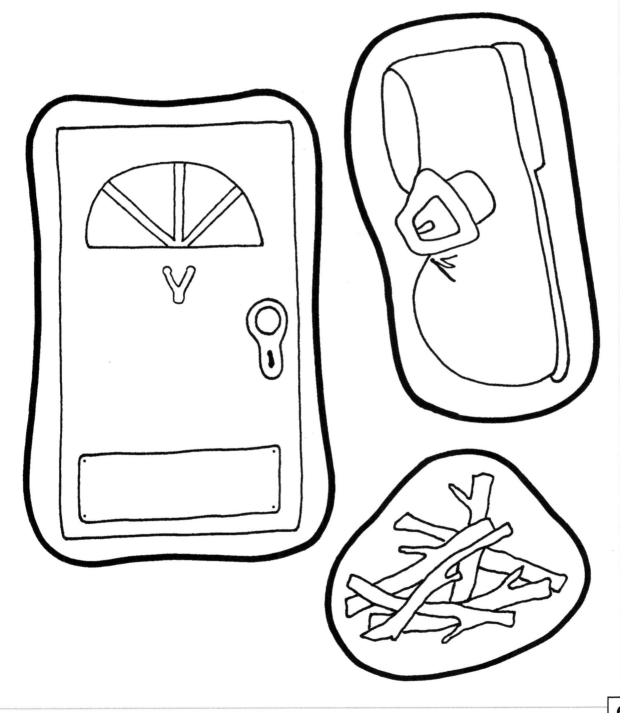

One, Two, Buckle My Shoe

The Three Little Kittens

Directions: Photocopy the patterns on pages 603-606. Use a black sharpie pen to trace the patterns onto pelon. Color them with crayons and cut them out.

Three little kittens, they lost their mittens,
And they began to cry,
"Oh, mother dear, we very greatly fear
Our mittens we have lost."
"What! Lost your mittens? You naughty kittens!
Then you shall have no pie."
"Meow! Meow! Meow! Meow!"

Three little kittens, they found their mittens,
And they began to cry,
"Oh, Mother dear, see here, see here!
Our mittens we have found!"
"What! Found your mittens? You darling kittens!
Now you shall have some pie."
"Purr! Purr! Purr! Purr!"

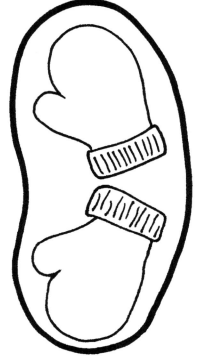

The Three Little Kittens

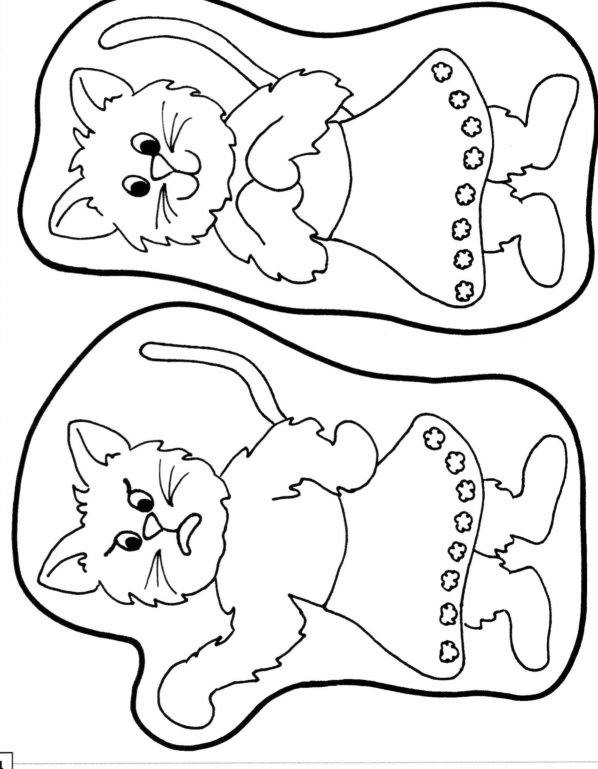

The Three Little Kittens

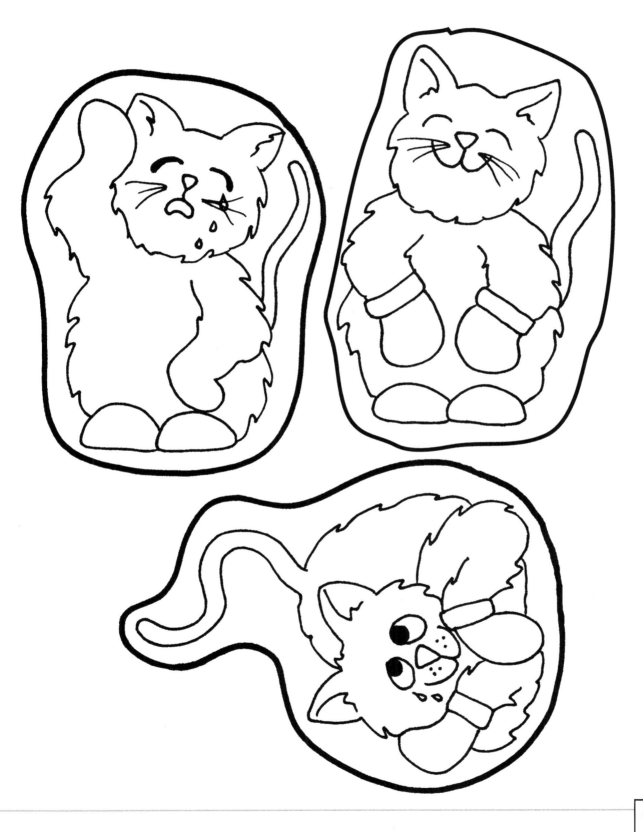

The Three Little Kittens

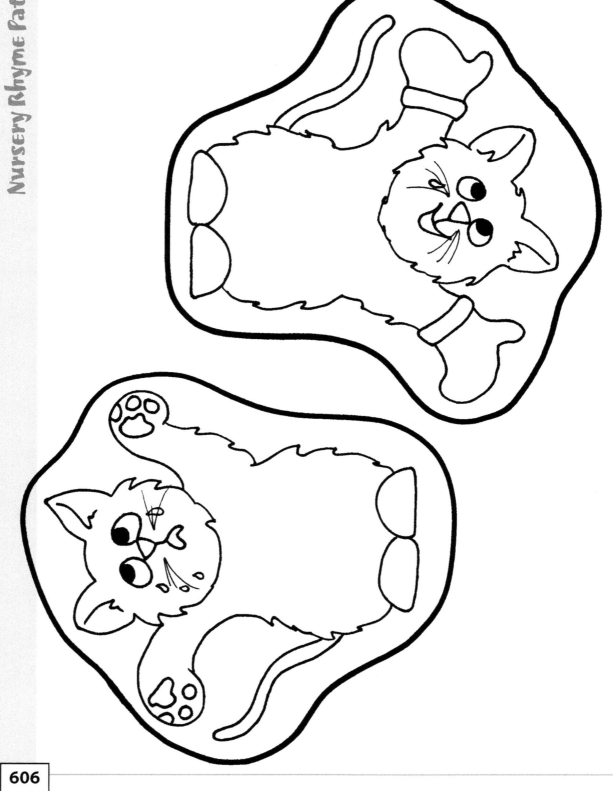

Old MacDonald Had a Farm Song Cards

Directions: Photocopy the cards on pages 607-610. Enlarge if desired. Color them and laminate them.

Old MacDonald Had a Farm Song Cards

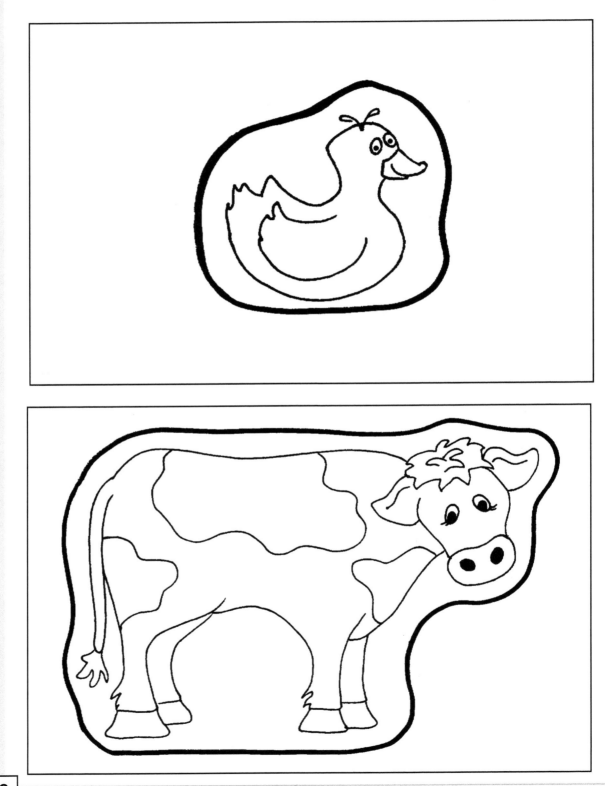

Old MacDonald Had a Farm Song Cards

Old MacDonald Had a Farm Song Cards

Twinkle, Twinkle, Little Star Song Cards

Directions: Photocopy the cards on pages 611-612. Enlarge if desired. Make two copies of the illustration on p. 612 so you can use them at the beginning and at the end of the song. Color them and laminate them.

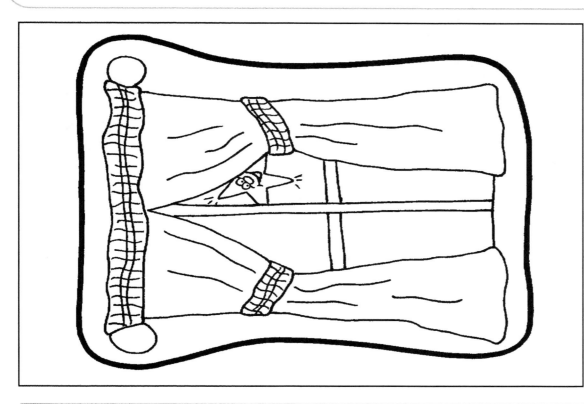

Twinkle, Twinkle, Little Star Song Cards

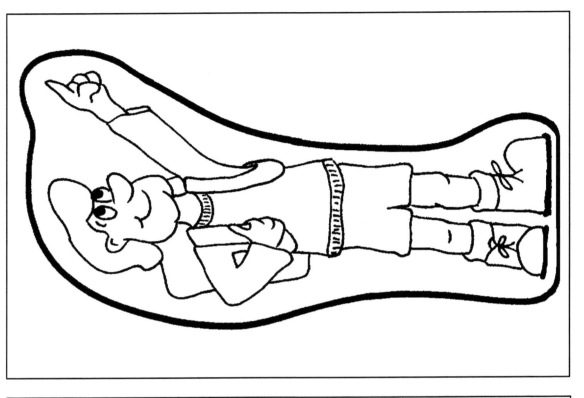

The Wheels on the Bus Song Cards

Directions: Photocopy the cards on pages 613-615. Color them, and laminate them.

The Wheels on the Bus Song Cards

The Wheels on the Bus Song Cards

Assessment

Child's name _____

Assessment Instrument

SKILL/CONCEPT (Mark with date of observation.)	NOT YET	EMERGING	ACCOMPLISHED
Points to body parts when asked.			
Eyes			
Ears			
Nose			
Mouth			
Chin			
Hair			
Hands and fingers			
Arms			
Feet and toes			
Legs			
Knees and elbows			
Describes the functions of body parts.			
Eyes			
Ears			
Nose			
Mouth			
Chin			
Hair			
Hands and fingers			
Arms			
Feet and toes			
Legs			
Knees and elbows			
Identifies facial expressions.			
Happy			
Sad			
Surprised			
Angry			
Frightened			
Recognizes shapes and patterns.			
Round			
Circle			
Square			
Stripes			

SKILL/CONCEPT (Mark with date of observation.)	NOT YET	EMERGING	ACCOMPLISHED
Identifies attributes.			
Big			
Little			
Short			
Long			
Tall			
Rough			
Smooth			
Soft			
Hard			
Loud			
Thin/Skinny			
Wide/Fat			
Recognizes colors.			
Red			
Yellow			
Blue			
Green			
Purple			
Orange			
Black			
White			
Identifies pairs of opposites.			
Big and Little			
Tall and Short			
Long and Short			
Up and Down/High and Low			
In/Inside and Out/Outside			
Over and Under			
Front/Forward and Back/Backward			
Fat and Skinny			
Day and Night			
Hard and Soft			
Fast and Slow			
Thick and Thin			
Loud and Soft			
Light and Heavy			
Understands spatial concepts.			
In/Inside			
Out/Outside			
On			
Off			

Assessment Instrument

SKILL/CONCEPT (Mark with date of observation.)	NOT YET	EMERGING	ACCOMPLISHED
Up			
Down			
Over/Above			
Under/Below			
Top, Middle, and Bottom			
First, Next, Last			
Can identify weather conditions.			
Sunny			
Windy			
Rainy			
Hot			
Cold			
Sings along with a simple song such as "Twinkle, Twinkle, Little Star" or "Itsy Bitsy Spider."			
Recites part of a simple rhyme such as "Humpty Dumpty" or "Hey, Diddle Diddle."			
Recognizes things that are alike and things that are different.			
Recognizes specific books by cover.			
Pretends to read books.			
Understands that books are handled in a special way.			
Enters into a book-sharing routine with primary caregiver.			
Demonstrates enjoyment of rhyming language and nonsense words.			
Labels objects in books.			
Listens to stories.			
Requests adult to read or write.			
Begins to show attentions to specific print, such as letters in names.			
Uses increasingly purposeful scribbling.			
Begins to distinguish between drawing and writing.			
Produces letter-like forms and scribbles with some features of writing.			

Index

Books, Games, Rhymes, and Songs Index

623

Complete Index

APPENDIX